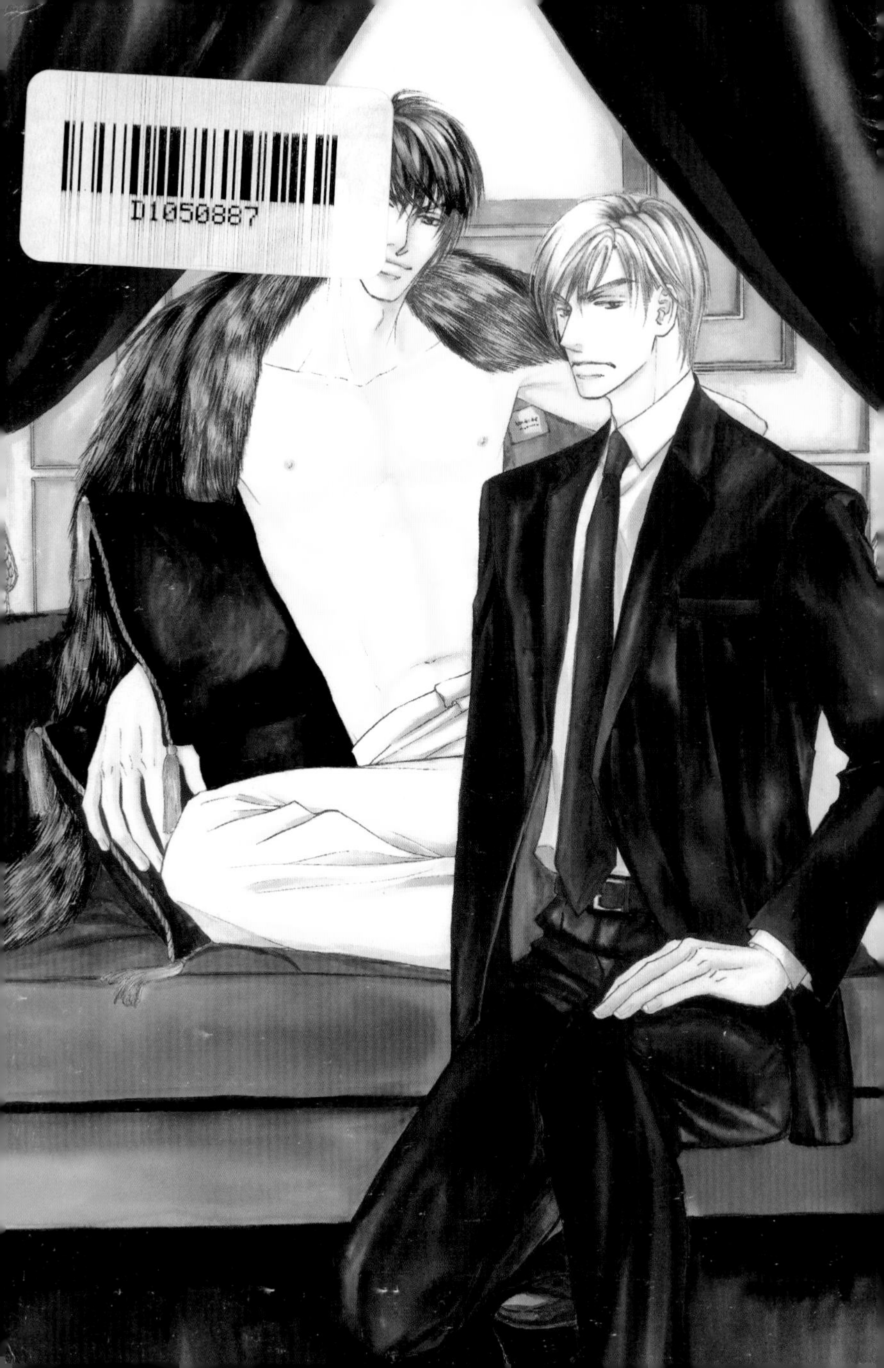

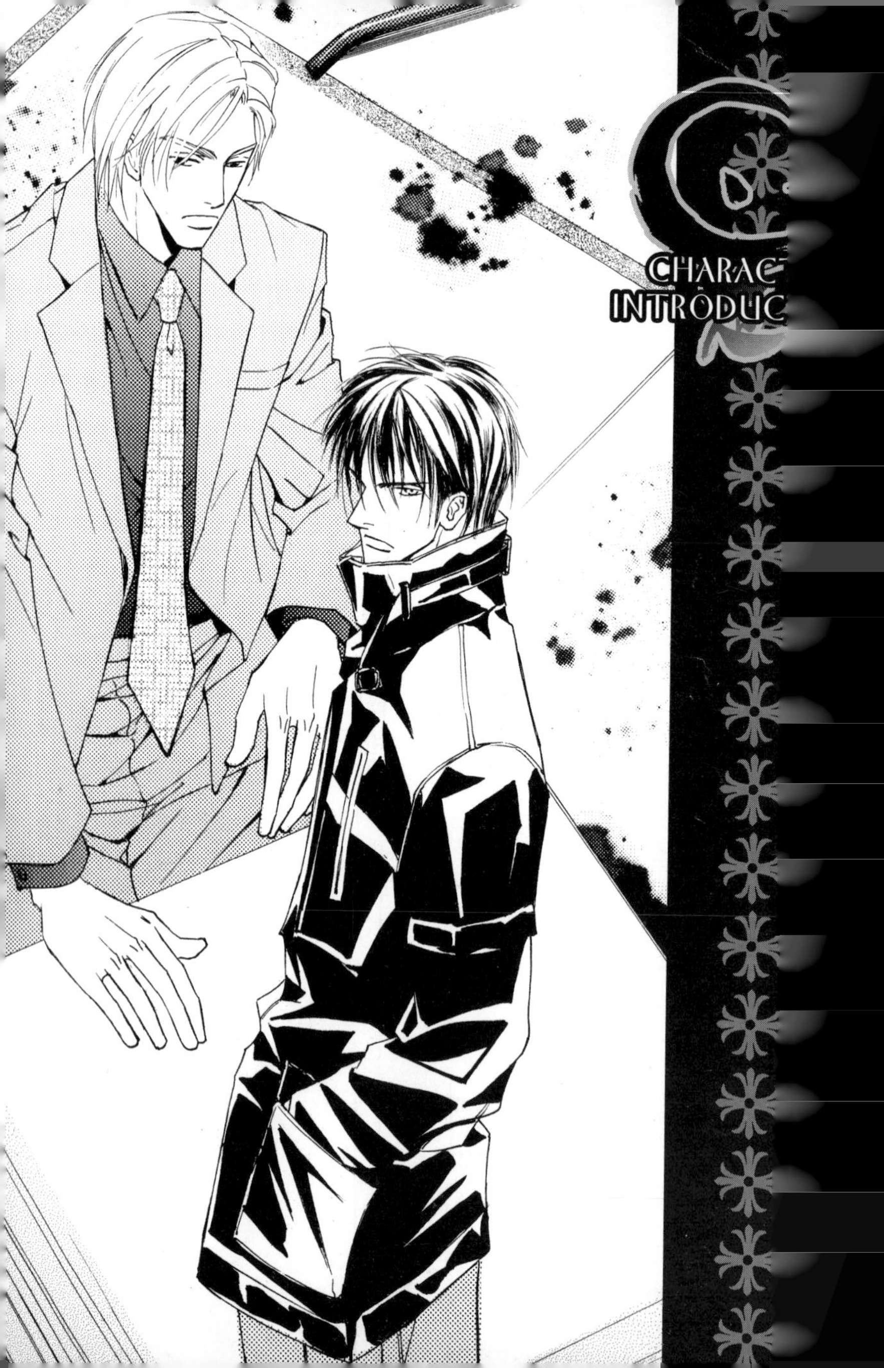
CHARACT
INTRODUC

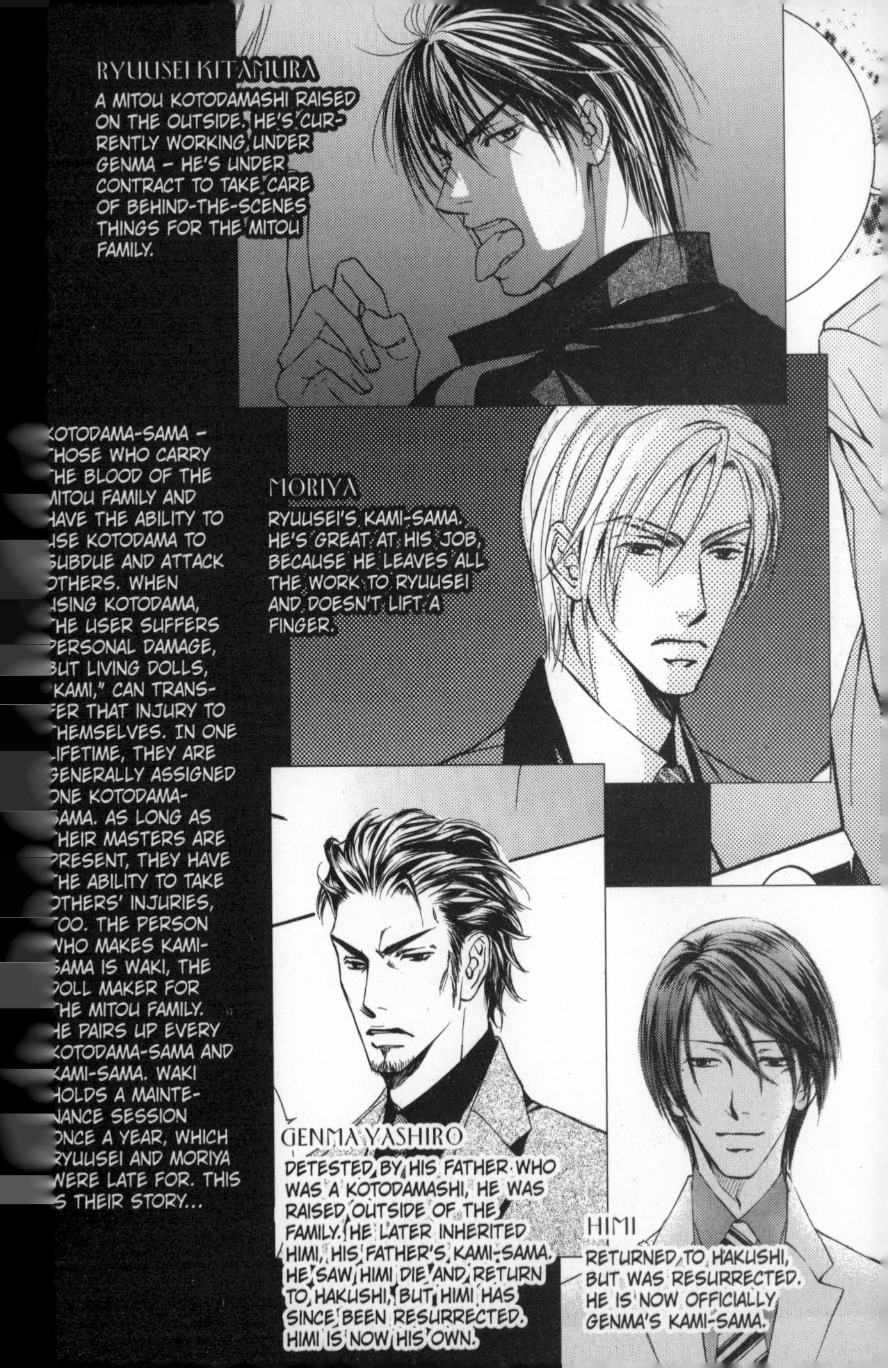
RYUUSEI KITAMURA
A MITOU KOTODAMASHI RAISED ON THE OUTSIDE. HE'S CURRENTLY WORKING UNDER GENMA – HE'S UNDER CONTRACT TO TAKE CARE OF BEHIND-THE-SCENES THINGS FOR THE MITOU FAMILY.
MORIYA
RYUUSEI'S KAMI-SAMA. HE'S GREAT AT HIS JOB, BECAUSE HE LEAVES ALL THE WORK TO RYUUSEI AND DOESN'T LIFT A FINGER.
HIMI
RETURNED TO HAKUSHI, BUT WAS RESURRECTED. HE IS NOW OFFICIALLY GENMA'S KAMI-SAMA.
GENMA YASHIRO
DETESTED BY HIS FATHER WHO WAS A KOTODAMASHI, HE WAS RAISED OUTSIDE OF THE FAMILY. HE LATER INHERITED HIMI, HIS FATHER'S KAMI-SAMA. HE SAW HIMI DIE AND RETURN TO HAKUSHI, BUT HIMI HAS SINCE BEEN RESURRECTED. HIMI IS NOW HIS OWN.
KOTODAMA-SAMA – THOSE WHO CARRY THE BLOOD OF THE MITOU FAMILY AND HAVE THE ABILITY TO USE KOTODAMA TO SUBDUE AND ATTACK OTHERS. WHEN USING KOTODAMA, THE USER SUFFERS PERSONAL DAMAGE, BUT LIVING DOLLS, "KAMI," CAN TRANSFER THAT INJURY TO THEMSELVES. IN ONE LIFETIME, THEY ARE GENERALLY ASSIGNED ONE KOTODAMA-SAMA. AS LONG AS THEIR MASTERS ARE PRESENT, THEY HAVE THE ABILITY TO TAKE OTHERS' INJURIES, TOO. THE PERSON WHO MAKES KAMI-SAMA IS WAKI, THE DOLL MAKER FOR THE MITOU FAMILY. HE PAIRS UP EVERY KOTODAMA-SAMA AND KAMI-SAMA. WAKI HOLDS A MAINTENANCE SESSION ONCE A YEAR, WHICH RYUUSEI AND MORIYA WERE LATE FOR. THIS IS THEIR STORY...

ZE是 5

Translation / Leona Wong

Senior Editor / Stephanie Donnelly

Graphic Design / Matt A.

Lettering / Shelby Peak

801 Media, Inc.
www.801media.com
contact@801media.com

ISBN-10: 1-934129-36-4
ISBN-13: 978-1-934129-36-4
First edition printed April 2010

10 9 8 7 6 5 4 3 2 1

Printed in Canada

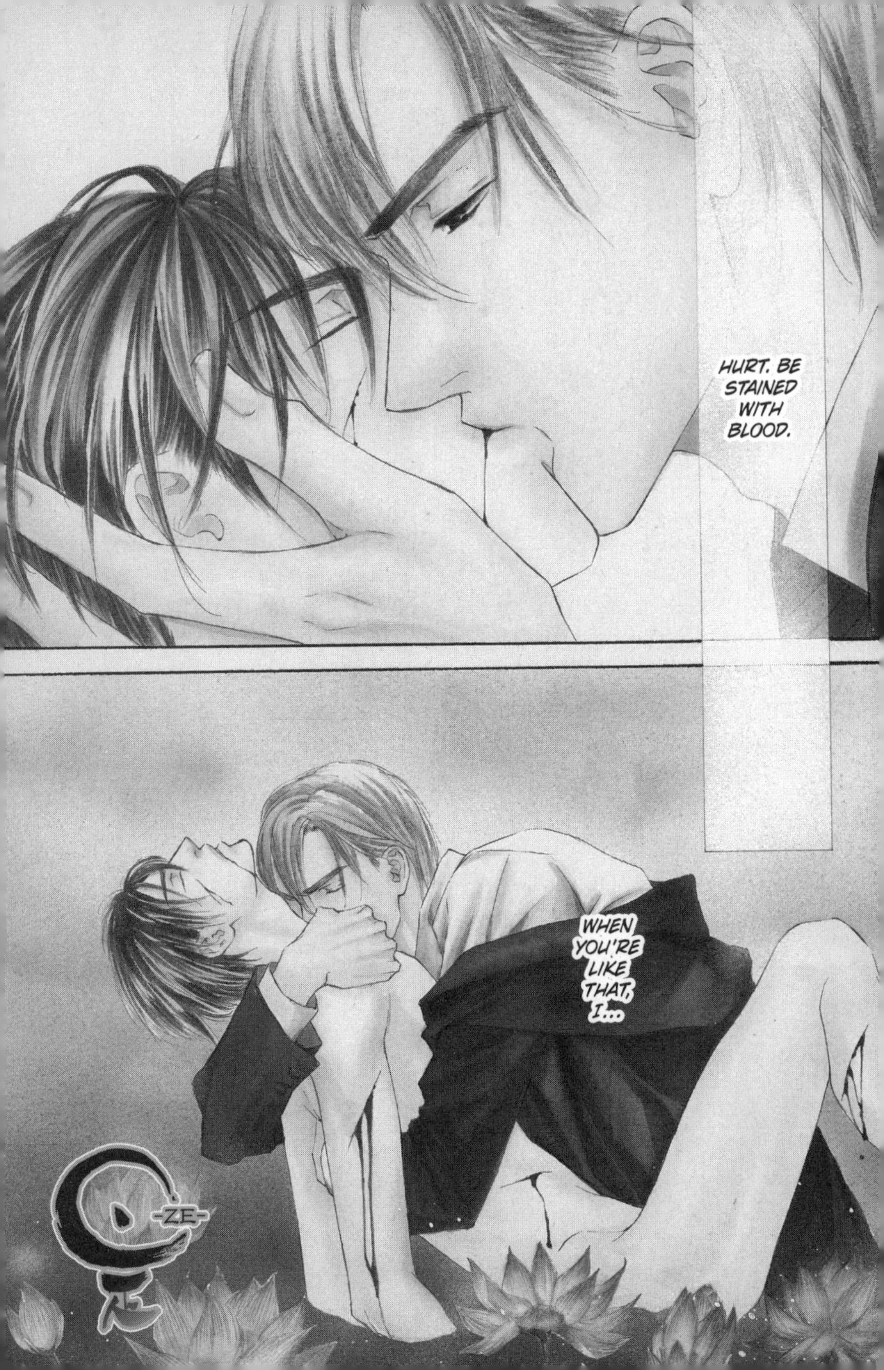
HURT. BE STAINED WITH BLOOD.
WHEN YOU'RE LIKE THAT, I...
-ZE-

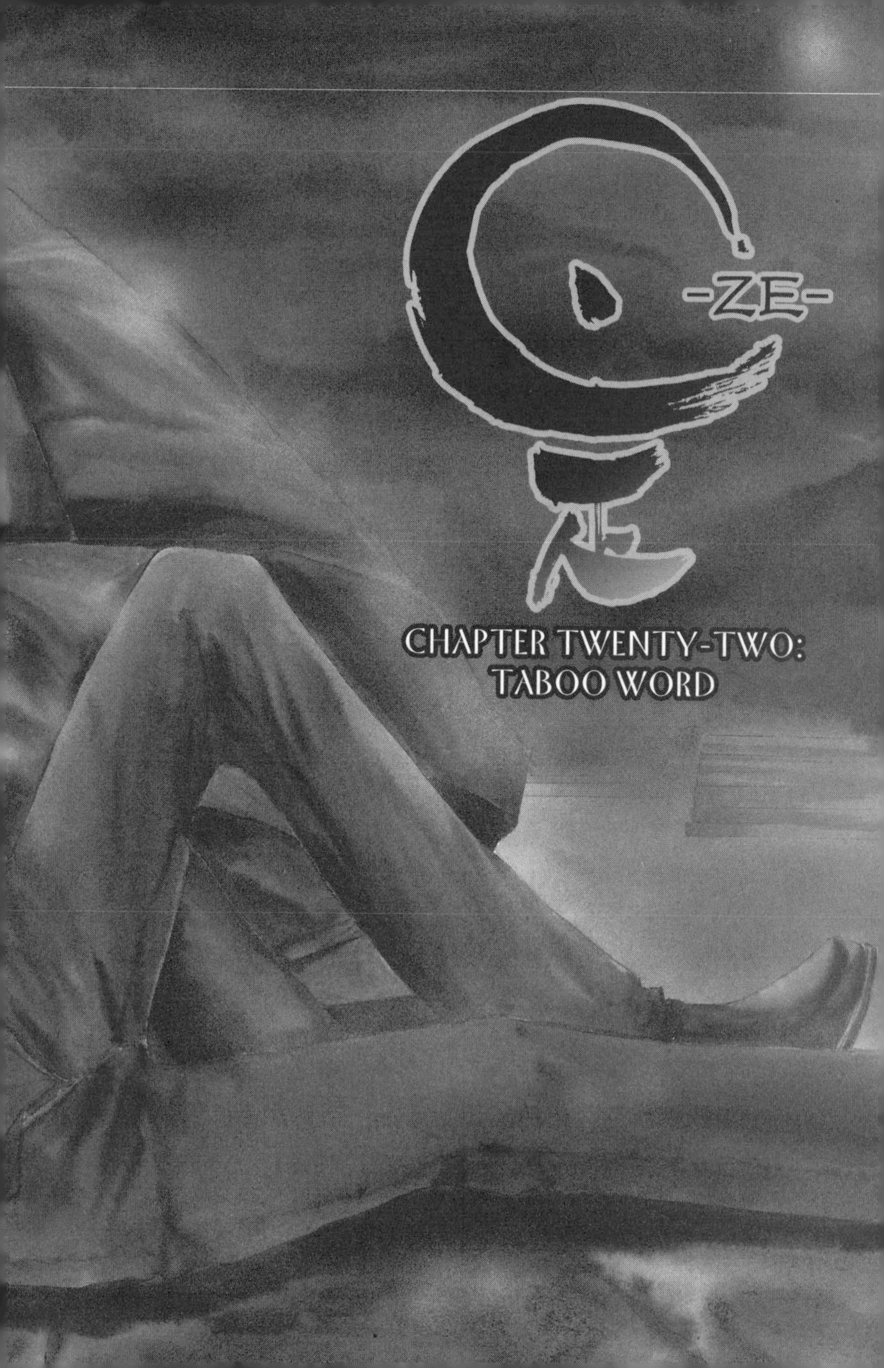
-ZE-

CHAPTER TWENTY-TWO: TABOO WORD

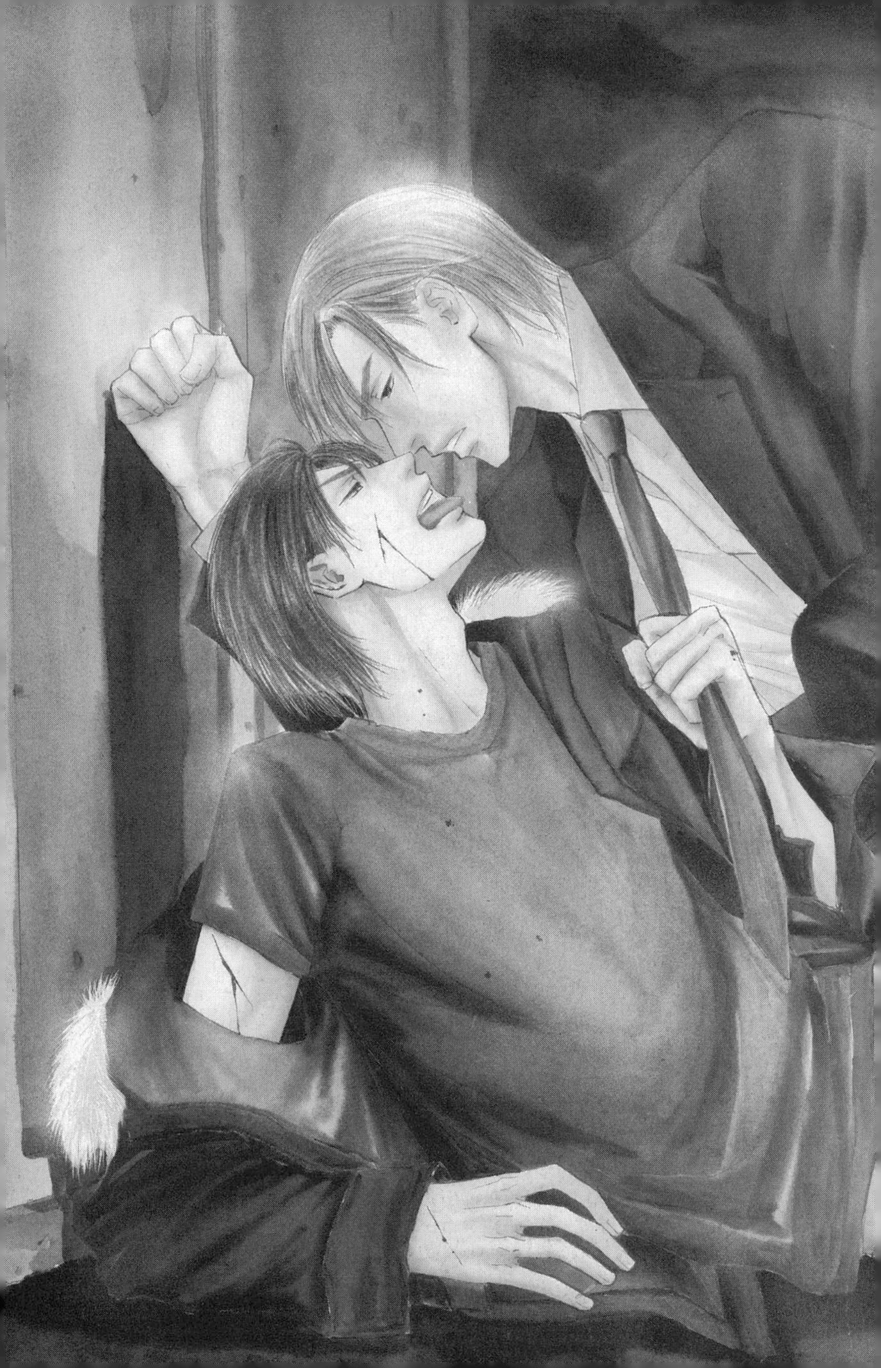

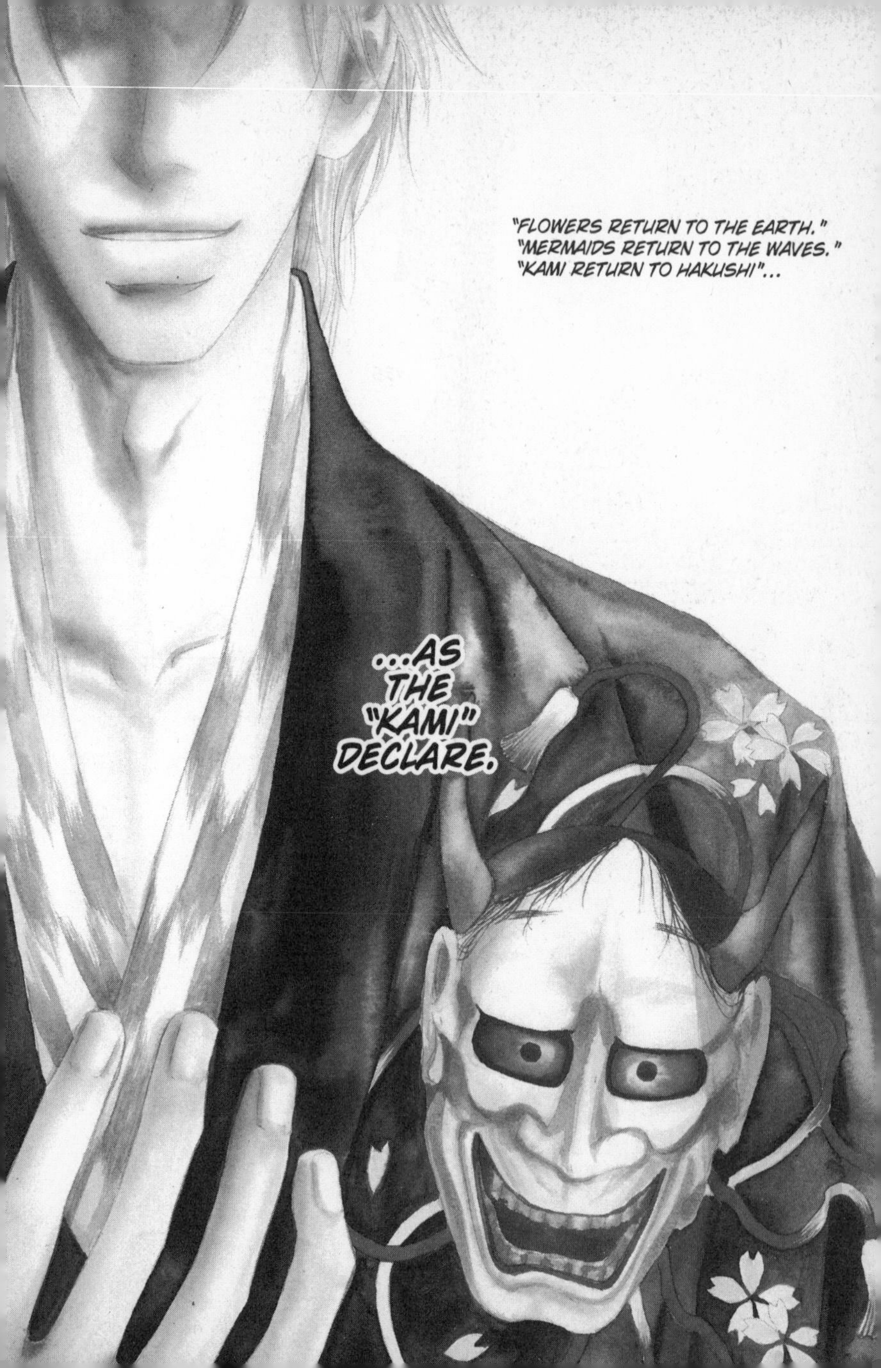
"FLOWERS RETURN TO THE EARTH."
"MERMAIDS RETURN TO THE WAVES."
"KAMI RETURN TO HAKUSHI"...
...AS THE "KAMI" DECLARE.

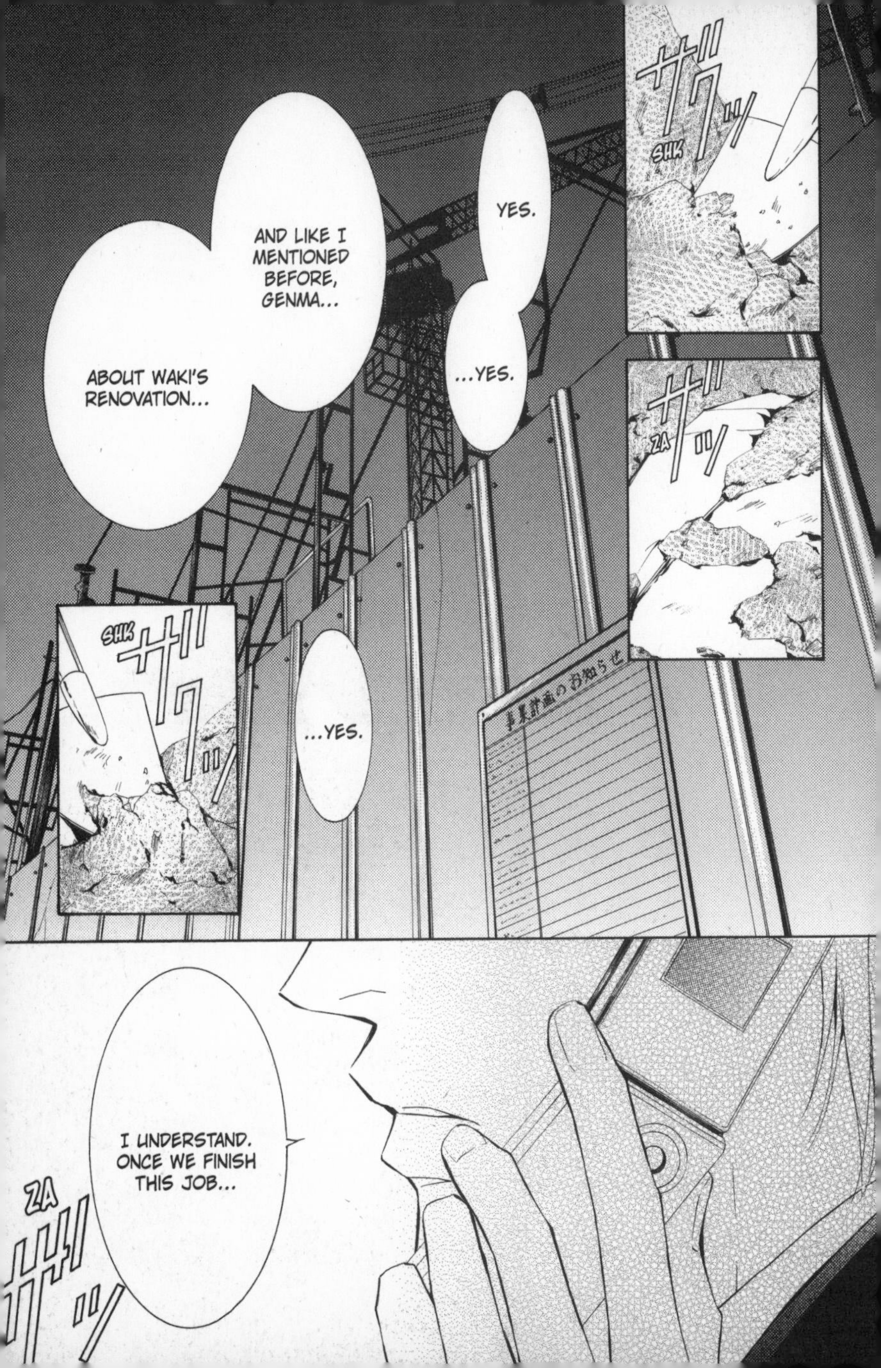
SHK
YES.
AND LIKE I MENTIONED BEFORE, GENMA...
...YES.
ABOUT WAKI'S RENOVATION...
ZA
...YES.
SHK
事業計画のお知らせ
I UNDERSTAND. ONCE WE FINISH THIS JOB...
ZA

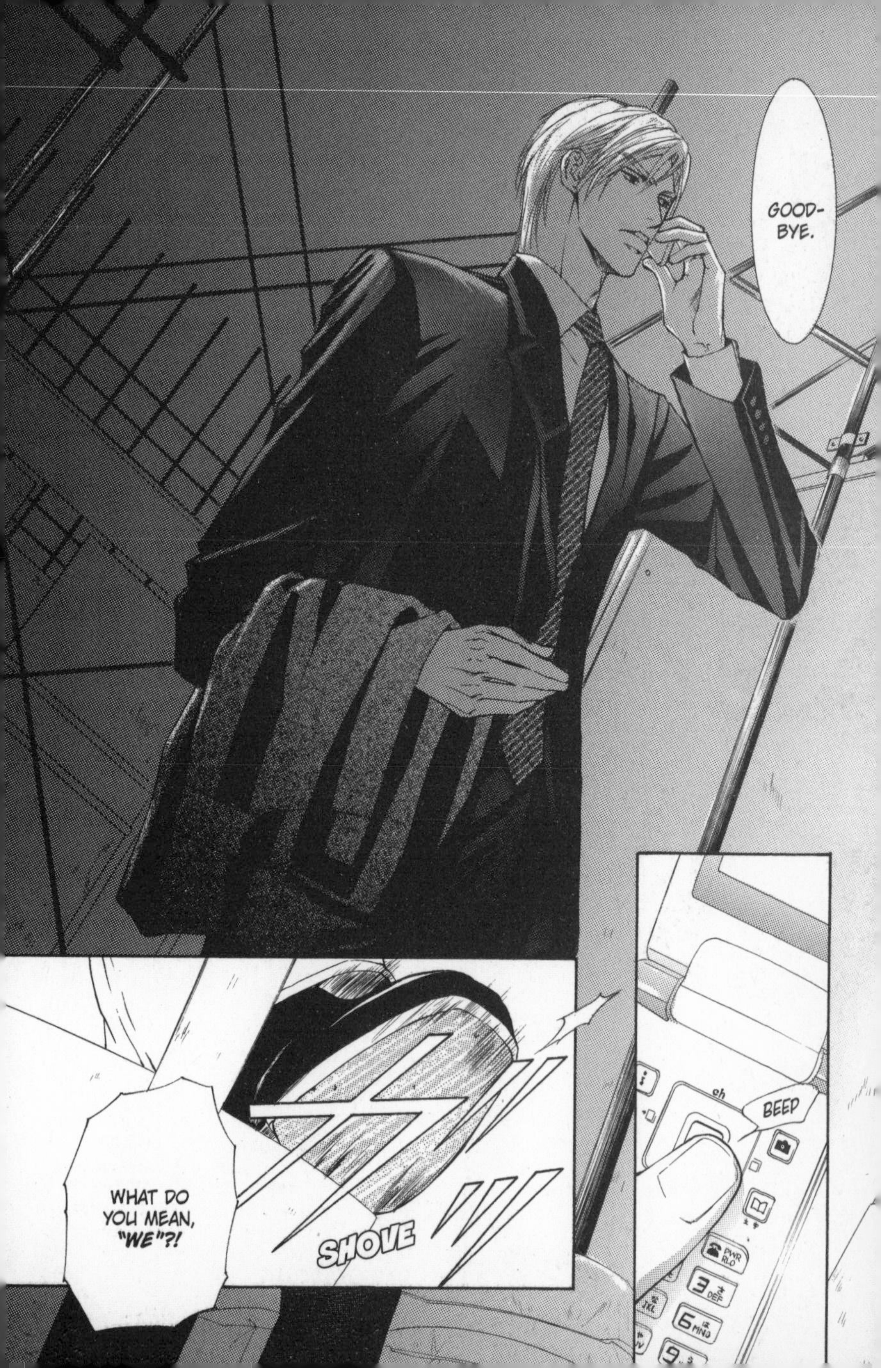
GOOD-BYE.
BEEP
SHOVE
WHAT DO YOU MEAN, "WE"?!

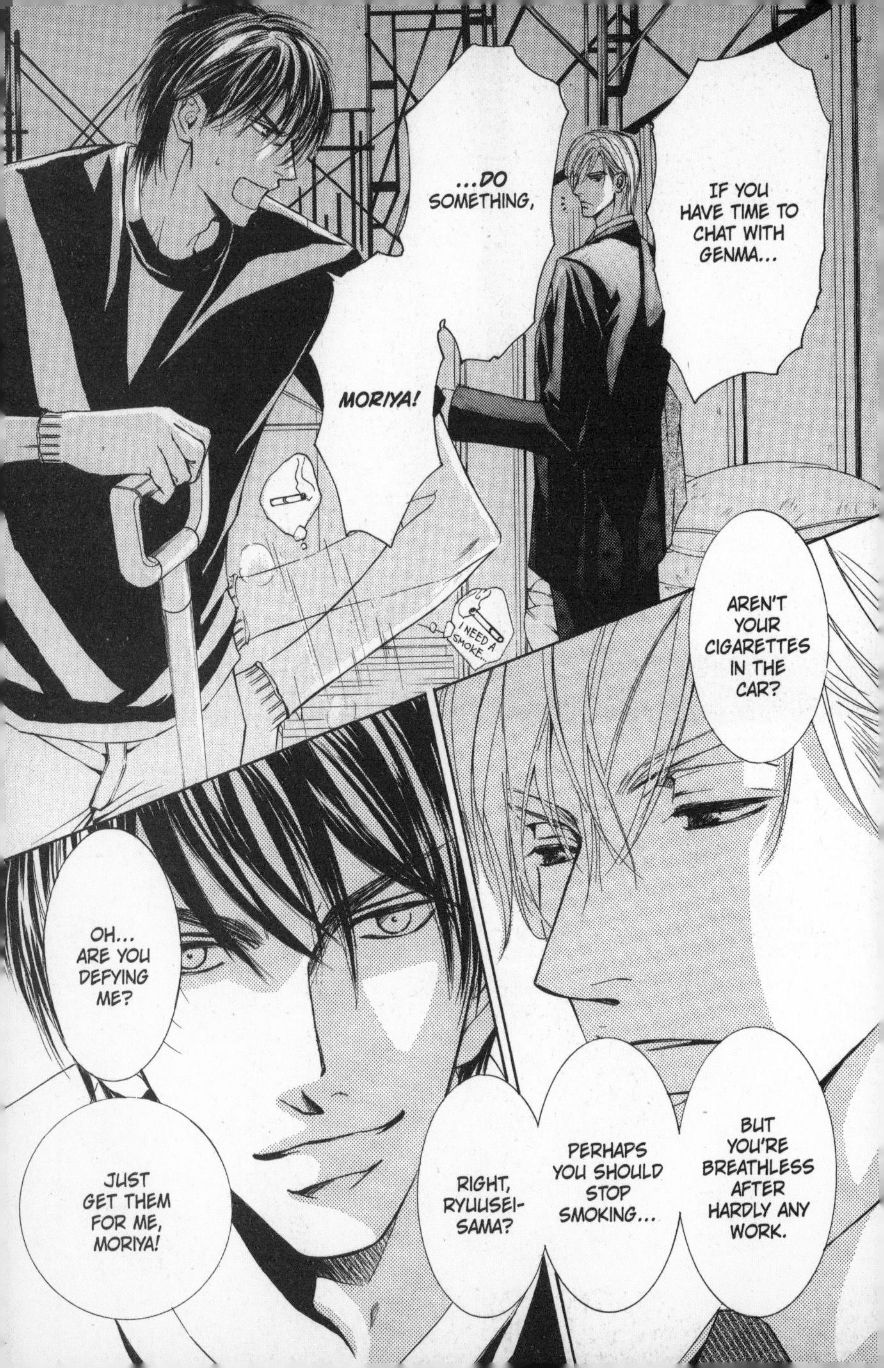
IF YOU HAVE TIME TO CHAT WITH GENMA...
...DO SOMETHING,
MORIYA!
I NEED A SMOKE...
AREN'T YOUR CIGARETTES IN THE CAR?
OH... ARE YOU DEFYING ME?
BUT YOU'RE BREATHLESS AFTER HARDLY ANY WORK.
PERHAPS YOU SHOULD STOP SMOKING...
RIGHT, RYUUSEI-SAMA?
JUST GET THEM FOR ME, MORIYA!

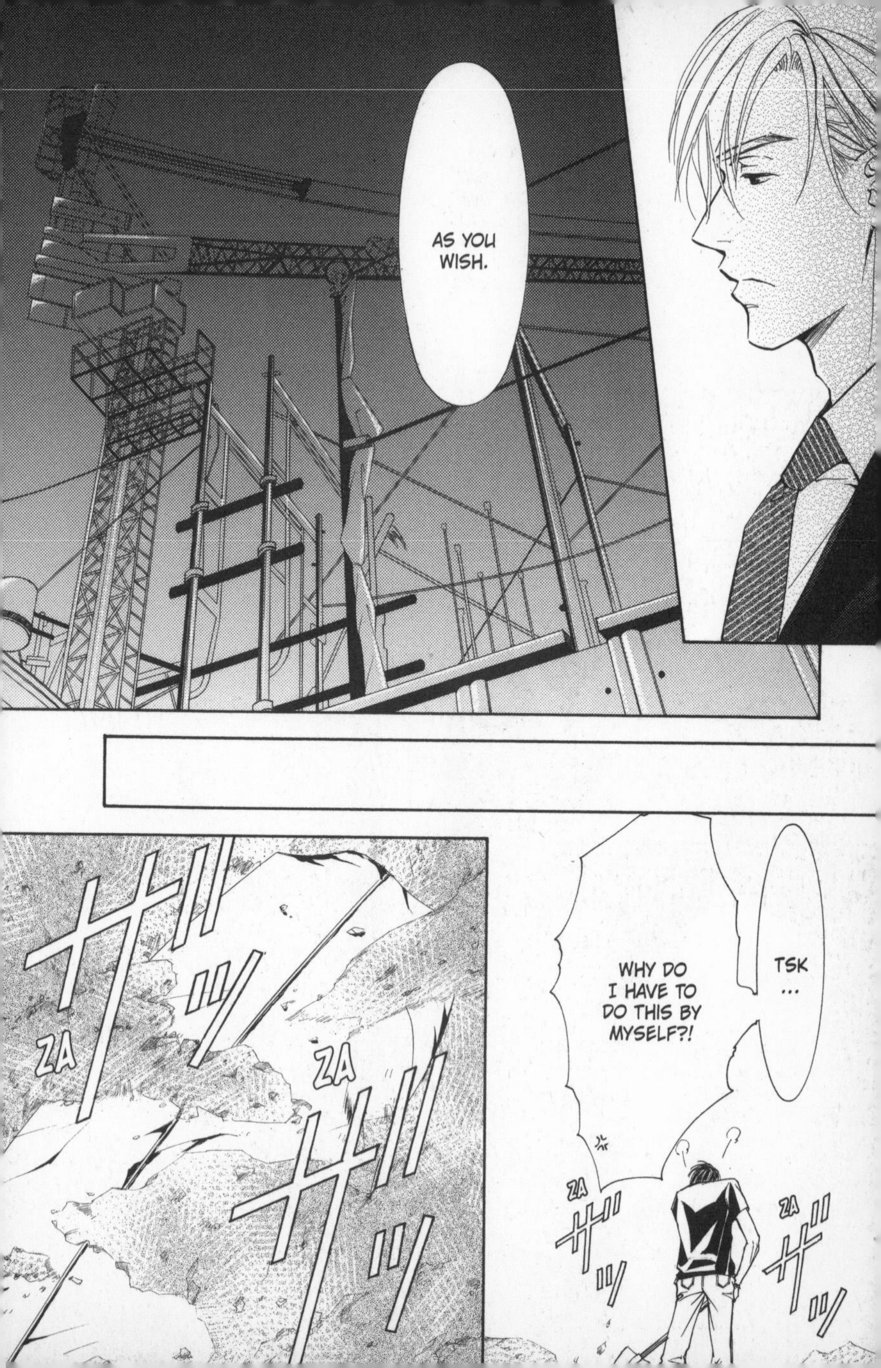
AS YOU WISH.
TSK ...
WHY DO I HAVE TO DO THIS BY MYSELF?!
ZA
ZA
ZA
ZA

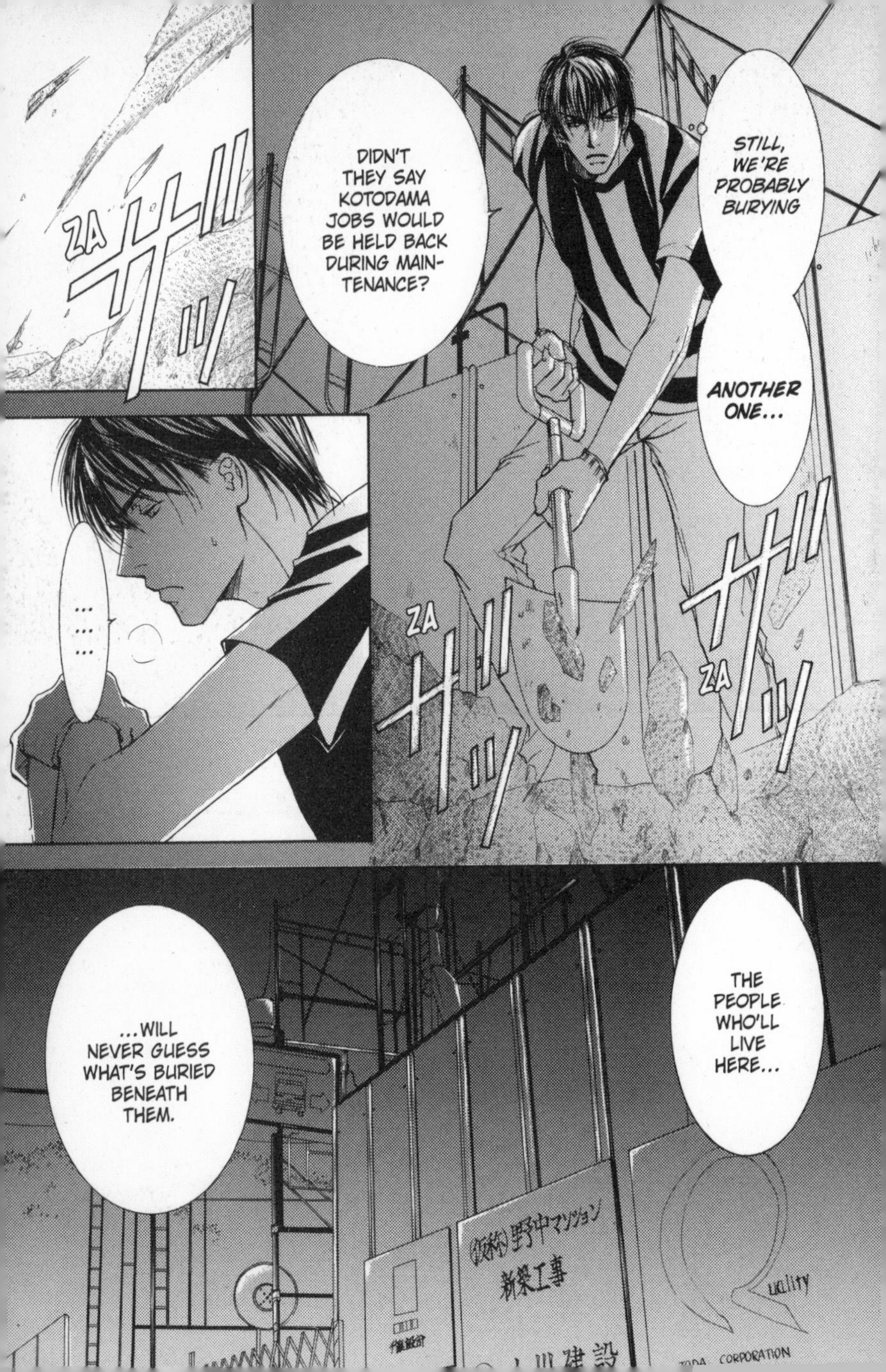
DIDN'T THEY SAY KOTODAMA JOBS WOULD BE HELD BACK DURING MAIN-TENANCE?
STILL, WE'RE PROBABLY BURYING
ANOTHER ONE...
ZA
ZA
ZA
...
...
...
THE PEOPLE WHO'LL LIVE HERE...
...WILL NEVER GUESS WHAT'S BURIED BENEATH THEM.
(仮称)野中マンション
新築工事
TODA CORPORATION

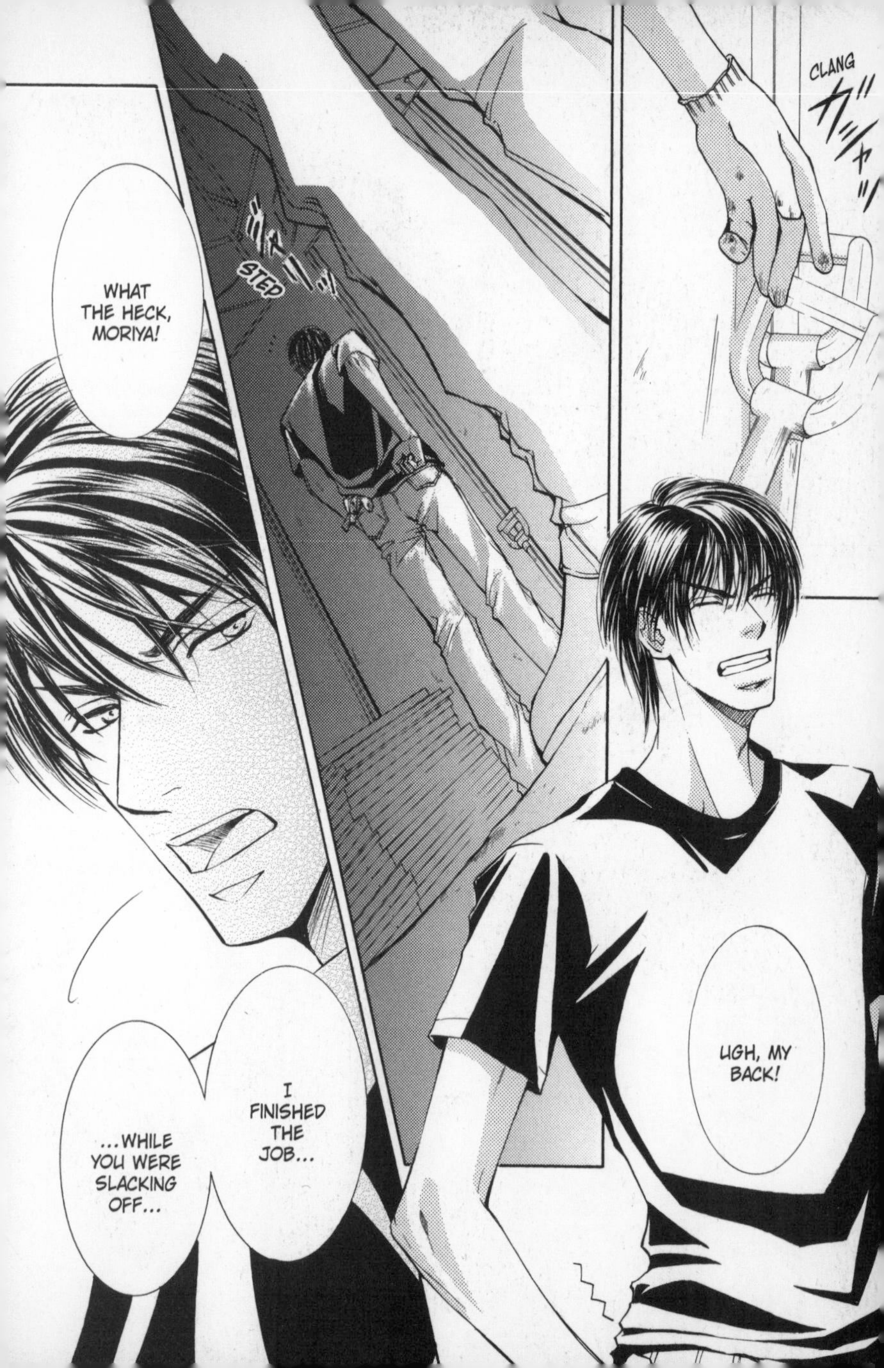
CLANG
UGH, MY BACK!
STEP
WHAT THE HECK, MORIYA!
I FINISHED THE JOB...
...WHILE YOU WERE SLACKING OFF...

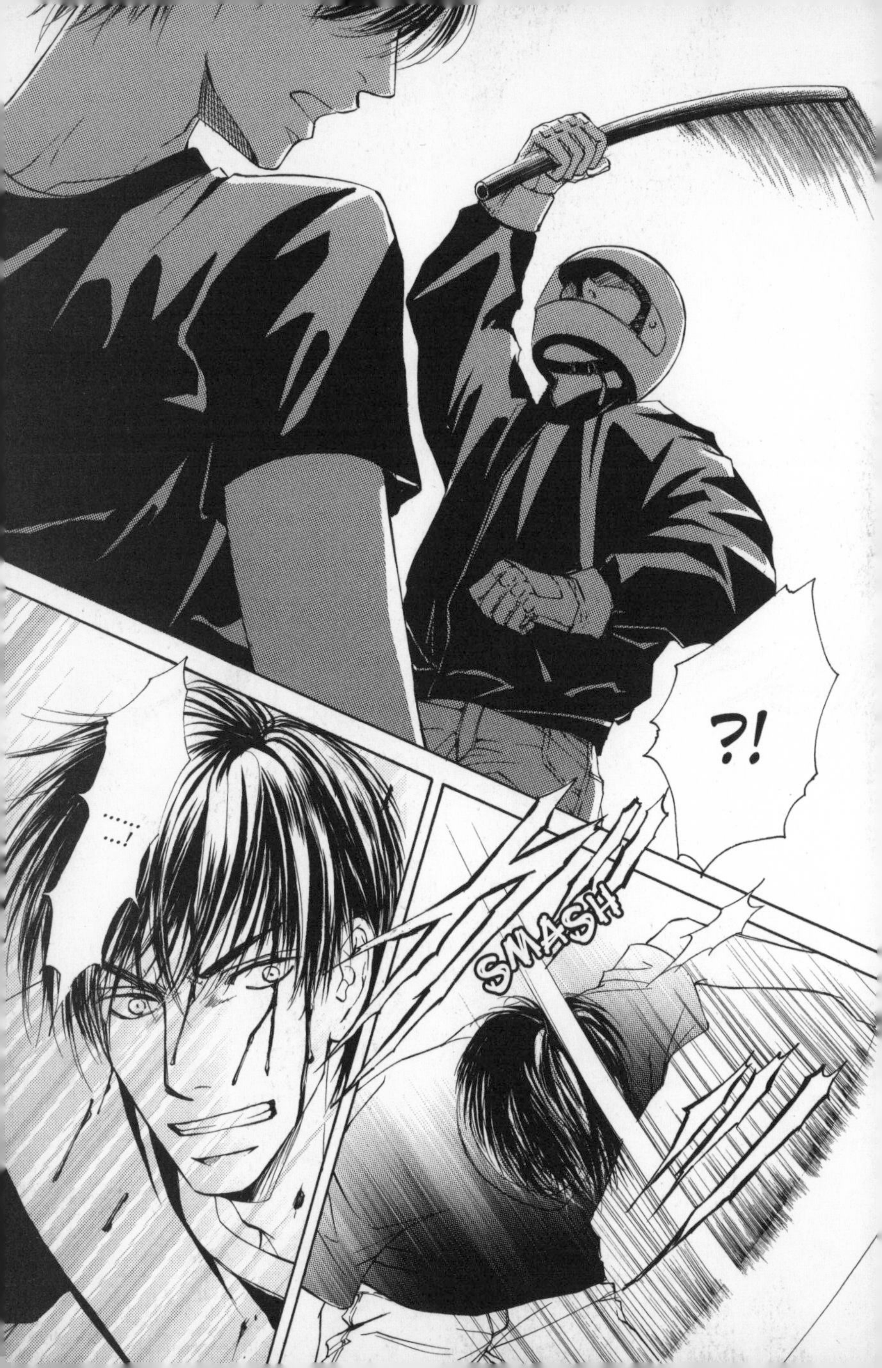
?!
SMASH
......
...!

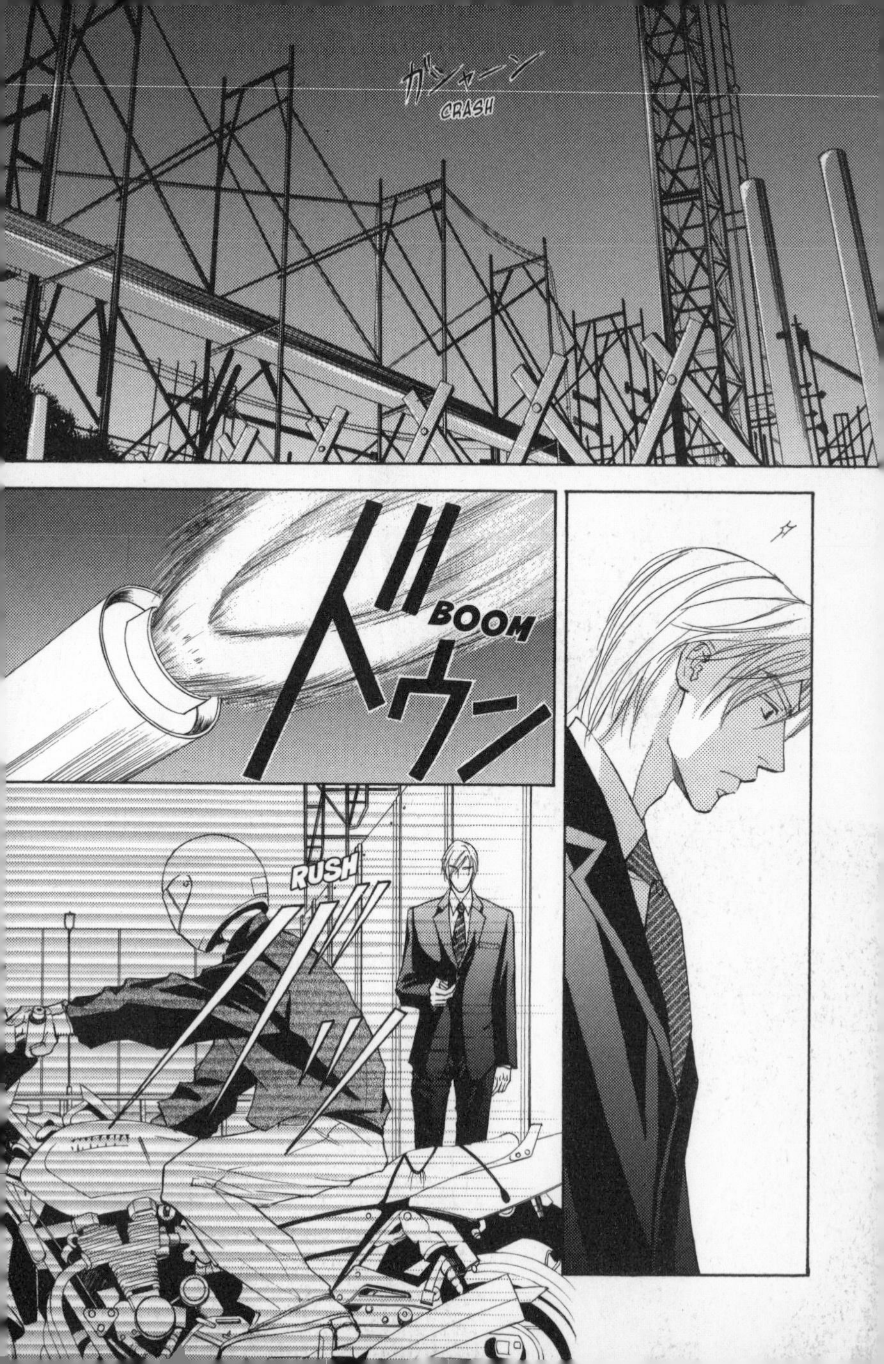
ガシャーン
CRASH
ドウーン
BOOM
RUSH

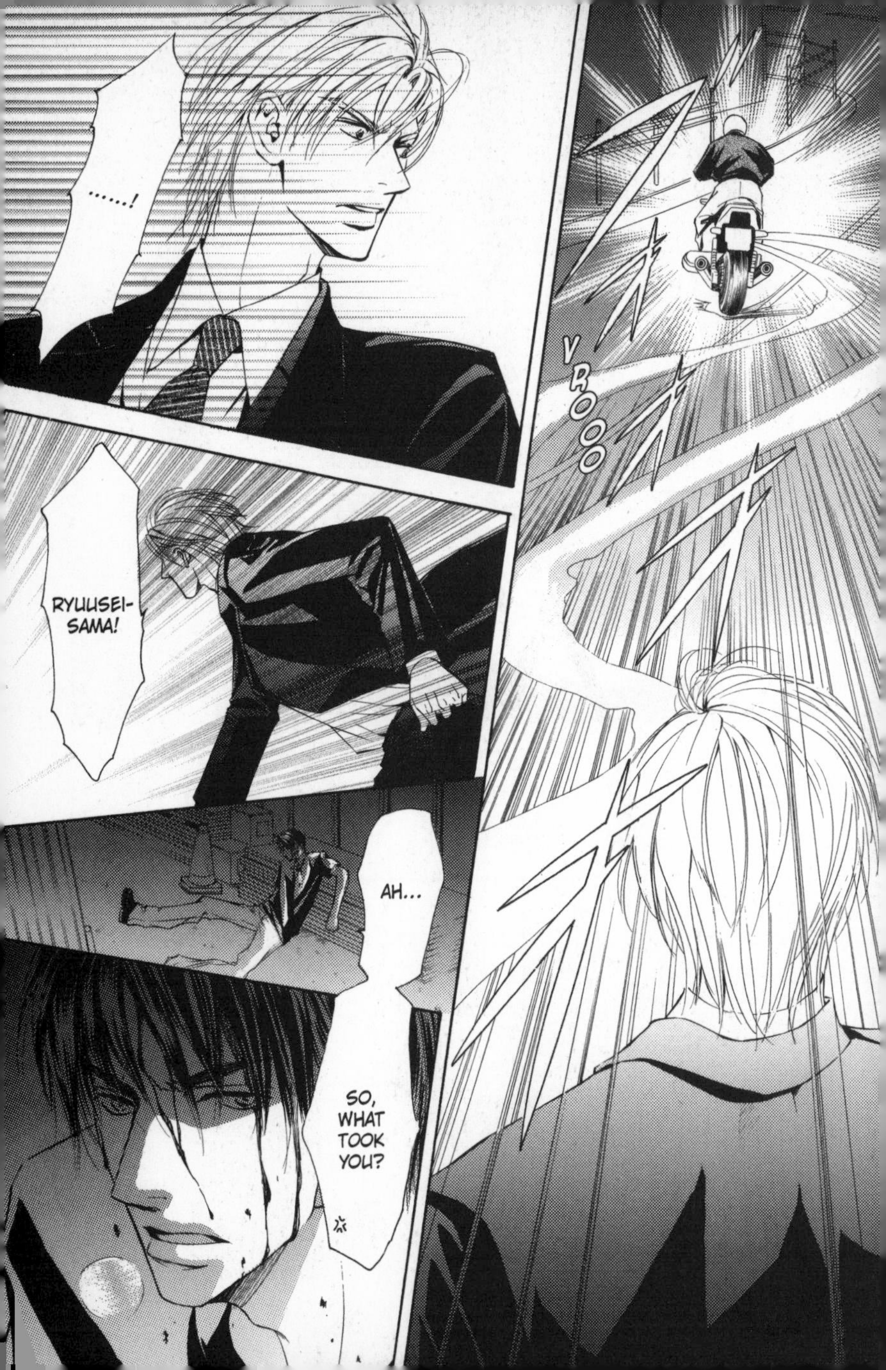
VROOOO
......!
RYUUSEI-SAMA!
AH...
SO, WHAT TOOK YOU?

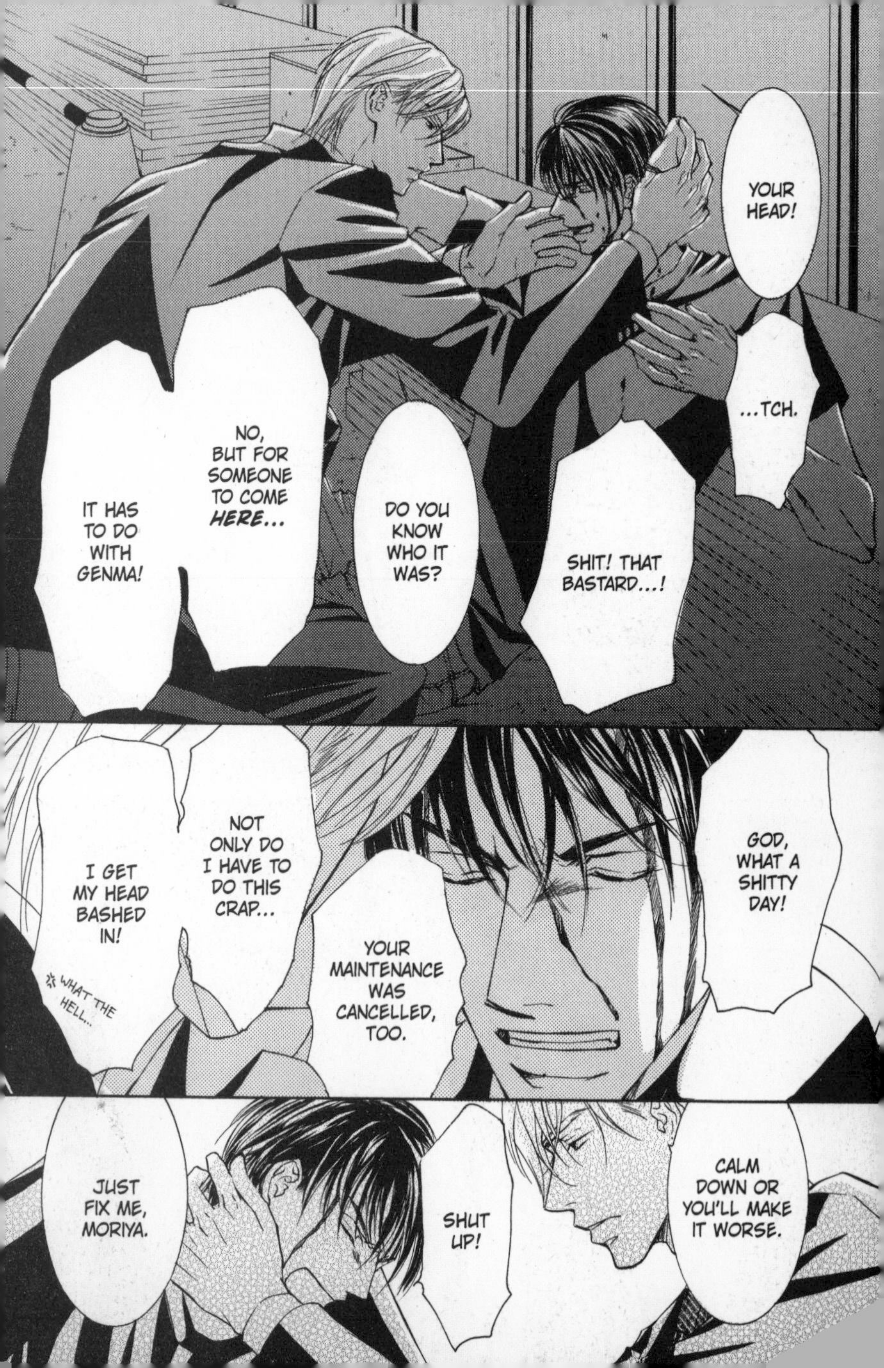
YOUR HEAD!
...TCH.
SHIT! THAT BASTARD...!
DO YOU KNOW WHO IT WAS?
NO, BUT FOR SOMEONE TO COME *HERE*...
IT HAS TO DO WITH GENMA!
GOD, WHAT A SHITTY DAY!
YOUR MAINTENANCE WAS CANCELLED, TOO.
NOT ONLY DO I HAVE TO DO THIS CRAP...
I GET MY HEAD BASHED IN!
WHAT THE HELL...
CALM DOWN OR YOU'LL MAKE IT WORSE.
SHUT UP!
JUST FIX ME, MORIYA.

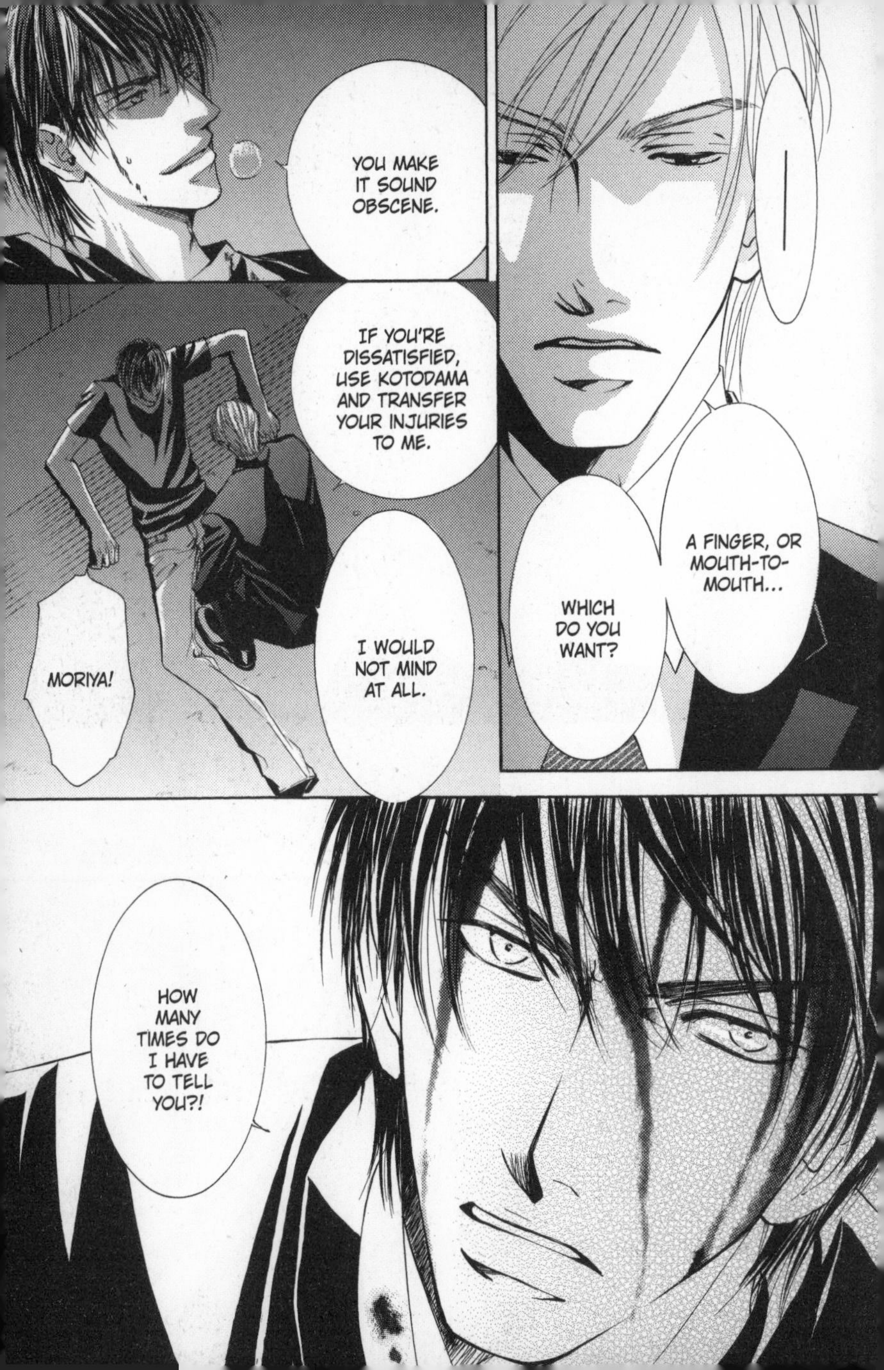
—
A FINGER, OR MOUTH-TO-MOUTH...
WHICH DO YOU WANT?
YOU MAKE IT SOUND OBSCENE.
IF YOU'RE DISSATISFIED, USE KOTODAMA AND TRANSFER YOUR INJURIES TO ME.
I WOULD NOT MIND AT ALL.
MORIYA!
HOW MANY TIMES DO I HAVE TO TELL YOU?!

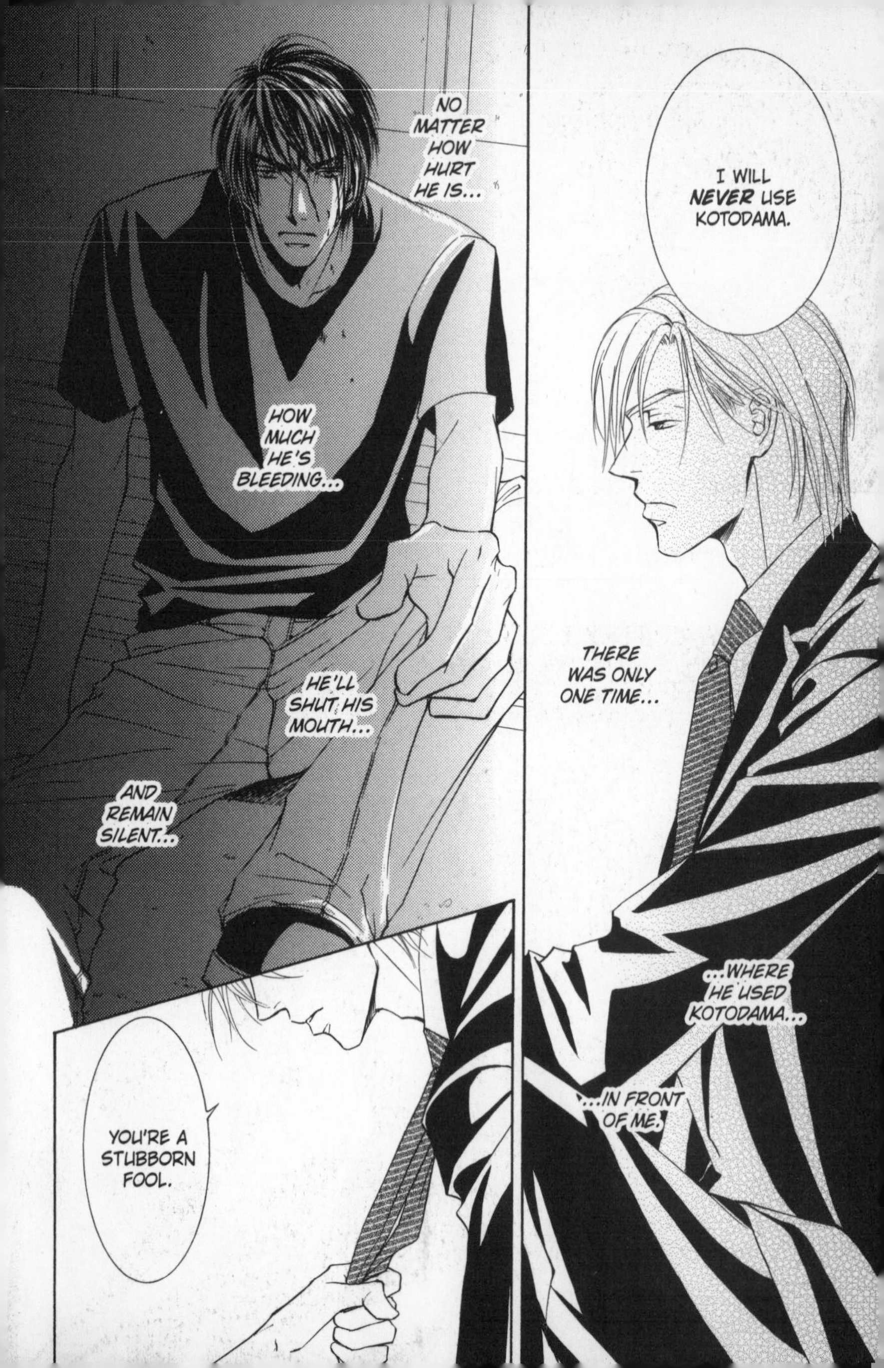
I WILL NEVER USE KOTODAMA.
THERE WAS ONLY ONE TIME...
...WHERE HE USED KOTODAMA...
...IN FRONT OF ME.
NO MATTER HOW HURT HE IS...
HOW MUCH HE'S BLEEDING...
HE'LL SHUT HIS MOUTH...
AND REMAIN SILENT...
YOU'RE A STUBBORN FOOL.

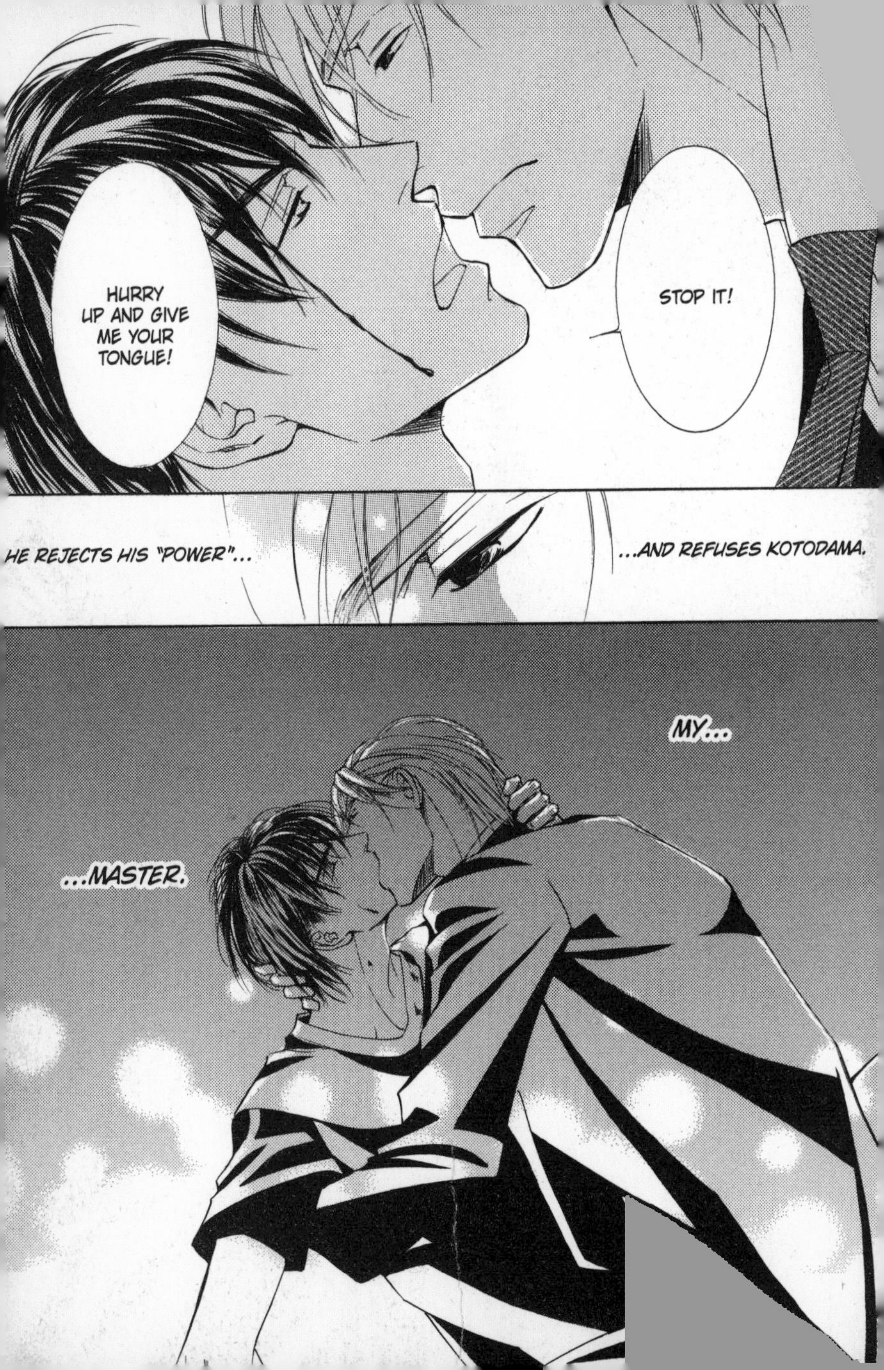
STOP IT!
HURRY UP AND GIVE ME YOUR TONGUE!
...AND REFUSES KOTODAMA.
HE REJECTS HIS "POWER"...
MY...
...MASTER.

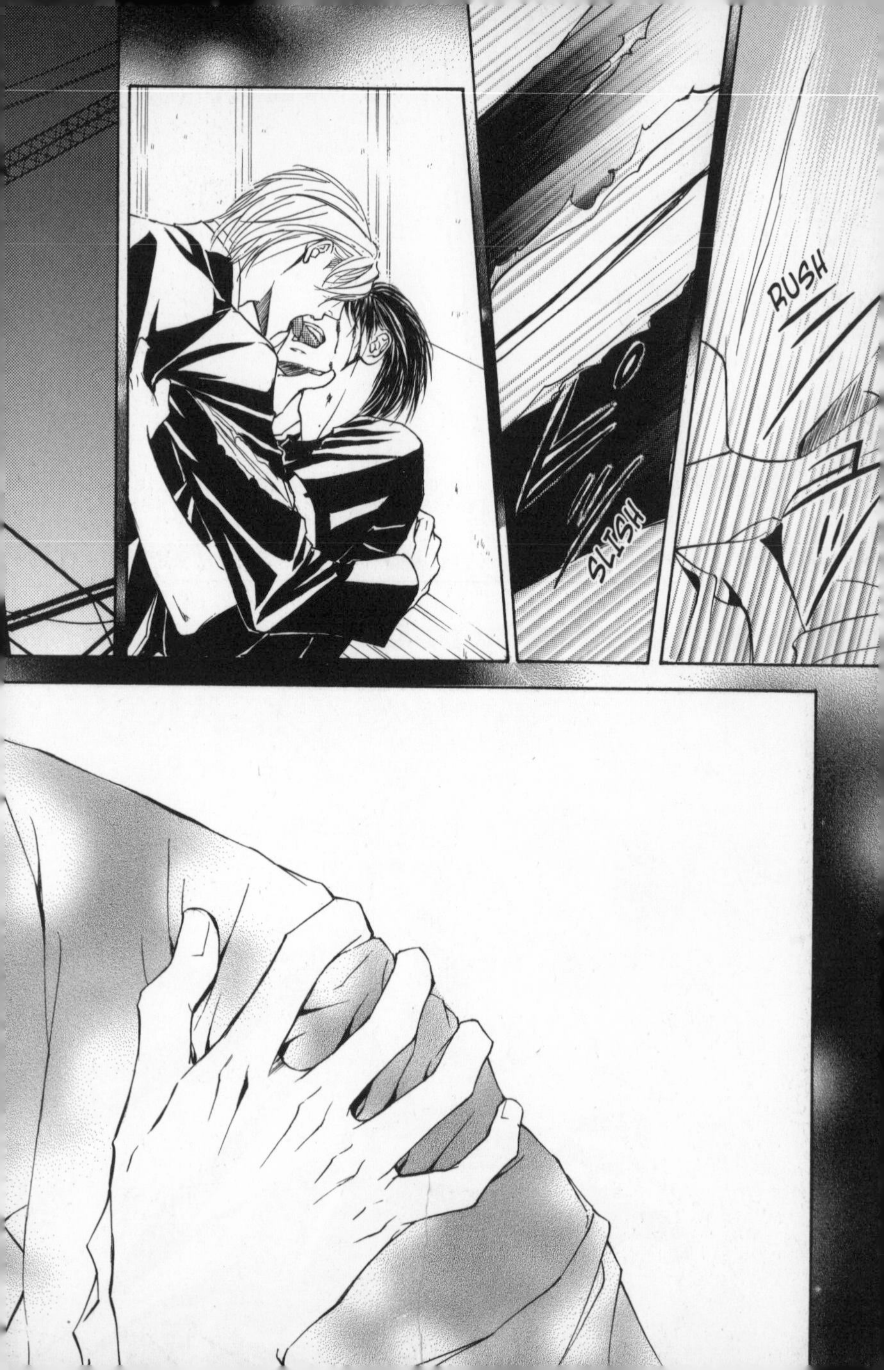
RUSH
SLISH

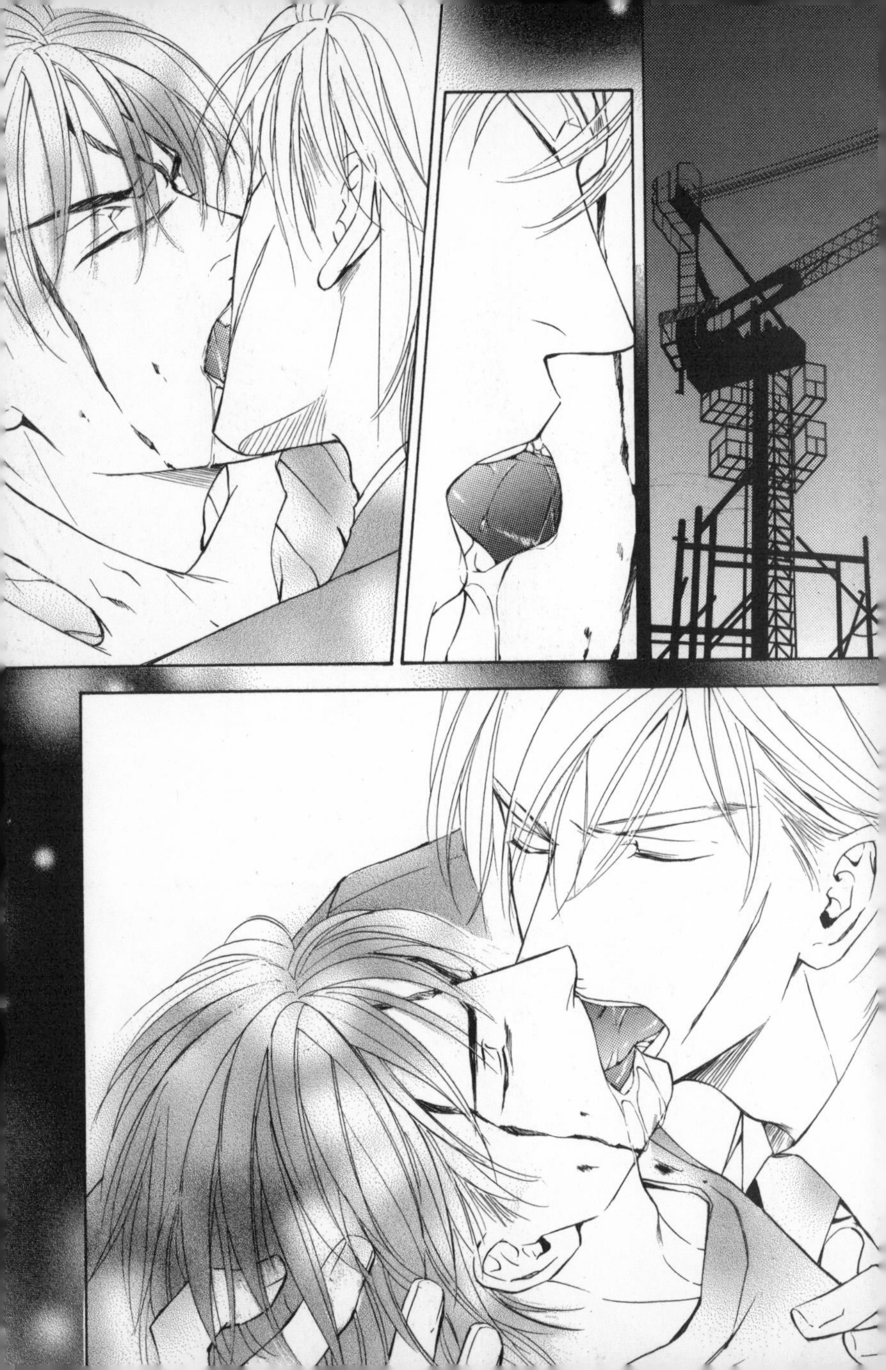

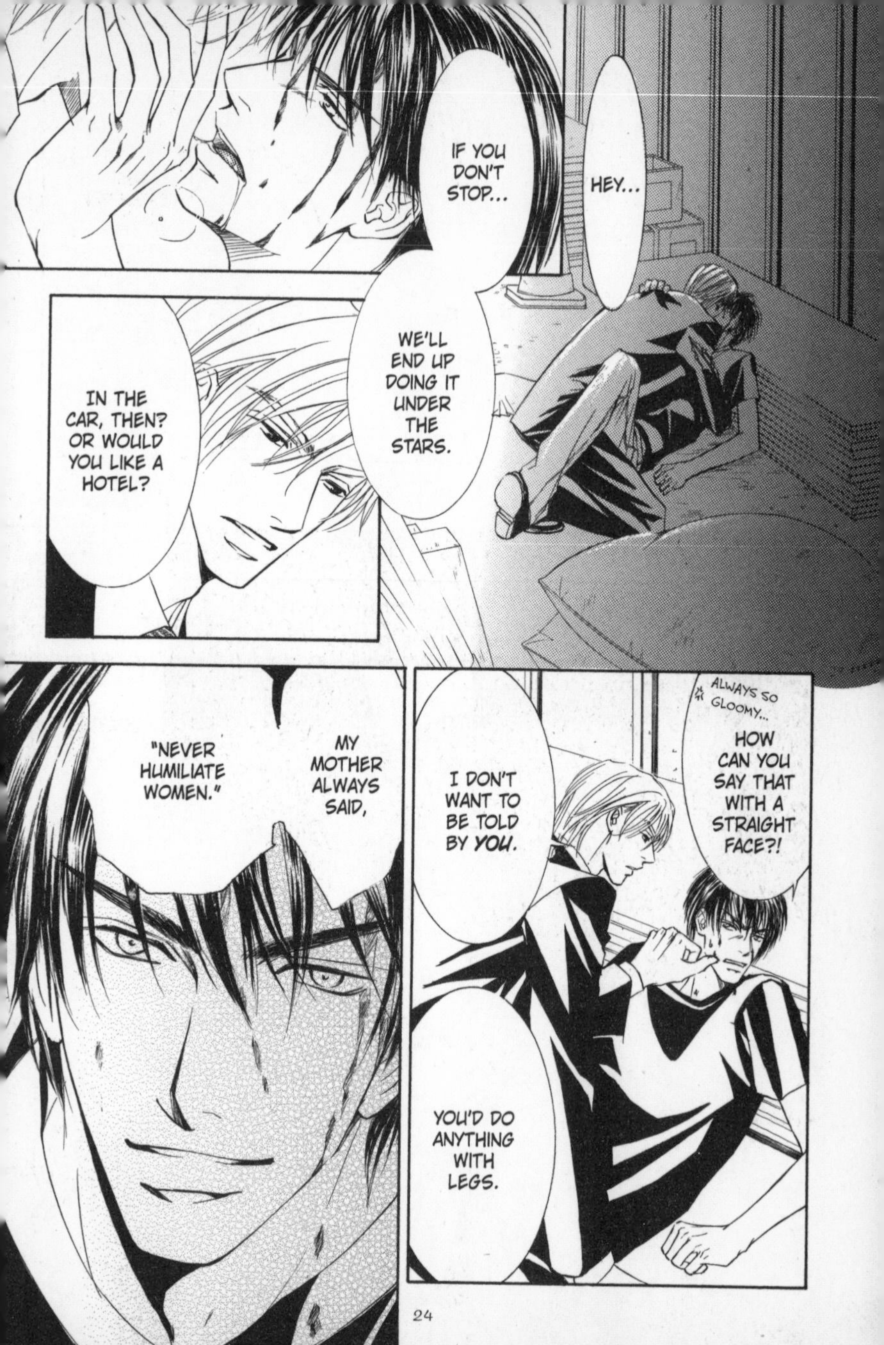
HEY...
IF YOU DON'T STOP...
WE'LL END UP DOING IT UNDER THE STARS.
IN THE CAR, THEN? OR WOULD YOU LIKE A HOTEL?
ALWAYS SO GLOOMY...
HOW CAN YOU SAY THAT WITH A STRAIGHT FACE?!
I DON'T WANT TO BE TOLD BY *YOU*.
YOU'D DO ANYTHING WITH LEGS.
MY MOTHER ALWAYS SAID,
"NEVER HUMILIATE WOMEN."

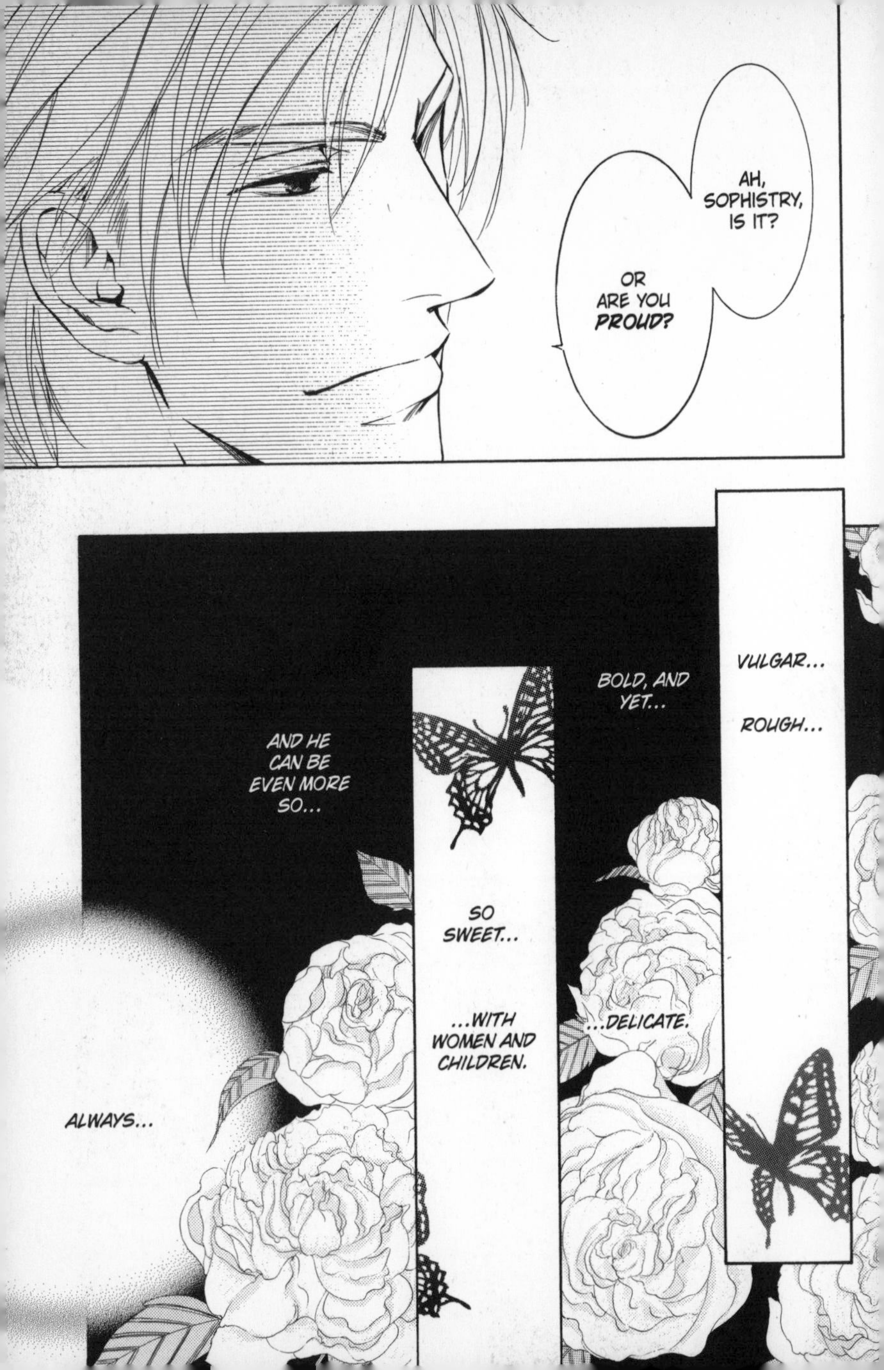
AH, SOPHISTRY, IS IT?
OR ARE YOU *PROUD?*
VULGAR...
ROUGH...
BOLD, AND YET...
...DELICATE.
SO SWEET...
...WITH WOMEN AND CHILDREN.
AND HE CAN BE EVEN MORE SO...
ALWAYS...

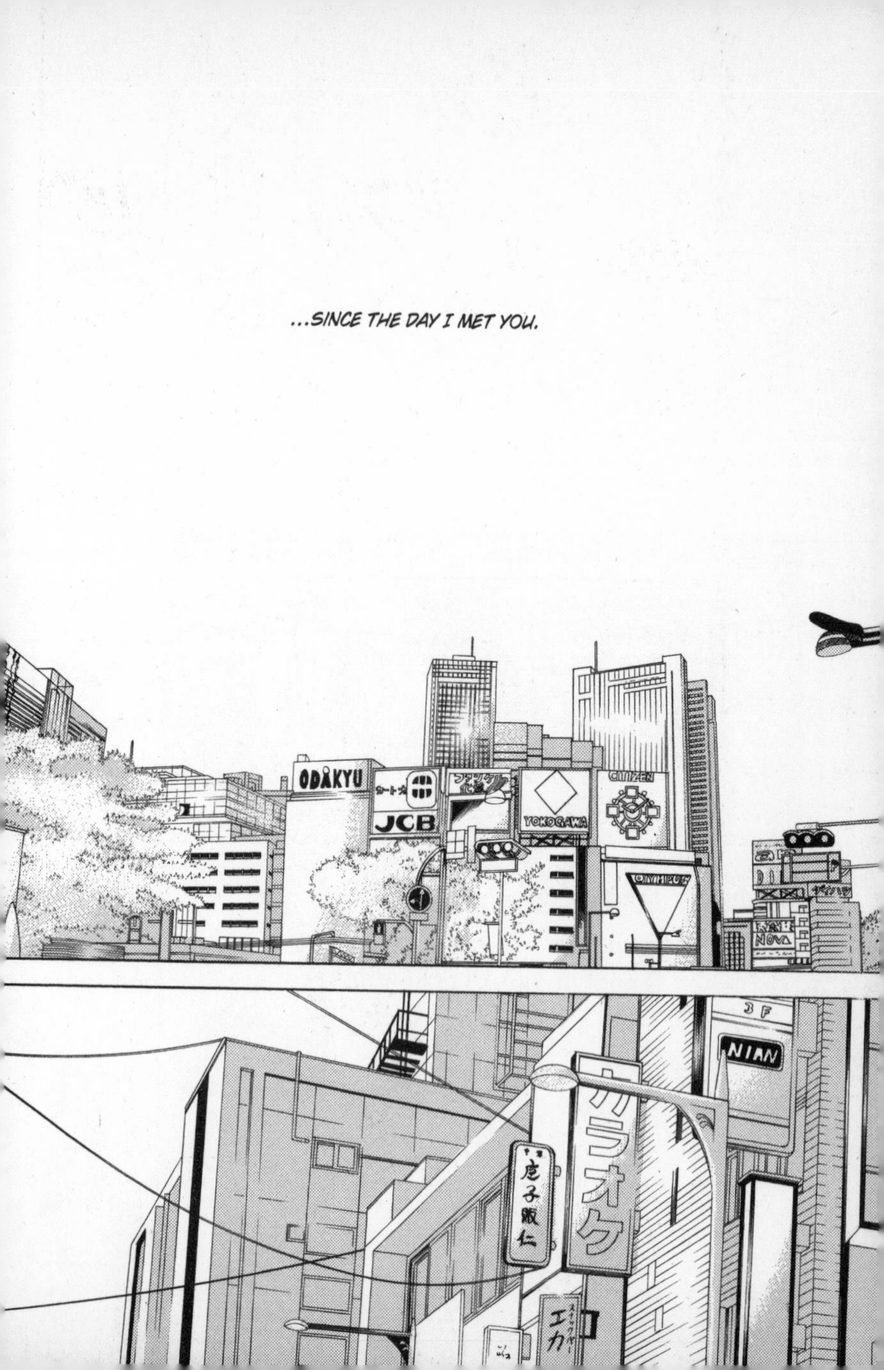
...SINCE THE DAY I MET YOU.
ODAKYU
JCB
YOKOGAWA
CITIZEN
OLYMPUS
NOVA
3F
NIAN
カラオケ

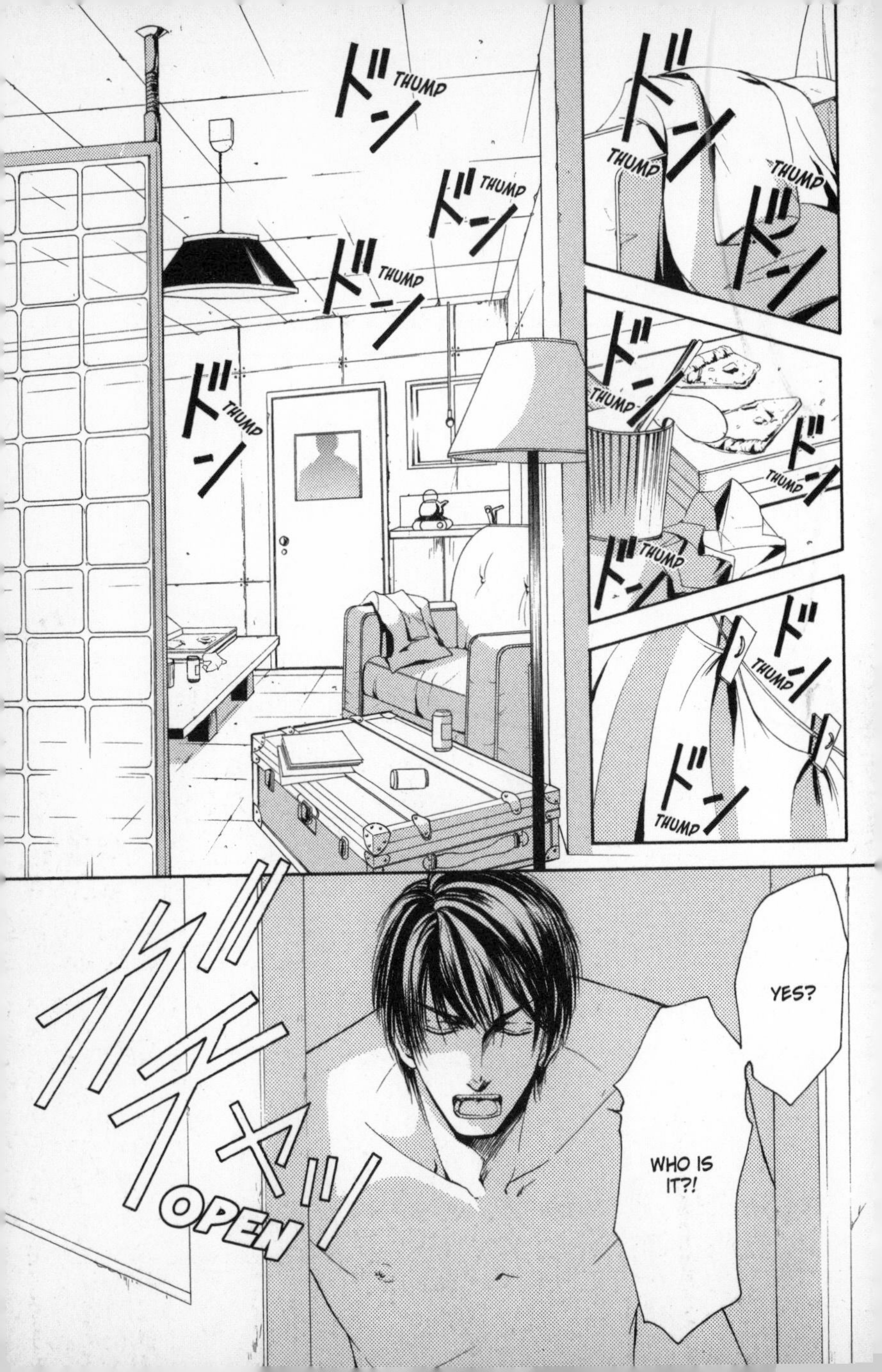

ドン THUMP
THUMP ドン
ドン THUMP
ドン THUMP
ドン THUMP
ドン THUMP
ドン THUMP
ドン THUMP
ドン THUMP
ドン THUMP
ドン THUMP
OPEN
YES?
WHO IS IT?!

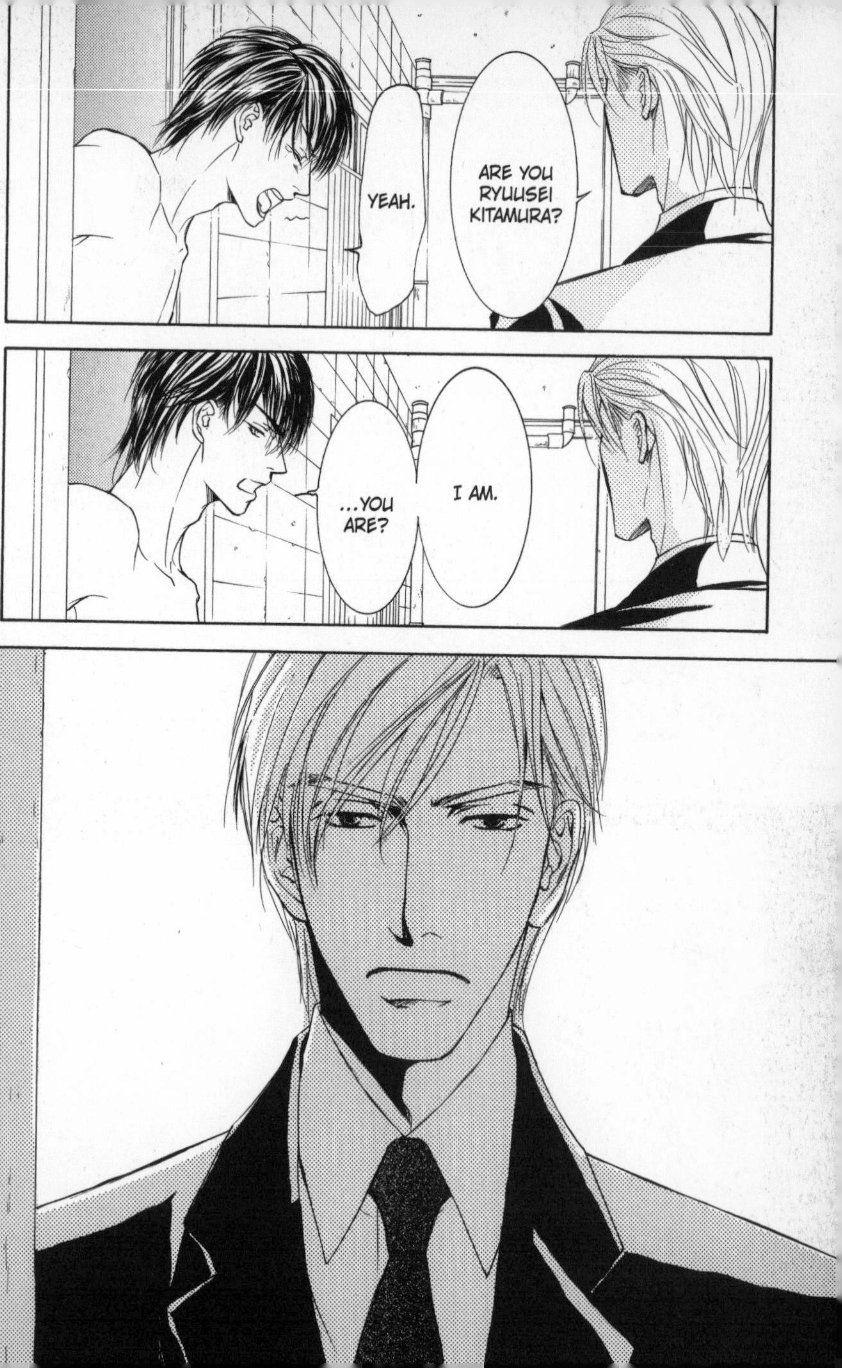
ARE YOU RYUUSEI KITAMURA?
YEAH.
I AM.
...YOU ARE?

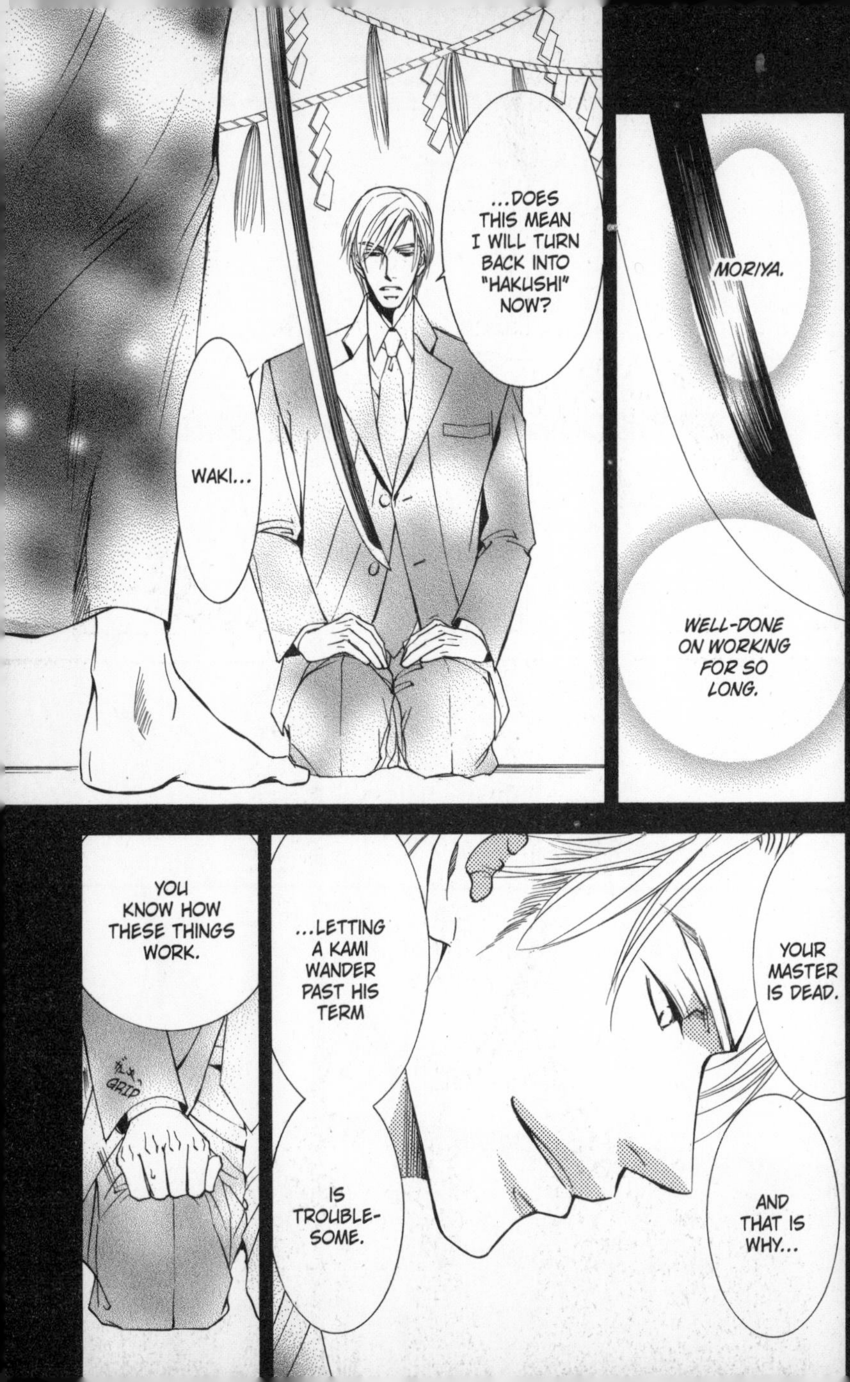
MORIYA.
WELL-DONE ON WORKING FOR SO LONG.
...DOES THIS MEAN I WILL TURN BACK INTO "HAKUSHI" NOW?
WAKI...
YOUR MASTER IS DEAD.
AND THAT IS WHY...
...LETTING A KAMI WANDER PAST HIS TERM
IS TROUBLESOME.
YOU KNOW HOW THESE THINGS WORK.
GRIP

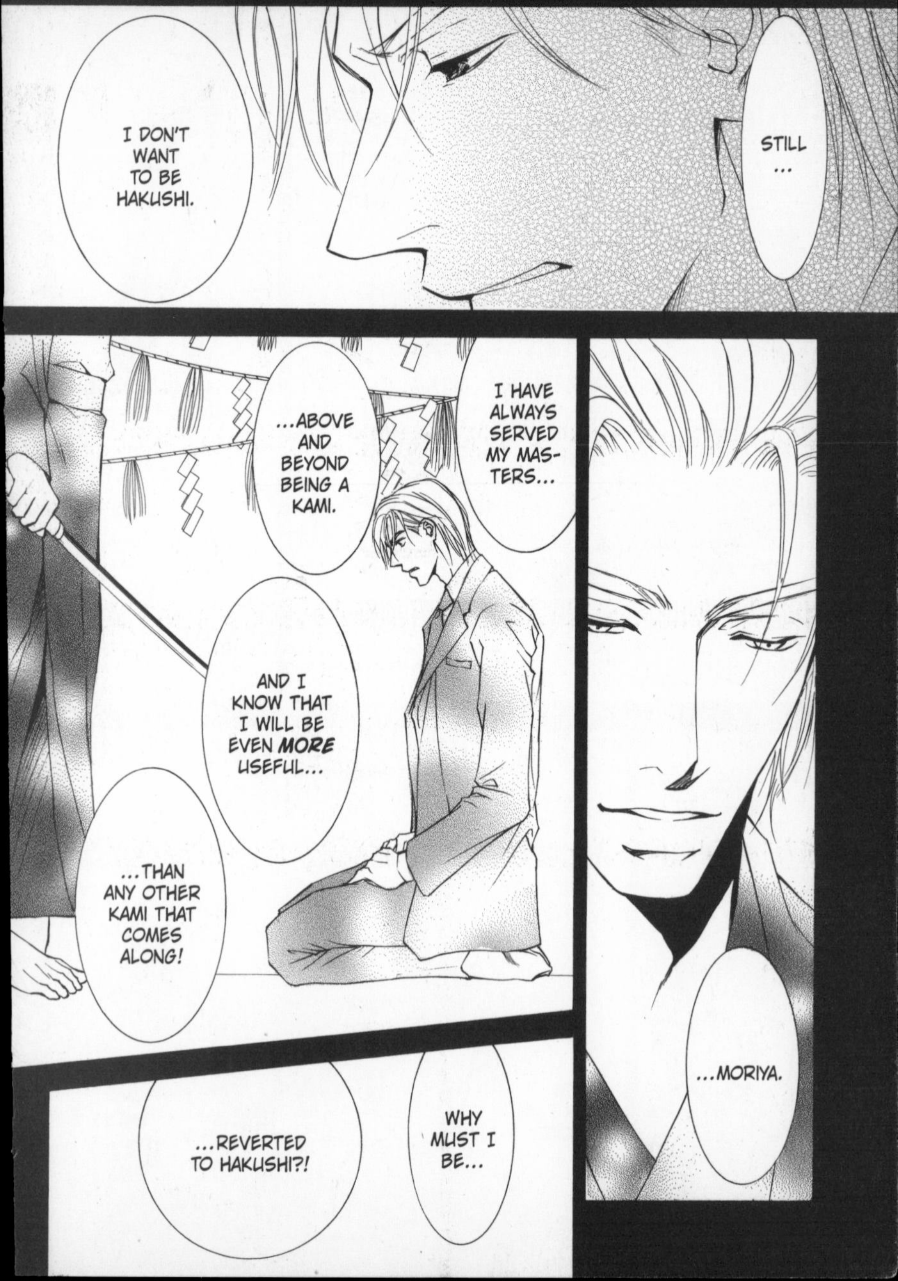
STILL ...
I DON'T WANT TO BE HAKUSHI.
...MORIYA.
I HAVE ALWAYS SERVED MY MAS- TERS...
...ABOVE AND BEYOND BEING A KAMI.
AND I KNOW THAT I WILL BE EVEN *MORE* USEFUL...
...THAN ANY OTHER KAMI THAT COMES ALONG!
WHY MUST I BE...
...REVERTED TO HAKUSHI?!

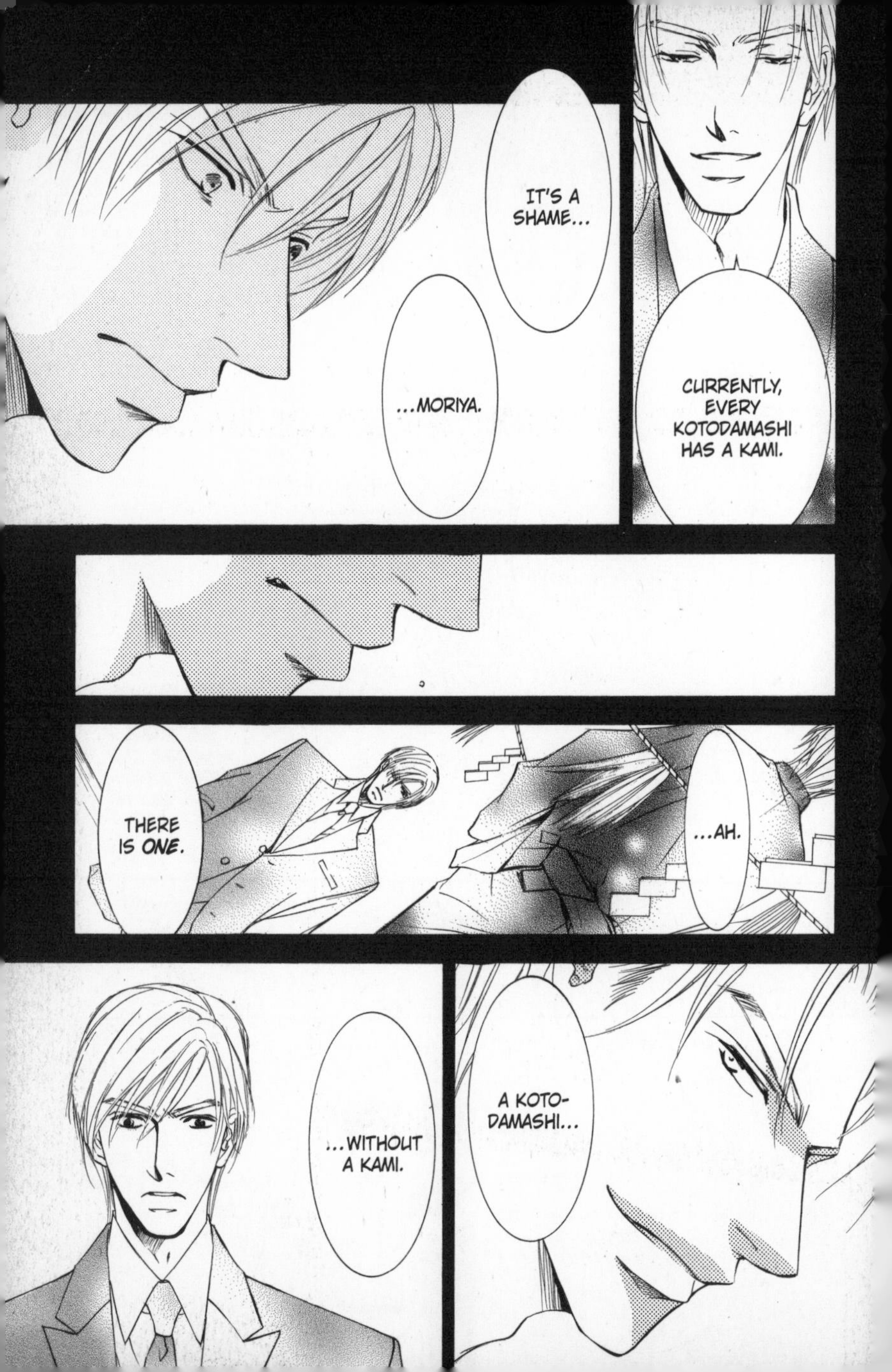
CURRENTLY, EVERY KOTODAMASHI HAS A KAMI.
IT'S A SHAME...
...MORIYA.
...AH.
THERE IS *ONE*.
A KOTO-DAMASHI...
...WITHOUT A KAMI.

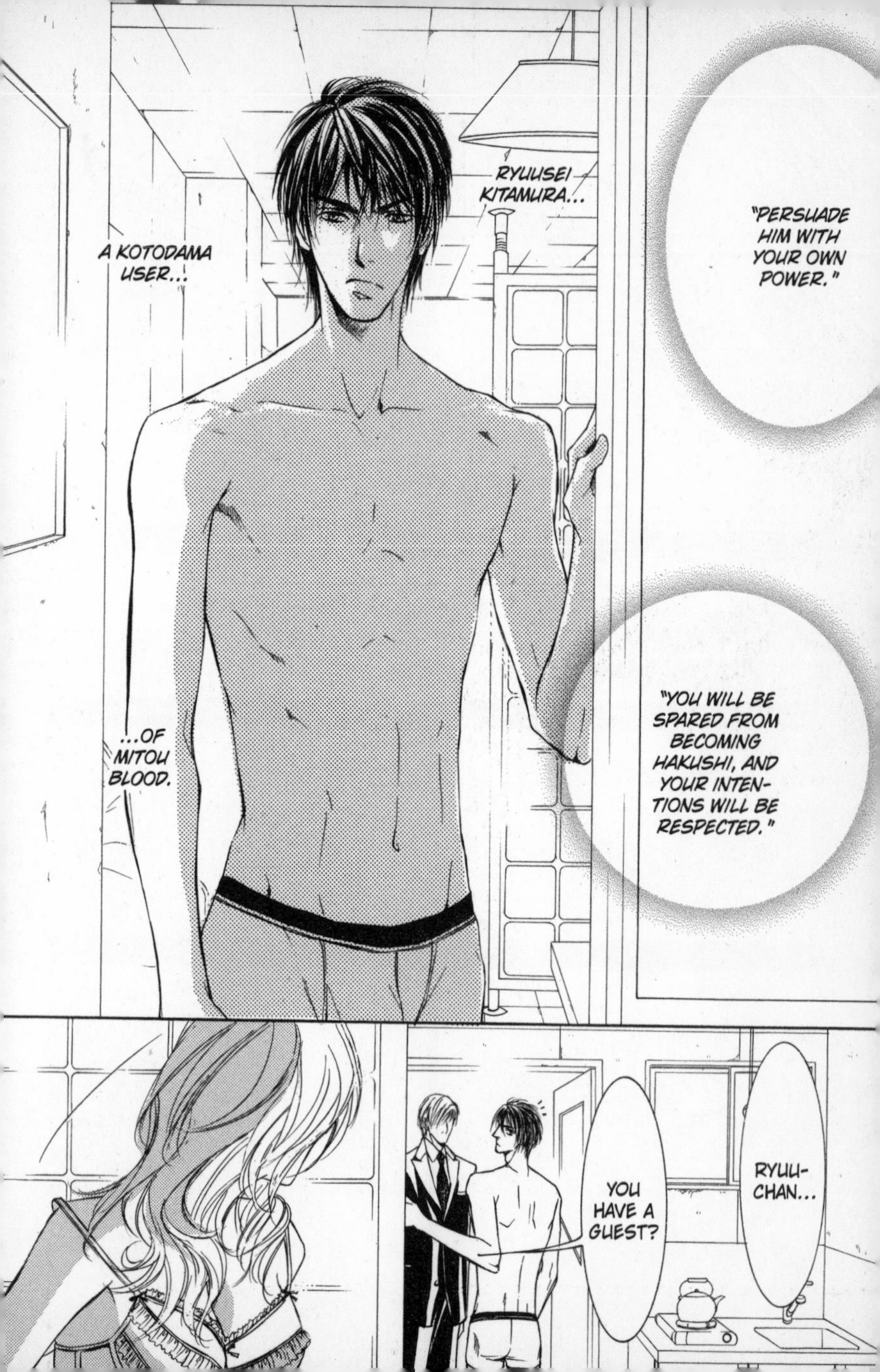
"PERSUADE HIM WITH YOUR OWN POWER."
"YOU WILL BE SPARED FROM BECOMING HAKUSHI, AND YOUR INTEN-TIONS WILL BE RESPECTED."
RYUUSEI KITAMURA...
A KOTODAMA USER...
...OF MITOU BLOOD.
RYUU-CHAN...
YOU HAVE A GUEST?

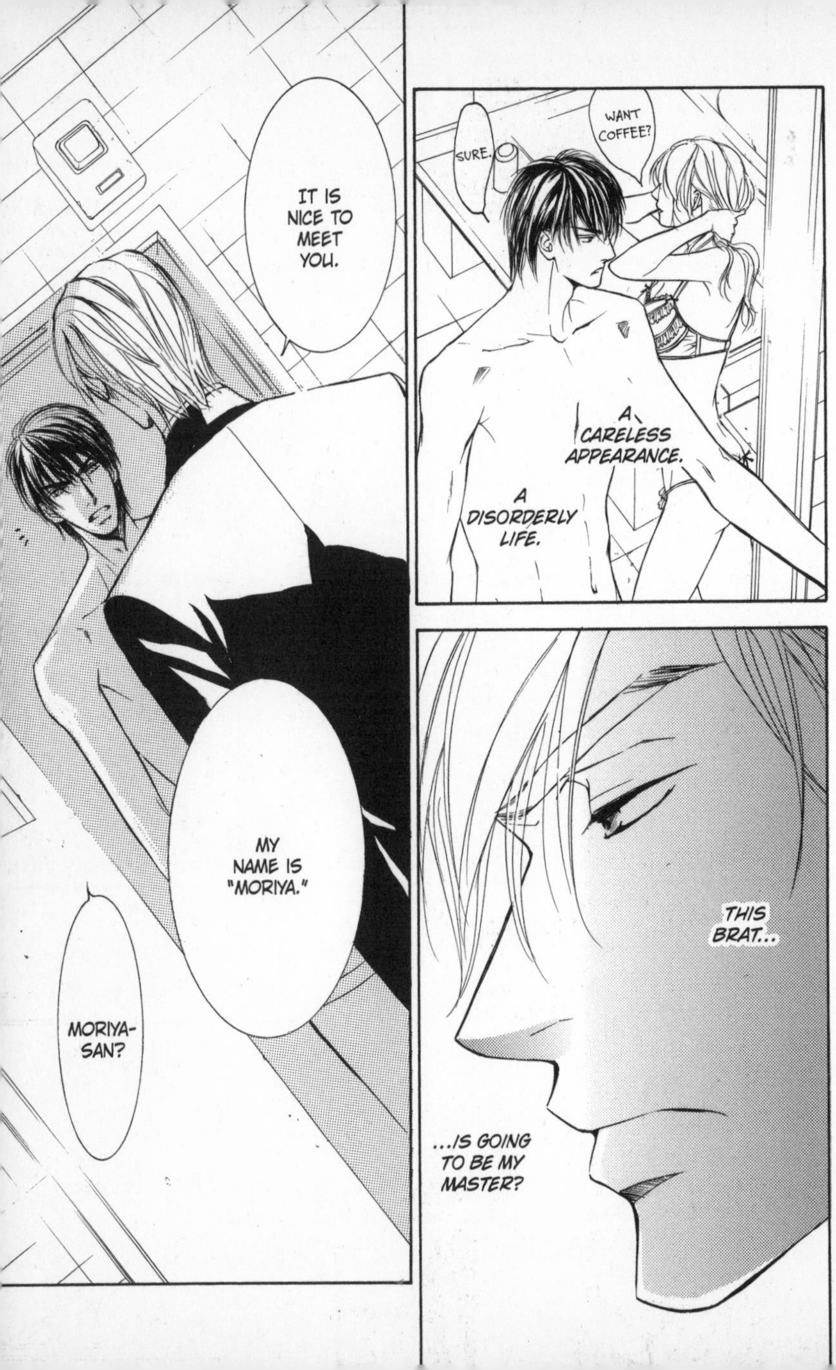
WANT COFFEE?
SURE.
A CARELESS APPEARANCE.
A DISORDERLY LIFE.
THIS BRAT...
...IS GOING TO BE MY MASTER?
IT IS NICE TO MEET YOU.
MY NAME IS "MORIYA."
MORIYA-SAN?

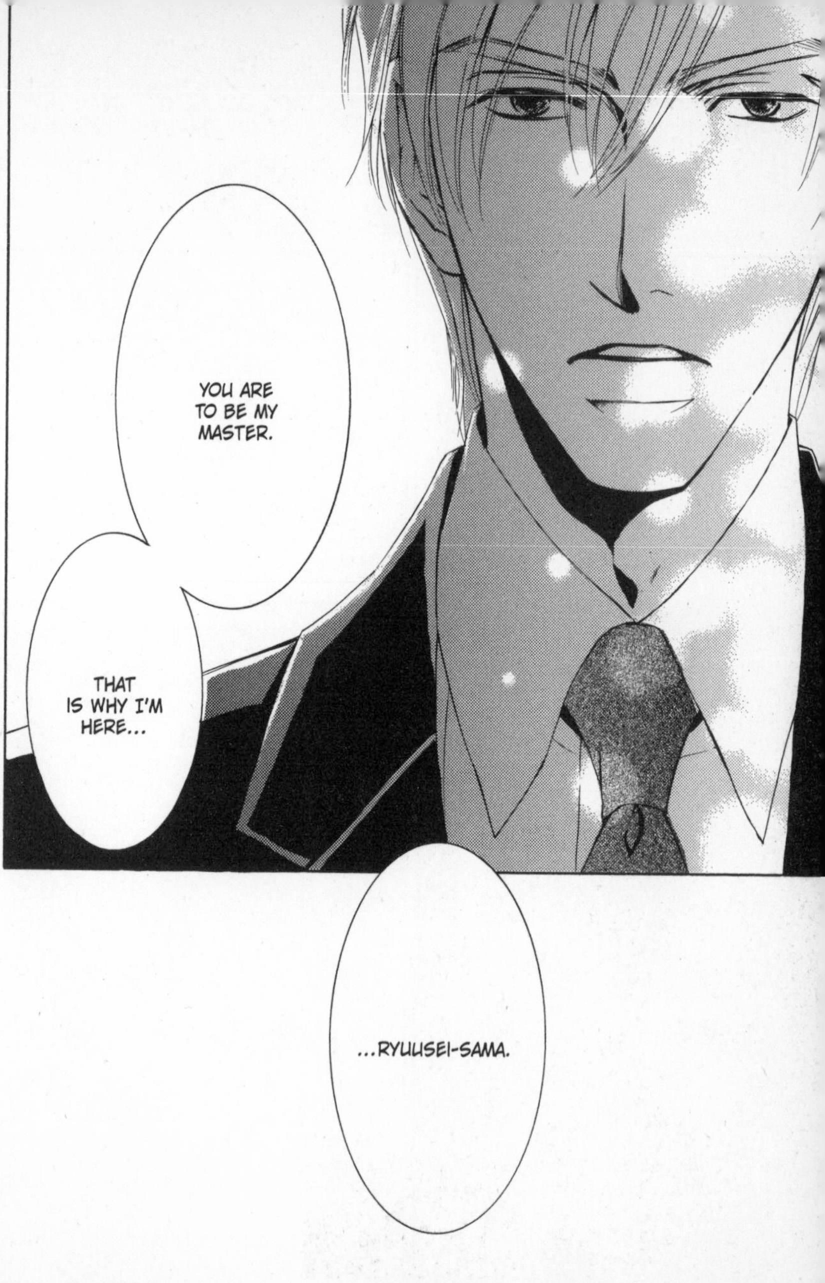
YOU ARE TO BE MY MASTER.
THAT IS WHY I'M HERE...
...RYUUSEI-SAMA.

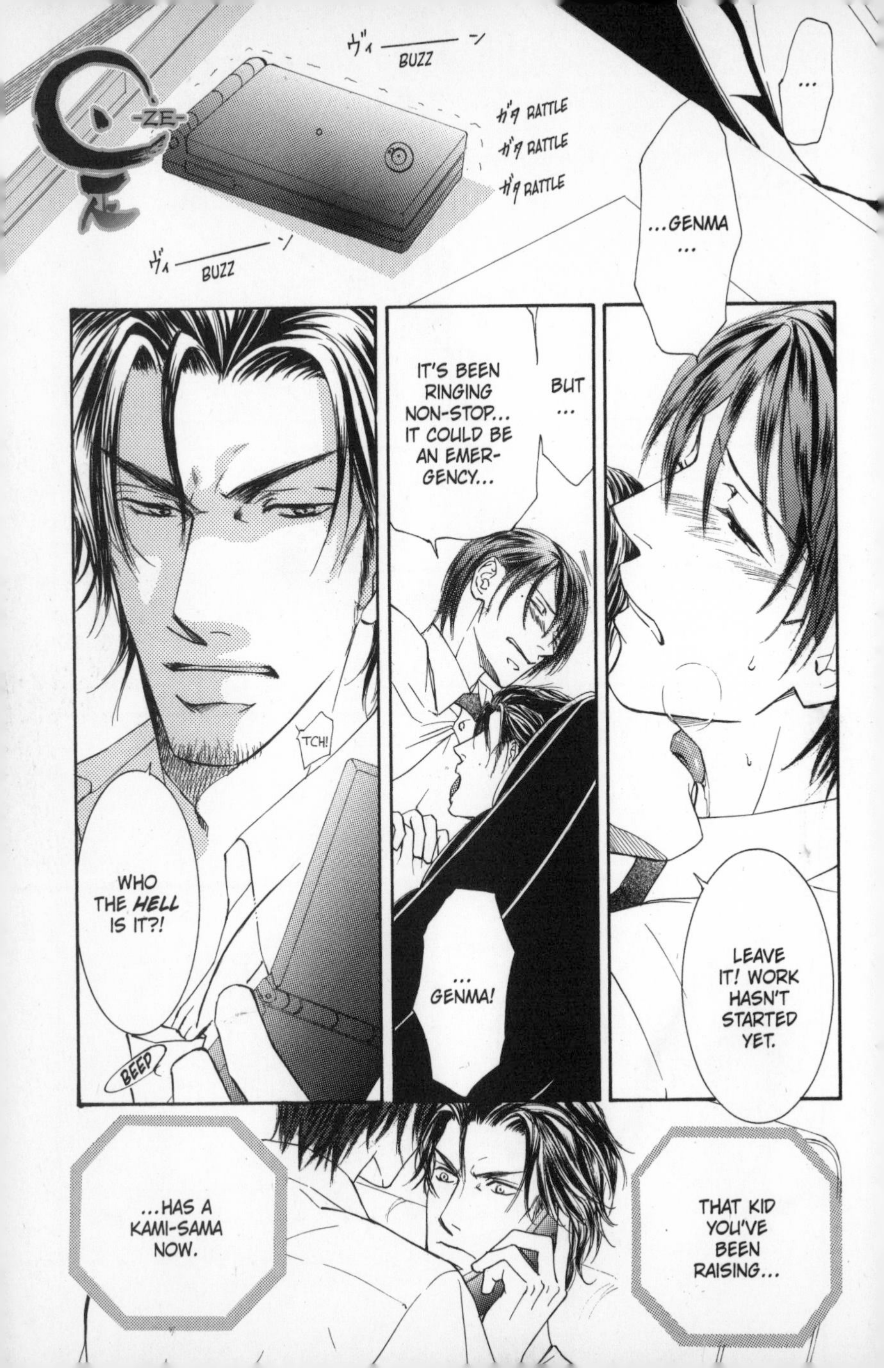
...
...GENMA ...
ヴィーーン BUZZ
ガタ RATTLE
ガタ RATTLE
ガタ RATTLE
ヴィーーン BUZZ
-ZE-
LEAVE IT! WORK HASN'T STARTED YET.
BUT ...
IT'S BEEN RINGING NON-STOP... IT COULD BE AN EMER-GENCY...
... GENMA!
TCH!
WHO THE HELL IS IT?!
BEEP
THAT KID YOU'VE BEEN RAISING...
...HAS A KAMI-SAMA NOW.

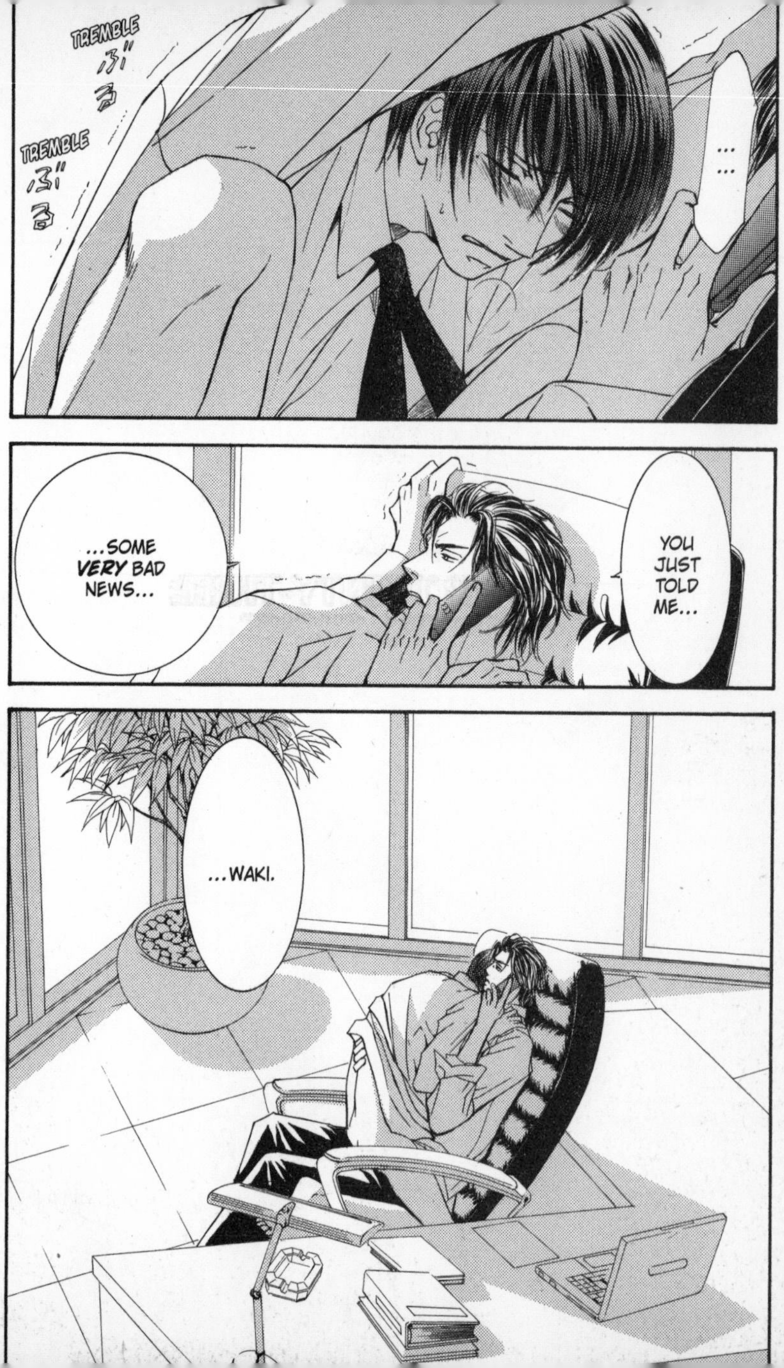
… …
TREMBLE ぶる
TREMBLE ぶる
YOU JUST TOLD ME…
…SOME VERY BAD NEWS…
…WAKI.

-ZE-

CHAPTER TWENTY-THREE: BEFORE A CHOICE

Konic
新宿
高崎
カメラ
駐車場
FUSAN BANK
富山銀行
FUSAN BANK
富山銀行
日本ダイナーズクラブ
FUJITA
新宿 ロビンソン
富山銀行

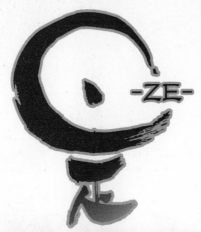

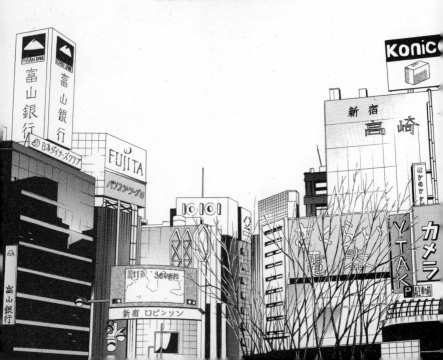

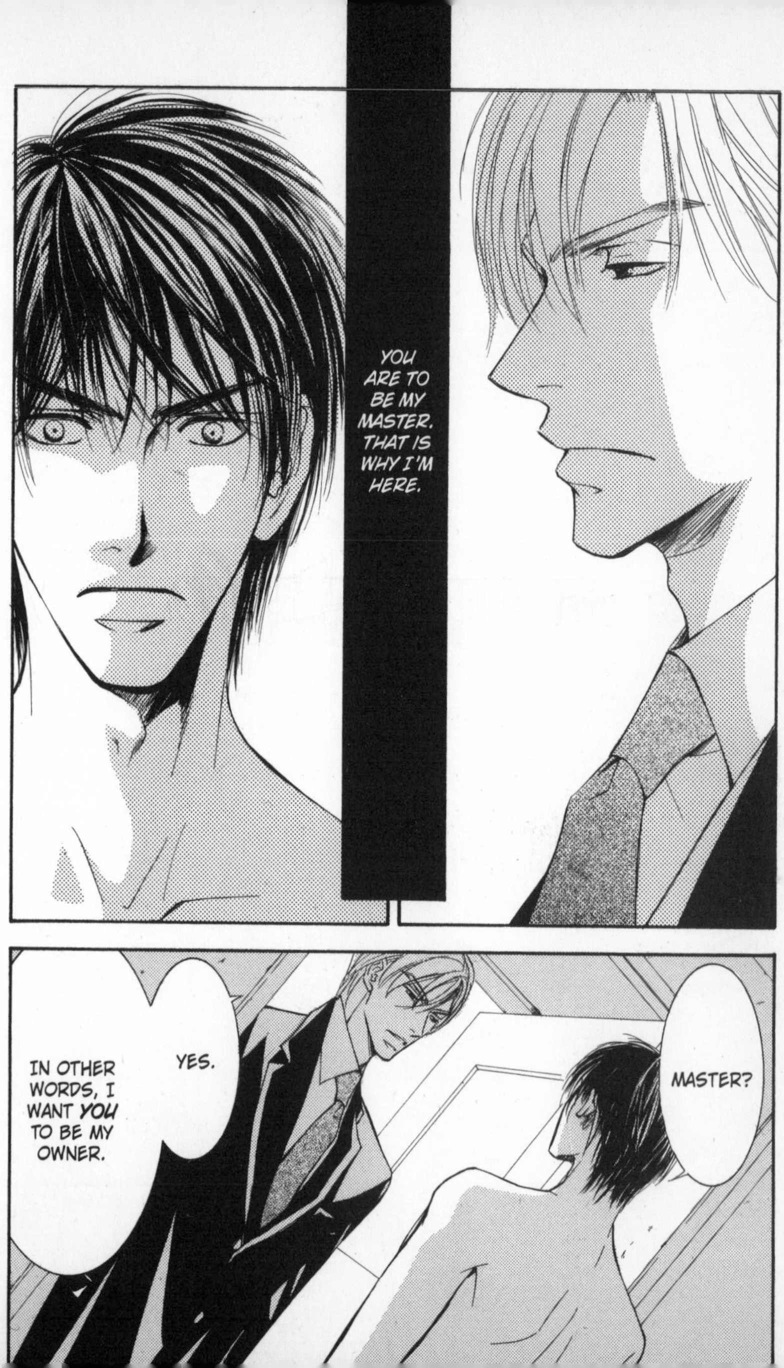
YOU ARE TO BE MY MASTER. THAT IS WHY I'M HERE.
MASTER?
YES.
IN OTHER WORDS, I WANT *YOU* TO BE MY OWNER.

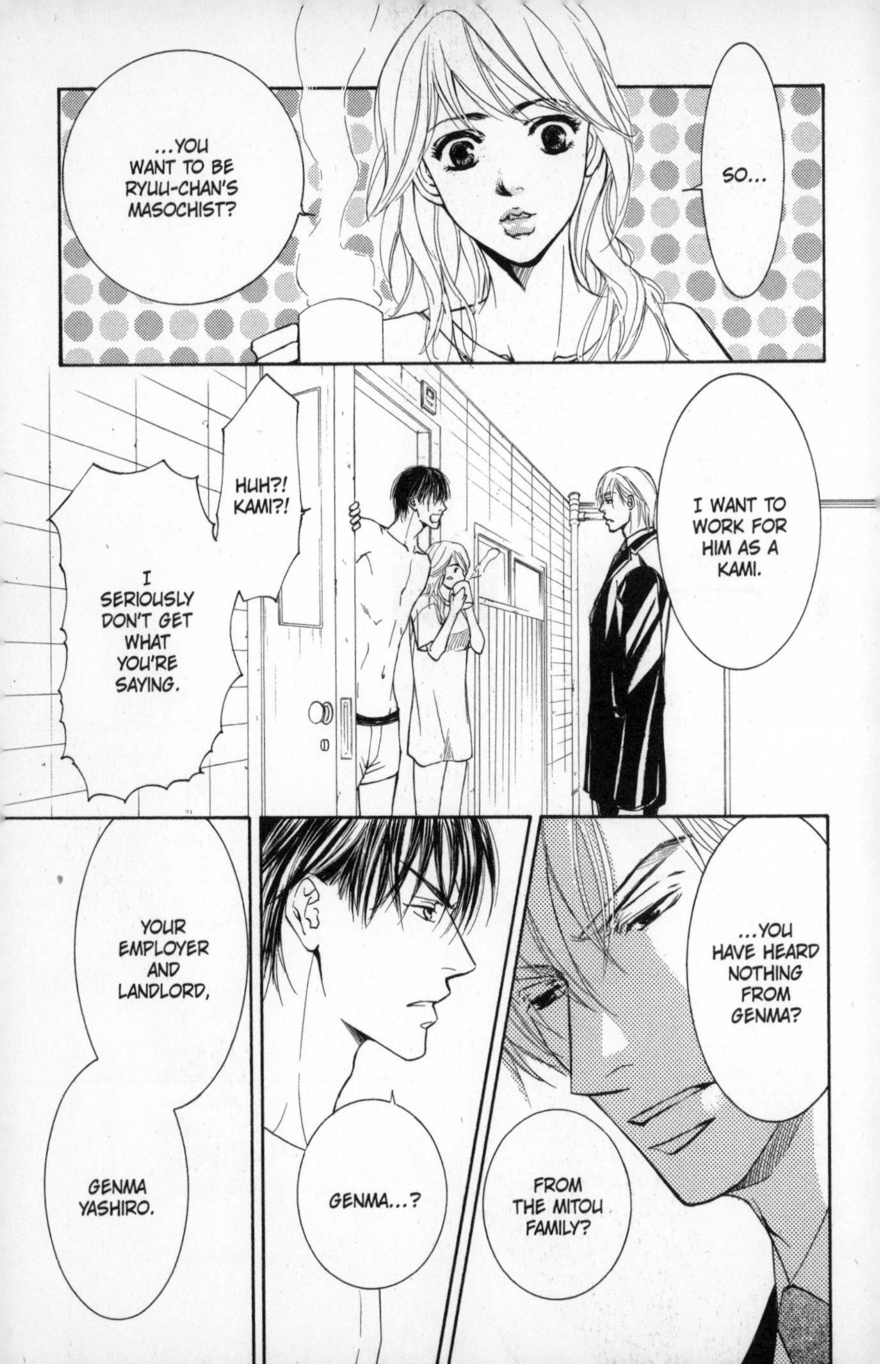
SO...
...YOU WANT TO BE RYUU-CHAN'S MASOCHIST?
I WANT TO WORK FOR HIM AS A KAMI.
HUH?! KAMI?!
I SERIOUSLY DON'T GET WHAT YOU'RE SAYING.
...YOU HAVE HEARD NOTHING FROM GENMA?
FROM THE MITOU FAMILY?
GENMA...?
YOUR EMPLOYER AND LANDLORD,
GENMA YASHIRO.

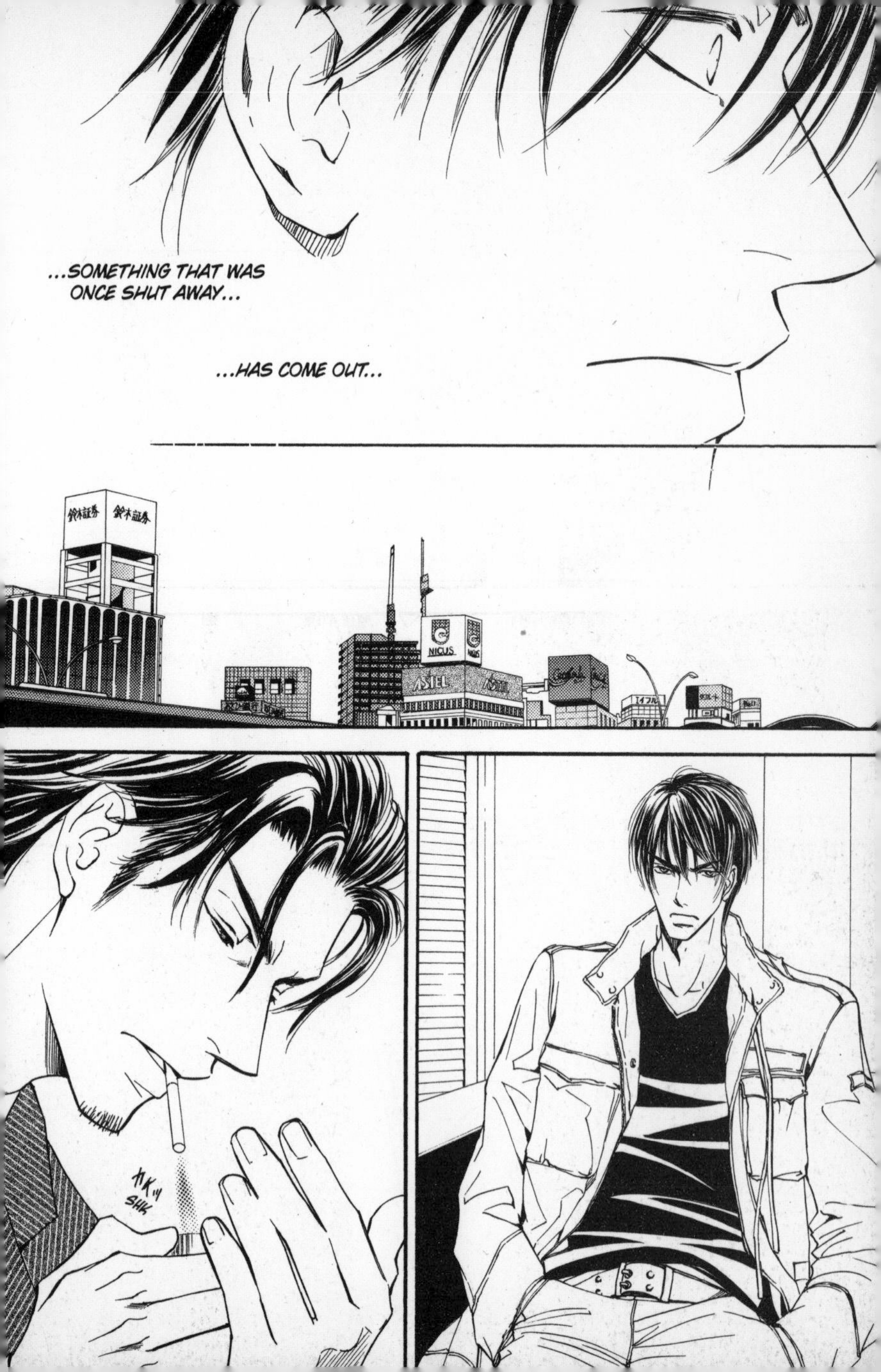
...SOMETHING THAT WAS ONCE SHUT AWAY...
...HAS COME OUT...
鈴木証券
鈴木証券
NICUS
ASTEL
SHK

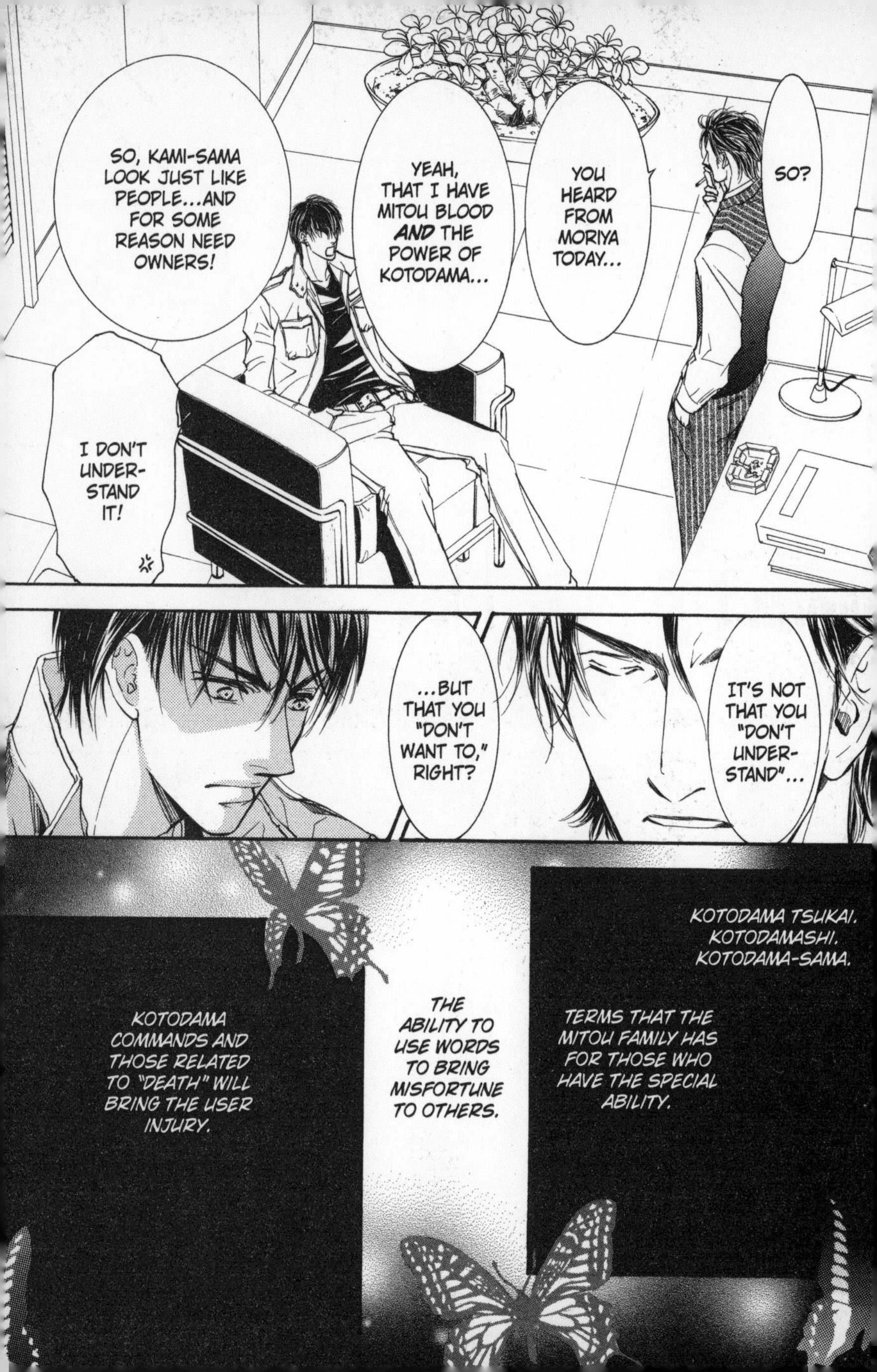
SO?
YOU HEARD FROM MORIYA TODAY...
YEAH, THAT I HAVE MITOU BLOOD **AND** THE POWER OF KOTODAMA...
SO, KAMI-SAMA LOOK JUST LIKE PEOPLE...AND FOR SOME REASON NEED OWNERS!
I DON'T UNDER-STAND IT!
IT'S NOT THAT YOU "DON'T UNDER-STAND"...
...BUT THAT YOU "DON'T WANT TO," RIGHT?
KOTODAMA TSUKAI. KOTODAMASHI. KOTODAMA-SAMA.
TERMS THAT THE MITOU FAMILY HAS FOR THOSE WHO HAVE THE SPECIAL ABILITY.
THE ABILITY TO USE WORDS TO BRING MISFORTUNE TO OTHERS.
KOTODAMA COMMANDS AND THOSE RELATED TO "DEATH" WILL BRING THE USER INJURY.

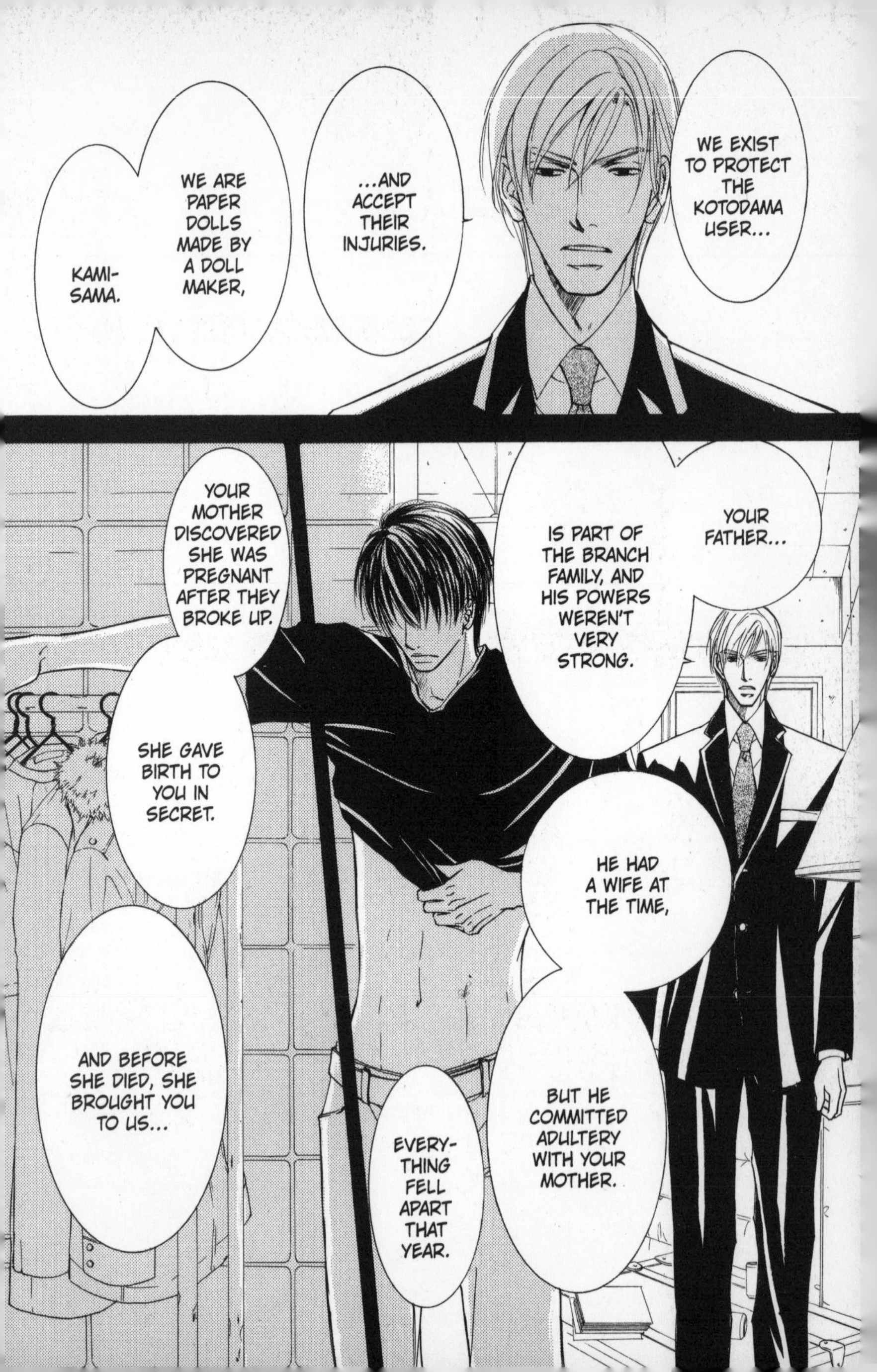
WE EXIST TO PROTECT THE KOTODAMA USER...
...AND ACCEPT THEIR INJURIES.
WE ARE PAPER DOLLS MADE BY A DOLL MAKER,
KAMI-SAMA.
YOUR FATHER...
IS PART OF THE BRANCH FAMILY, AND HIS POWERS WEREN'T VERY STRONG.
HE HAD A WIFE AT THE TIME,
BUT HE COMMITTED ADULTERY WITH YOUR MOTHER.
EVERY-THING FELL APART THAT YEAR.
YOUR MOTHER DISCOVERED SHE WAS PREGNANT AFTER THEY BROKE UP.
SHE GAVE BIRTH TO YOU IN SECRET.
AND BEFORE SHE DIED, SHE BROUGHT YOU TO US...

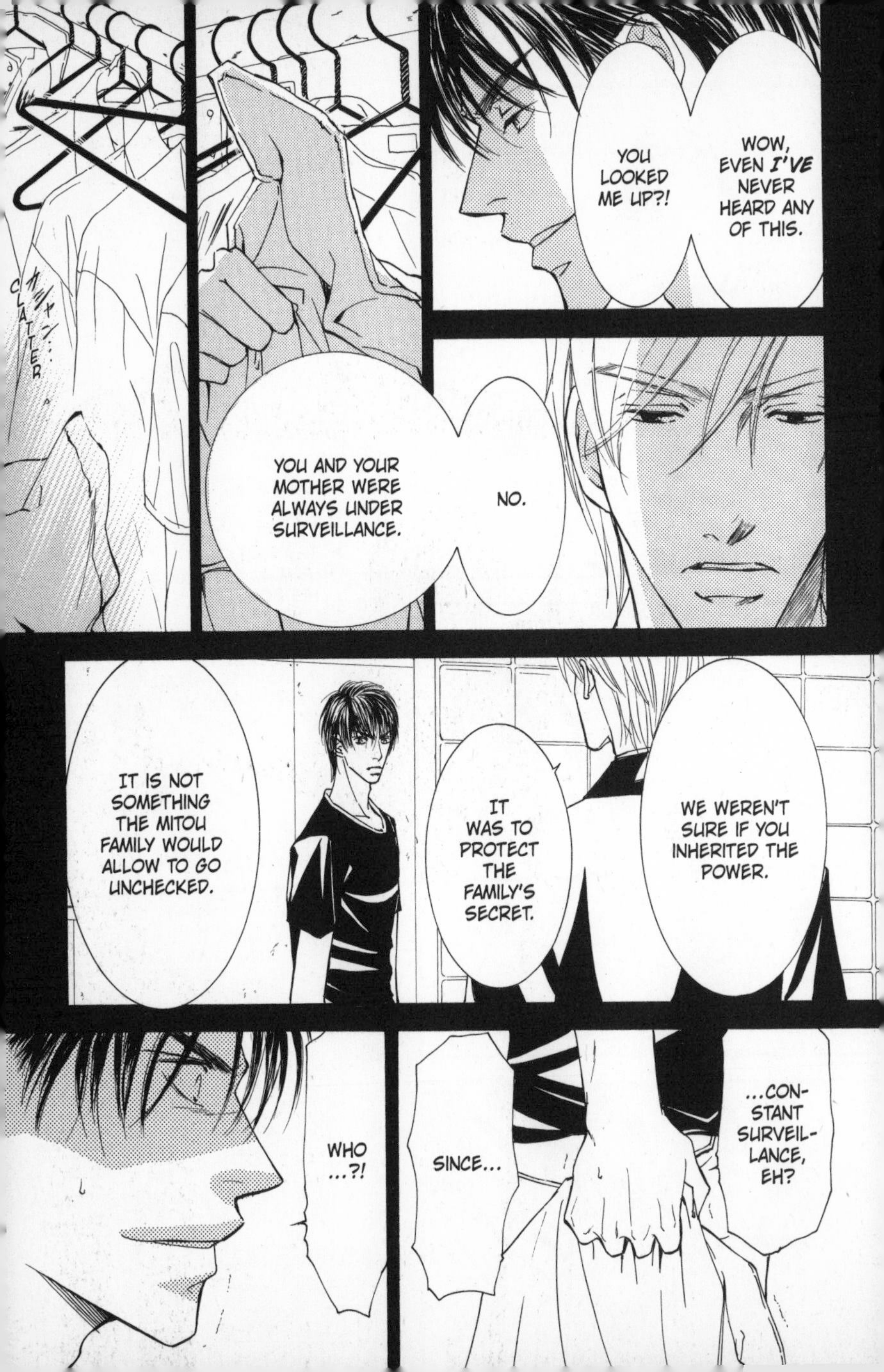
WOW, EVEN I'VE NEVER HEARD ANY OF THIS.
YOU LOOKED ME UP?!
CLATTER
NO.
YOU AND YOUR MOTHER WERE ALWAYS UNDER SURVEILLANCE.
WE WEREN'T SURE IF YOU INHERITED THE POWER.
IT WAS TO PROTECT THE FAMILY'S SECRET.
IT IS NOT SOMETHING THE MITOU FAMILY WOULD ALLOW TO GO UNCHECKED.
...CON-STANT SURVEIL-LANCE, EH?
SINCE...
WHO ...?!

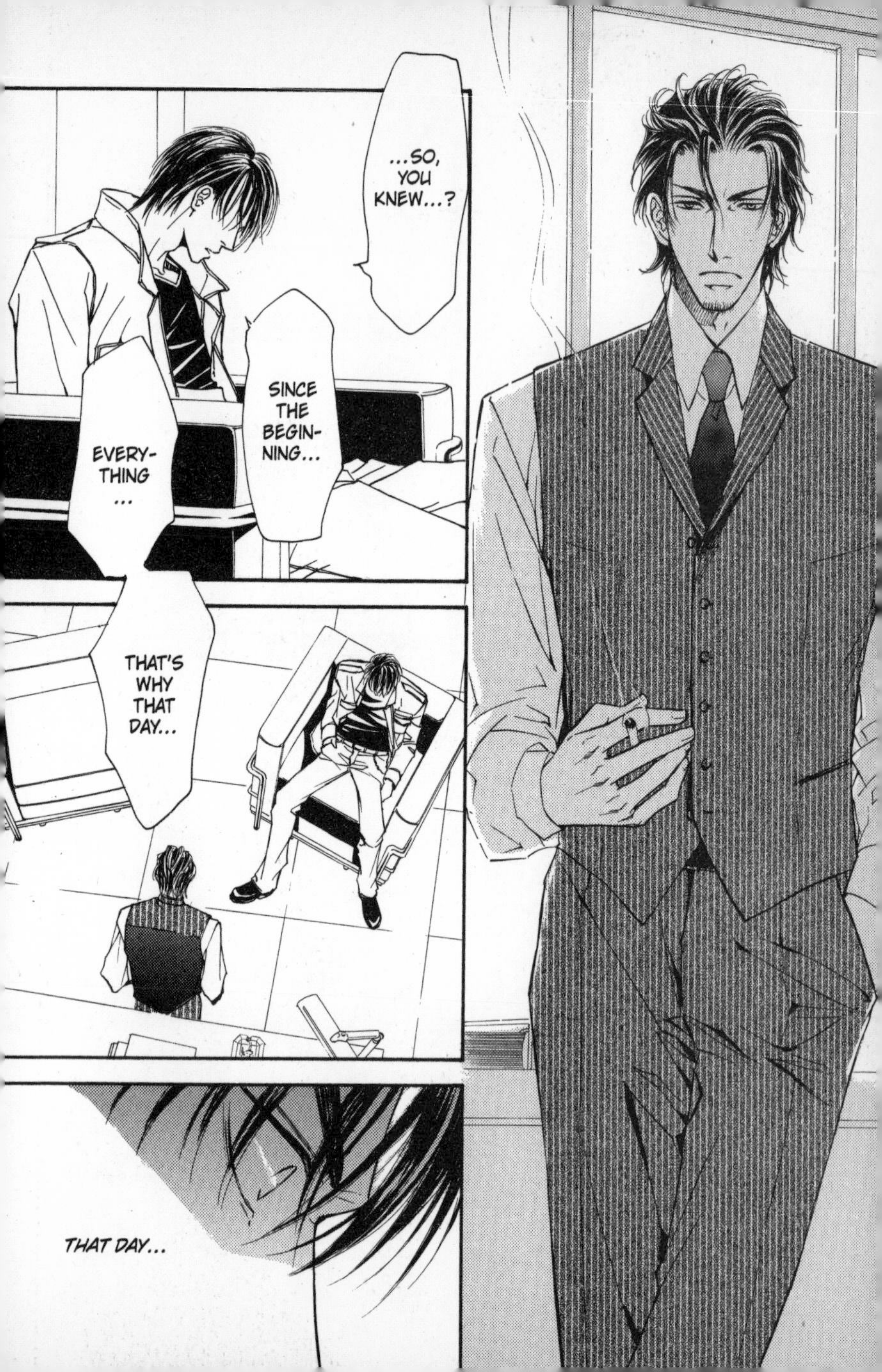
...SO, YOU KNEW...?
SINCE THE BEGIN-NING...
EVERY-THING ...
THAT'S WHY THAT DAY...
THAT DAY...

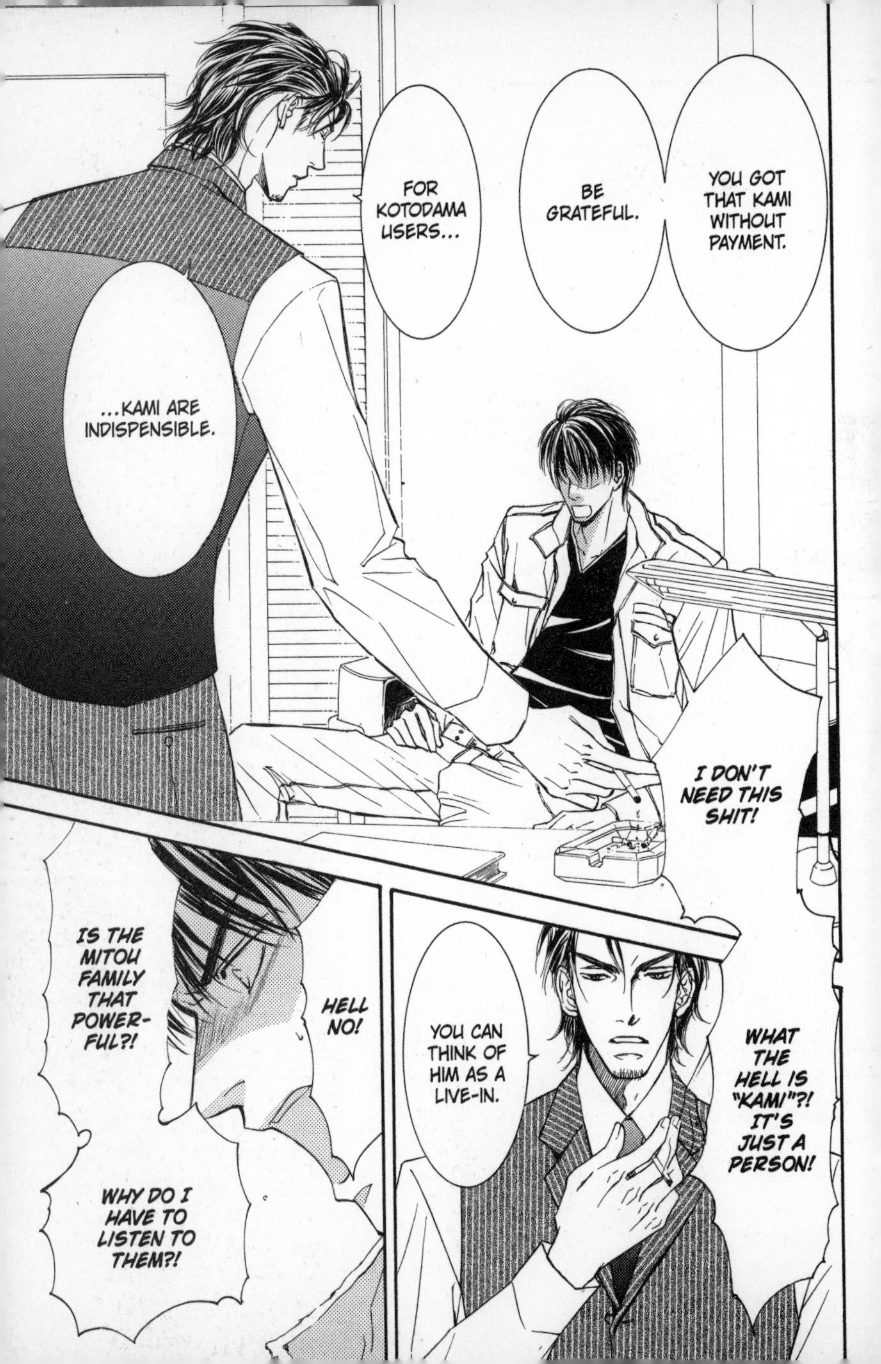
YOU GOT THAT KAMI WITHOUT PAYMENT.
BE GRATEFUL.
FOR KOTODAMA USERS...
...KAMI ARE INDISPENSIBLE.
I DON'T NEED THIS SHIT!
WHAT THE HELL IS "KAMI"?! IT'S JUST A PERSON!
YOU CAN THINK OF HIM AS A LIVE-IN.
HELL NO!
IS THE MITOU FAMILY THAT POWER-FUL?!
WHY DO I HAVE TO LISTEN TO THEM?!

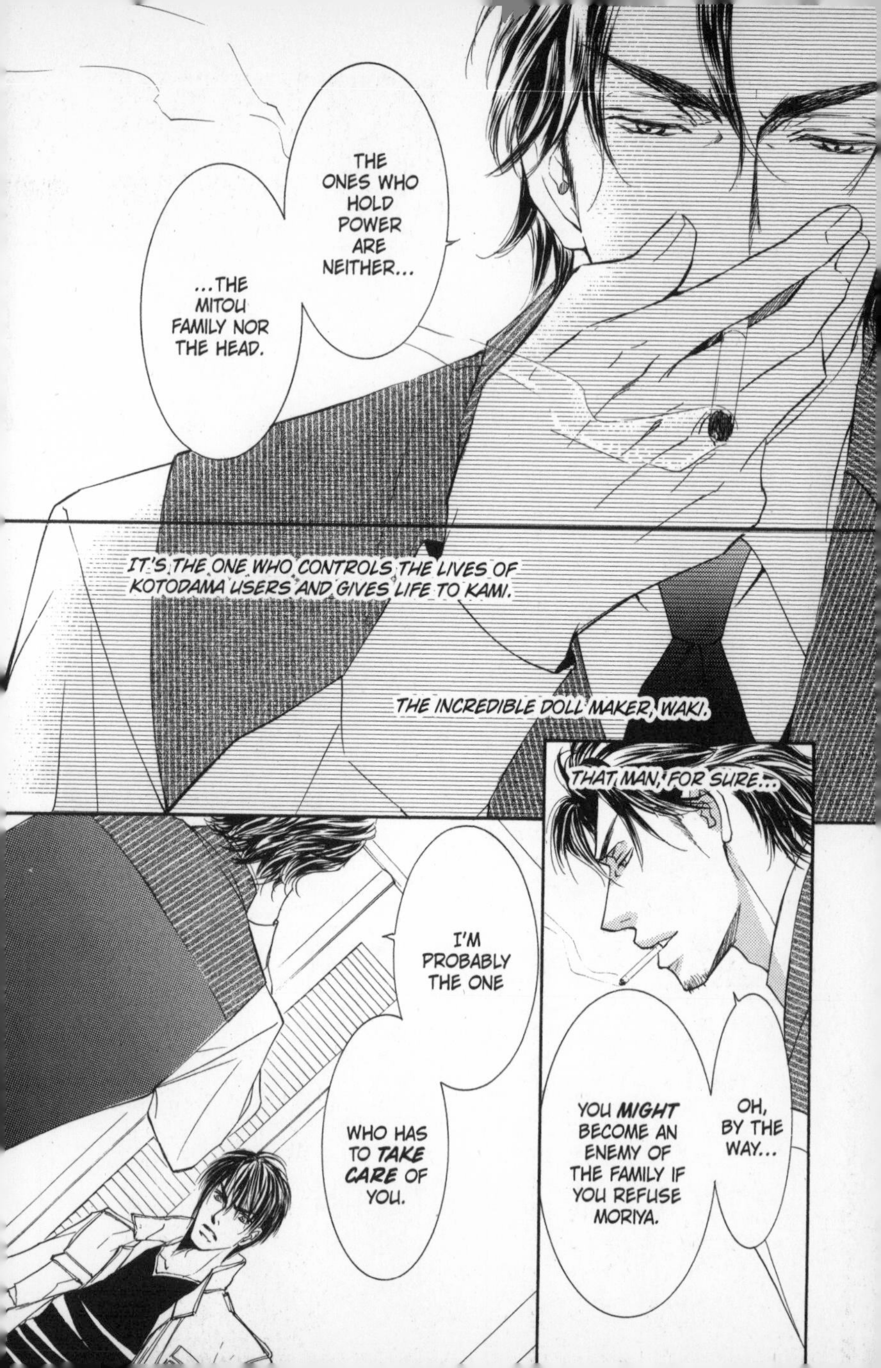
THE ONES WHO HOLD POWER ARE NEITHER...
...THE MITOU FAMILY NOR THE HEAD.
IT'S THE ONE WHO CONTROLS THE LIVES OF KOTODAMA USERS AND GIVES LIFE TO KAMI.
THE INCREDIBLE DOLL MAKER, WAKI.
THAT MAN, FOR SURE...
OH, BY THE WAY...
YOU *MIGHT* BECOME AN ENEMY OF THE FAMILY IF YOU REFUSE MORIYA.
I'M PROBABLY THE ONE
WHO HAS TO *TAKE CARE* OF YOU.

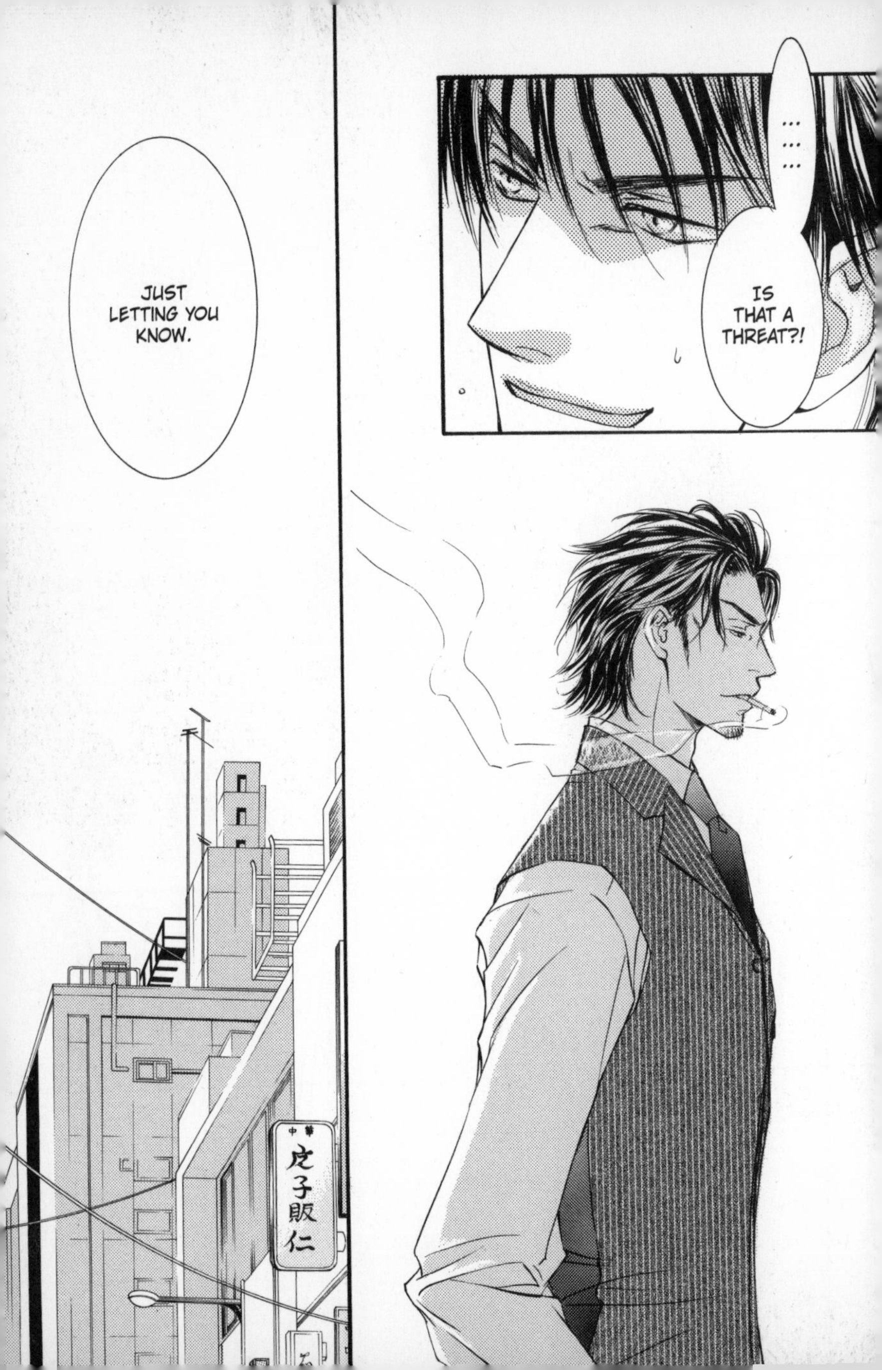
....
IS THAT A THREAT?!
JUST LETTING YOU KNOW.
中華

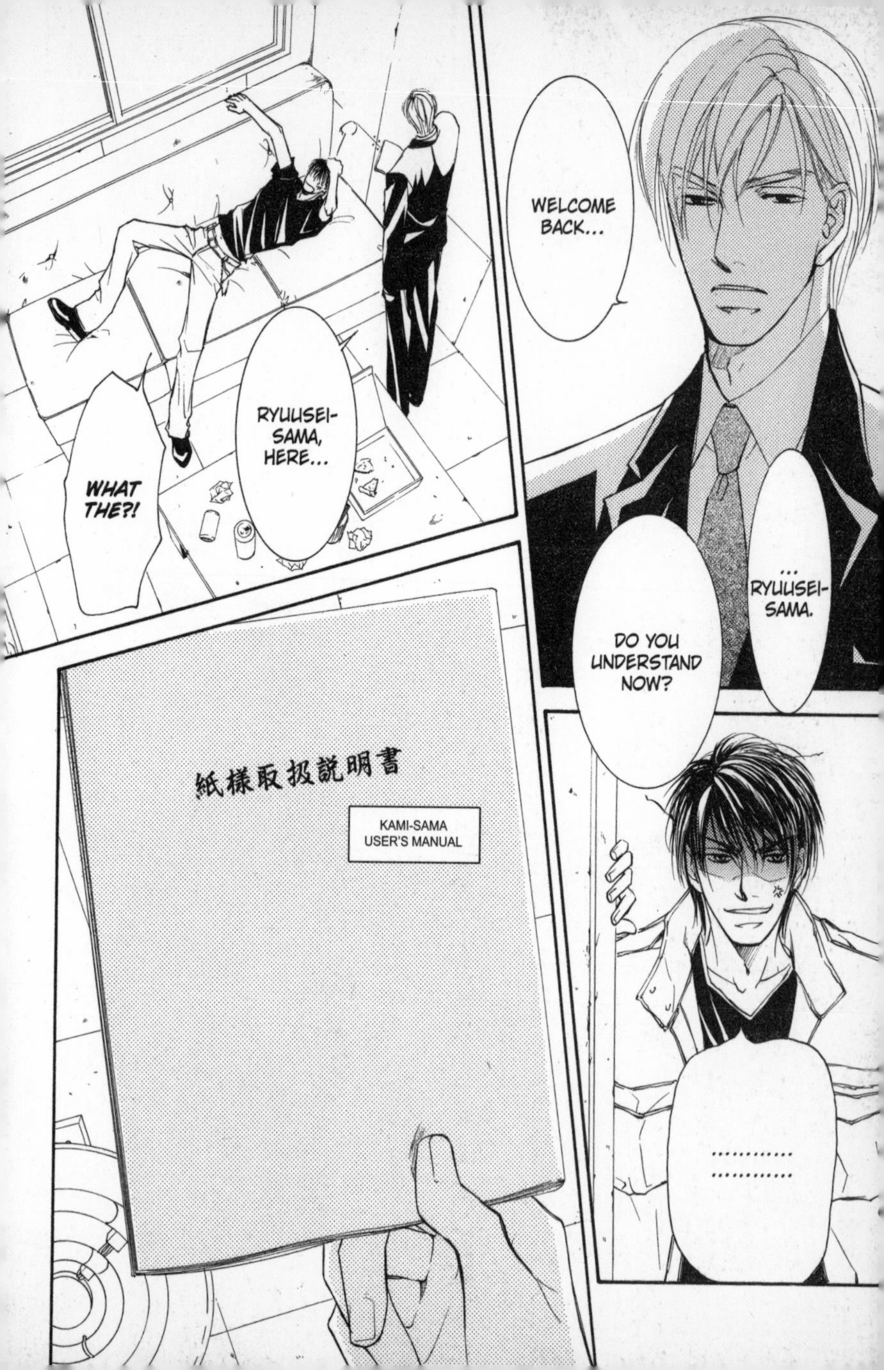
WELCOME BACK...
...RYUUSEI-SAMA.
DO YOU UNDERSTAND NOW?
RYUUSEI-SAMA, HERE...
WHAT THE?!
....
....
紙様取扱説明書
KAMI-SAMA USER'S MANUAL

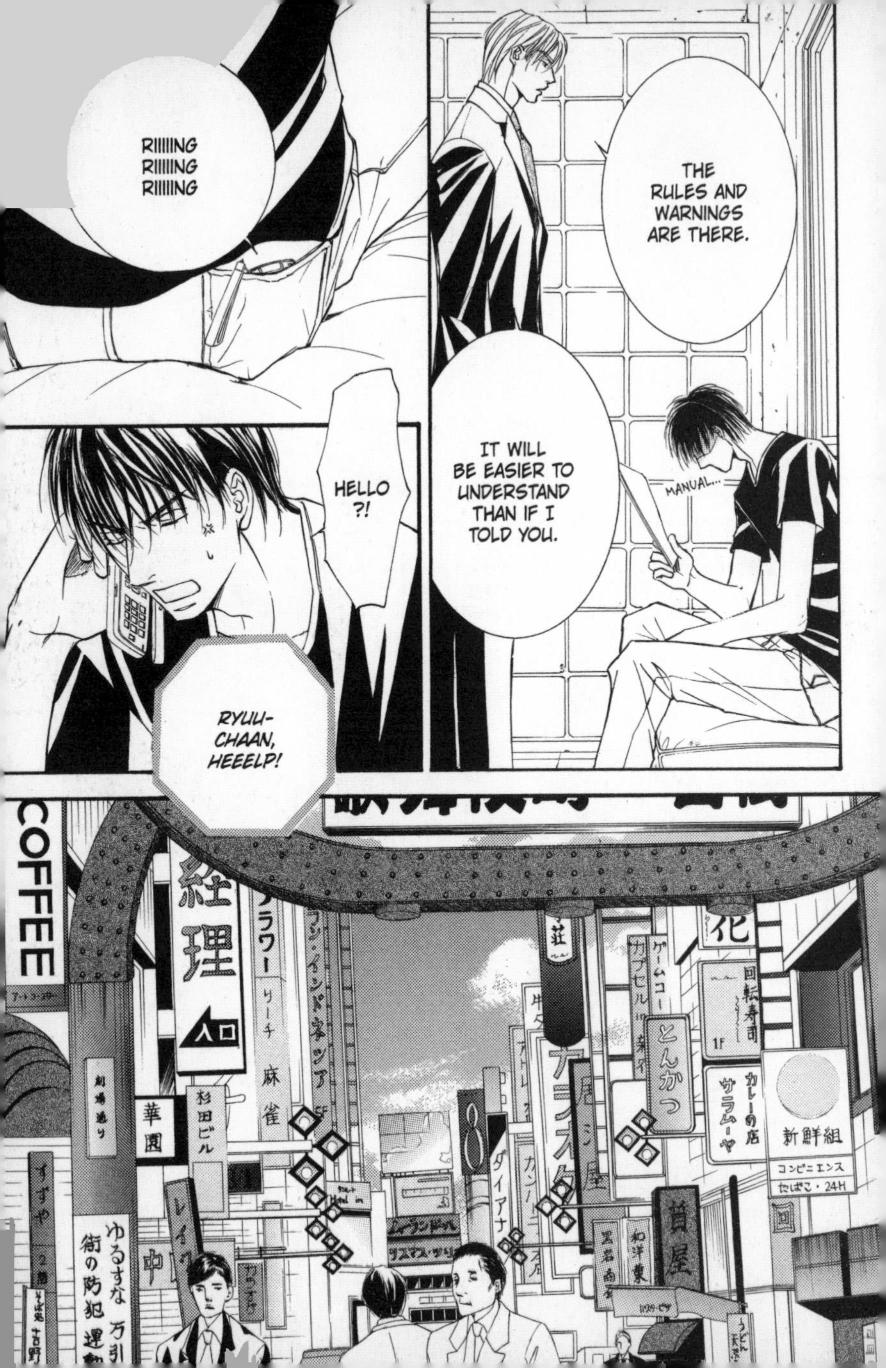
THE RULES AND WARNINGS ARE THERE.
IT WILL BE EASIER TO UNDERSTAND THAN IF I TOLD YOU.
MANUAL...
RIIIING RIIIING RIIIING
HELLO ?!
RYUU-CHAAN, HEEELP!
COFFEE
入口
杉田ビル
麻雀
とんかつ
回転寿司
カレーの店
新鮮組
コンビニエンス
たばこ・24H
質屋
ゆるすな 万引
街の防犯運動

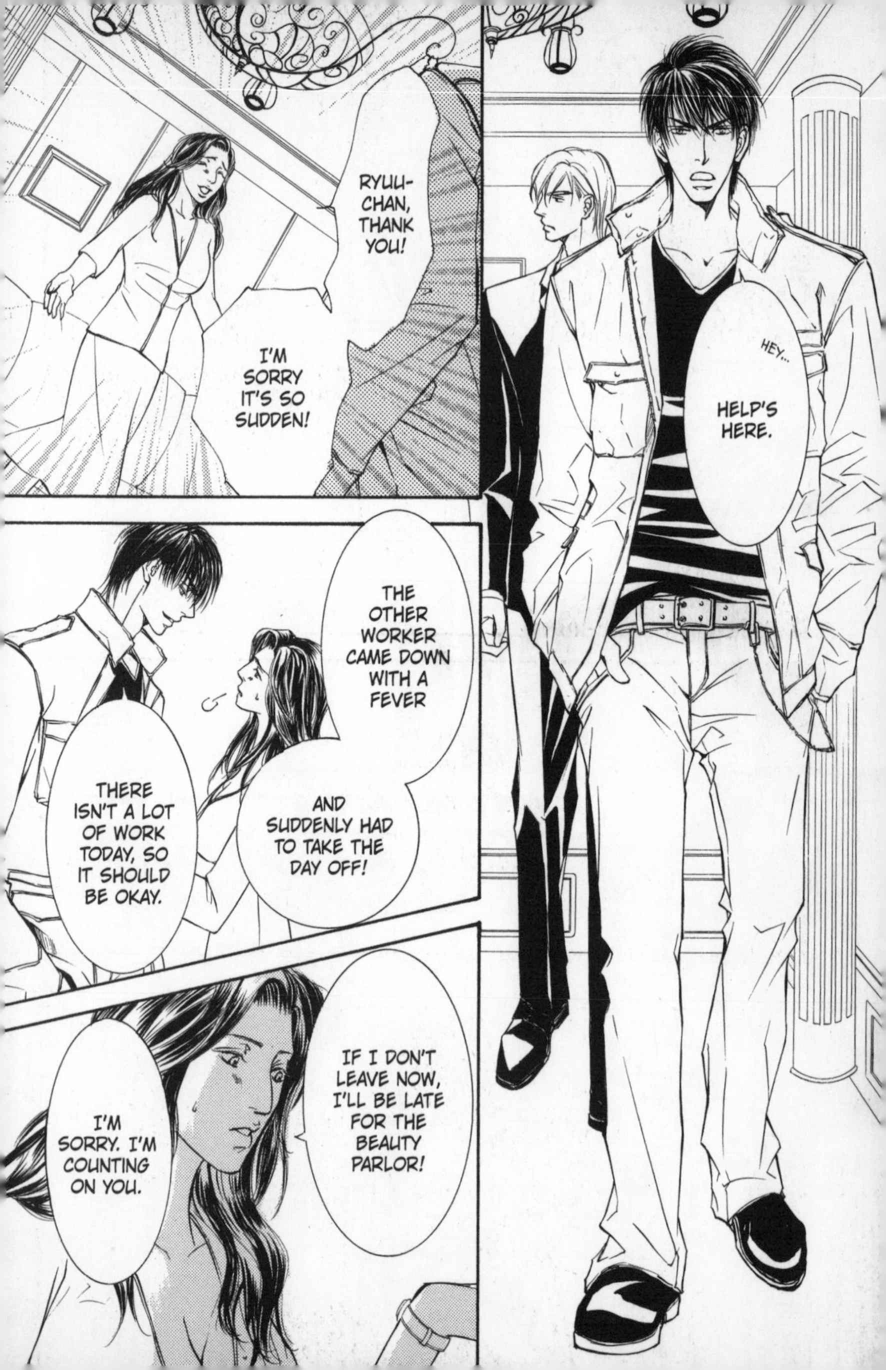
HEY...
HELP'S HERE.
RYUU-CHAN, THANK YOU!
I'M SORRY IT'S SO SUDDEN!
THE OTHER WORKER CAME DOWN WITH A FEVER
AND SUDDENLY HAD TO TAKE THE DAY OFF!
THERE ISN'T A LOT OF WORK TODAY, SO IT SHOULD BE OKAY.
IF I DON'T LEAVE NOW, I'LL BE LATE FOR THE BEAUTY PARLOR!
I'M SORRY. I'M COUNTING ON YOU.

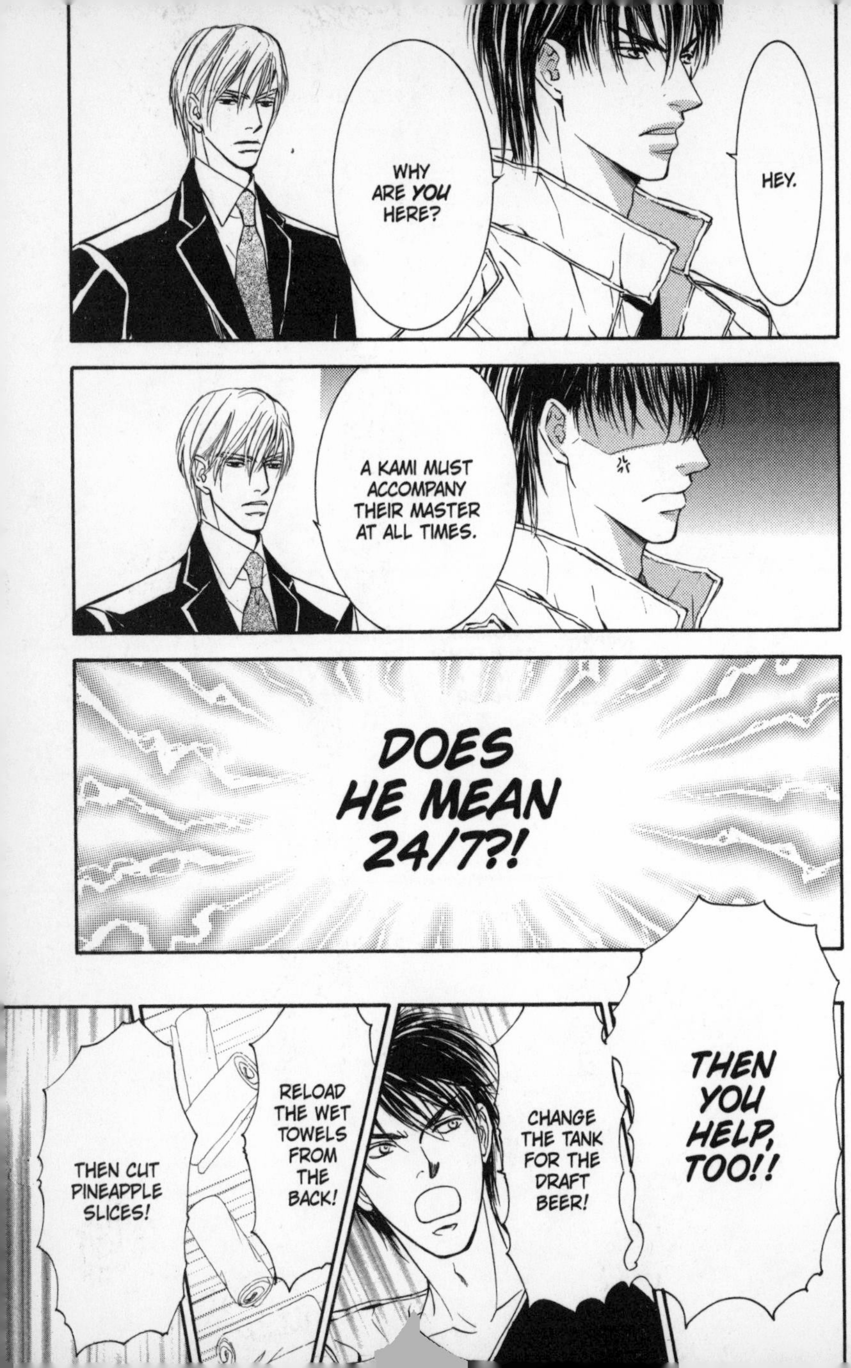
HEY.
WHY ARE YOU HERE?
A KAMI MUST ACCOMPANY THEIR MASTER AT ALL TIMES.
DOES HE MEAN 24/7?!
THEN YOU HELP, TOO!!
CHANGE THE TANK FOR THE DRAFT BEER!
RELOAD THE WET TOWELS FROM THE BACK!
THEN CUT PINEAPPLE SLICES!

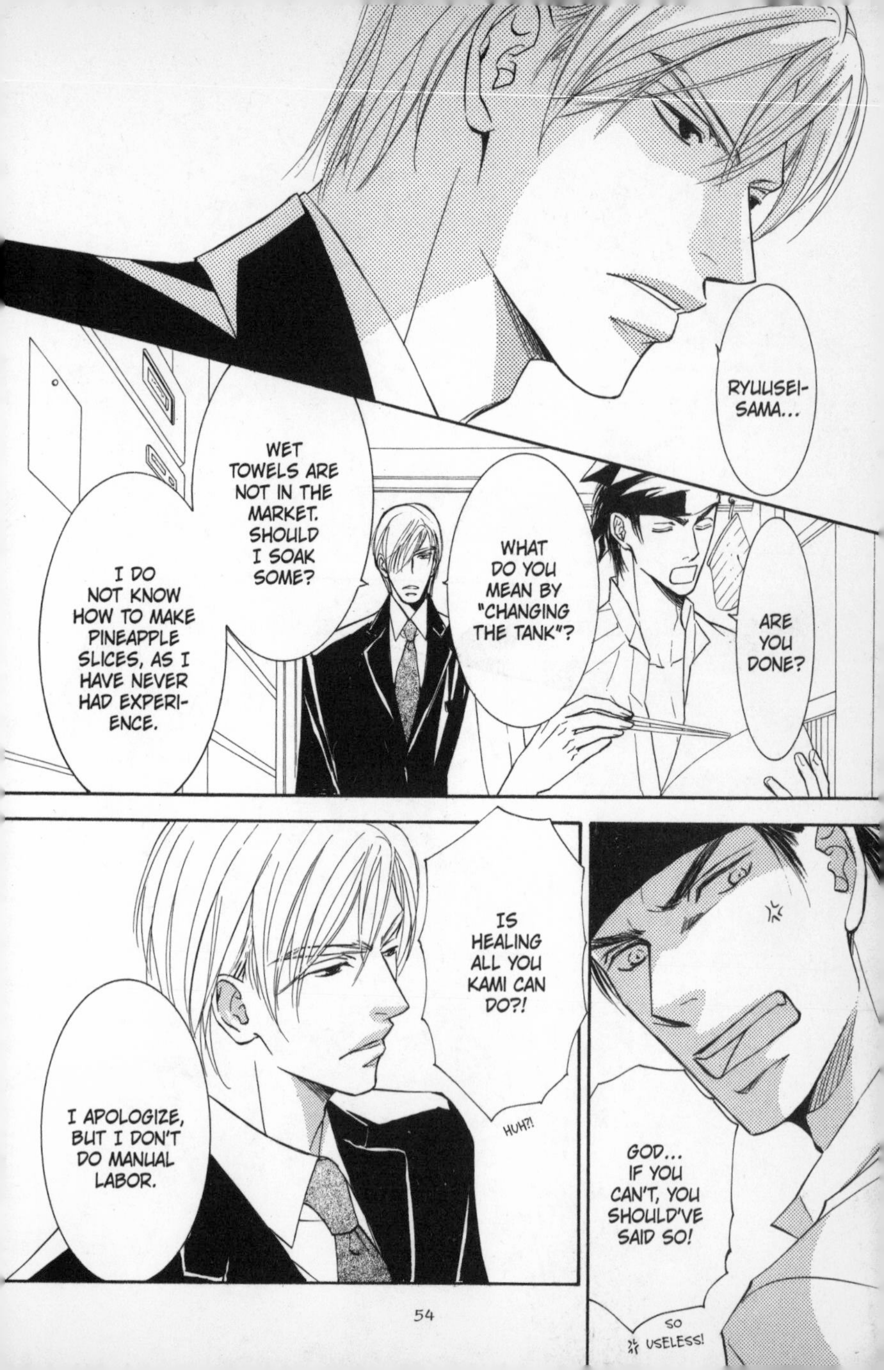
RYUUSEI-SAMA...
ARE YOU DONE?
WHAT DO YOU MEAN BY "CHANGING THE TANK"?
WET TOWELS ARE NOT IN THE MARKET. SHOULD I SOAK SOME?
I DO NOT KNOW HOW TO MAKE PINEAPPLE SLICES, AS I HAVE NEVER HAD EXPERI-ENCE.
GOD... IF YOU CAN'T, YOU SHOULD'VE SAID SO!
SO USELESS!
IS HEALING ALL YOU KAMI CAN DO?!
HUH?!
I APOLOGIZE, BUT I DON'T DO MANUAL LABOR.

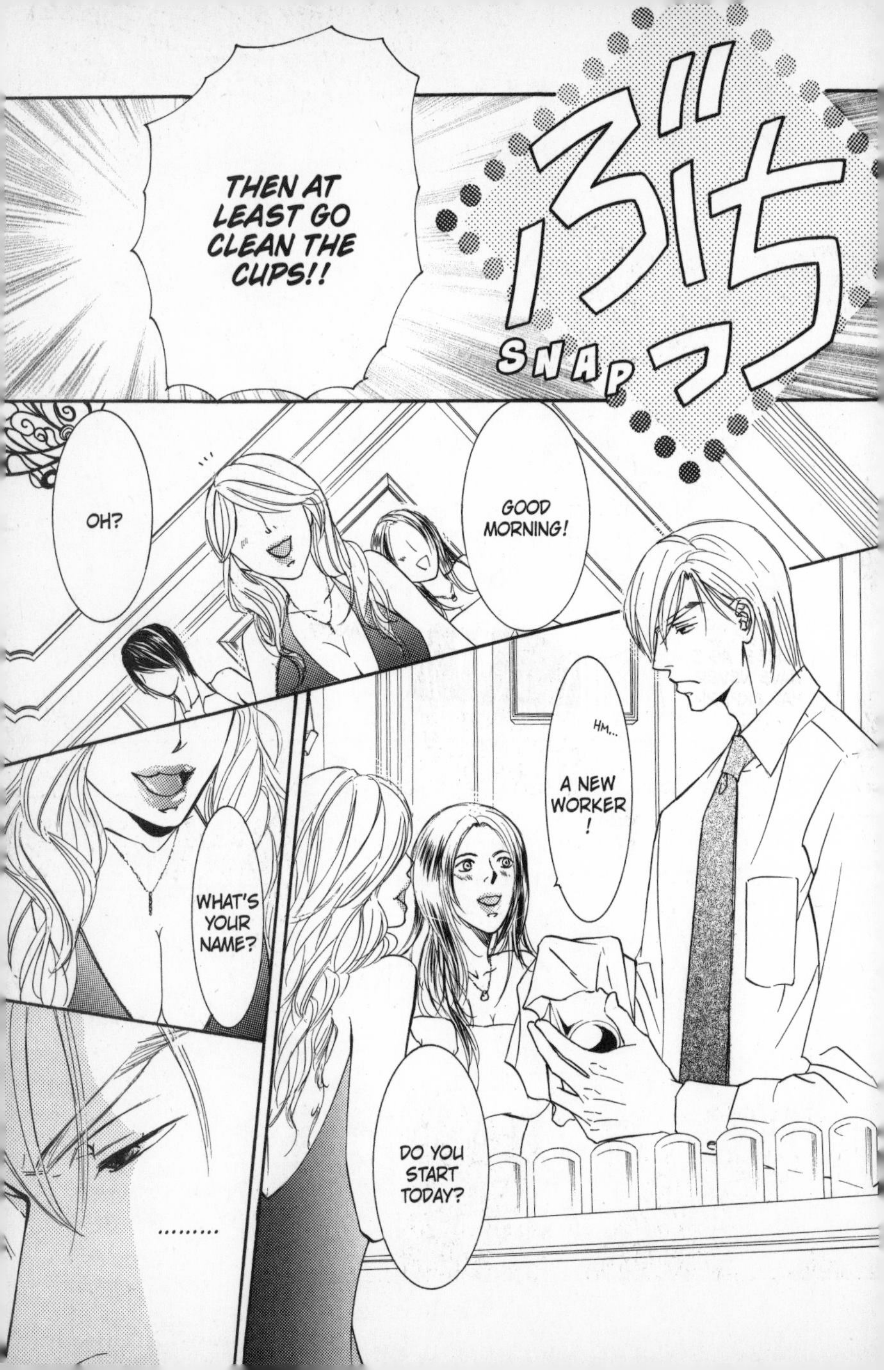
THEN AT LEAST GO CLEAN THE CUPS!!
ぶちっ
SNAP
GOOD MORNING!
OH?
HM... A NEW WORKER!
DO YOU START TODAY?
WHAT'S YOUR NAME?
....

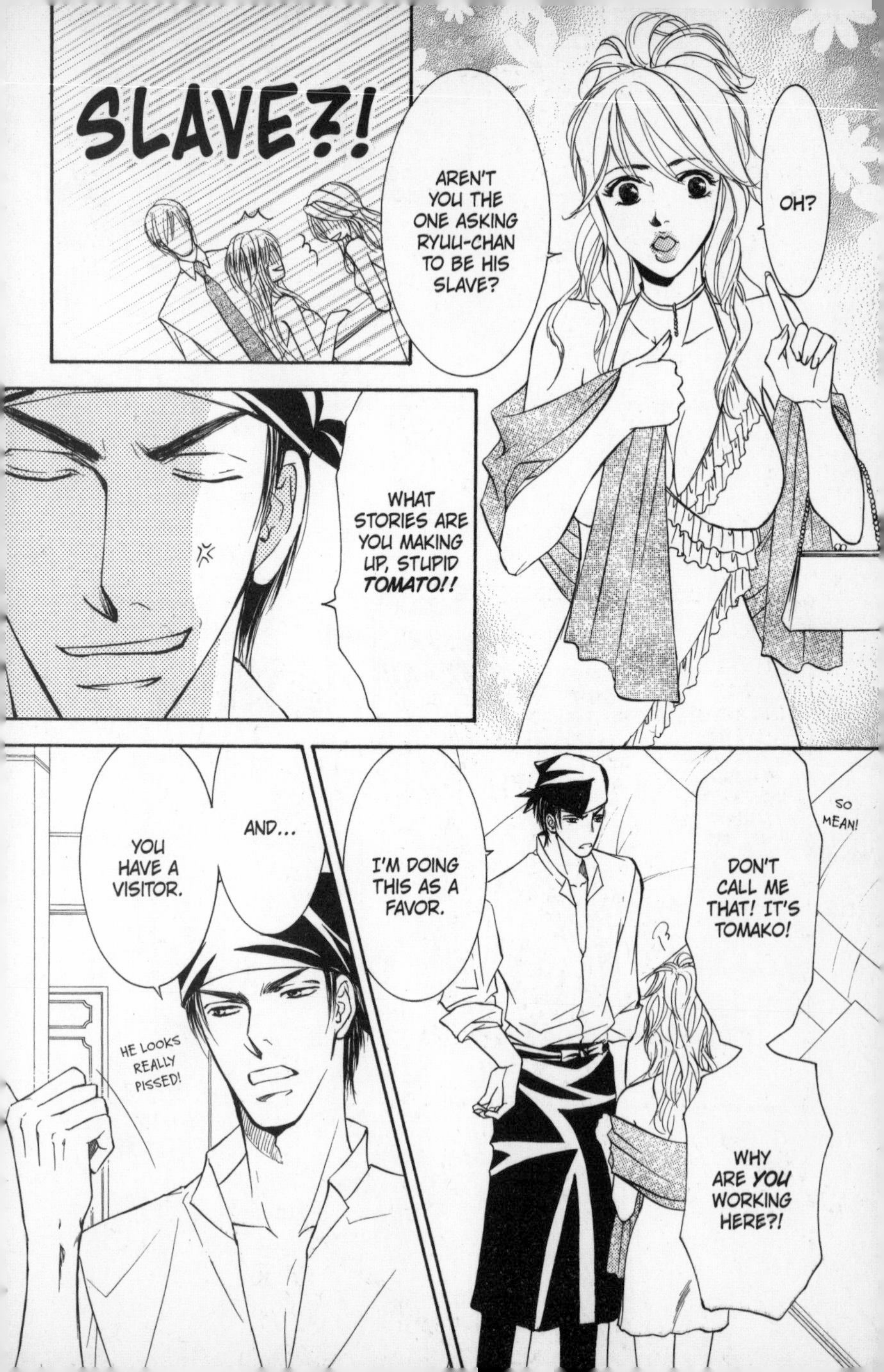
OH?
AREN'T YOU THE ONE ASKING RYUU-CHAN TO BE HIS SLAVE?
SLAVE?!
WHAT STORIES ARE YOU MAKING UP, STUPID *TOMATO!!*
SO MEAN!
DON'T CALL ME THAT! IT'S TOMAKO!
WHY ARE *YOU* WORKING HERE?!
I'M DOING THIS AS A FAVOR.
AND...
YOU HAVE A VISITOR.
HE LOOKS REALLY PISSED!

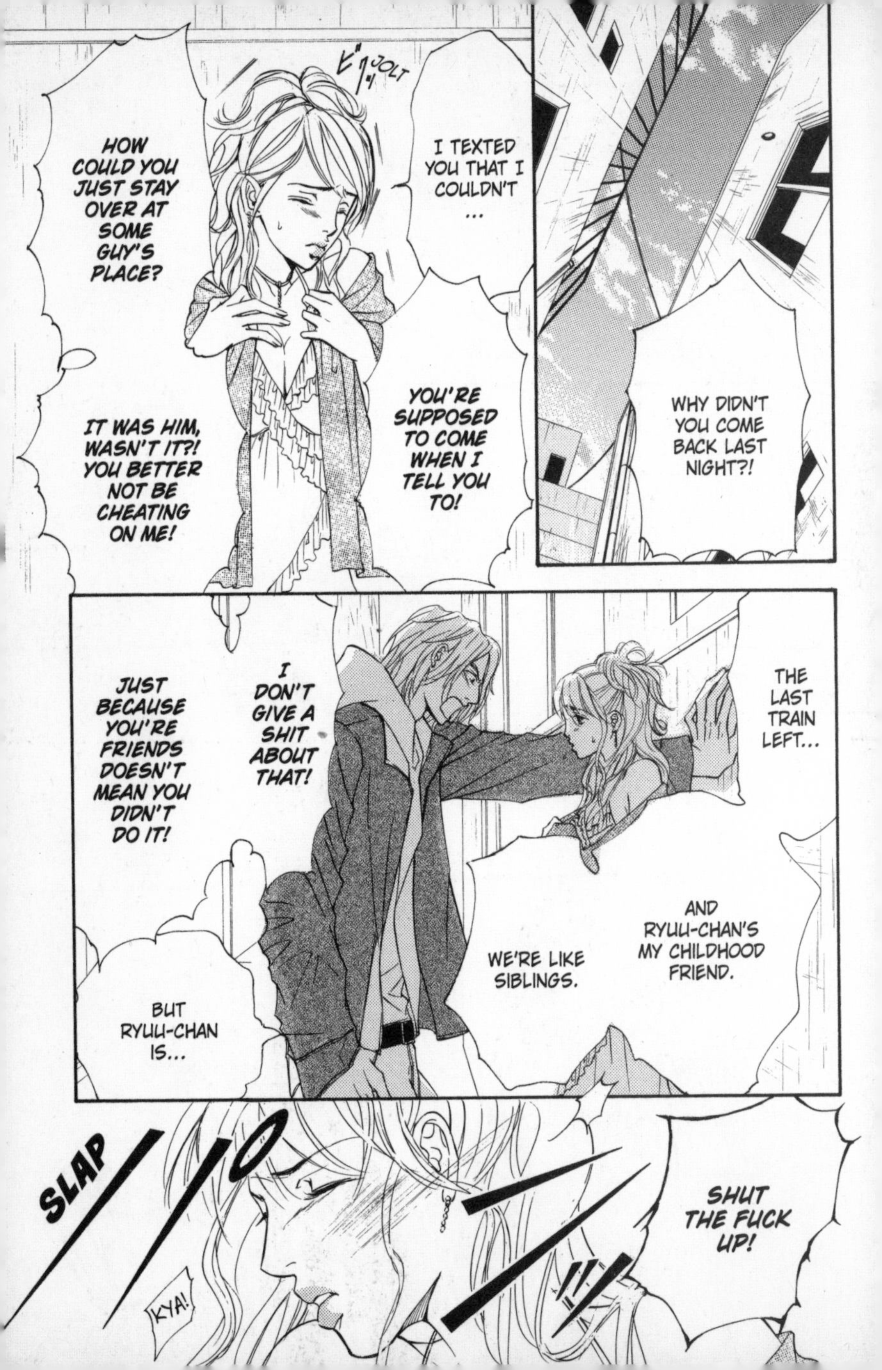
WHY DIDN'T YOU COME BACK LAST NIGHT?!
JOLT
I TEXTED YOU THAT I COULDN'T ...
HOW COULD YOU JUST STAY OVER AT SOME GUY'S PLACE?
YOU'RE SUPPOSED TO COME WHEN I TELL YOU TO!
IT WAS HIM, WASN'T IT?! YOU BETTER NOT BE CHEATING ON ME!
THE LAST TRAIN LEFT...
I DON'T GIVE A SHIT ABOUT THAT!
JUST BECAUSE YOU'RE FRIENDS DOESN'T MEAN YOU DIDN'T DO IT!
AND RYUU-CHAN'S MY CHILDHOOD FRIEND.
WE'RE LIKE SIBLINGS.
BUT RYUU-CHAN IS...
SHUT THE FUCK UP!
SLAP
KYA!

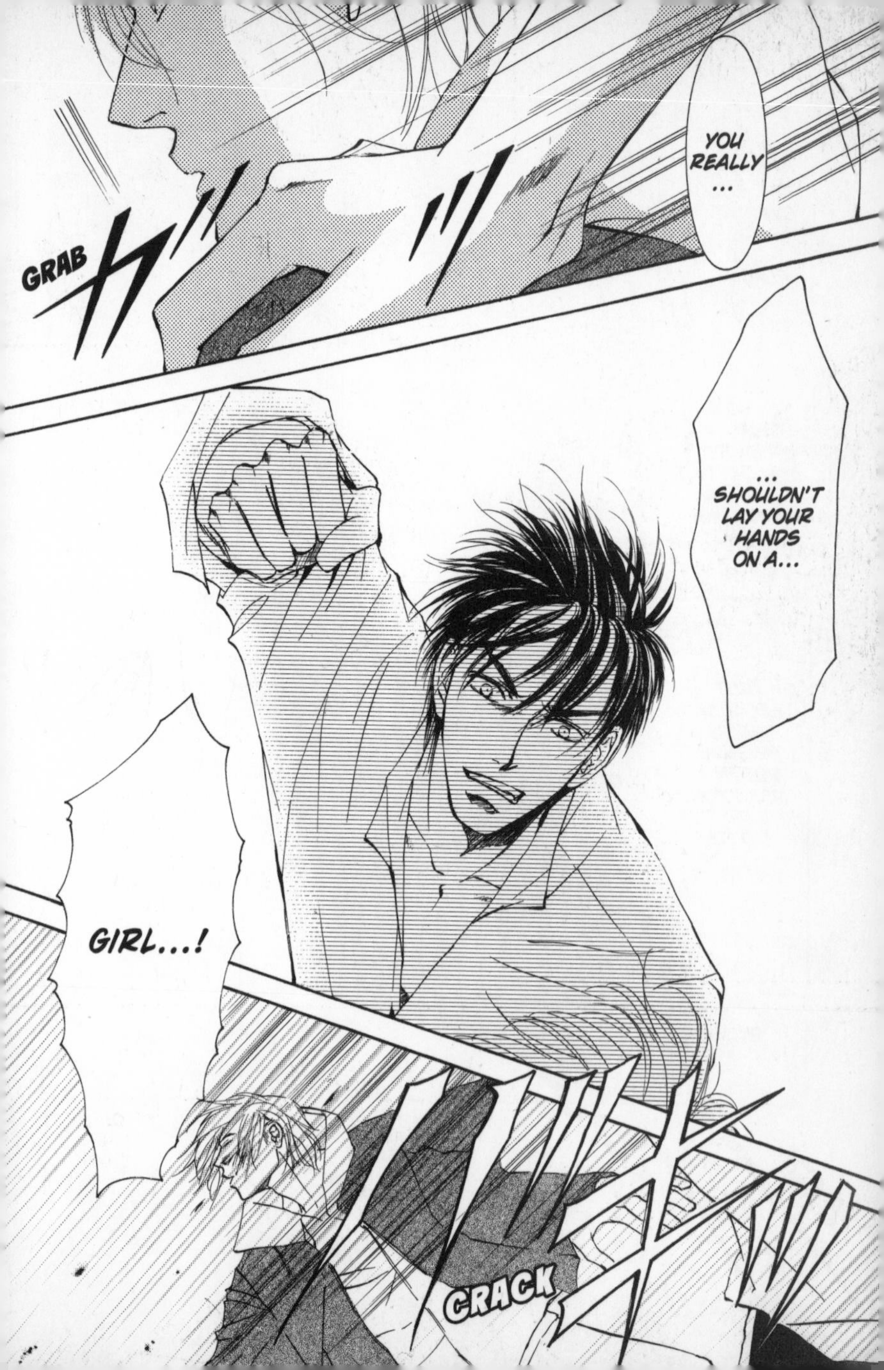
YOU REALLY ...
GRAB
... SHOULDN'T LAY YOUR HANDS ON A...
GIRL...!
CRACK

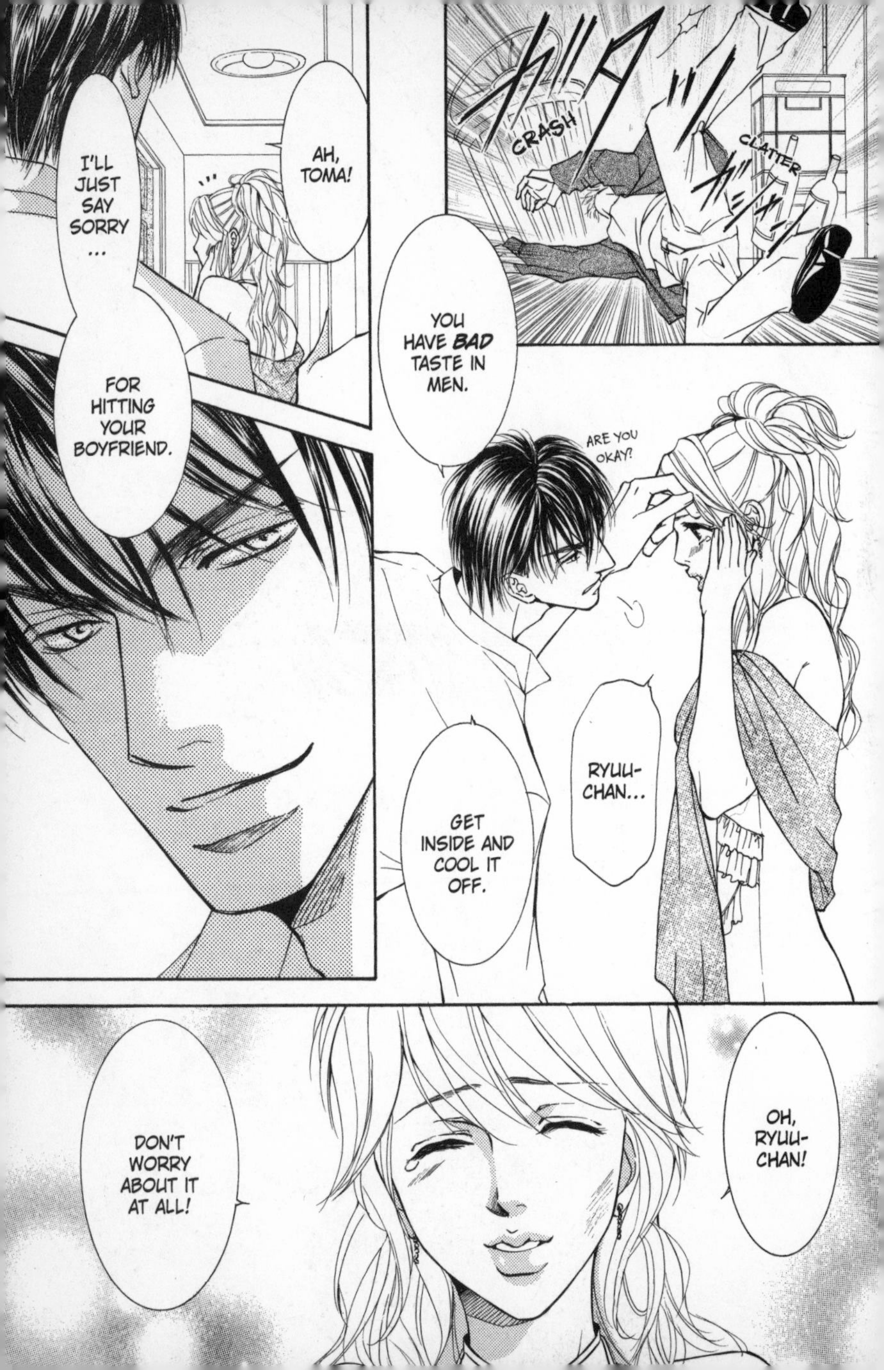
CRASH
CLATTER
AH, TOMA!
I'LL JUST SAY SORRY...
FOR HITTING YOUR BOYFRIEND.
YOU HAVE *BAD* TASTE IN MEN.
ARE YOU OKAY?
RYUU-CHAN...
GET INSIDE AND COOL IT OFF.
OH, RYUU-CHAN!
DON'T WORRY ABOUT IT AT ALL!

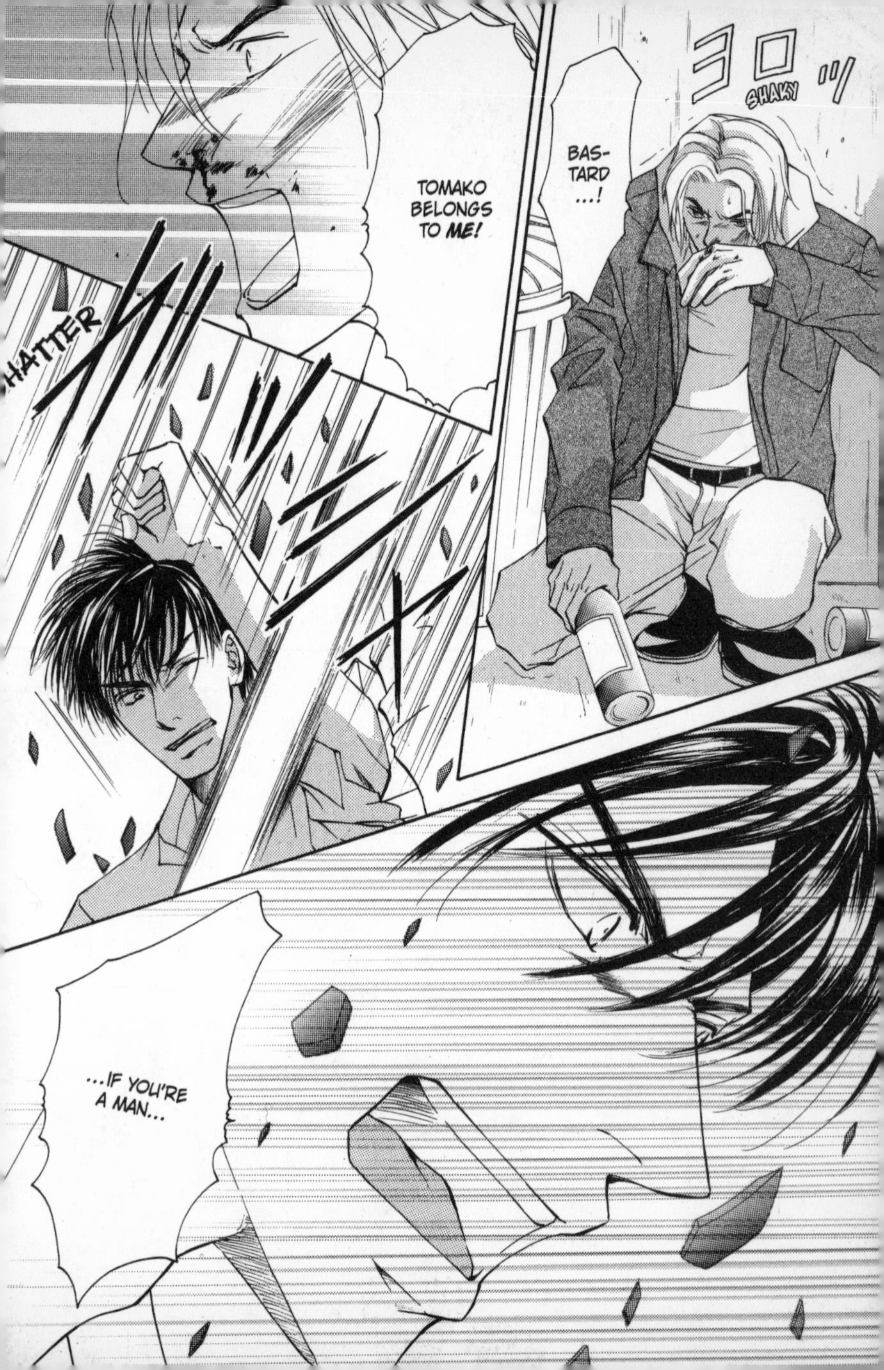
ヨロッ
SHAKY
BAS-TARD ...!
TOMAKO BELONGS TO ME!
HATTER
...IF YOU'RE A MAN...

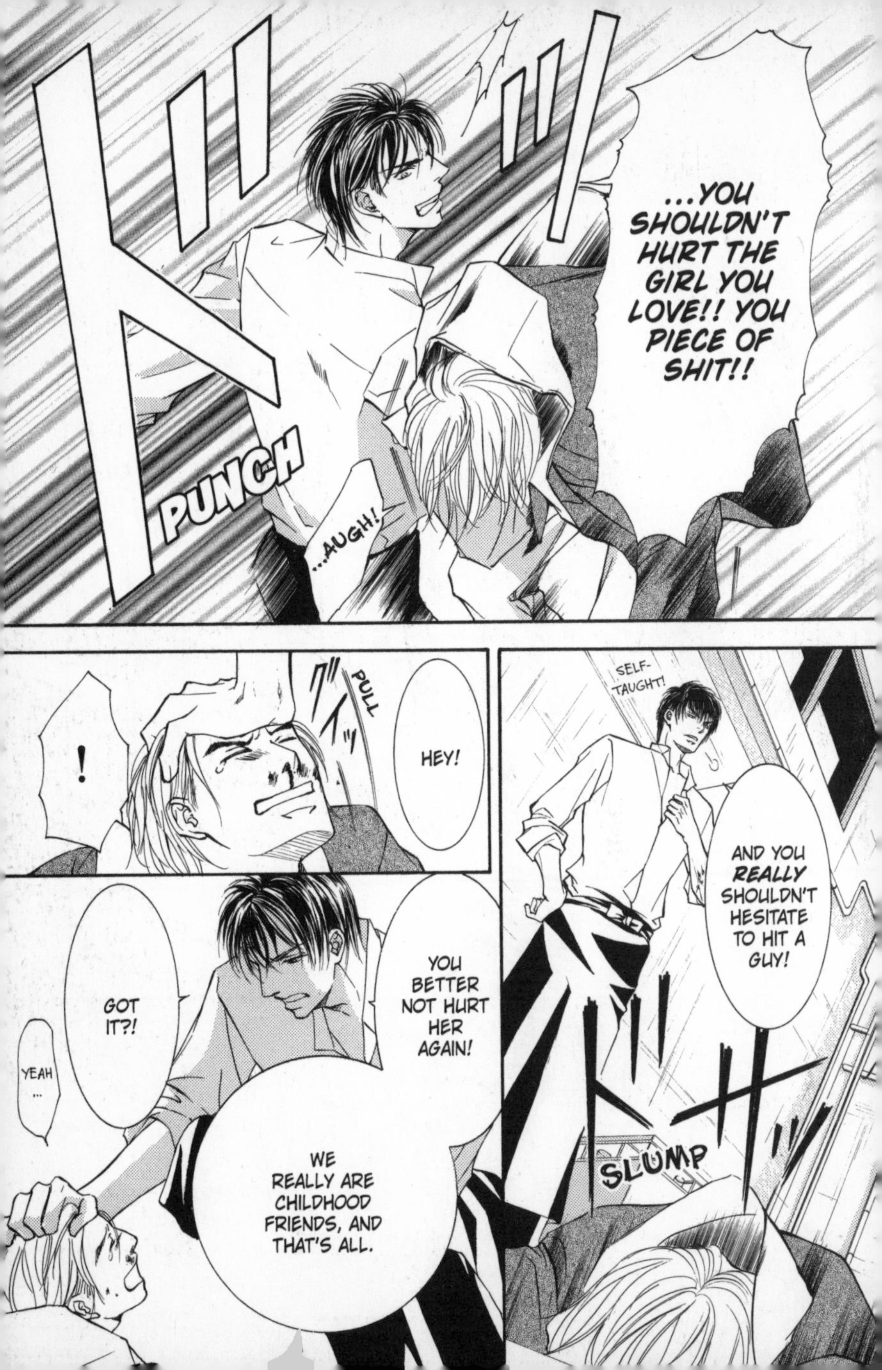
...YOU SHOULDN'T HURT THE GIRL YOU LOVE!! YOU PIECE OF SHIT!!
PUNCH
...AUGH!
SELF-TAUGHT!
AND YOU REALLY SHOULDN'T HESITATE TO HIT A GUY!
SLUMP
PULL
HEY!
!
YOU BETTER NOT HURT HER AGAIN!
GOT IT?!
YEAH ...
WE REALLY ARE CHILDHOOD FRIENDS, AND THAT'S ALL.

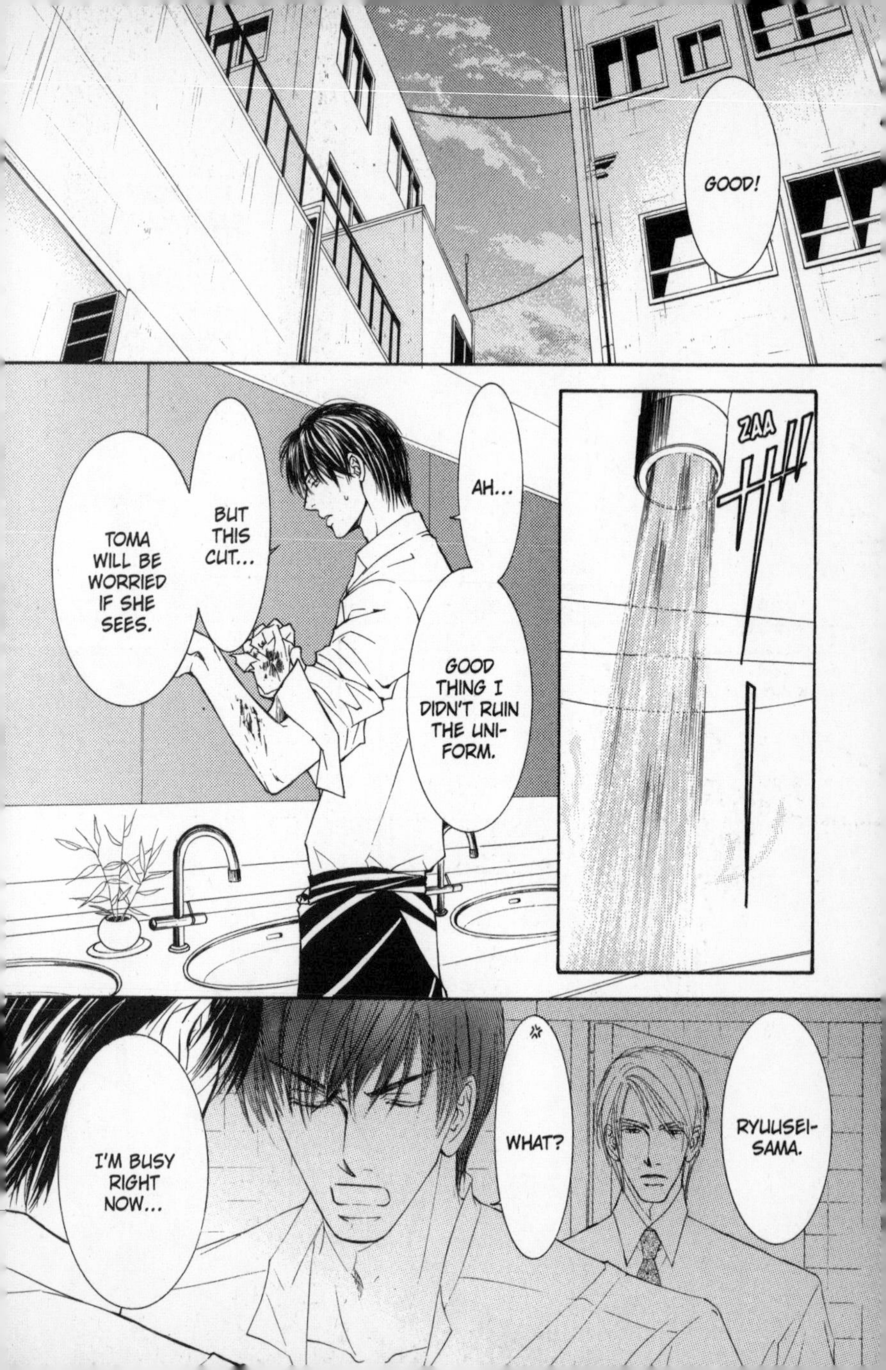
GOOD!
ZAA
AH...
GOOD THING I DIDN'T RUIN THE UNIFORM.
BUT THIS CUT...
TOMA WILL BE WORRIED IF SHE SEES.
RYUUSEI-SAMA.
WHAT?
I'M BUSY RIGHT NOW...

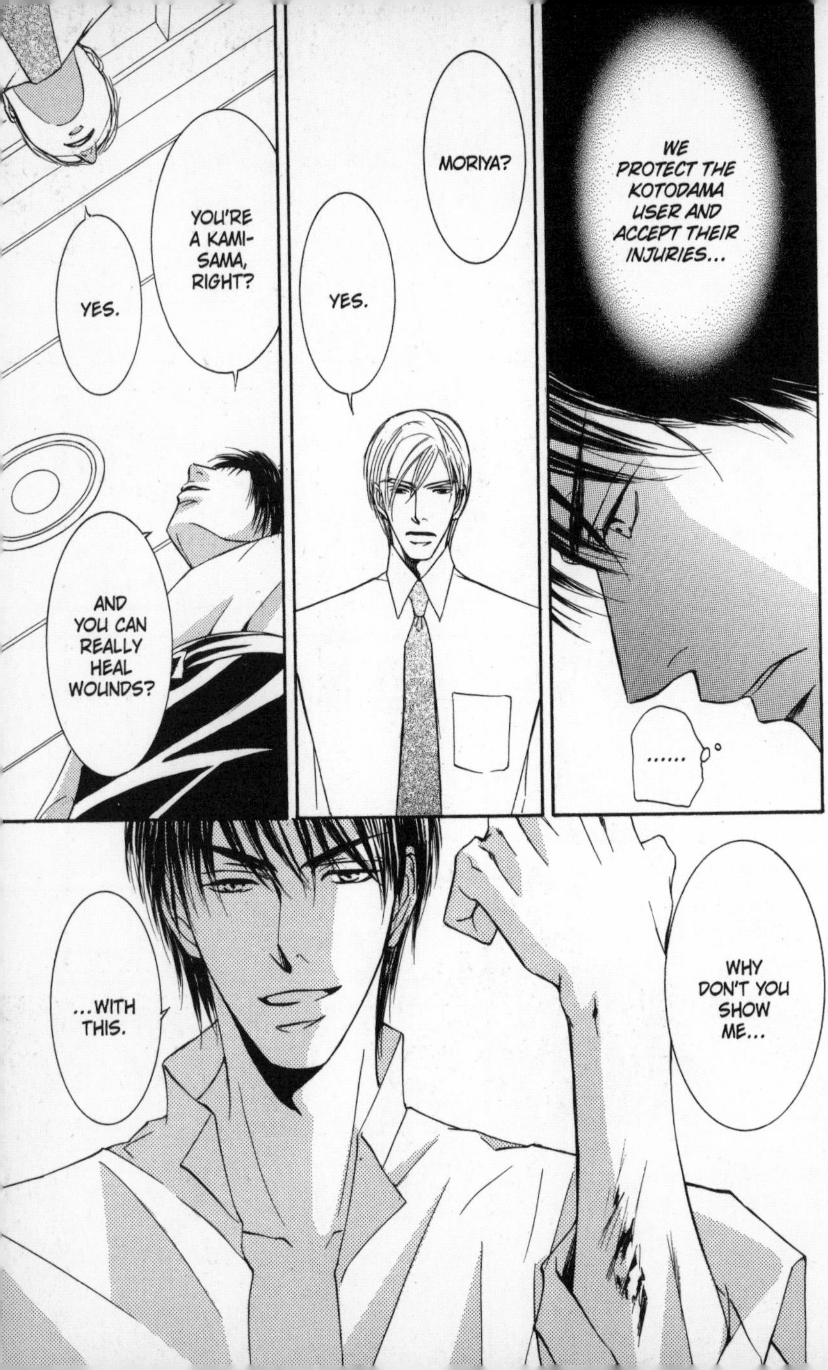
WE PROTECT THE KOTODAMA USER AND ACCEPT THEIR INJURIES...
......
MORIYA?
YES.
YOU'RE A KAMI-SAMA, RIGHT?
YES.
AND YOU CAN REALLY HEAL WOUNDS?
WHY DON'T YOU SHOW ME...
...WITH THIS.

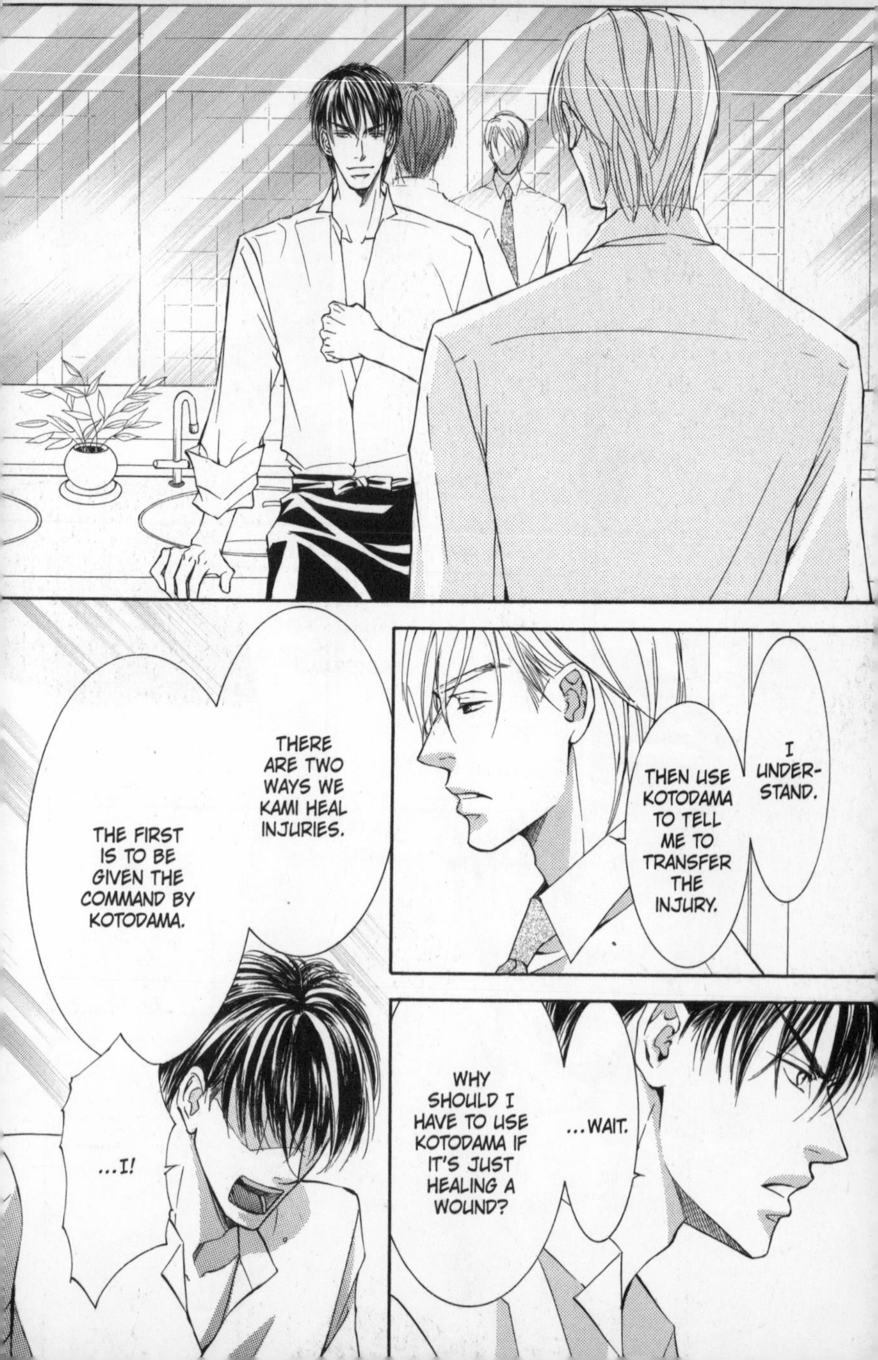
I UNDER-STAND.
THEN USE KOTODAMA TO TELL ME TO TRANSFER THE INJURY.
THERE ARE TWO WAYS WE KAMI HEAL INJURIES.
THE FIRST IS TO BE GIVEN THE COMMAND BY KOTODAMA.
...WAIT.
WHY SHOULD I HAVE TO USE KOTODAMA IF IT'S JUST HEALING A WOUND?
...I!

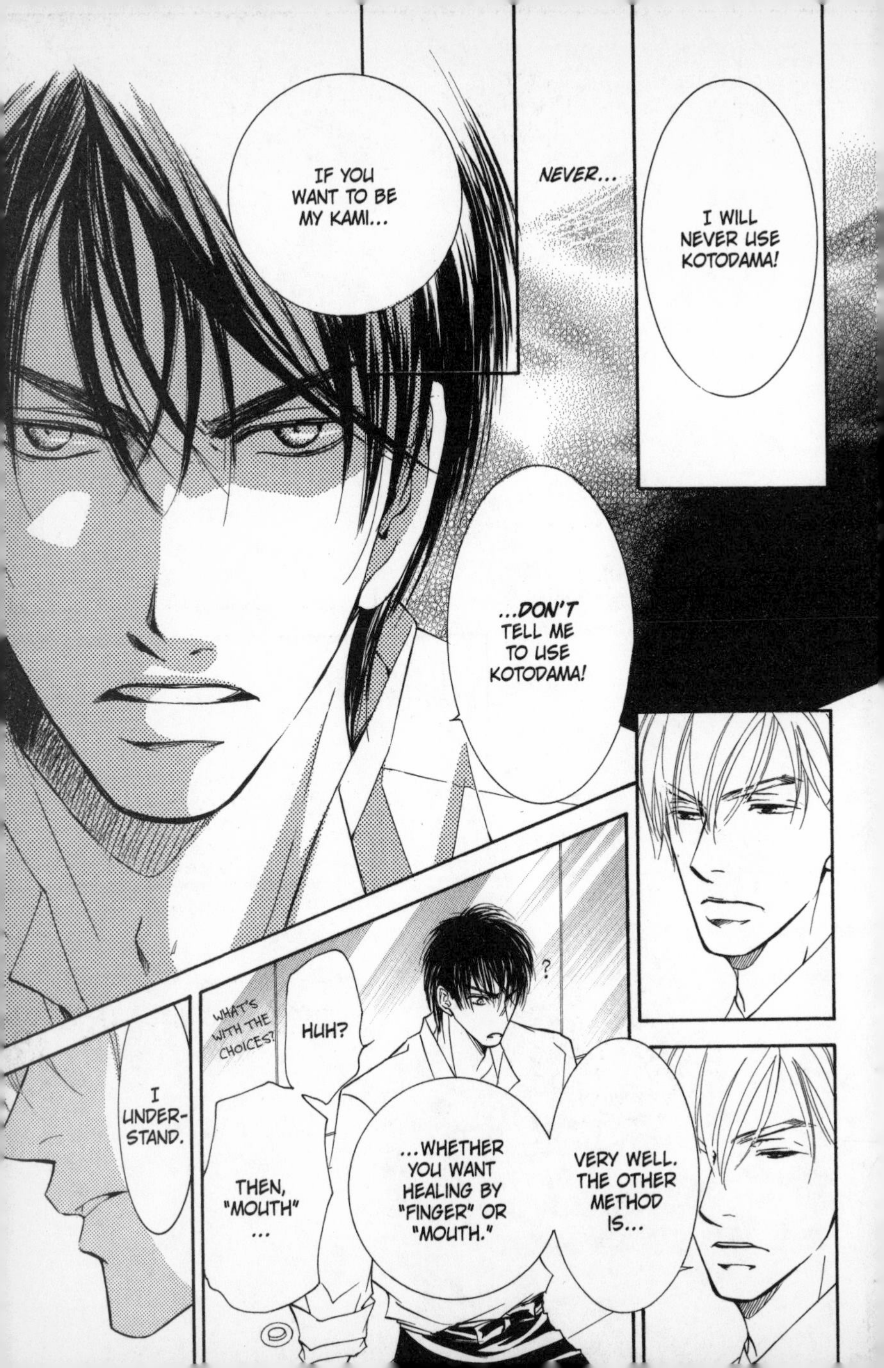
I WILL NEVER USE KOTODAMA!
NEVER...
IF YOU WANT TO BE MY KAMI...
...DON'T TELL ME TO USE KOTODAMA!
VERY WELL. THE OTHER METHOD IS...
...WHETHER YOU WANT HEALING BY "FINGER" OR "MOUTH."
?
HUH?
WHAT'S WITH THE CHOICES?
THEN, "MOUTH" ...
I UNDER-STAND.

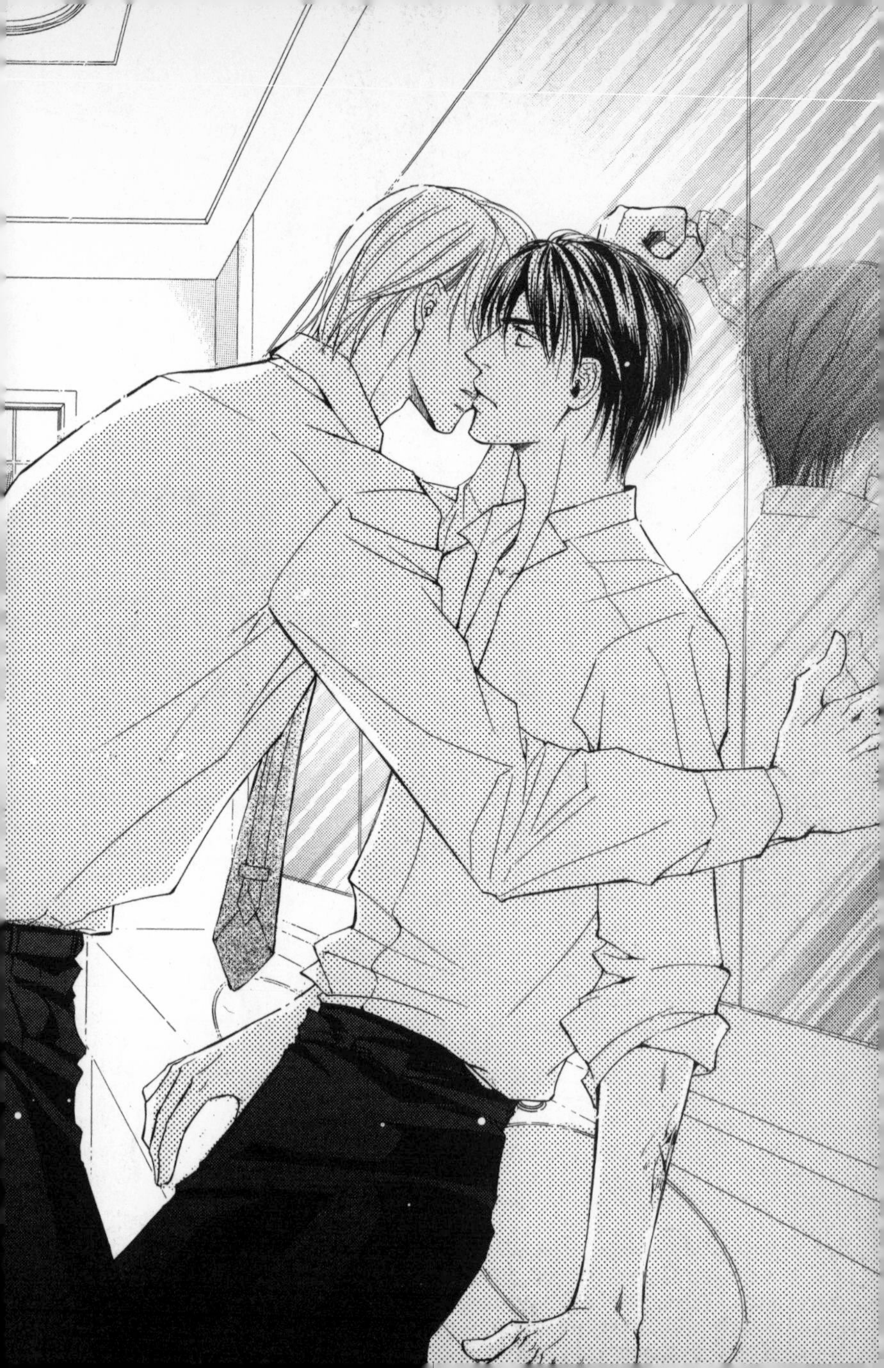

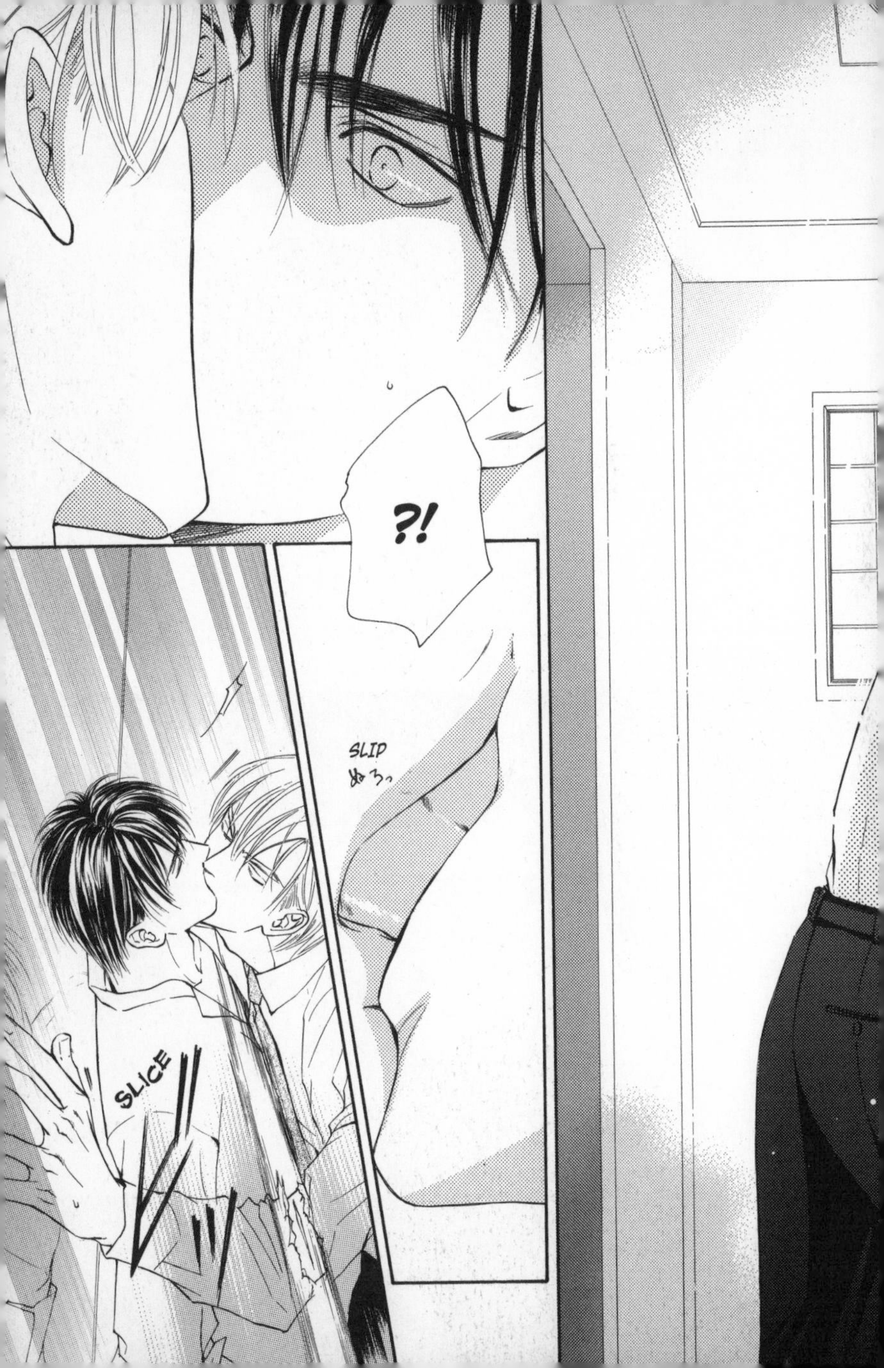
?!
SLIP
ぬるっ
SLICE

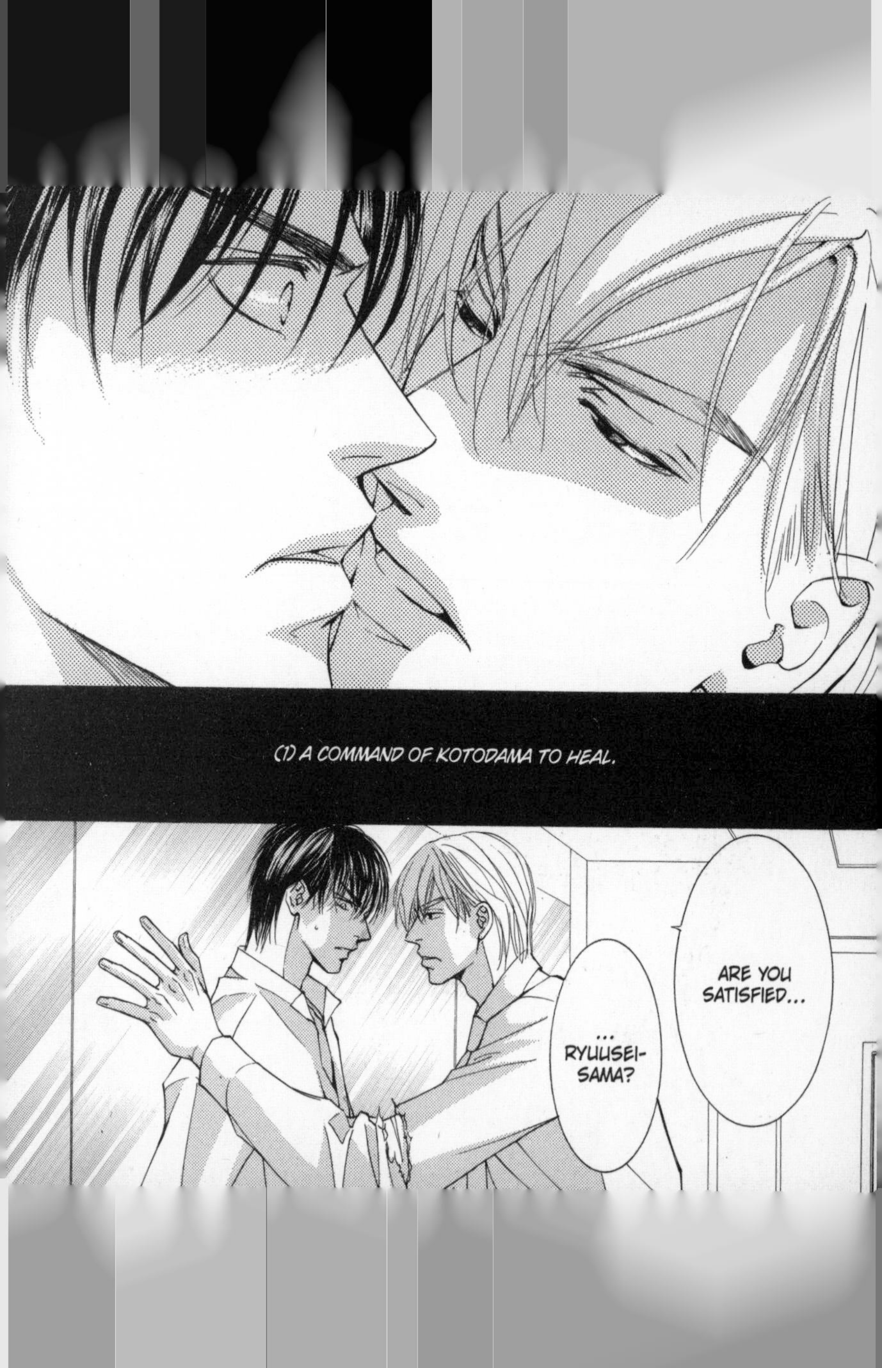
(1) A COMMAND OF KOTODAMA TO HEAL.
ARE YOU SATISFIED...
... RYUUSEI-SAMA?

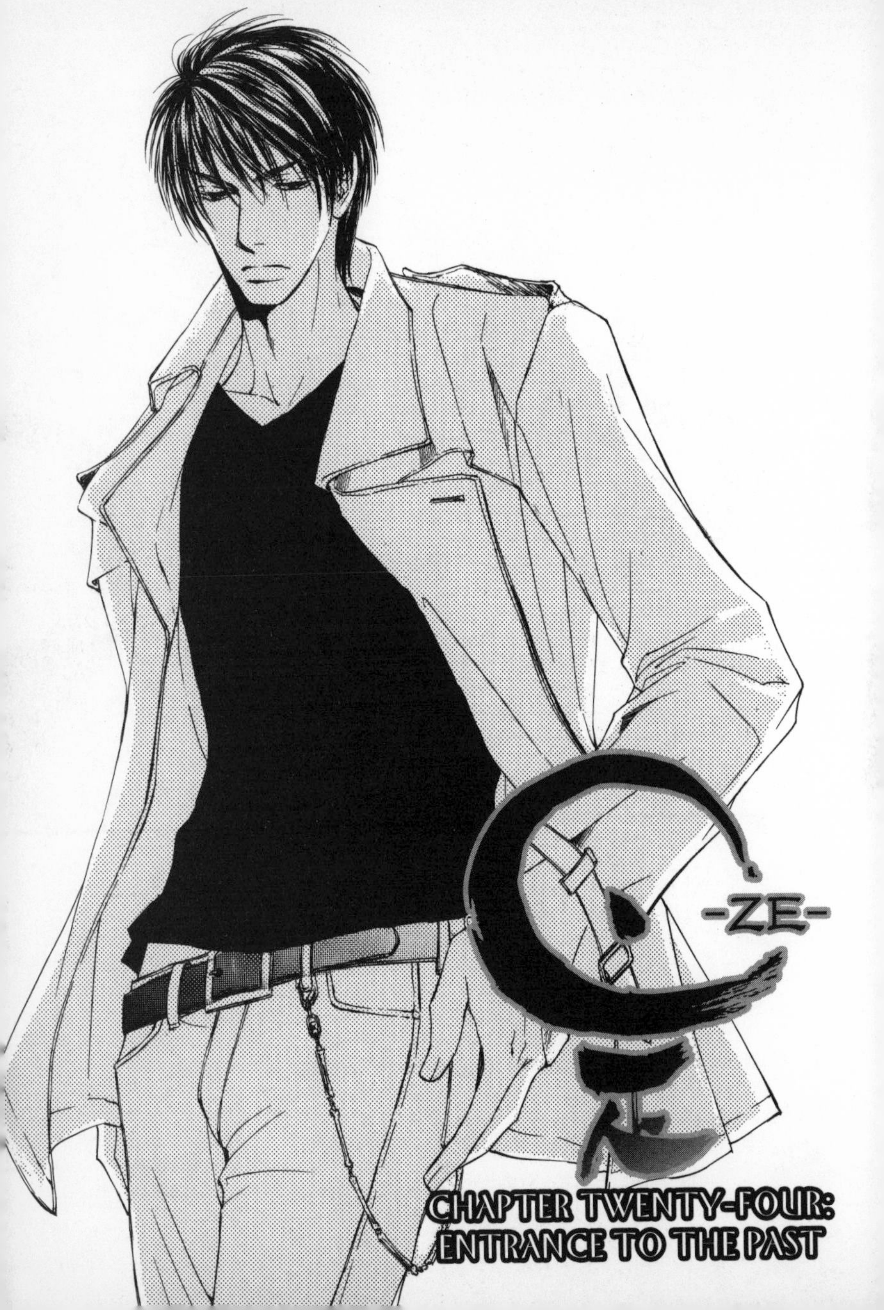
-ZE-
CHAPTER TWENTY-FOUR:
ENTRANCE TO THE PAST

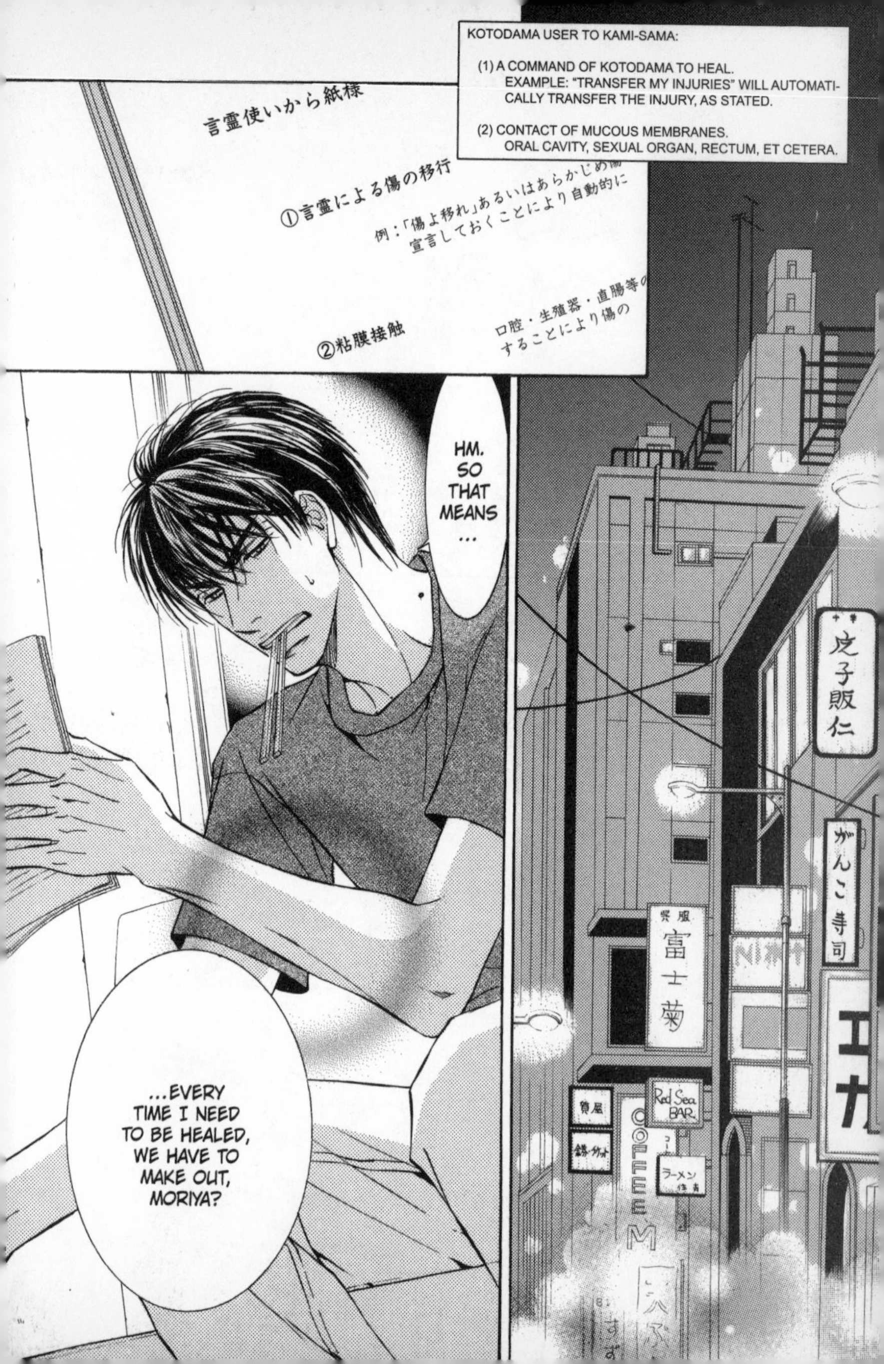
Red Sea BAR
COFFEE
ラーメン
KOTODAMA USER TO KAMI-SAMA:
(1) A COMMAND OF KOTODAMA TO HEAL.
EXAMPLE: "TRANSFER MY INJURIES" WILL AUTOMATICALLY TRANSFER THE INJURY, AS STATED.
(2) CONTACT OF MUCOUS MEMBRANES.
ORAL CAVITY, SEXUAL ORGAN, RECTUM, ET CETERA.
言霊使いから紙様
①言霊による傷の移行
例：「傷よ移れ」あるいはあらかじめ傷
宣言しておくことにより自動的に
②粘膜接触
口腔・生殖器・直腸等の
することにより傷の
HM. SO THAT MEANS...
...EVERY TIME I NEED TO BE HEALED, WE HAVE TO MAKE OUT, MORIYA?

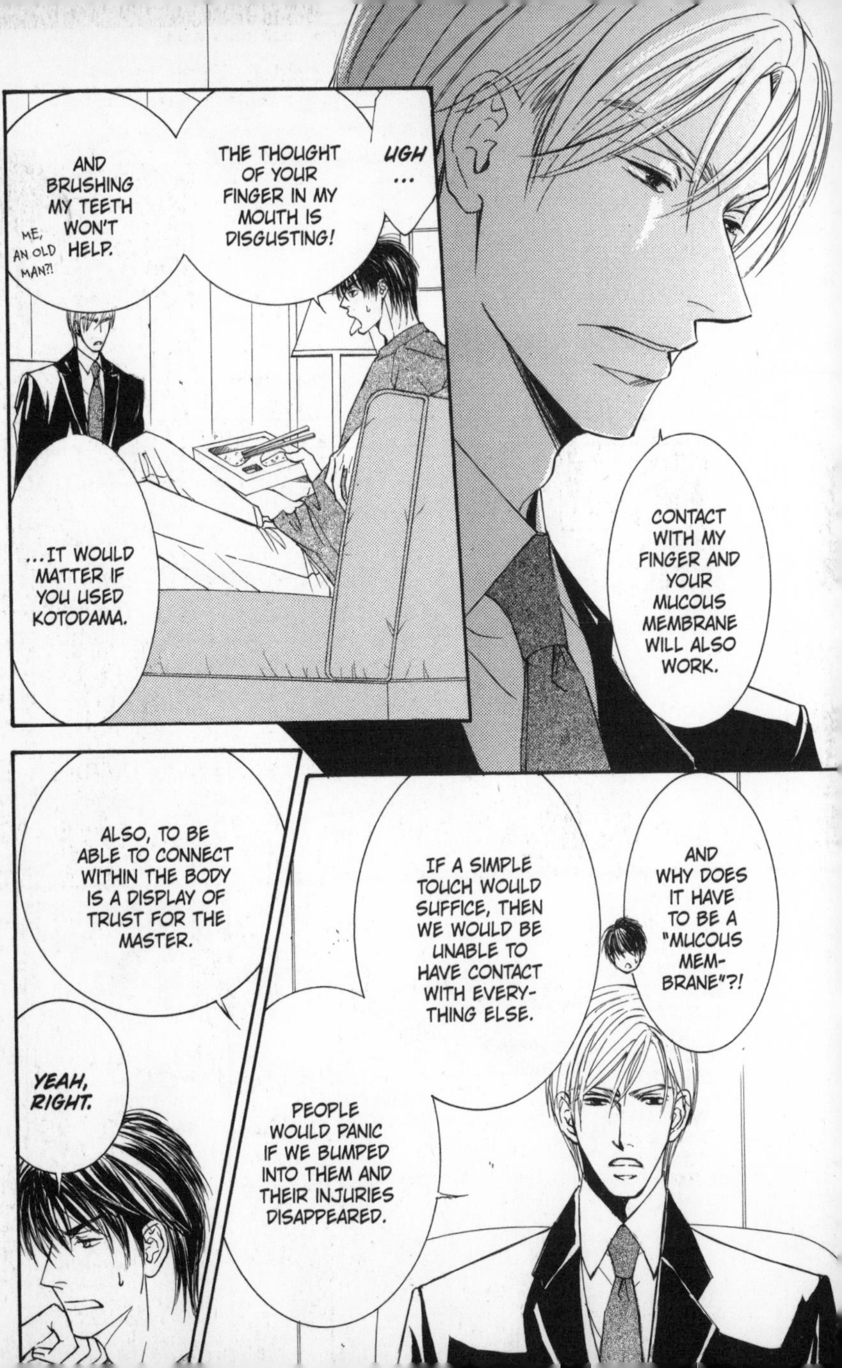
UGH ...
THE THOUGHT OF YOUR FINGER IN MY MOUTH IS DISGUSTING!
AND BRUSHING MY TEETH WON'T HELP.
ME, AN OLD MAN?!
...IT WOULD MATTER IF YOU USED KOTODAMA.
CONTACT WITH MY FINGER AND YOUR MUCOUS MEMBRANE WILL ALSO WORK.
AND WHY DOES IT HAVE TO BE A "MUCOUS MEM-BRANE"?!
IF A SIMPLE TOUCH WOULD SUFFICE, THEN WE WOULD BE UNABLE TO HAVE CONTACT WITH EVERY-THING ELSE.
PEOPLE WOULD PANIC IF WE BUMPED INTO THEM AND THEIR INJURIES DISAPPEARED.
ALSO, TO BE ABLE TO CONNECT WITHIN THE BODY IS A DISPLAY OF TRUST FOR THE MASTER.
YEAH, RIGHT.

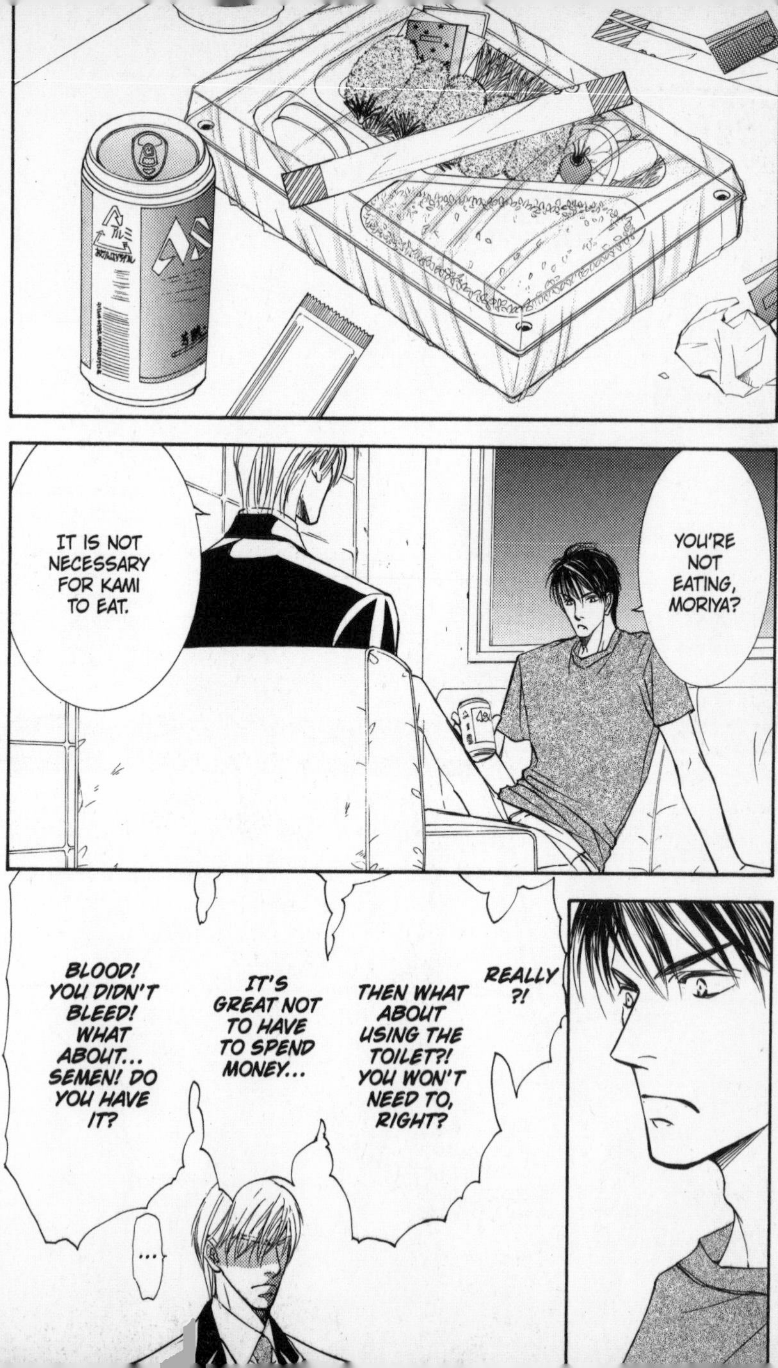
YOU'RE NOT EATING, MORIYA?
IT IS NOT NECESSARY FOR KAMI TO EAT.
REALLY ?!
THEN WHAT ABOUT USING THE TOILET?! YOU WON'T NEED TO, RIGHT?
IT'S GREAT NOT TO HAVE TO SPEND MONEY...
BLOOD! YOU DIDN'T BLEED! WHAT ABOUT... SEMEN! DO YOU HAVE IT?
...

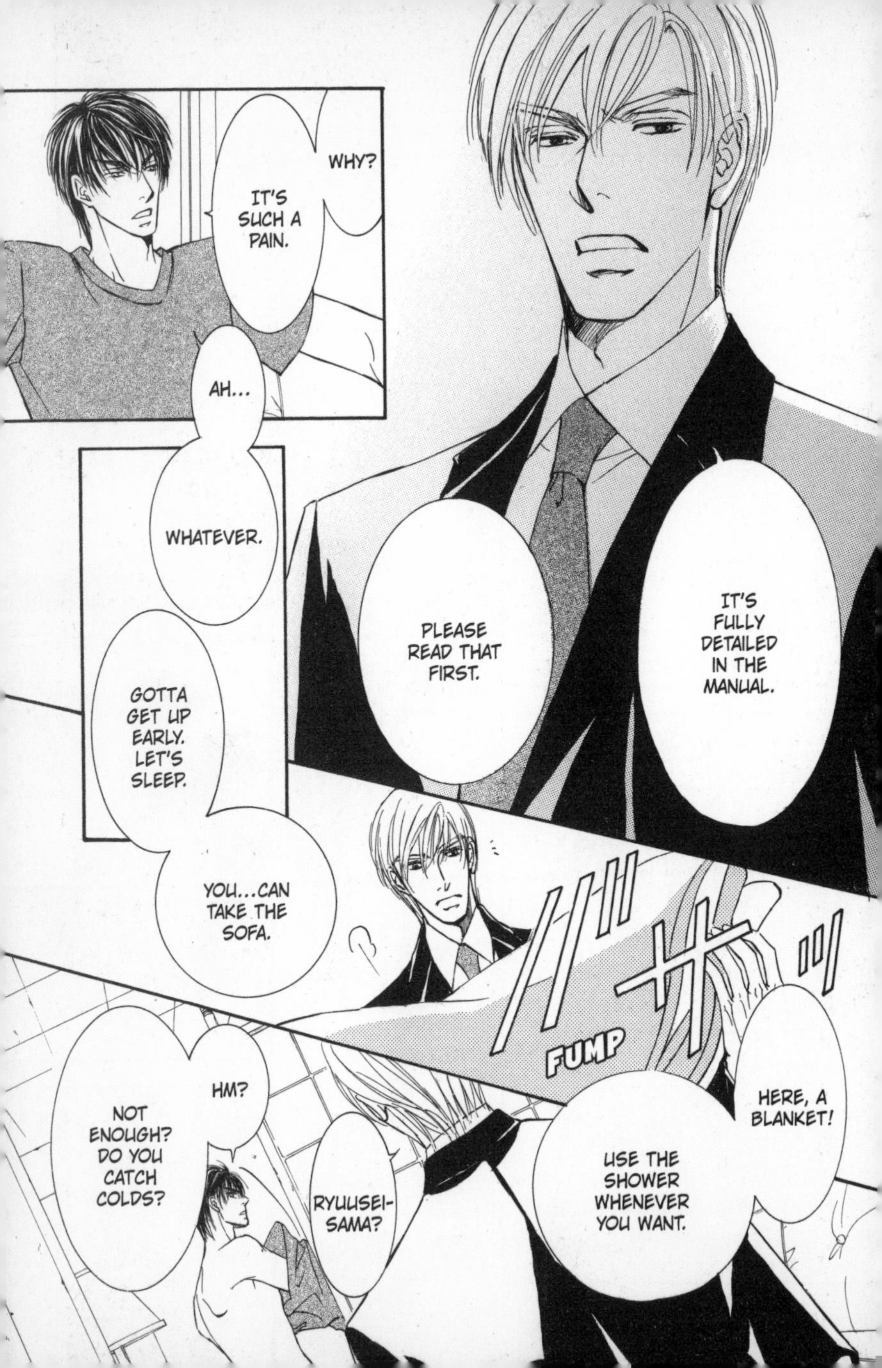
IT'S FULLY DETAILED IN THE MANUAL.
PLEASE READ THAT FIRST.
WHY?
IT'S SUCH A PAIN.
AH...
WHATEVER.
GOTTA GET UP EARLY. LET'S SLEEP.
YOU...CAN TAKE THE SOFA.
FUMP
HERE, A BLANKET!
USE THE SHOWER WHENEVER YOU WANT.
RYUUSEI-SAMA?
HM?
NOT ENOUGH? DO YOU CATCH COLDS?

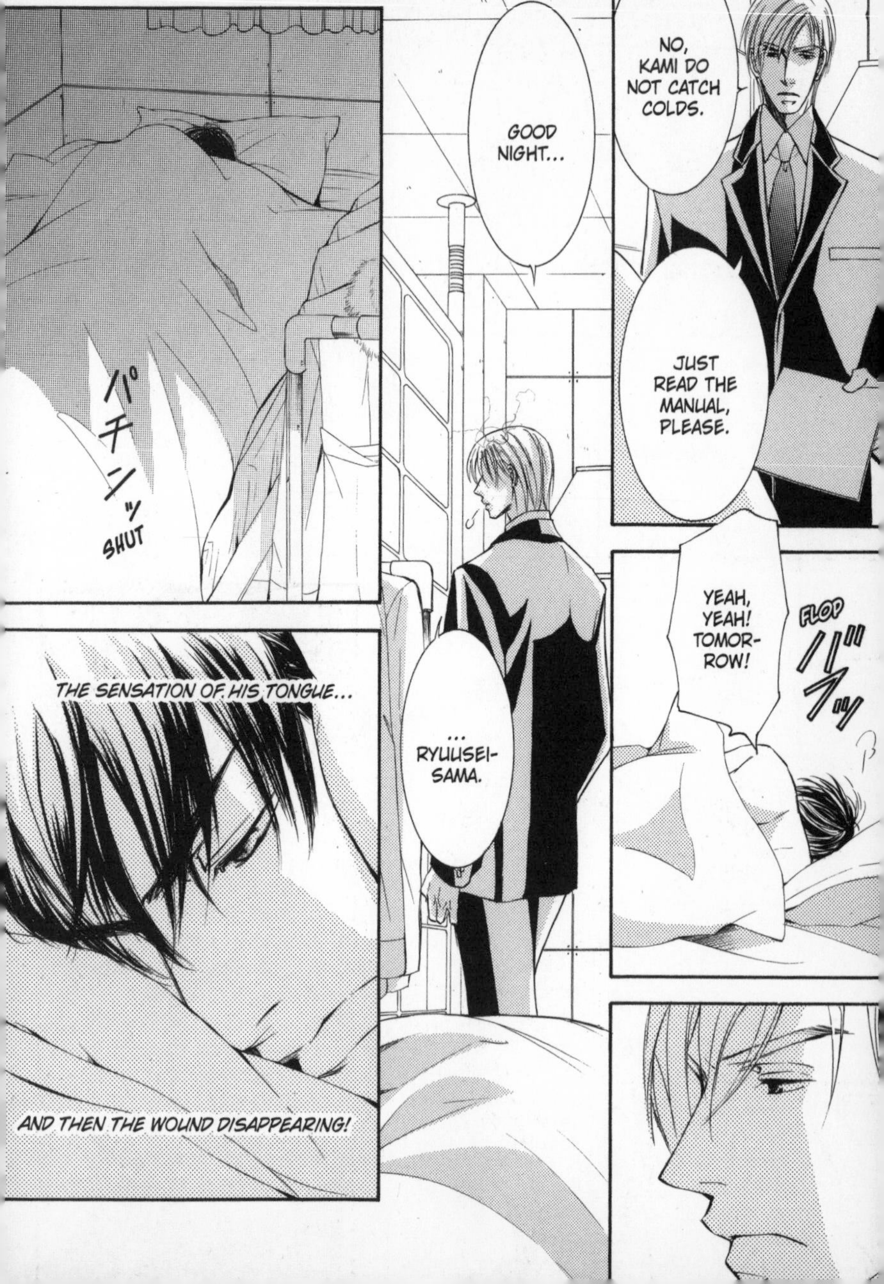
NO, KAMI DO NOT CATCH COLDS.
JUST READ THE MANUAL, PLEASE.
YEAH, YEAH! TOMORROW!
バフッ
FLOP
GOOD NIGHT...
... RYUUSEI-SAMA.
パチンッ
SHUT
THE SENSATION OF HIS TONGUE...
AND THEN THE WOUND DISAPPEARING!

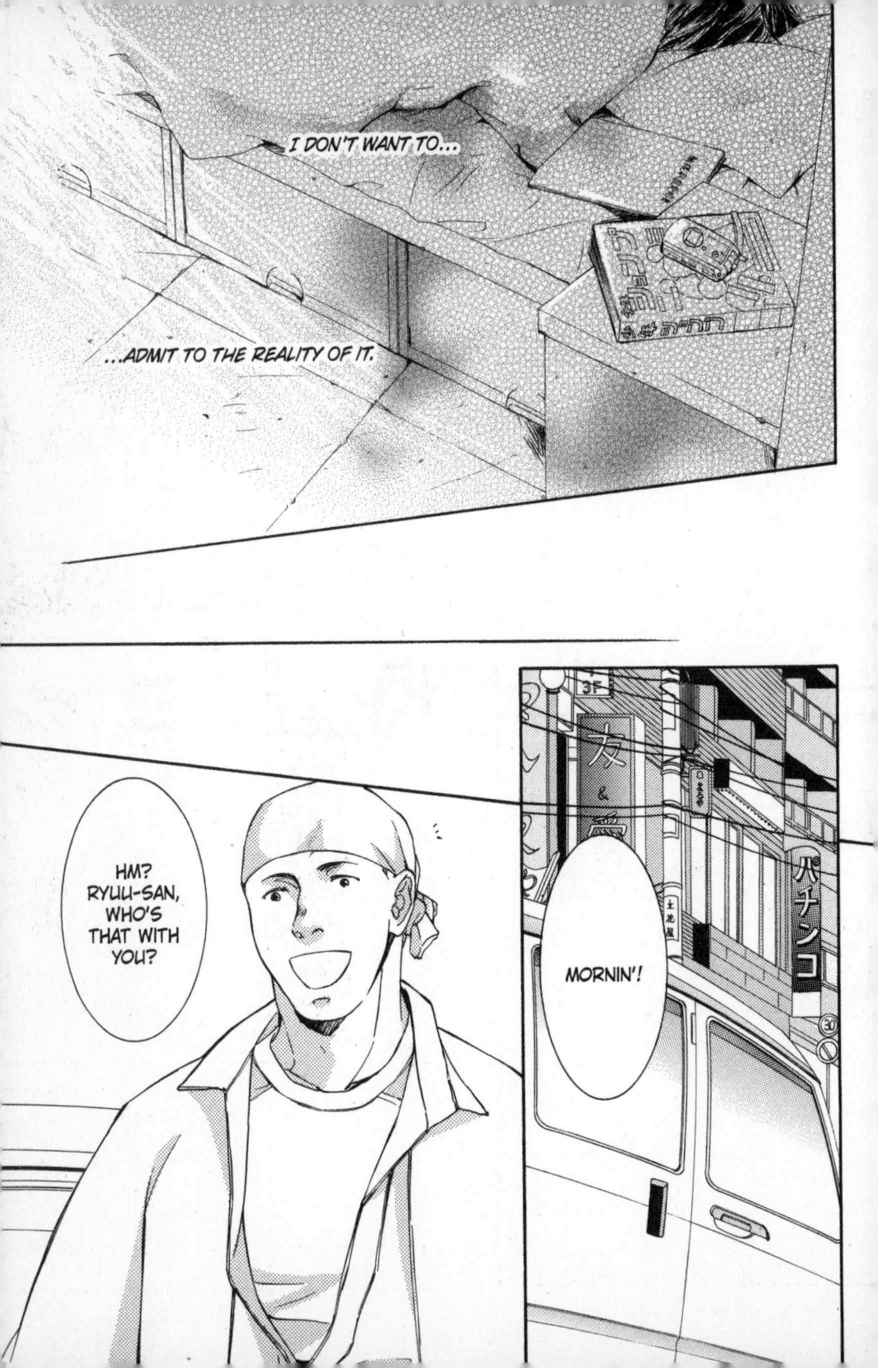
I DON'T WANT TO...
...ADMIT TO THE REALITY OF IT.
3F
パチンコ
MORNIN'!
HM? RYUU-SAN, WHO'S THAT WITH YOU?

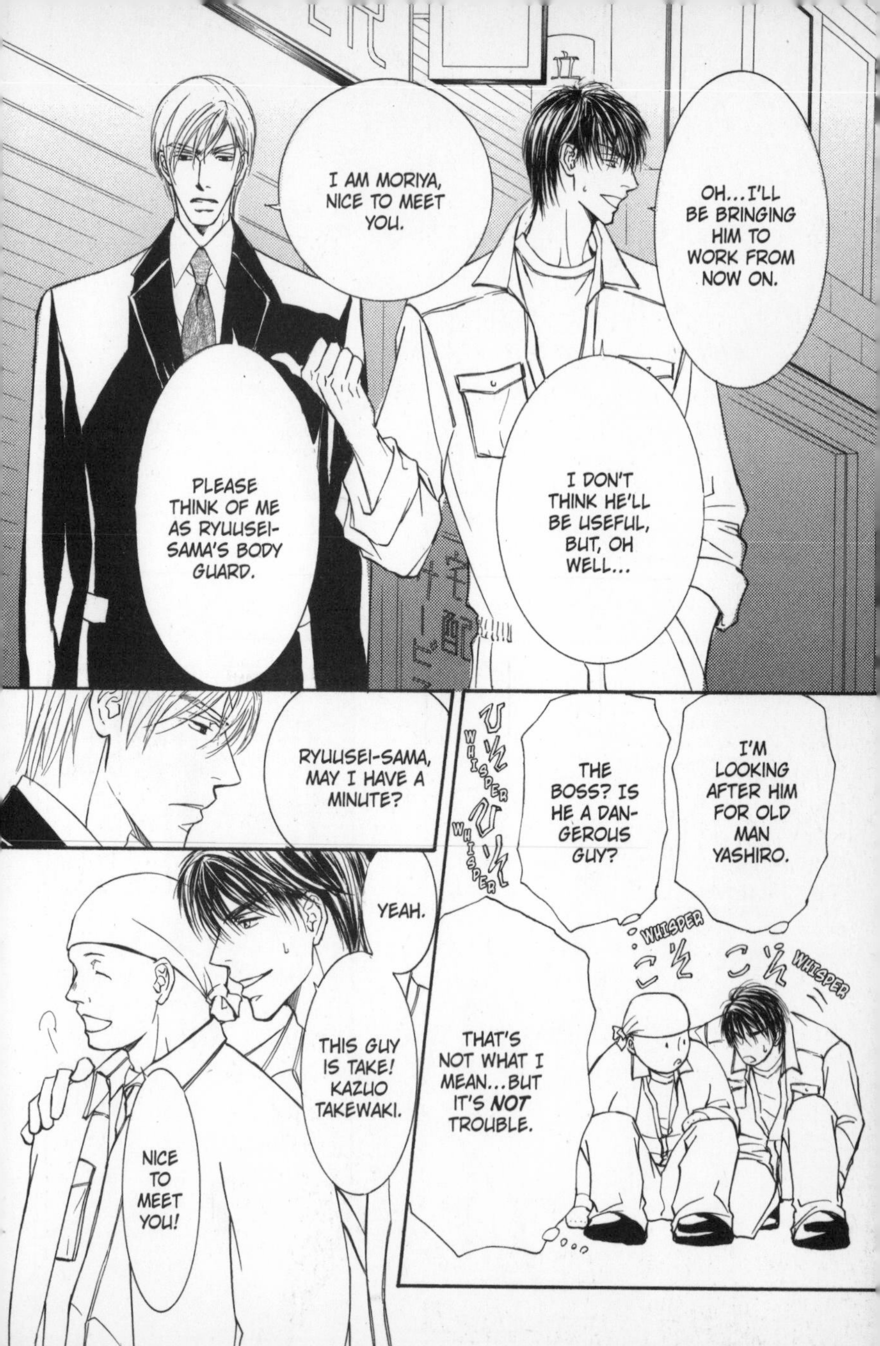
OH...I'LL BE BRINGING HIM TO WORK FROM NOW ON.
I AM MORIYA, NICE TO MEET YOU.
I DON'T THINK HE'LL BE USEFUL, BUT, OH WELL...
PLEASE THINK OF ME AS RYUUSEI-SAMA'S BODY GUARD.
I'M LOOKING AFTER HIM FOR OLD MAN YASHIRO.
THE BOSS? IS HE A DANGEROUS GUY?
WHISPER
WHISPER
WHISPER
WHISPER
THAT'S NOT WHAT I MEAN...BUT IT'S *NOT* TROUBLE.
RYUUSEI-SAMA, MAY I HAVE A MINUTE?
YEAH.
THIS GUY IS TAKE! KAZUO TAKEWAKI.
NICE TO MEET YOU!

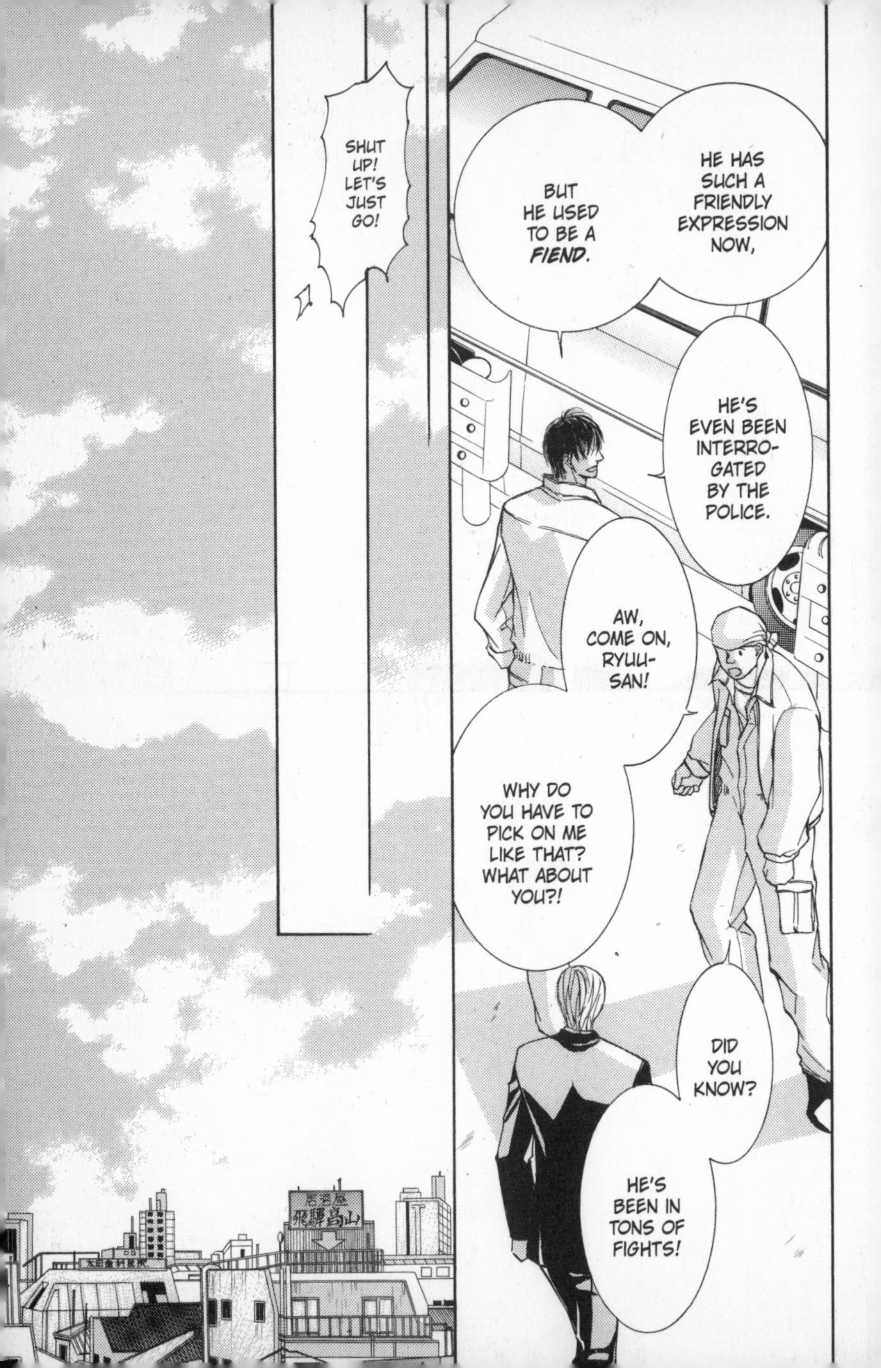
HE HAS SUCH A FRIENDLY EXPRESSION NOW,
BUT HE USED TO BE A *FIEND*.
HE'S EVEN BEEN INTERRO-GATED BY THE POLICE.
AW, COME ON, RYUU-SAN!
WHY DO YOU HAVE TO PICK ON ME LIKE THAT? WHAT ABOUT YOU?!
DID YOU KNOW?
HE'S BEEN IN TONS OF FIGHTS!
SHUT UP! LET'S JUST GO!

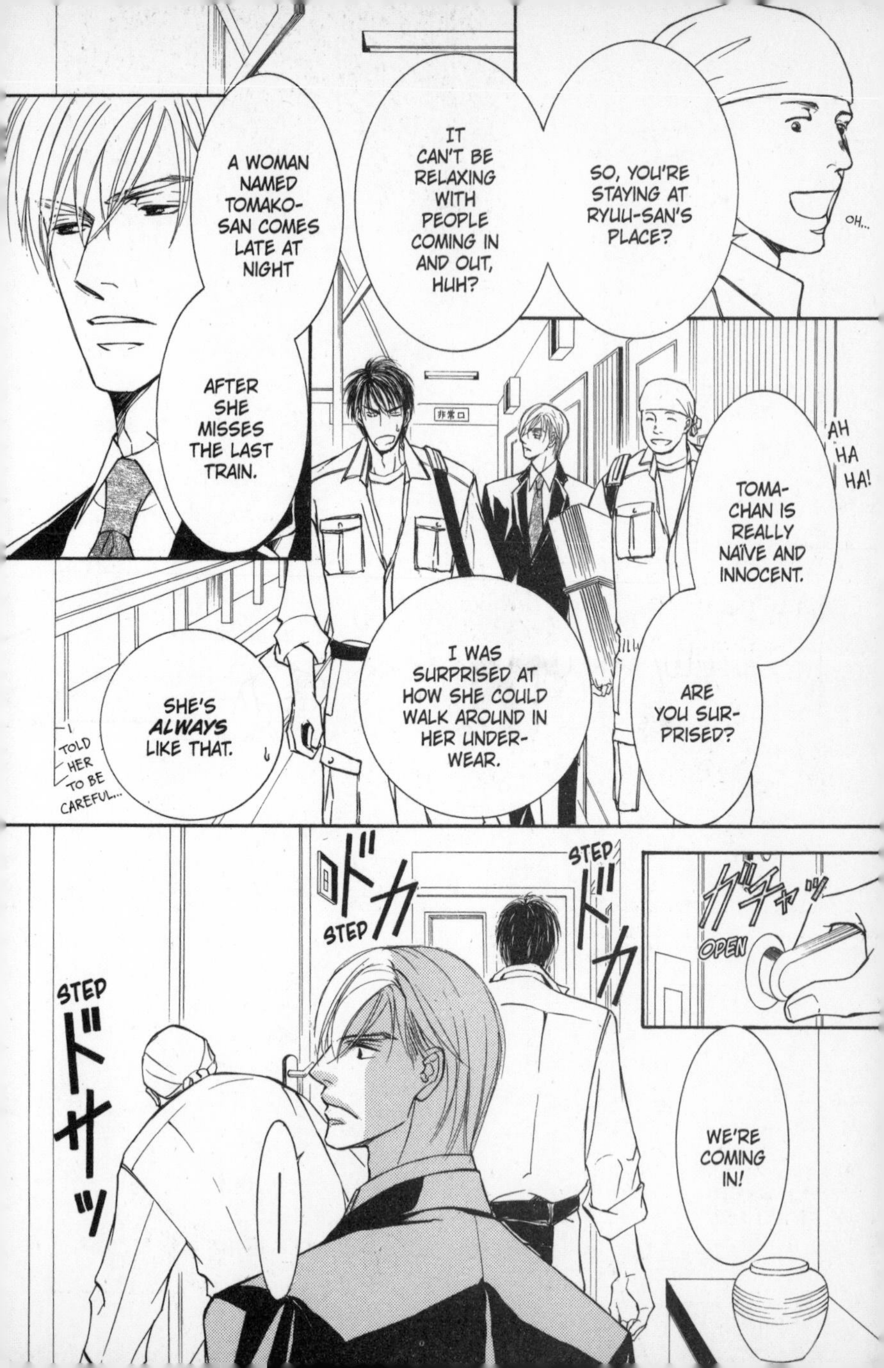

OH...
SO, YOU'RE STAYING AT RYUU-SAN'S PLACE?
IT CAN'T BE RELAXING WITH PEOPLE COMING IN AND OUT, HUH?
A WOMAN NAMED TOMAKO-SAN COMES LATE AT NIGHT
AFTER SHE MISSES THE LAST TRAIN.
非常口
AH HA HA!
TOMA-CHAN IS REALLY NAÏVE AND INNOCENT.
ARE YOU SURPRISED?
I WAS SURPRISED AT HOW SHE COULD WALK AROUND IN HER UNDER-WEAR.
SHE'S ***ALWAYS*** LIKE THAT.
I TOLD HER TO BE CAREFUL...
ガチャッ
OPEN
WE'RE COMING IN!
STEP
ドカ
STEP
ドカ
STEP
ドサッ

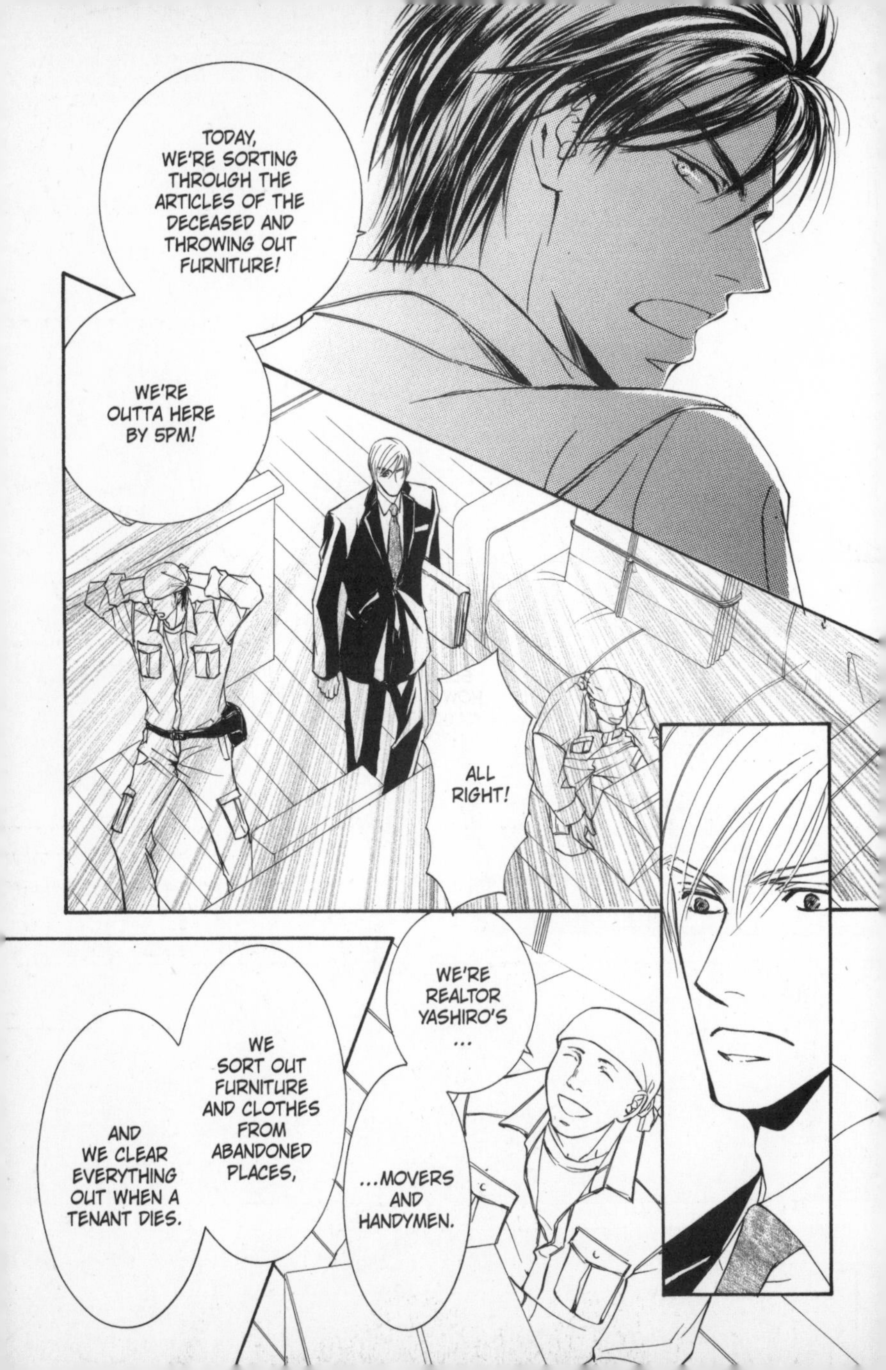
TODAY, WE'RE SORTING THROUGH THE ARTICLES OF THE DECEASED AND THROWING OUT FURNITURE!
WE'RE OUTTA HERE BY 5PM!
ALL RIGHT!
WE'RE REALTOR YASHIRO'S ...
...MOVERS AND HANDYMEN.
WE SORT OUT FURNITURE AND CLOTHES FROM ABANDONED PLACES,
AND WE CLEAR EVERYTHING OUT WHEN A TENANT DIES.

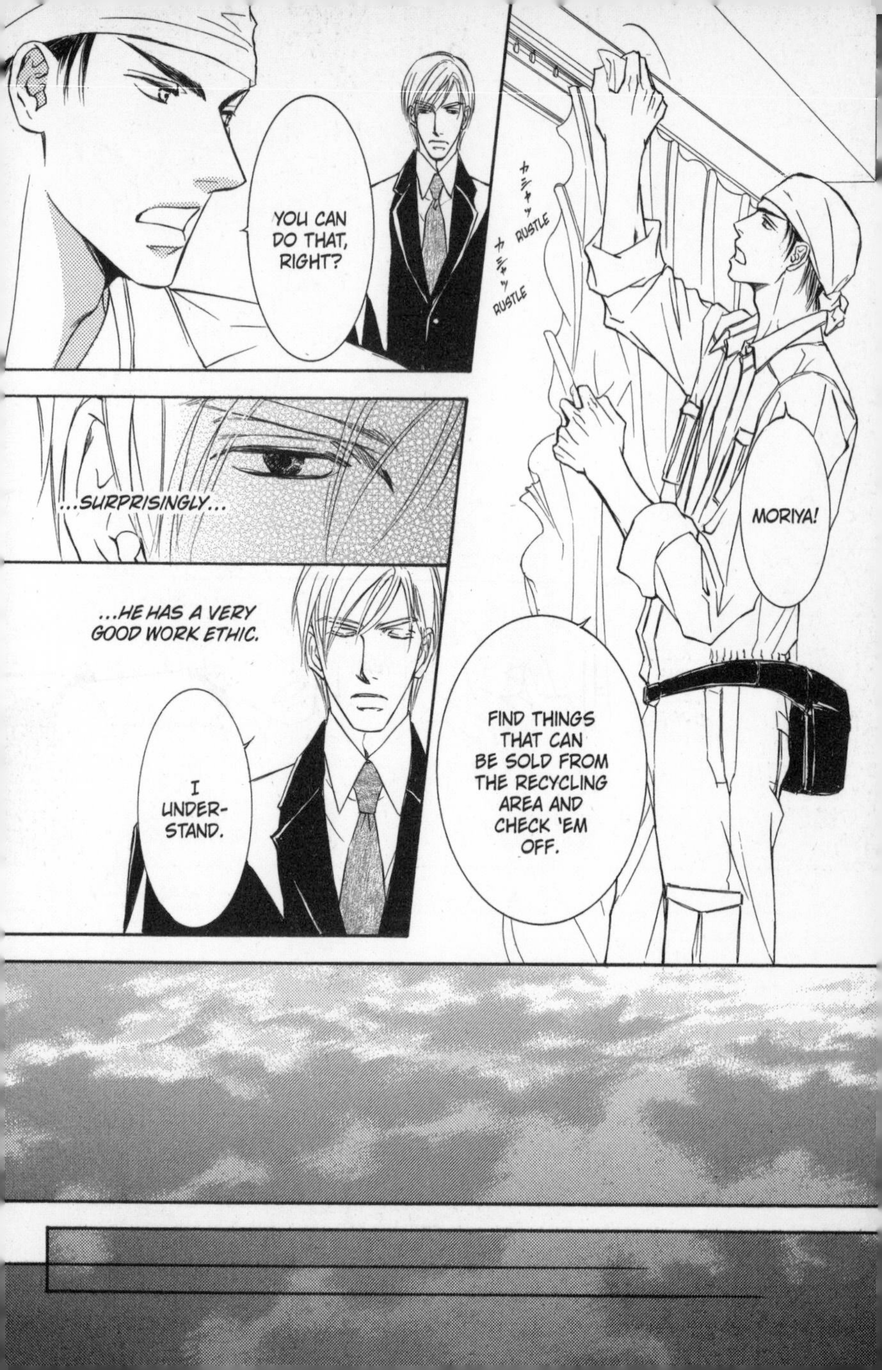
カシャッ RUSTLE
カシャッ RUSTLE
MORIYA!
FIND THINGS THAT CAN BE SOLD FROM THE RECYCLING AREA AND CHECK 'EM OFF.
YOU CAN DO THAT, RIGHT?
...SURPRISINGLY...
...HE HAS A VERY GOOD WORK ETHIC.
I UNDER-STAND.

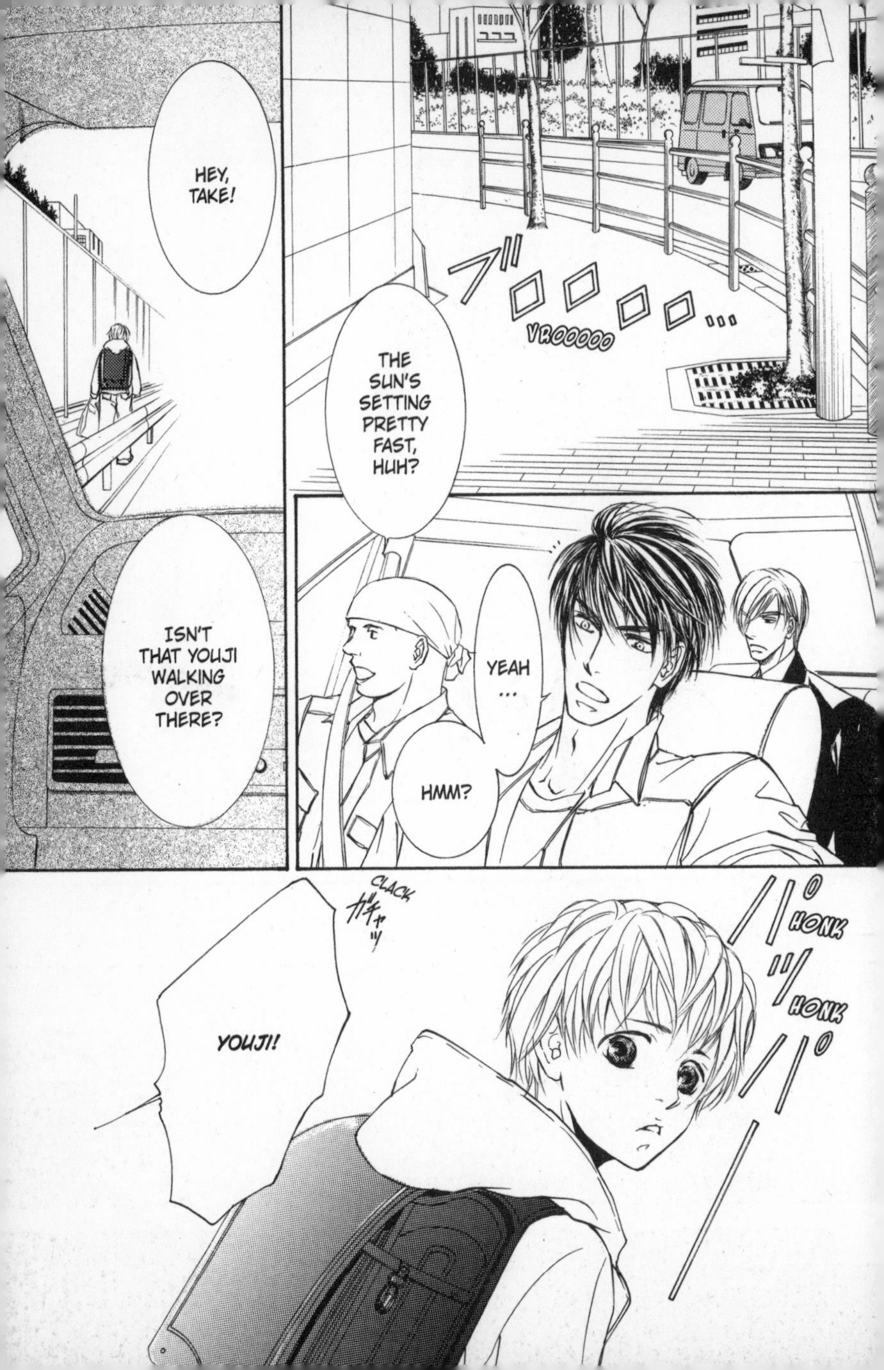
VROOOOO
THE SUN'S SETTING PRETTY FAST, HUH?
YEAH ...
HMM?
HEY, TAKE!
ISN'T THAT YOUJI WALKING OVER THERE?
HONK
HONK
CLACK
YOUJI!

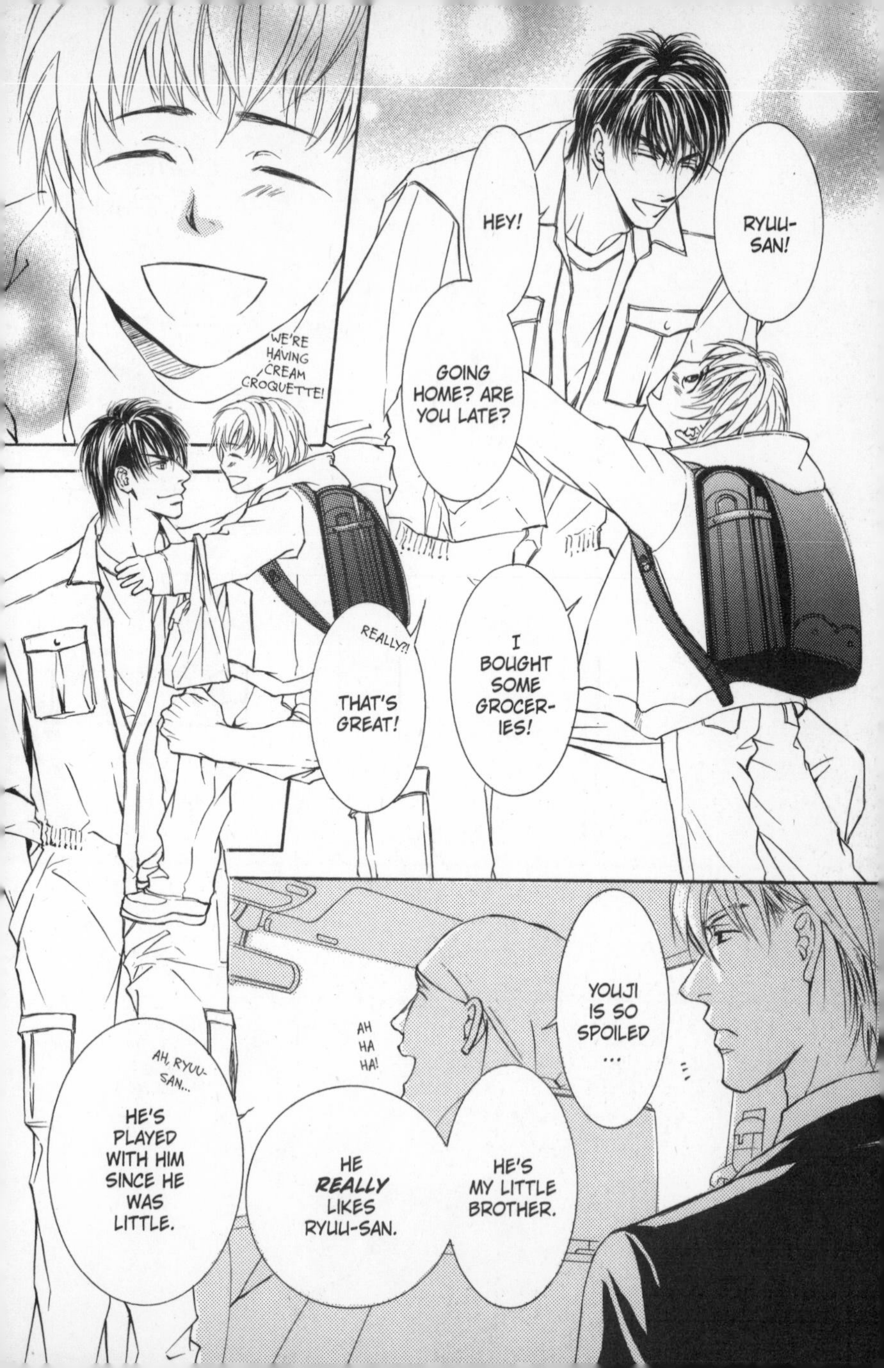
RYUU-SAN!
HEY!
GOING HOME? ARE YOU LATE?
I BOUGHT SOME GROCER-IES!
WE'RE HAVING CREAM CROQUETTE!
REALLY?!
THAT'S GREAT!
YOUJI IS SO SPOILED ...
AH HA HA!
HE'S MY LITTLE BROTHER.
HE *REALLY* LIKES RYUU-SAN.
AH, RYUU-SAN...
HE'S PLAYED WITH HIM SINCE HE WAS LITTLE.

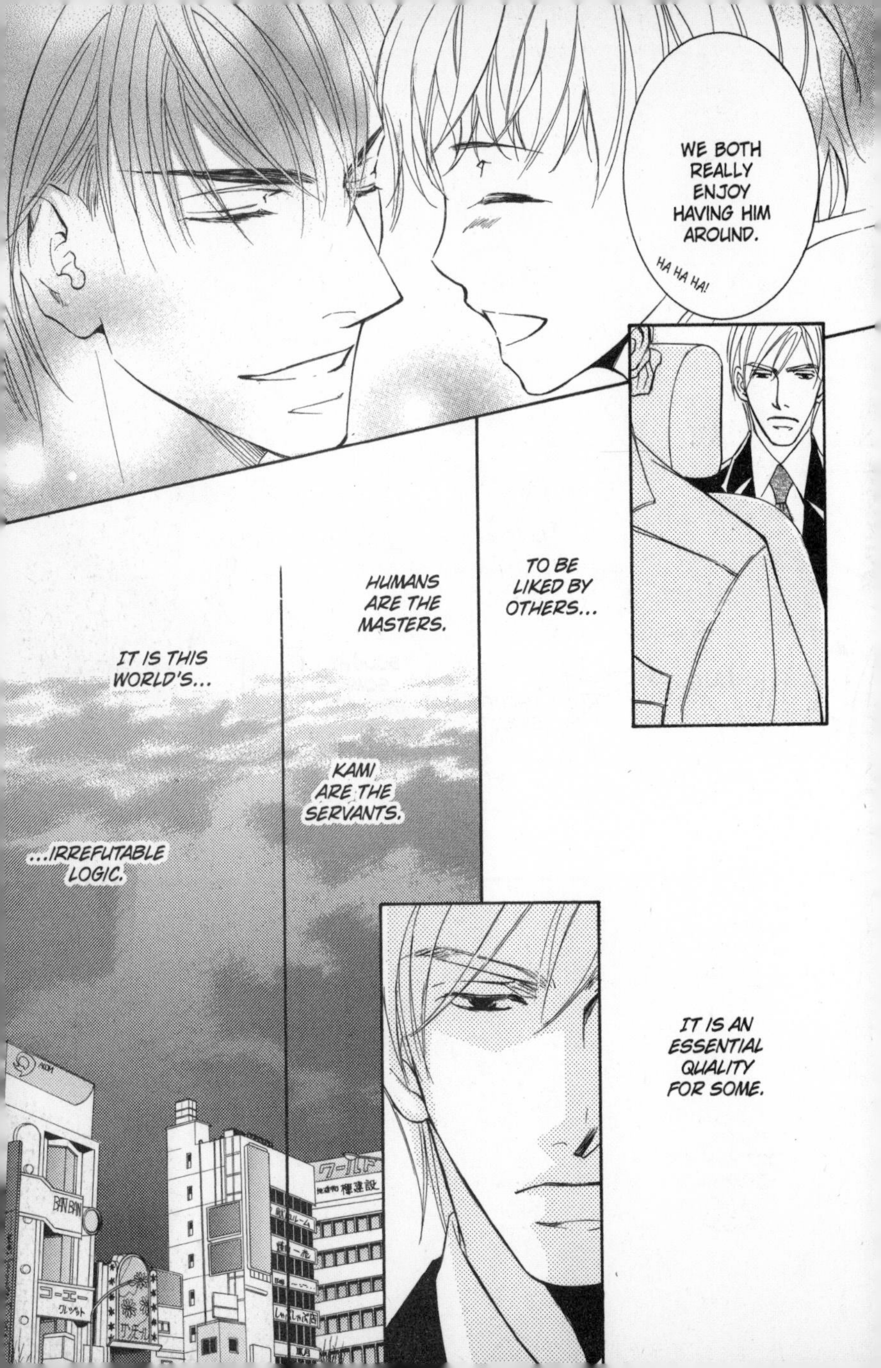
WE BOTH REALLY ENJOY HAVING HIM AROUND.
HA HA HA!
TO BE LIKED BY OTHERS...
IT IS AN ESSENTIAL QUALITY FOR SOME.
HUMANS ARE THE MASTERS.
KAMI ARE THE SERVANTS.
IT IS THIS WORLD'S...
...IRREFUTABLE LOGIC.

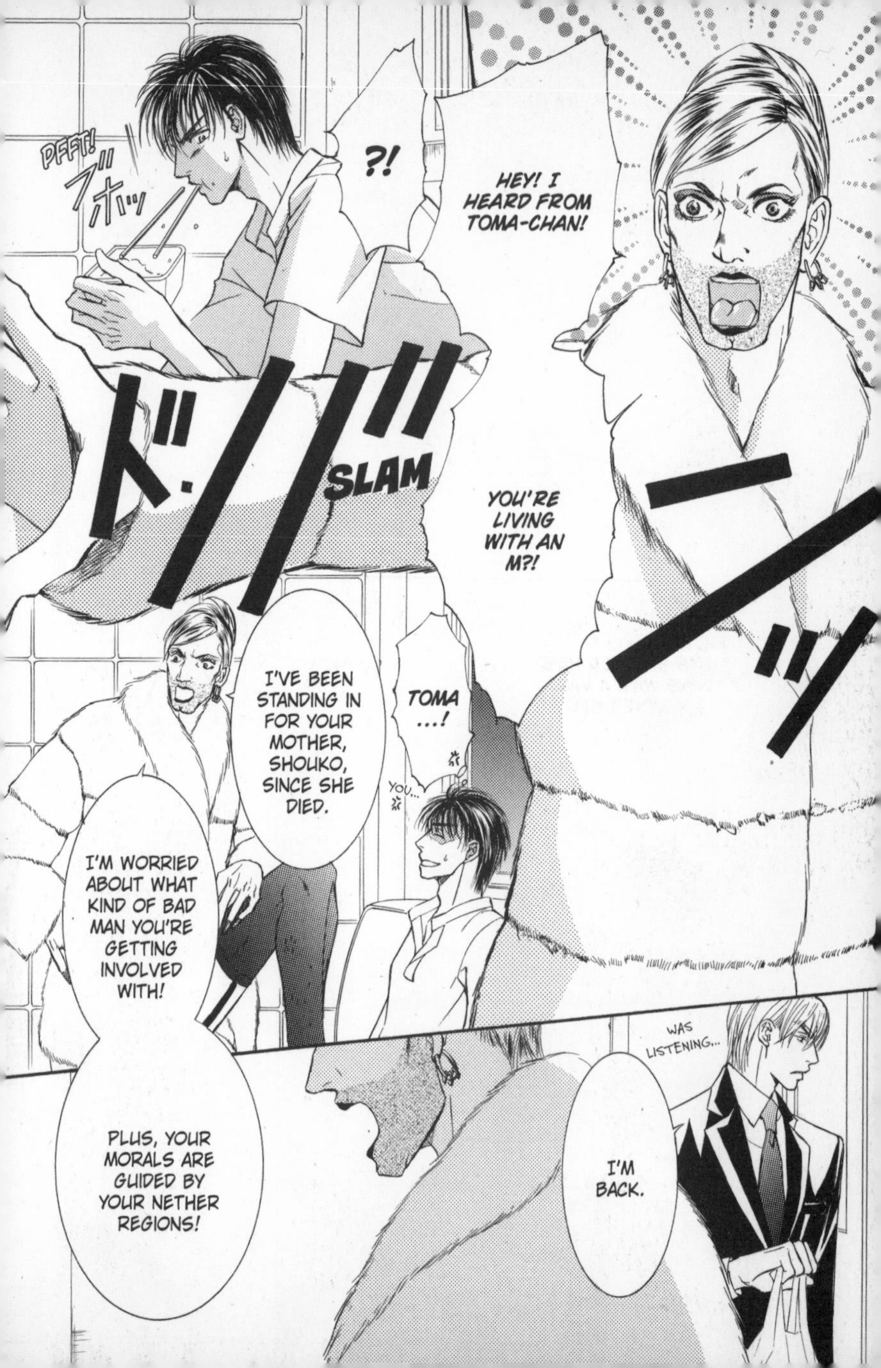
HEY! I HEARD FROM TOMA-CHAN!
YOU'RE LIVING WITH AN M?!
SLAM
PFFT!
?!
TOMA ...!
YOU...
I'VE BEEN STANDING IN FOR YOUR MOTHER, SHOUKO, SINCE SHE DIED.
I'M WORRIED ABOUT WHAT KIND OF BAD MAN YOU'RE GETTING INVOLVED WITH!
WAS LISTENING...
I'M BACK.
PLUS, YOUR MORALS ARE GUIDED BY YOUR NETHER REGIONS!

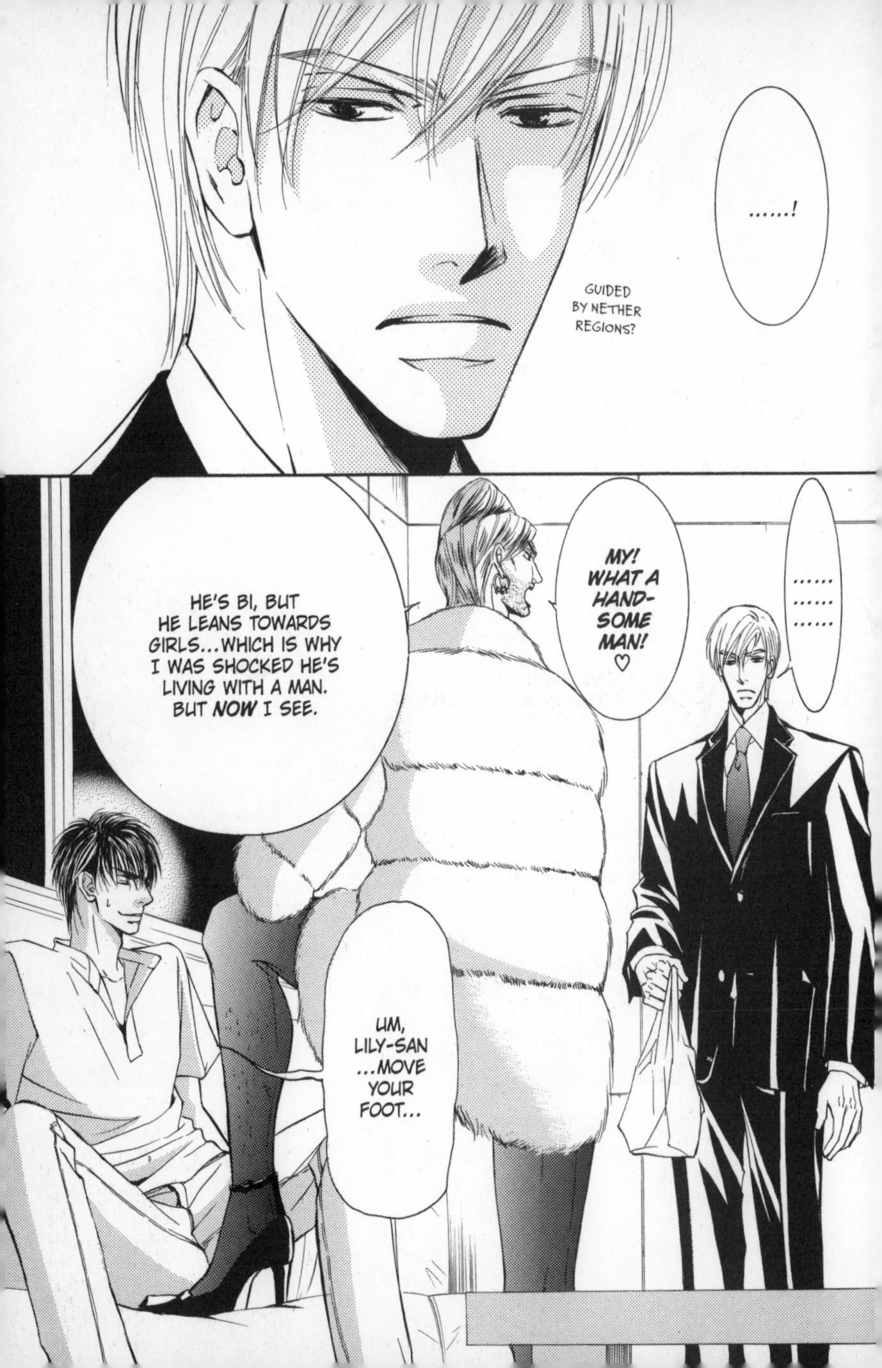
......!
GUIDED BY NETHER REGIONS?
....
....
....
MY! WHAT A HAND-SOME MAN! ♡
HE'S BI, BUT HE LEANS TOWARDS GIRLS...WHICH IS WHY I WAS SHOCKED HE'S LIVING WITH A MAN. BUT NOW I SEE.
UM, LILY-SAN ...MOVE YOUR FOOT...

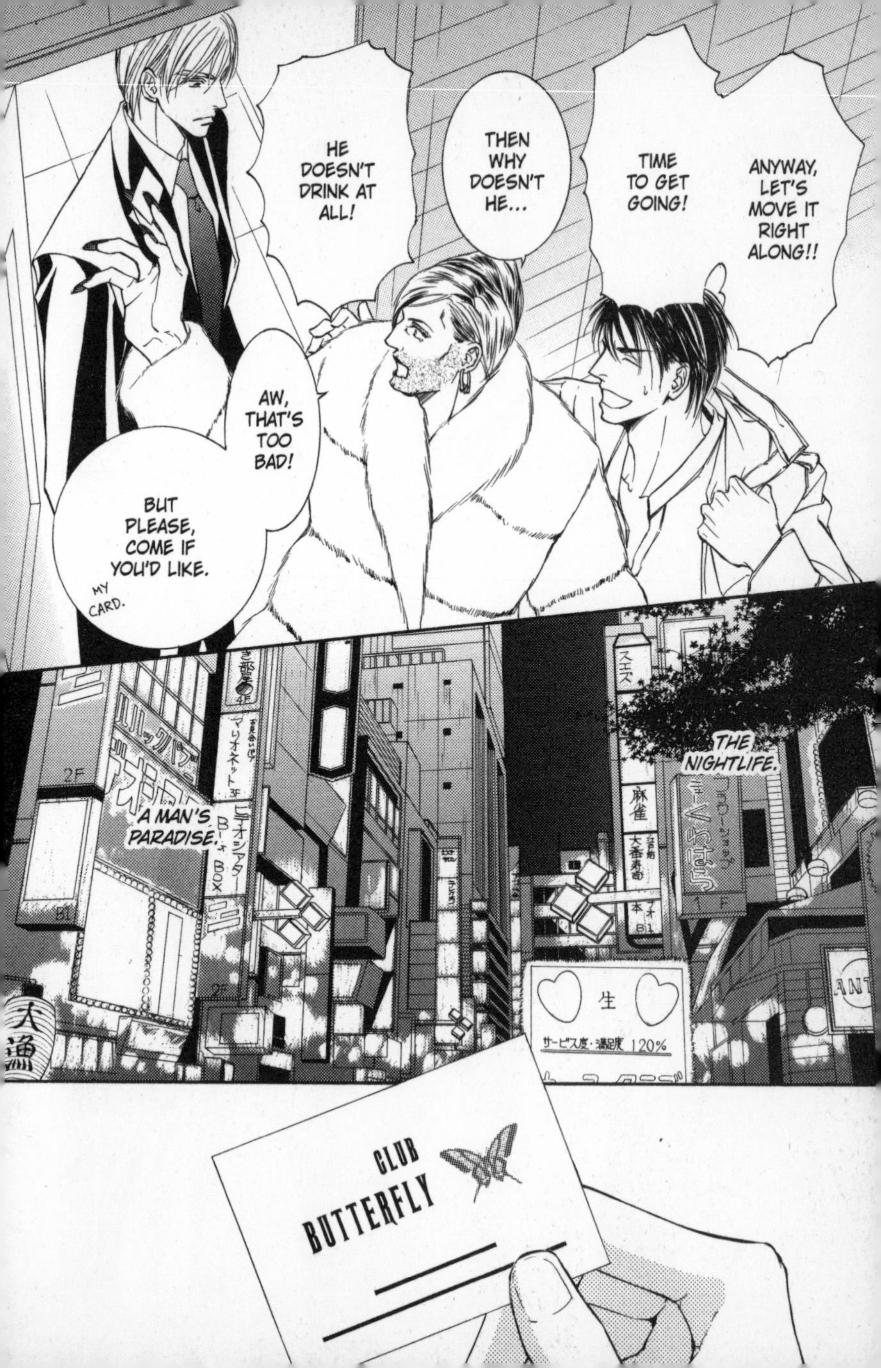
TIME TO GET GOING!
ANYWAY, LET'S MOVE IT RIGHT ALONG!!
THEN WHY DOESN'T HE...
HE DOESN'T DRINK AT ALL!
AW, THAT'S TOO BAD!
BUT PLEASE, COME IF YOU'D LIKE.
MY CARD.
THE NIGHTLIFE.
A MAN'S PARADISE.
麻雀
生
サービス度・満足度 120%
大漁
CLUB BUTTERFLY

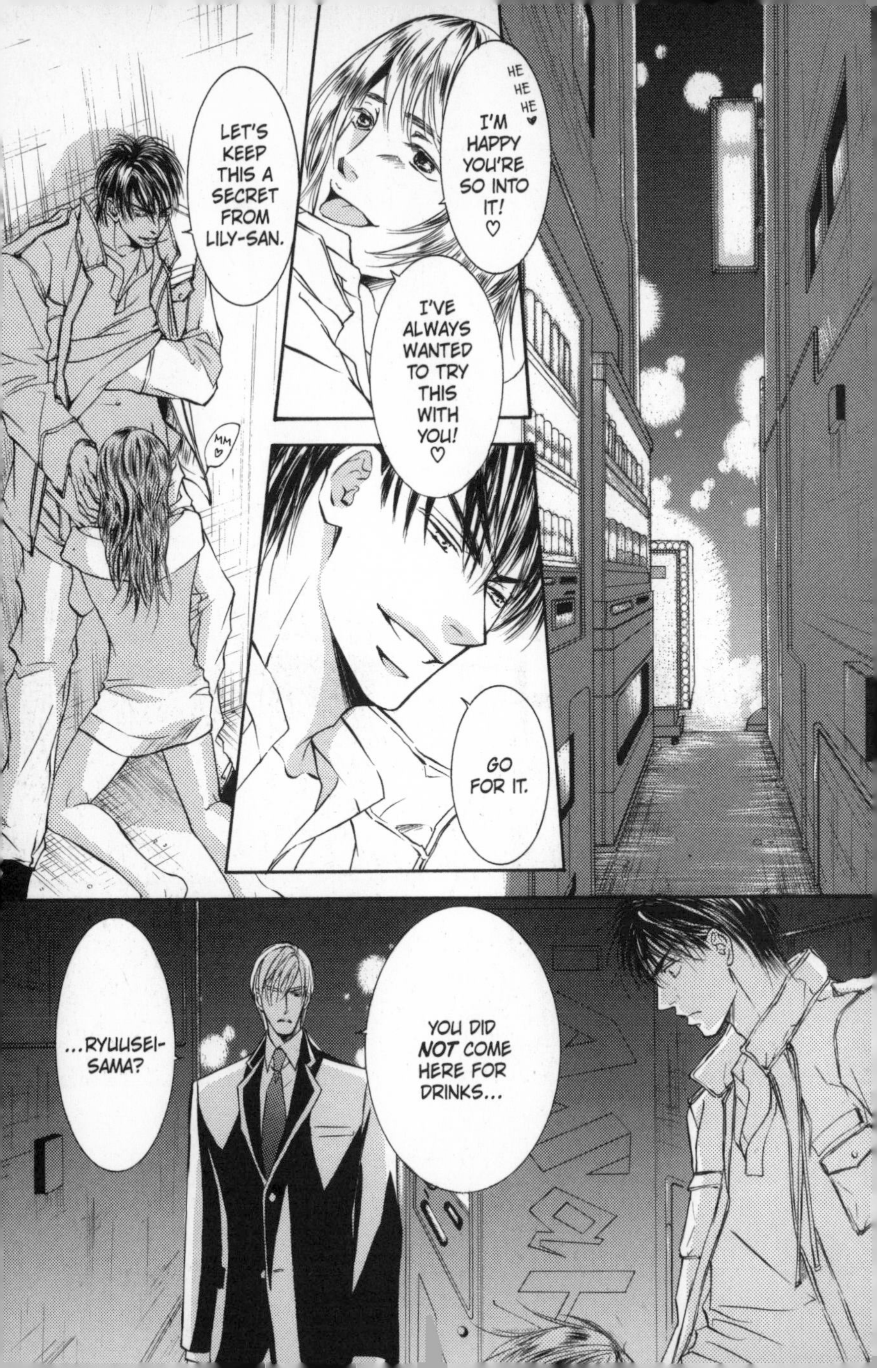
HE HE HE
I'M HAPPY YOU'RE SO INTO IT! ♡
I'VE ALWAYS WANTED TO TRY THIS WITH YOU! ♡
GO FOR IT.
LET'S KEEP THIS A SECRET FROM LILY-SAN.
MM ♡
YOU DID **NOT** COME HERE FOR DRINKS...
...RYUUSEI-SAMA?

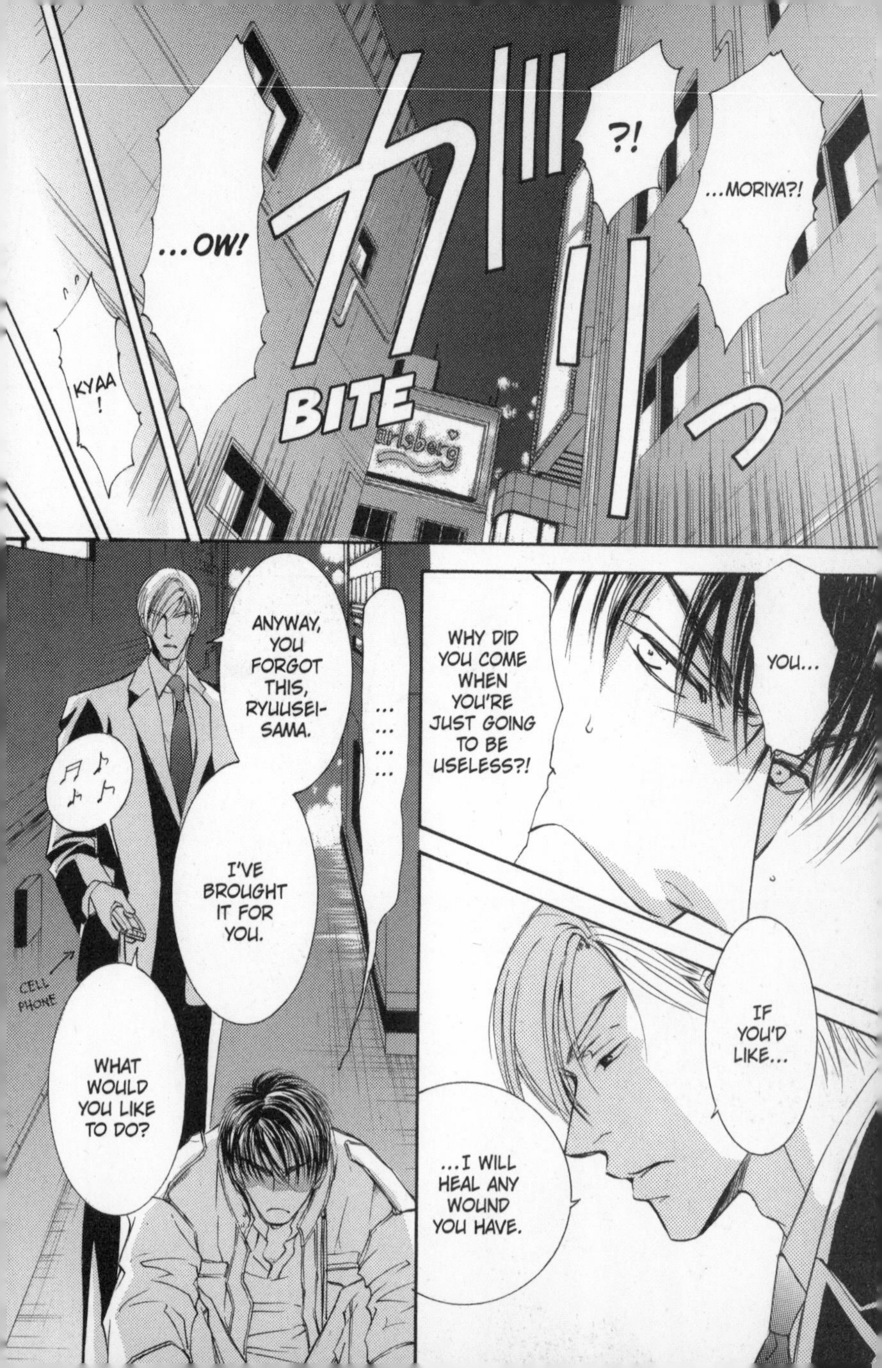
?!
...MORIYA?!
BITE
...OW!
KYAA!
YOU...
WHY DID YOU COME WHEN YOU'RE JUST GOING TO BE USELESS?!
IF YOU'D LIKE...
...I WILL HEAL ANY WOUND YOU HAVE.
ANYWAY, YOU FORGOT THIS, RYUUSEI-SAMA.
....
I'VE BROUGHT IT FOR YOU.
WHAT WOULD YOU LIKE TO DO?
CELL PHONE

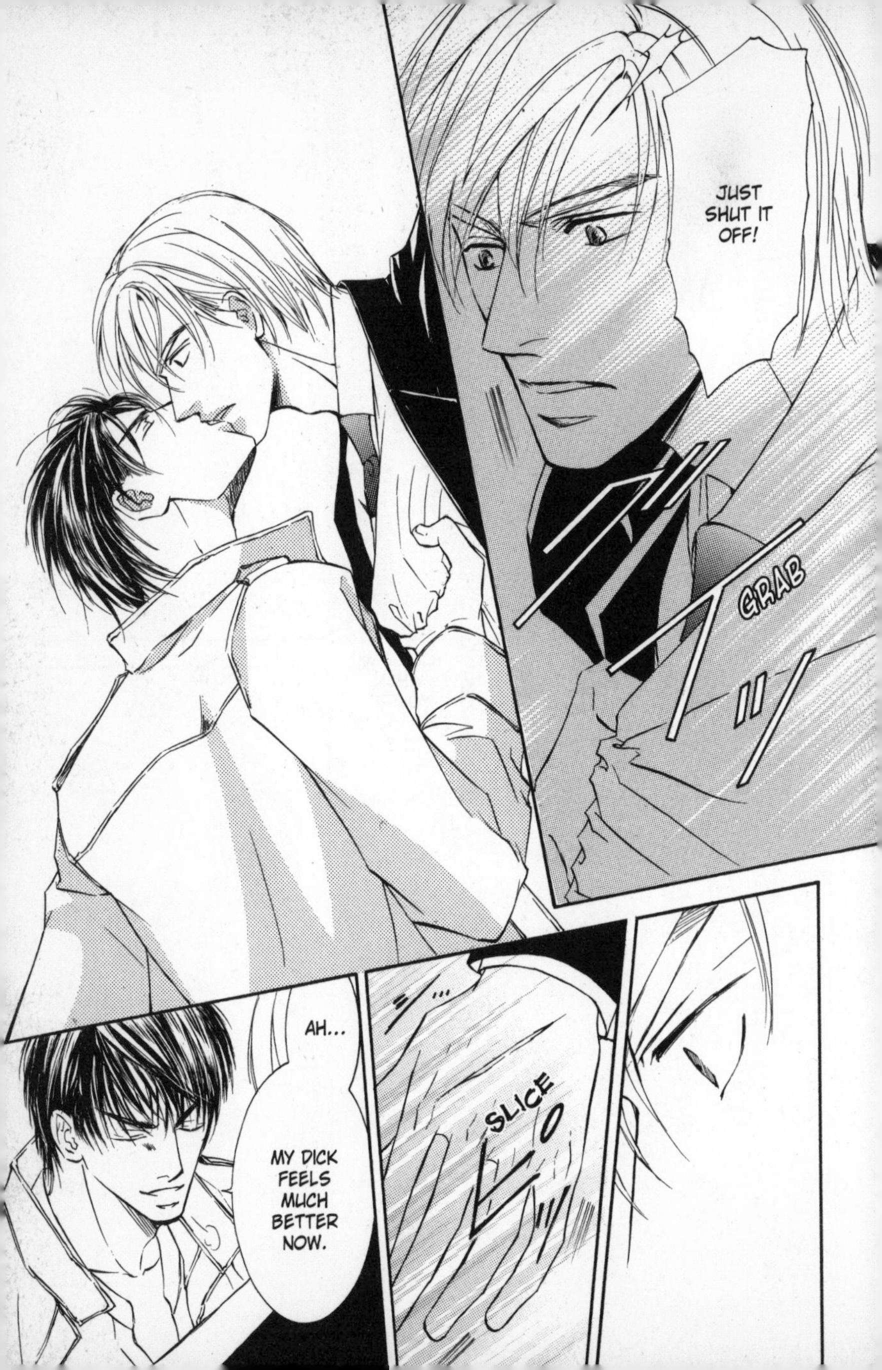
JUST SHUT IT OFF!
GRAB
SLICE
AH...
MY DICK FEELS MUCH BETTER NOW.

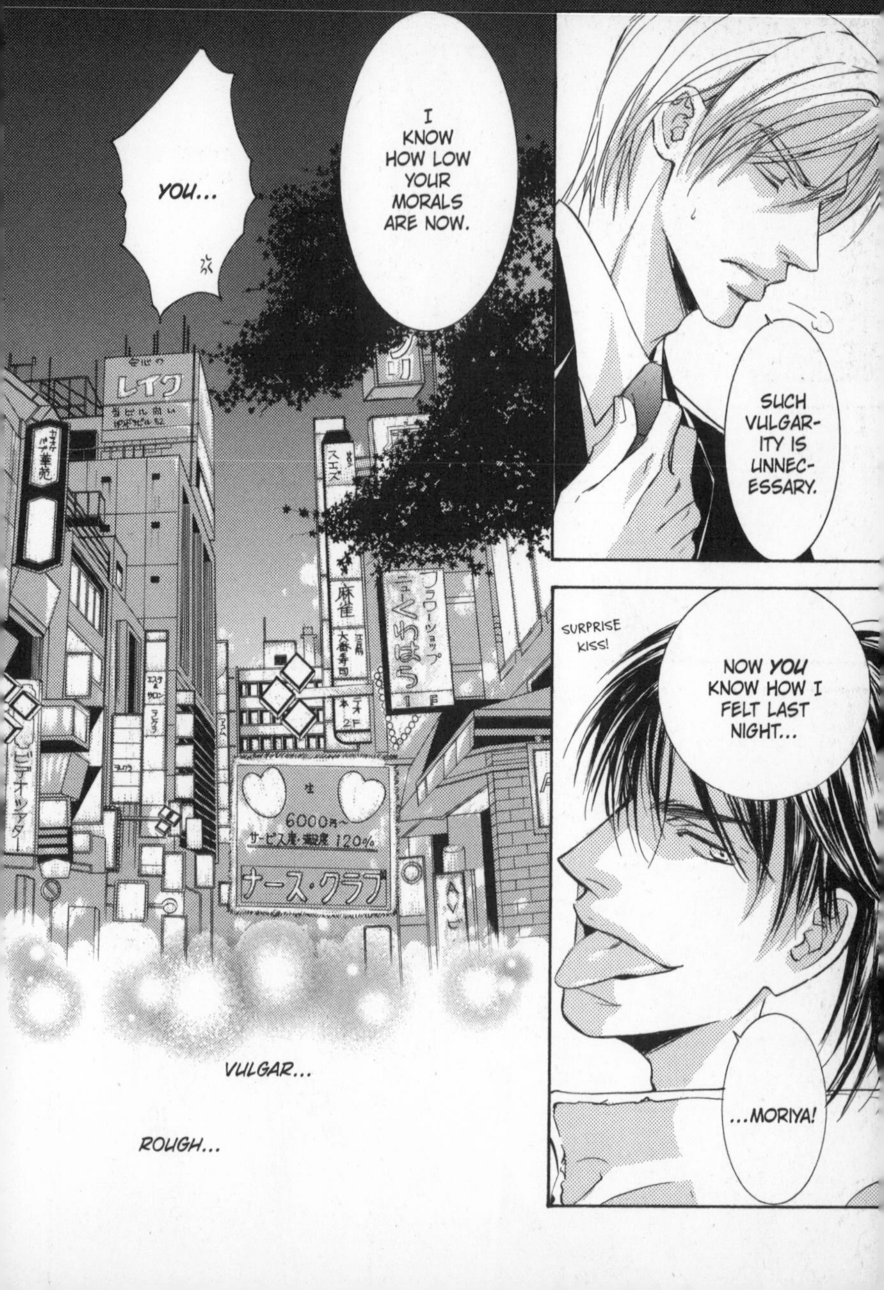
SUCH VULGARITY IS UNNECESSARY.
NOW *YOU* KNOW HOW I FELT LAST NIGHT...
SURPRISE KISS!
...MORIYA!
I KNOW HOW LOW YOUR MORALS ARE NOW.
YOU...
レイク
麻雀
ナース・クラブ
VULGAR...
ROUGH...

...HIS STRENGTH...

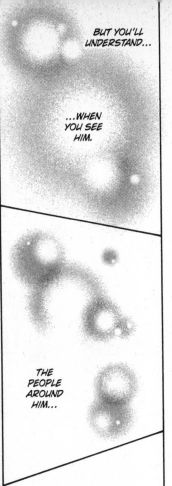

BUT YOU'LL UNDERSTAND...

...WHEN YOU SEE HIM.

THE PEOPLE AROUND HIM...

HIS KINDNESS...

AND...

...HIS RECKLESS-NESS.

YO! YOU'RE LATE...

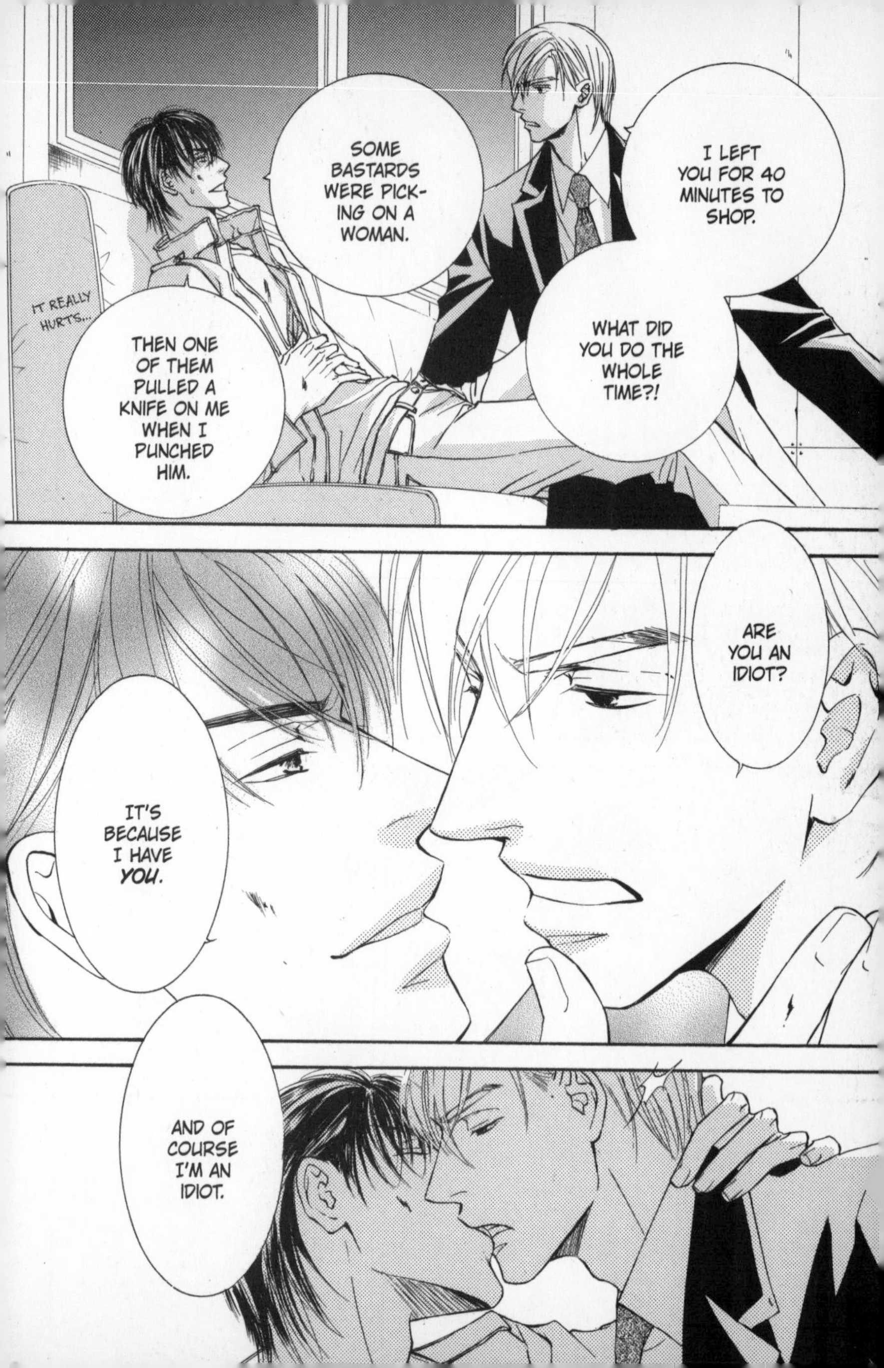
I LEFT YOU FOR 40 MINUTES TO SHOP.
WHAT DID YOU DO THE WHOLE TIME?!
SOME BASTARDS WERE PICK-ING ON A WOMAN.
THEN ONE OF THEM PULLED A KNIFE ON ME WHEN I PUNCHED HIM.
IT REALLY HURTS...
ARE YOU AN IDIOT?
IT'S BECAUSE I HAVE *YOU*.
AND OF COURSE I'M AN IDIOT.

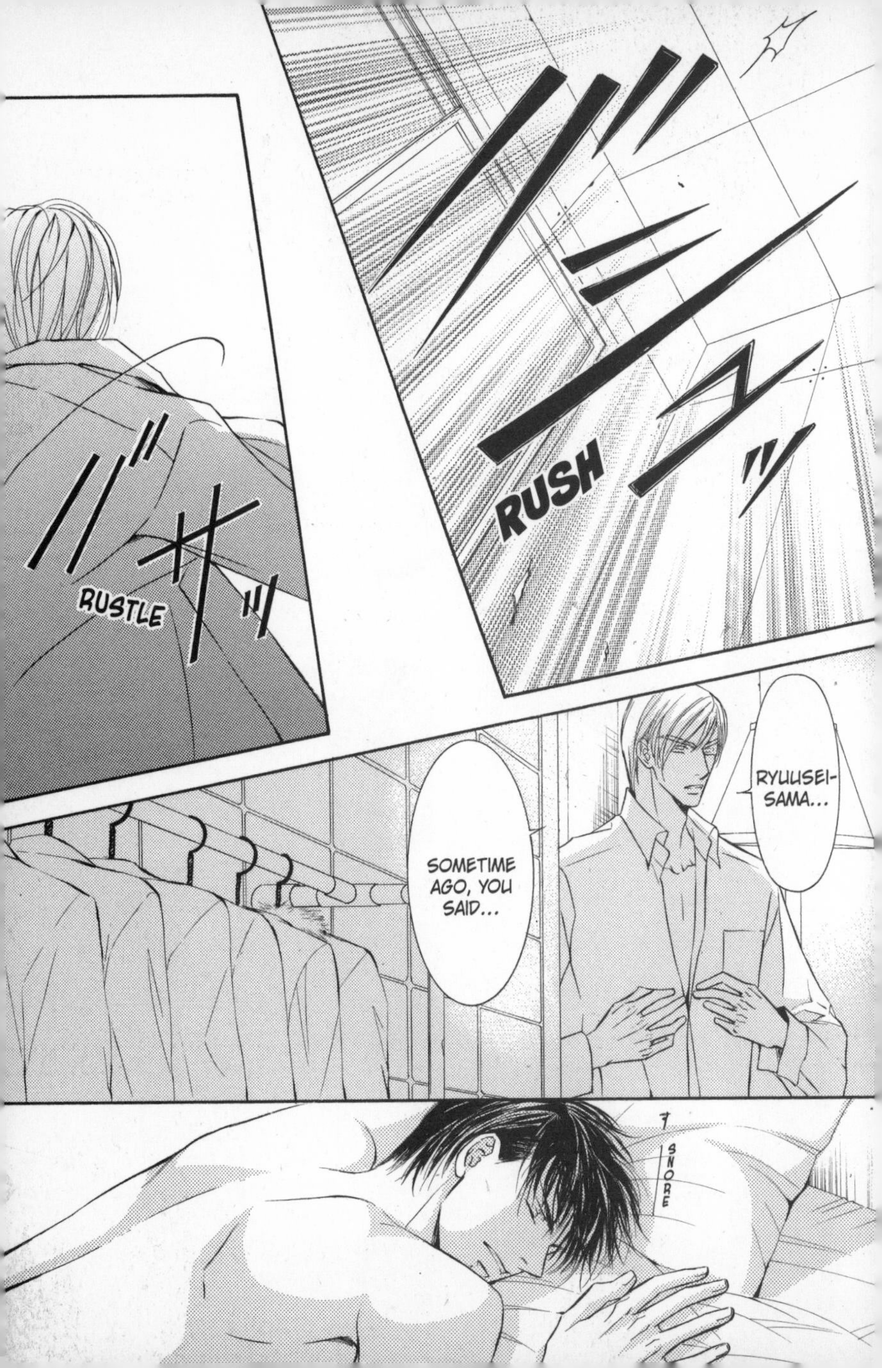
RUSH
RUSTLE
RYUUSEI-SAMA...
SOMETIME AGO, YOU SAID...
SNORE

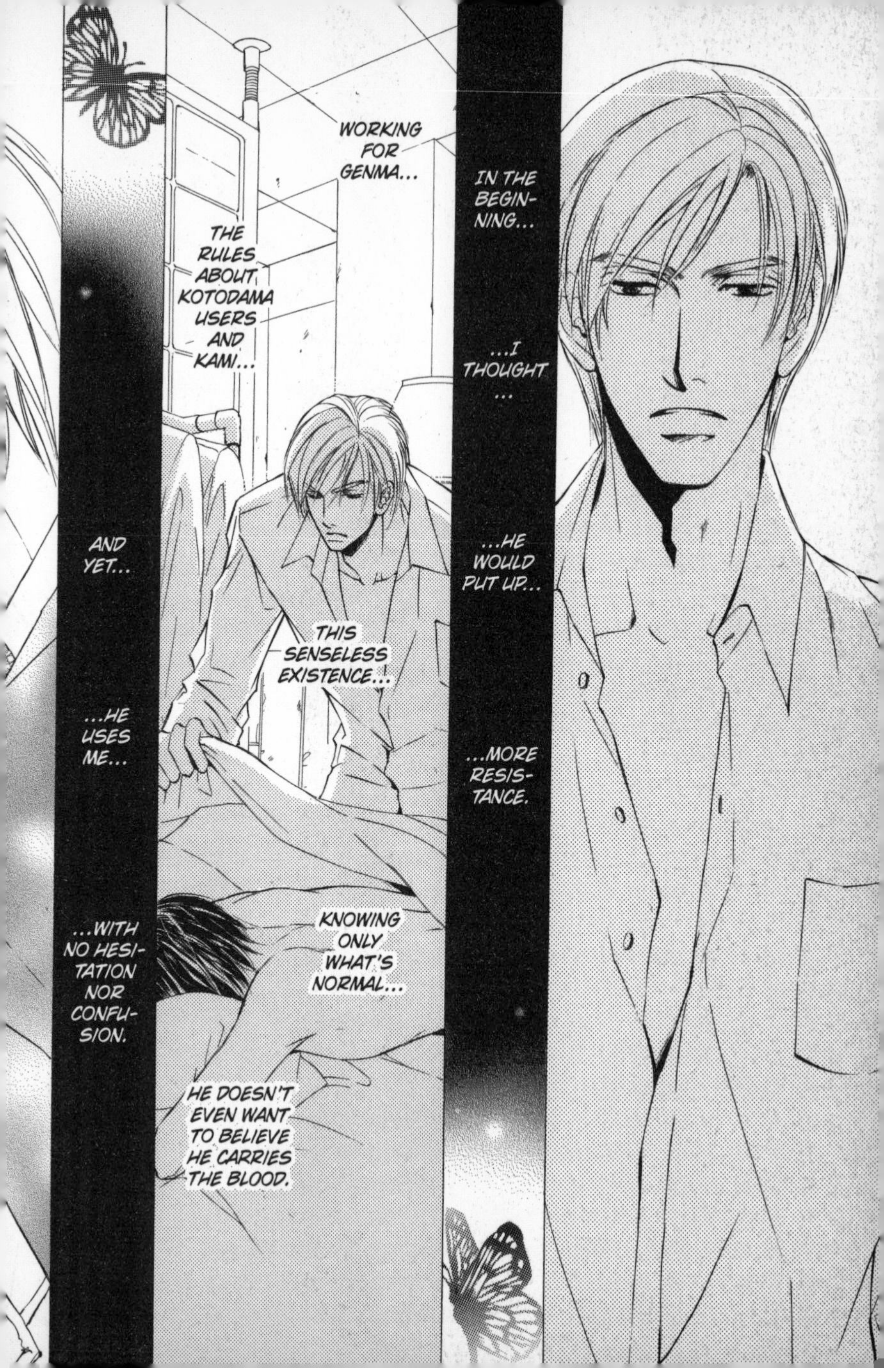
IN THE BEGINNING...
...I THOUGHT...
...HE WOULD PUT UP...
...MORE RESISTANCE.
WORKING FOR GENMA...
THE RULES ABOUT KOTODAMA USERS AND KAMI...
THIS SENSELESS EXISTENCE...
KNOWING ONLY WHAT'S NORMAL...
HE DOESN'T EVEN WANT TO BELIEVE HE CARRIES THE BLOOD.
AND YET...
...HE USES ME...
...WITH NO HESITATION NOR CONFUSION.

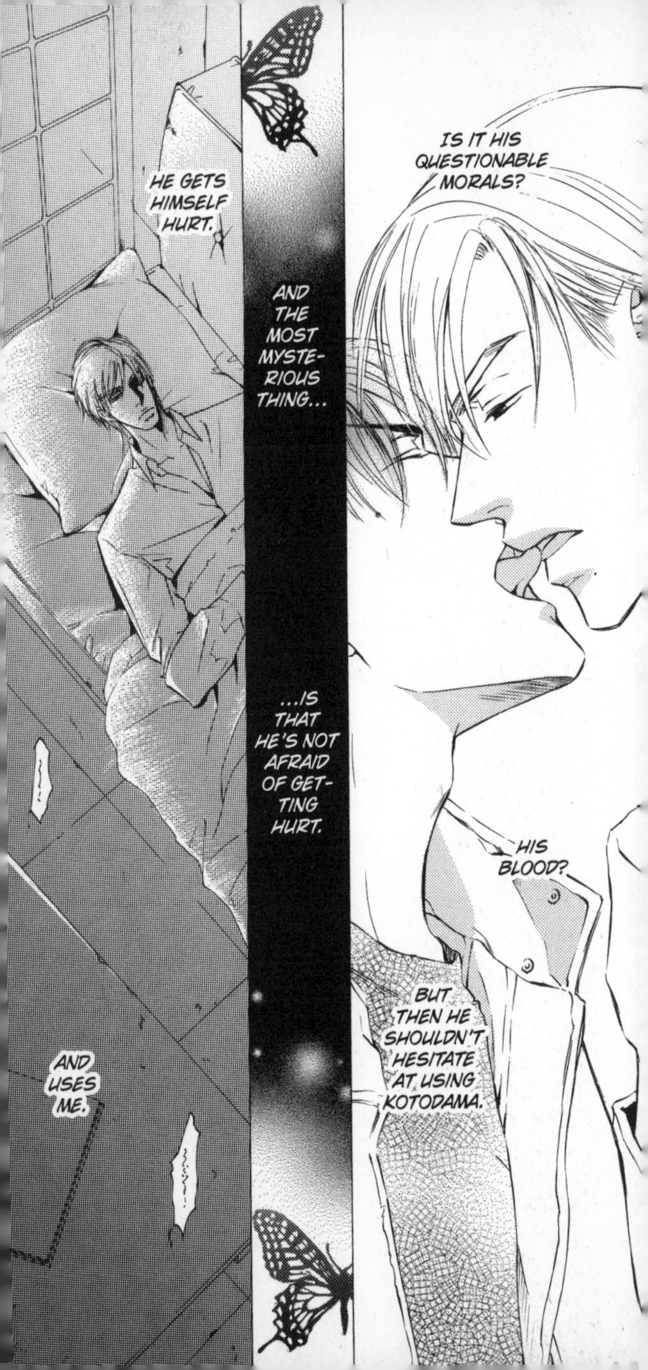
IS IT HIS QUESTIONABLE MORALS?
HIS BLOOD?
BUT THEN HE SHOULDN'T HESITATE AT USING KOTODAMA.
AND THE MOST MYSTE-RIOUS THING...
...IS THAT HE'S NOT AFRAID OF GET-TING HURT.
HE GETS HIMSELF HURT.
AND USES ME.

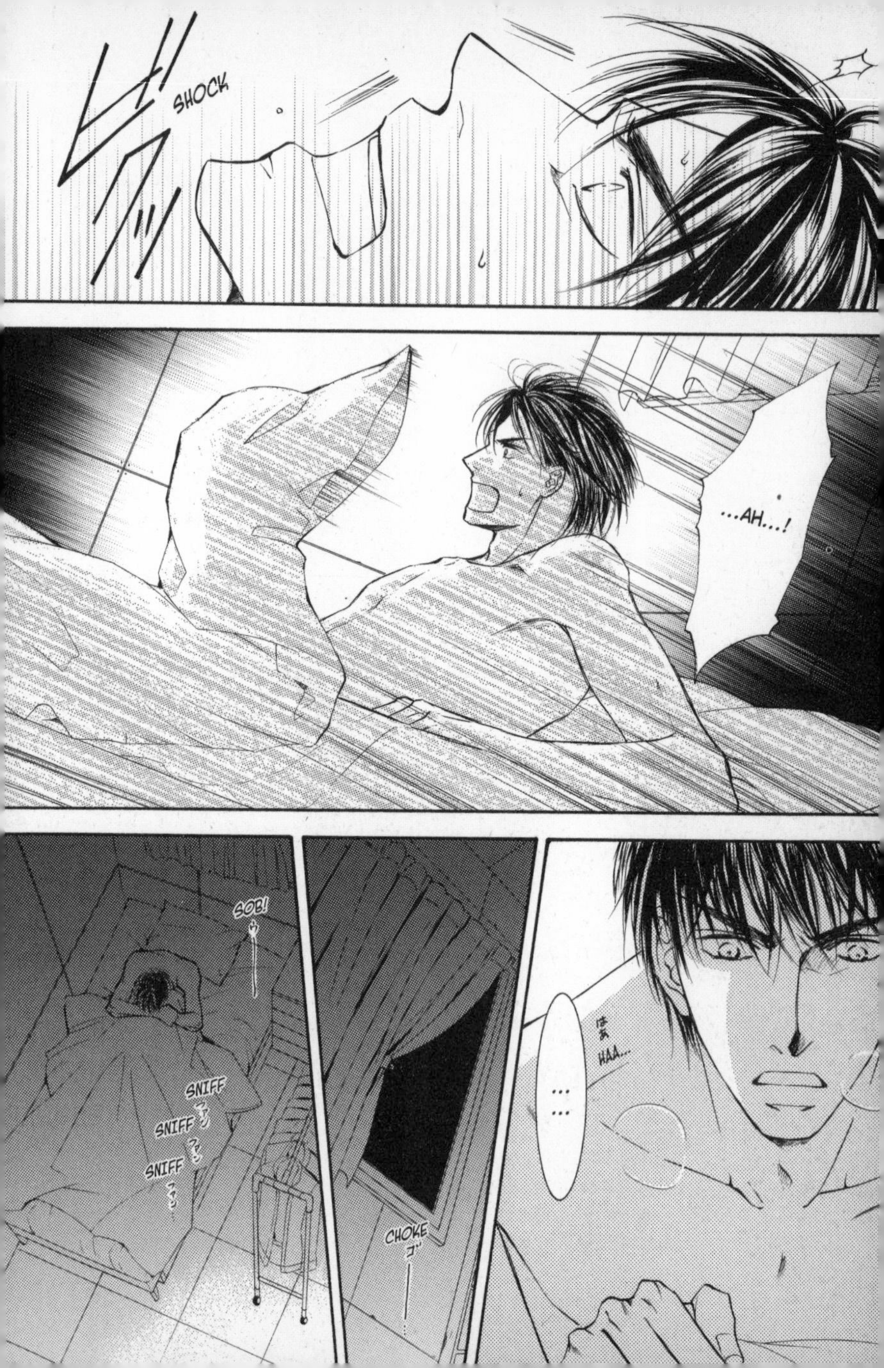
ビクッ
SHOCK
...AH...!
HAA...
......
CHOKE
SOB!
SNIFF
SNIFF
SNIFF

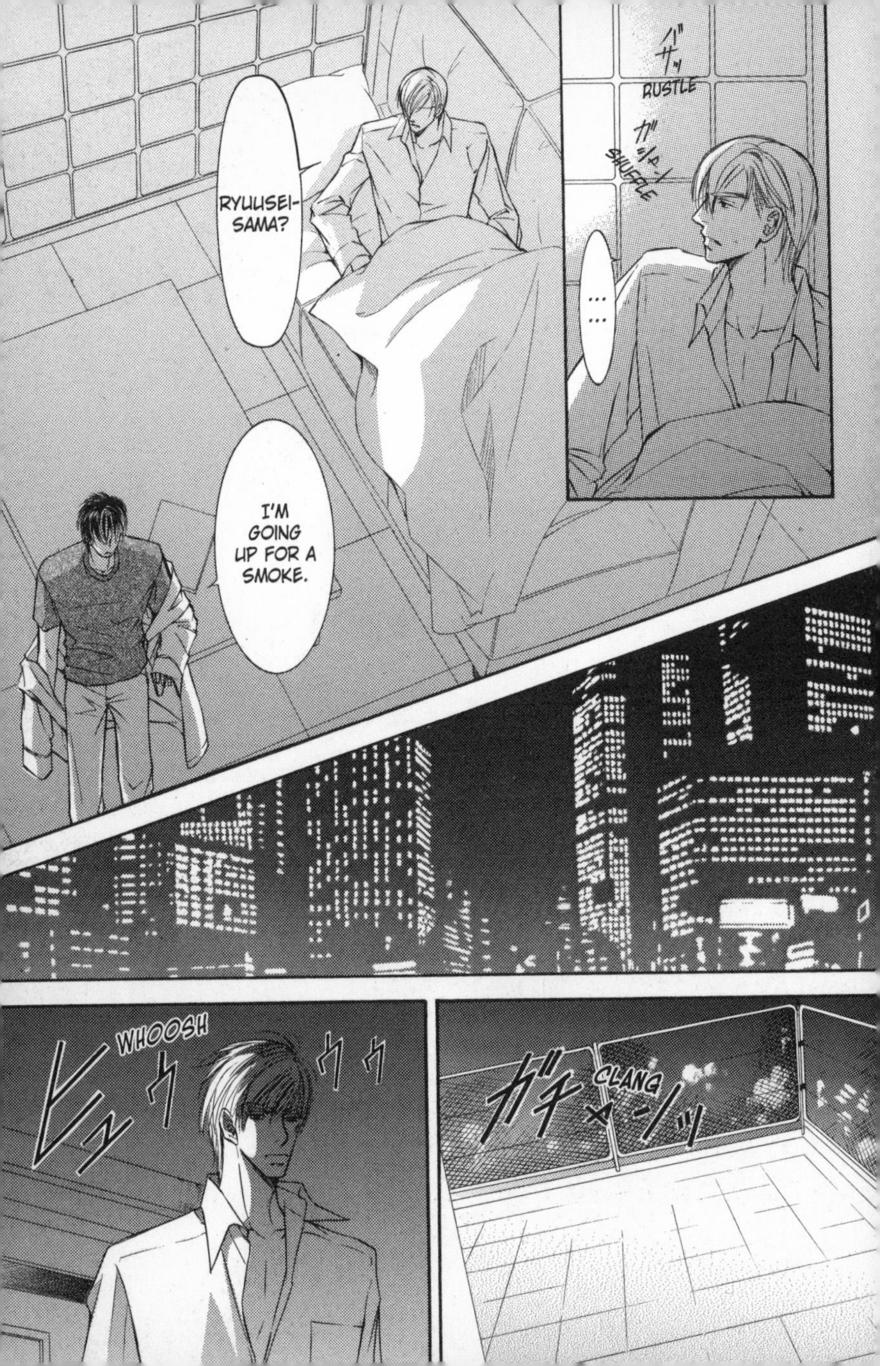
RUSTLE
SHUFFLE
……
RYUUSEI-SAMA?
I'M GOING UP FOR A SMOKE.
CLANG
WHOOSH

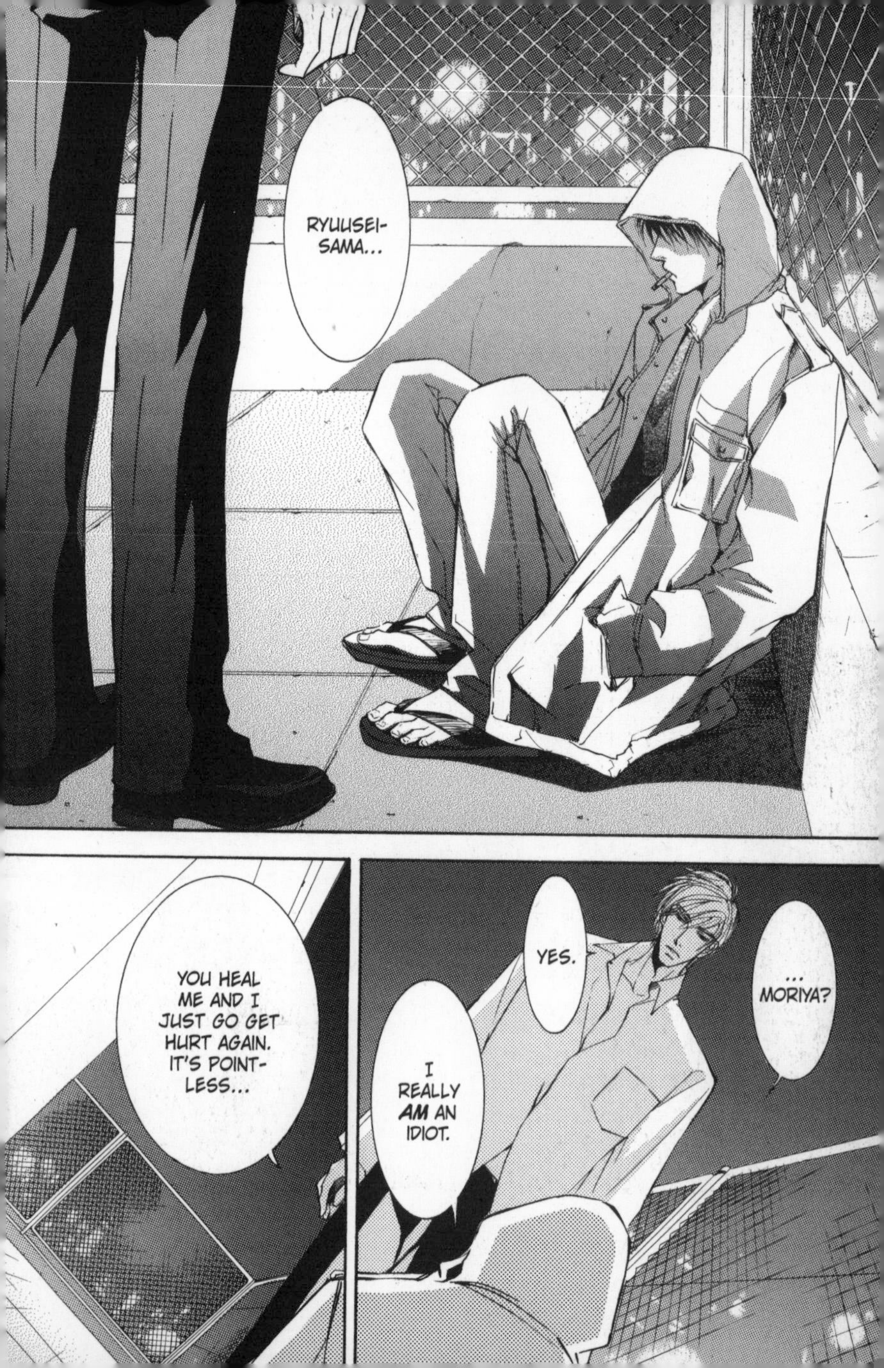
RYUUSEI-SAMA...
...MORIYA?
YES.
I REALLY **AM** AN IDIOT.
YOU HEAL ME AND I JUST GO GET HURT AGAIN. IT'S POINTLESS...

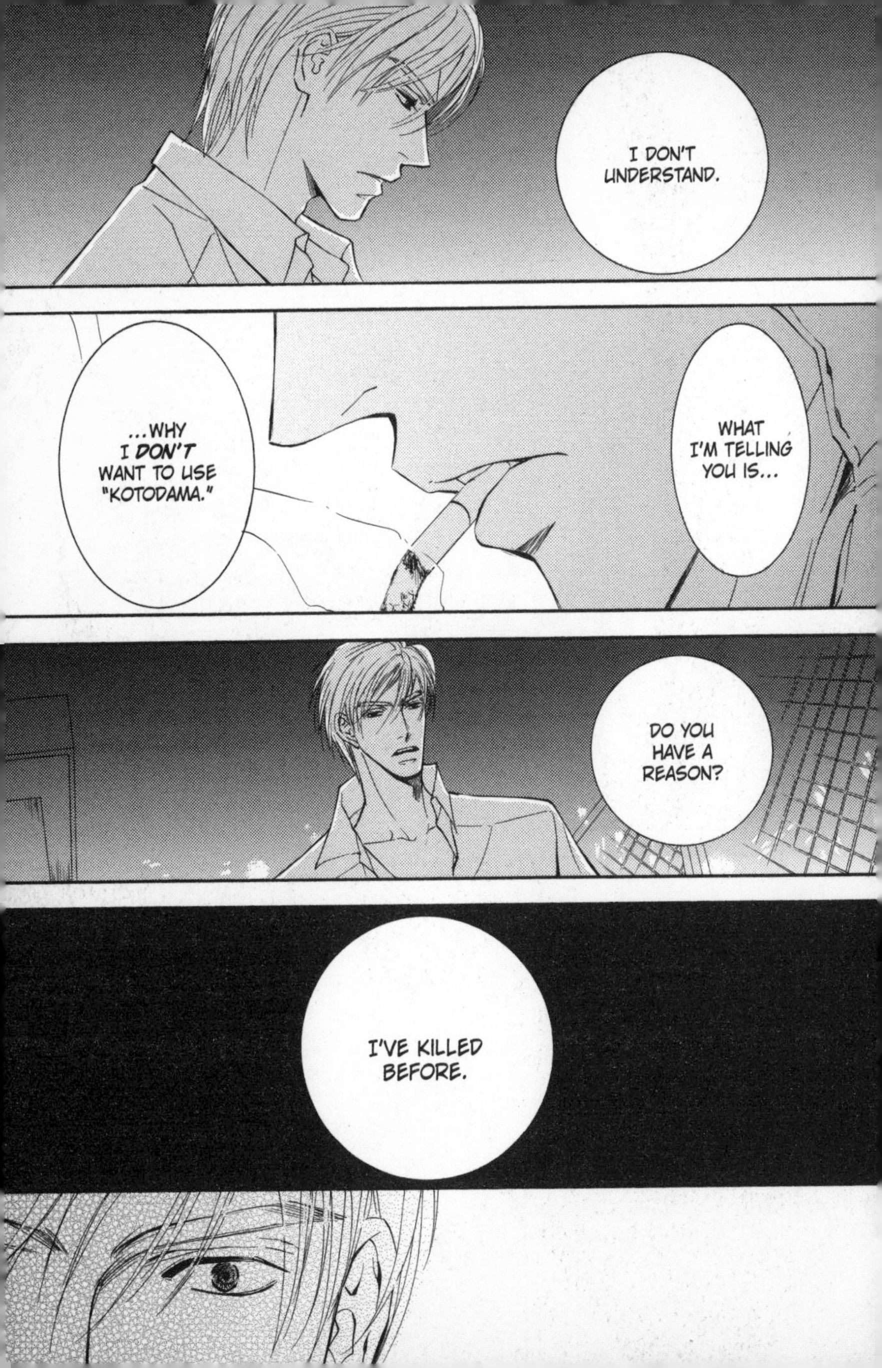
I DON'T UNDERSTAND.
WHAT I'M TELLING YOU IS...
...WHY I DON'T WANT TO USE "KOTODAMA."
DO YOU HAVE A REASON?
I'VE KILLED BEFORE.

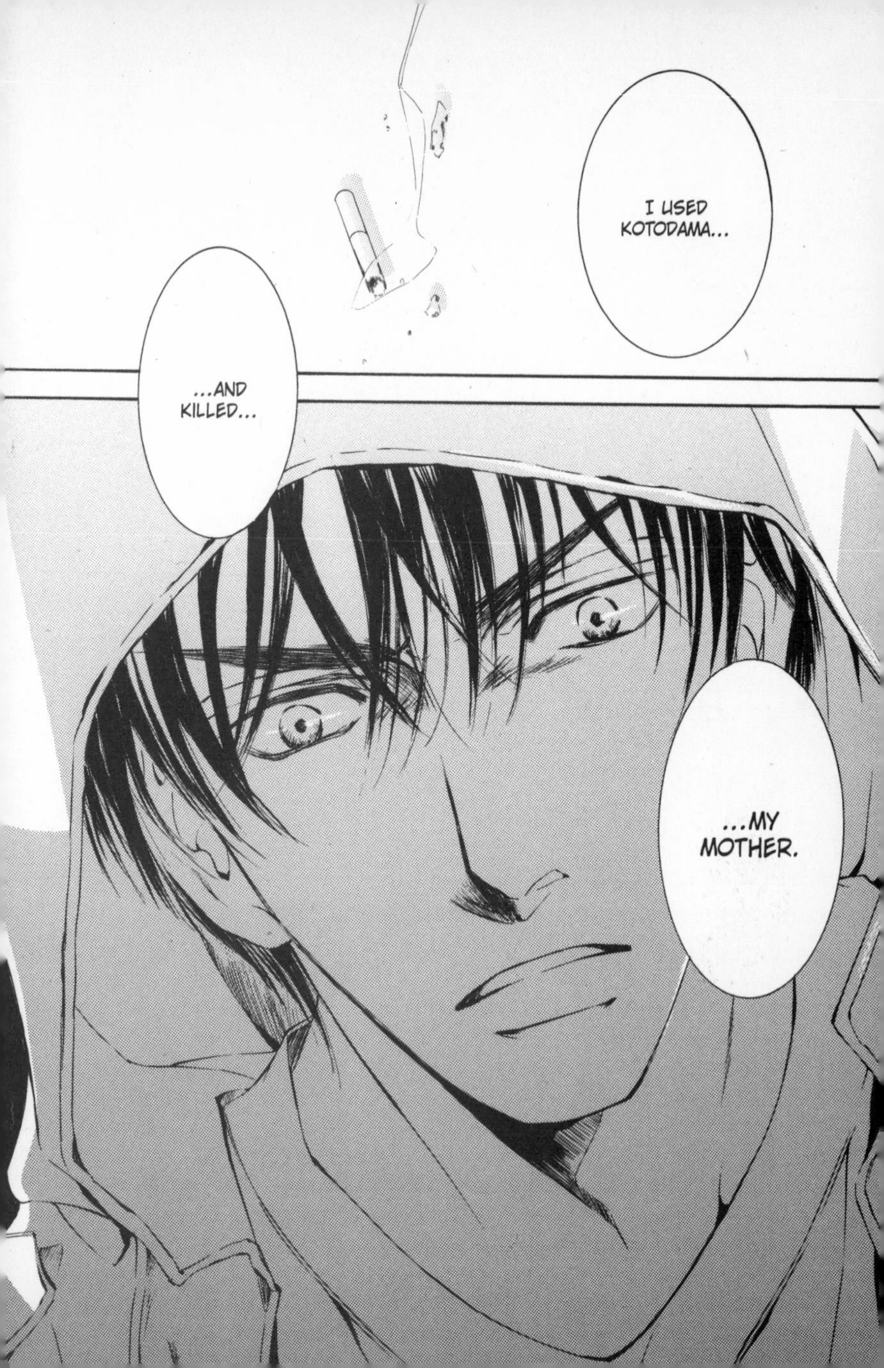
I USED KOTODAMA...
...AND KILLED...
...MY MOTHER.

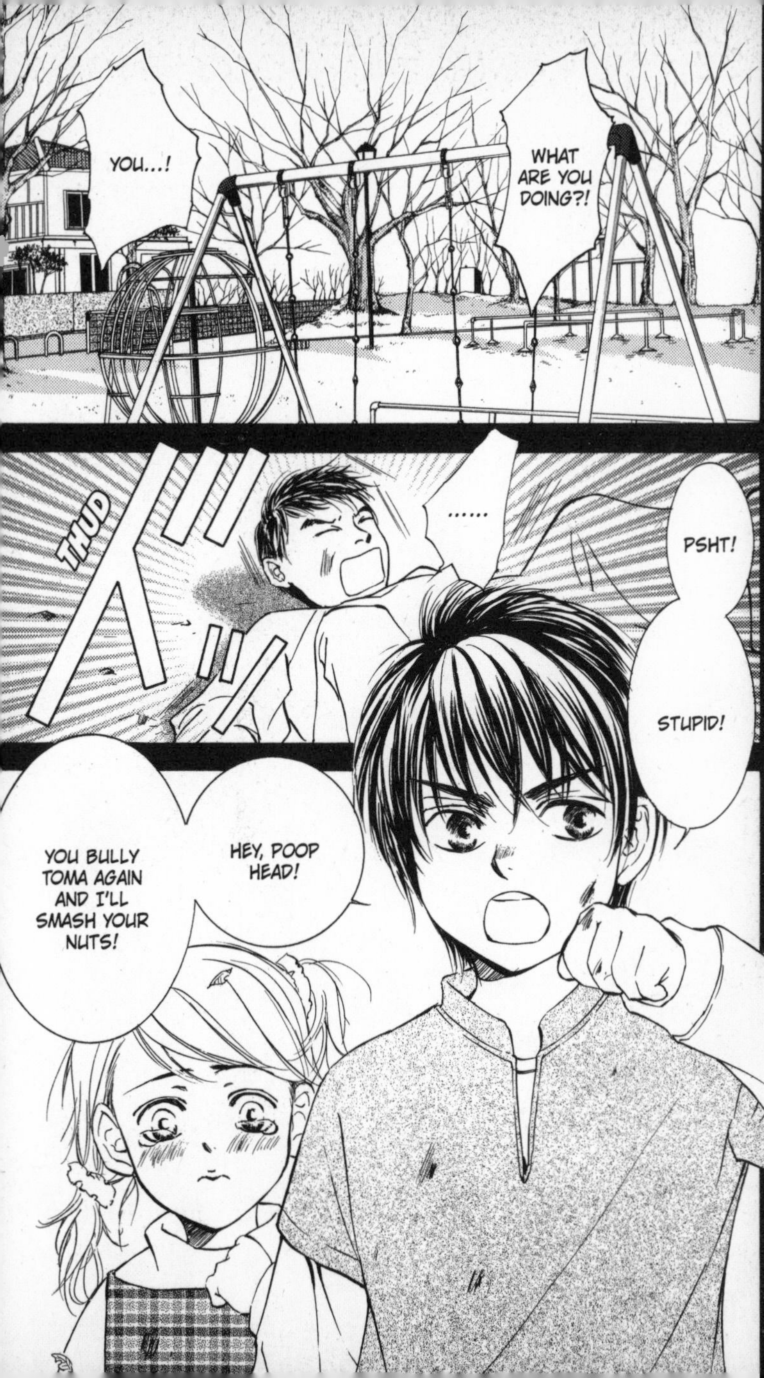
WHAT ARE YOU DOING?!
YOU...!
PSHT!
STUPID!
......
THUD
HEY, POOP HEAD!
YOU BULLY TOMA AGAIN AND I'LL SMASH YOUR NUTS!

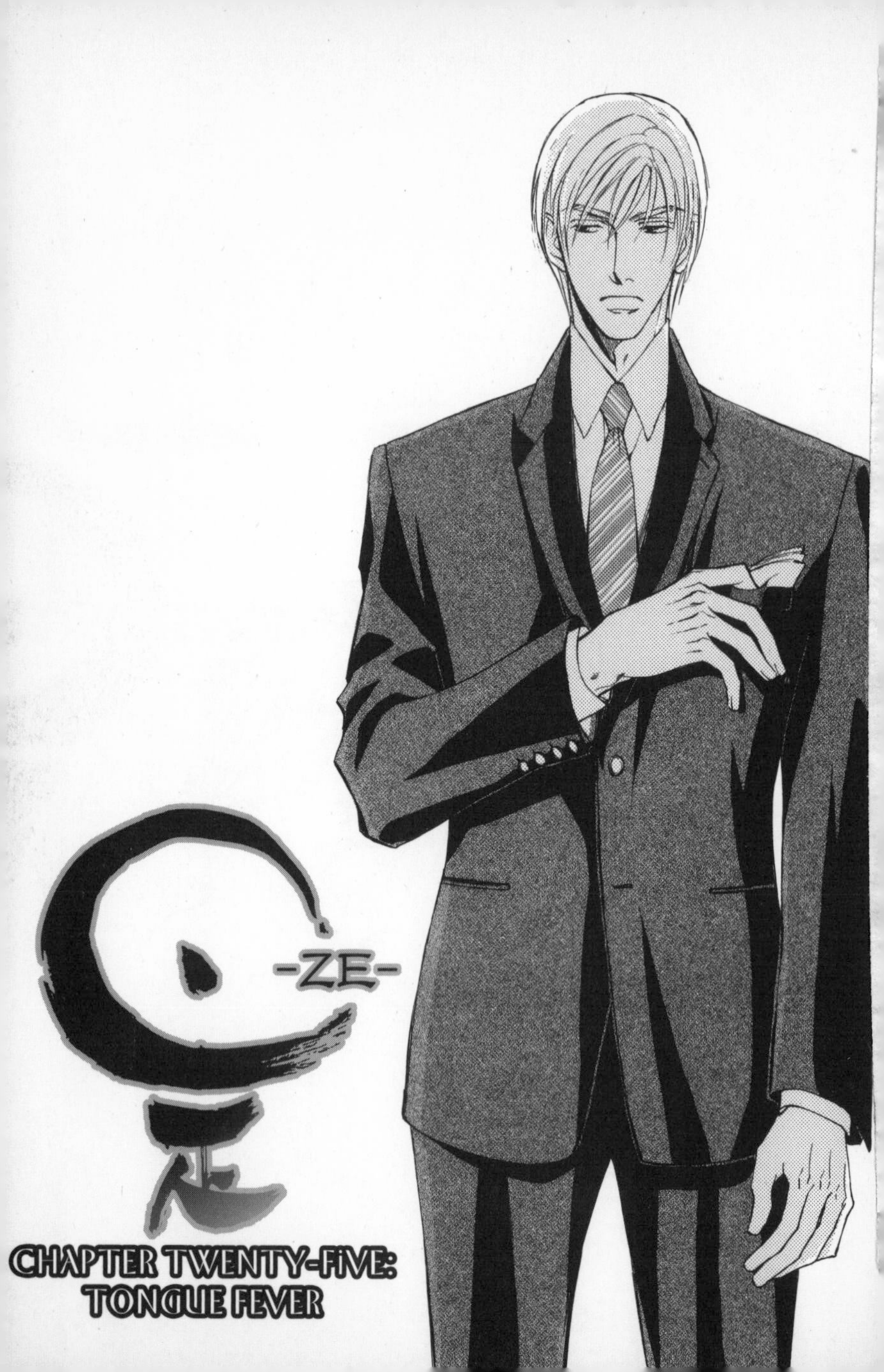
-ZE-
CHAPTER TWENTY-FIVE:
TONGUE FEVER

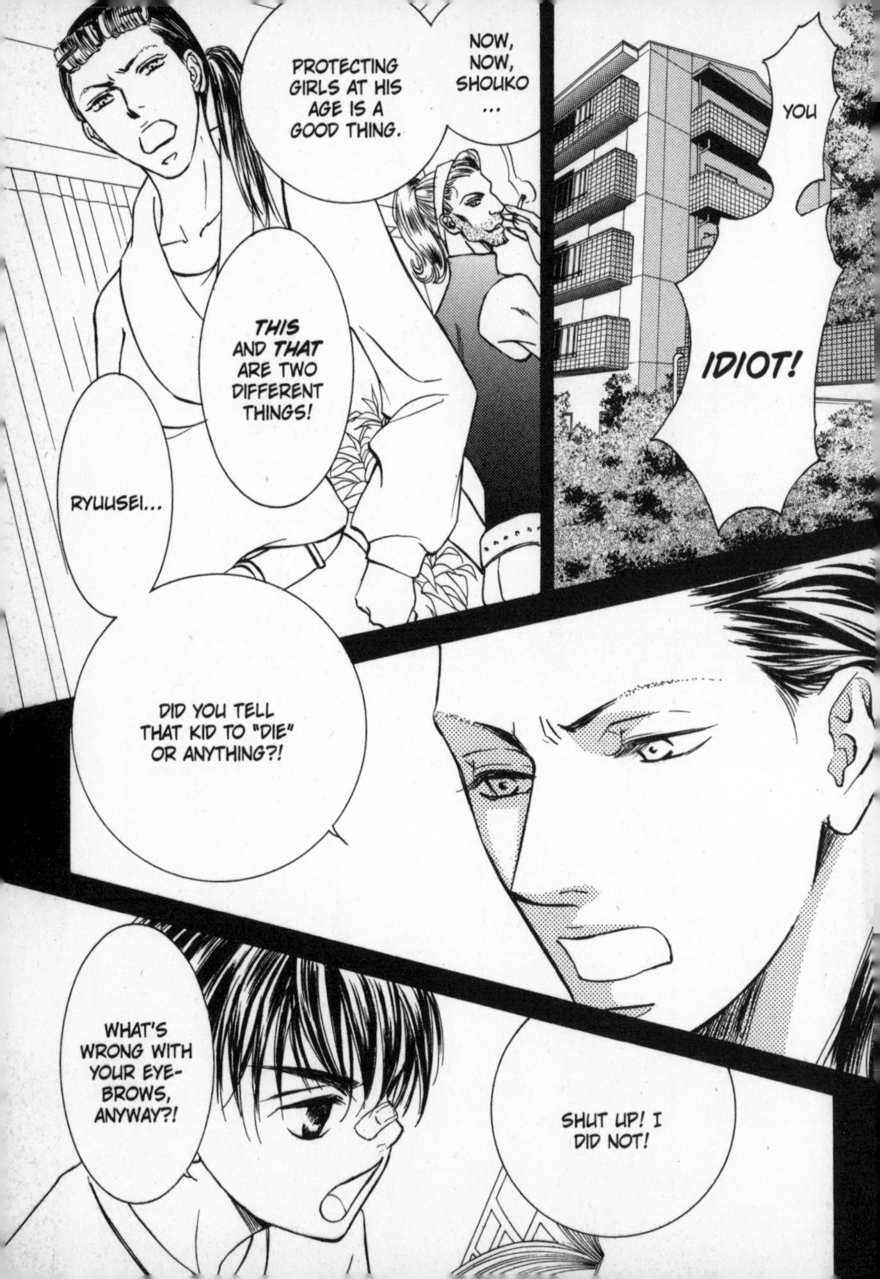
YOU
IDIOT!
NOW, NOW, SHOUKO ...
PROTECTING GIRLS AT HIS AGE IS A GOOD THING.
THIS AND *THAT* ARE TWO DIFFERENT THINGS!
RYUUSEI...
DID YOU TELL THAT KID TO "DIE" OR ANYTHING?!
SHUT UP! I DID NOT!
WHAT'S WRONG WITH YOUR EYE-BROWS, ANYWAY?!

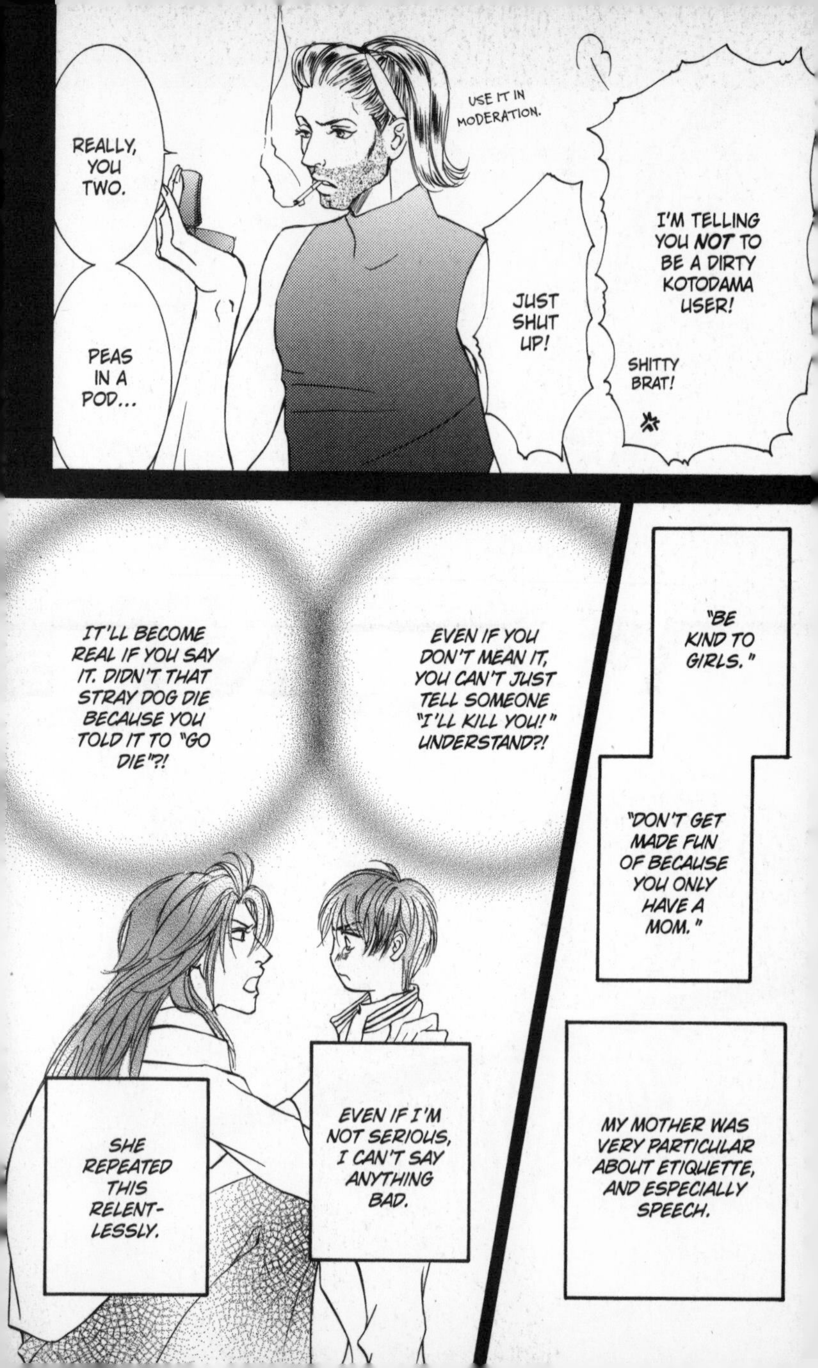
I'M TELLING YOU **NOT** TO BE A DIRTY KOTODAMA USER!
SHITTY BRAT!
JUST SHUT UP!
USE IT IN MODERATION.
REALLY, YOU TWO.
PEAS IN A POD...
"BE KIND TO GIRLS."
"DON'T GET MADE FUN OF BECAUSE YOU ONLY HAVE A MOM."
MY MOTHER WAS VERY PARTICULAR ABOUT ETIQUETTE, AND ESPECIALLY SPEECH.
EVEN IF YOU DON'T MEAN IT, YOU CAN'T JUST TELL SOMEONE "I'LL KILL YOU!" UNDERSTAND?!
IT'LL BECOME REAL IF YOU SAY IT. DIDN'T THAT STRAY DOG DIE BECAUSE YOU TOLD IT TO "GO DIE"?!
EVEN IF I'M NOT SERIOUS, I CAN'T SAY ANYTHING BAD.
SHE REPEATED THIS RELENT-LESSLY.

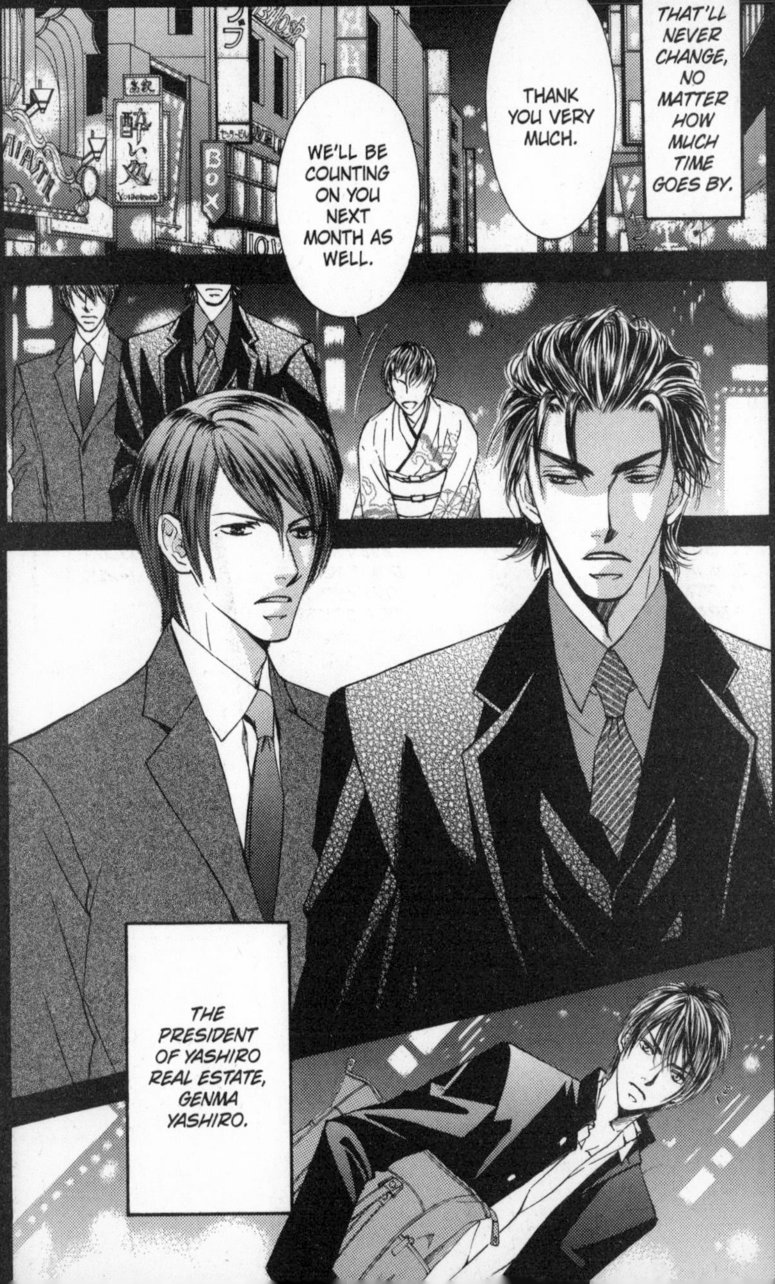
THAT'LL NEVER CHANGE, NO MATTER HOW MUCH TIME GOES BY.
THANK YOU VERY MUCH.
WE'LL BE COUNTING ON YOU NEXT MONTH AS WELL.
THE PRESIDENT OF YASHIRO REAL ESTATE, GENMA YASHIRO.

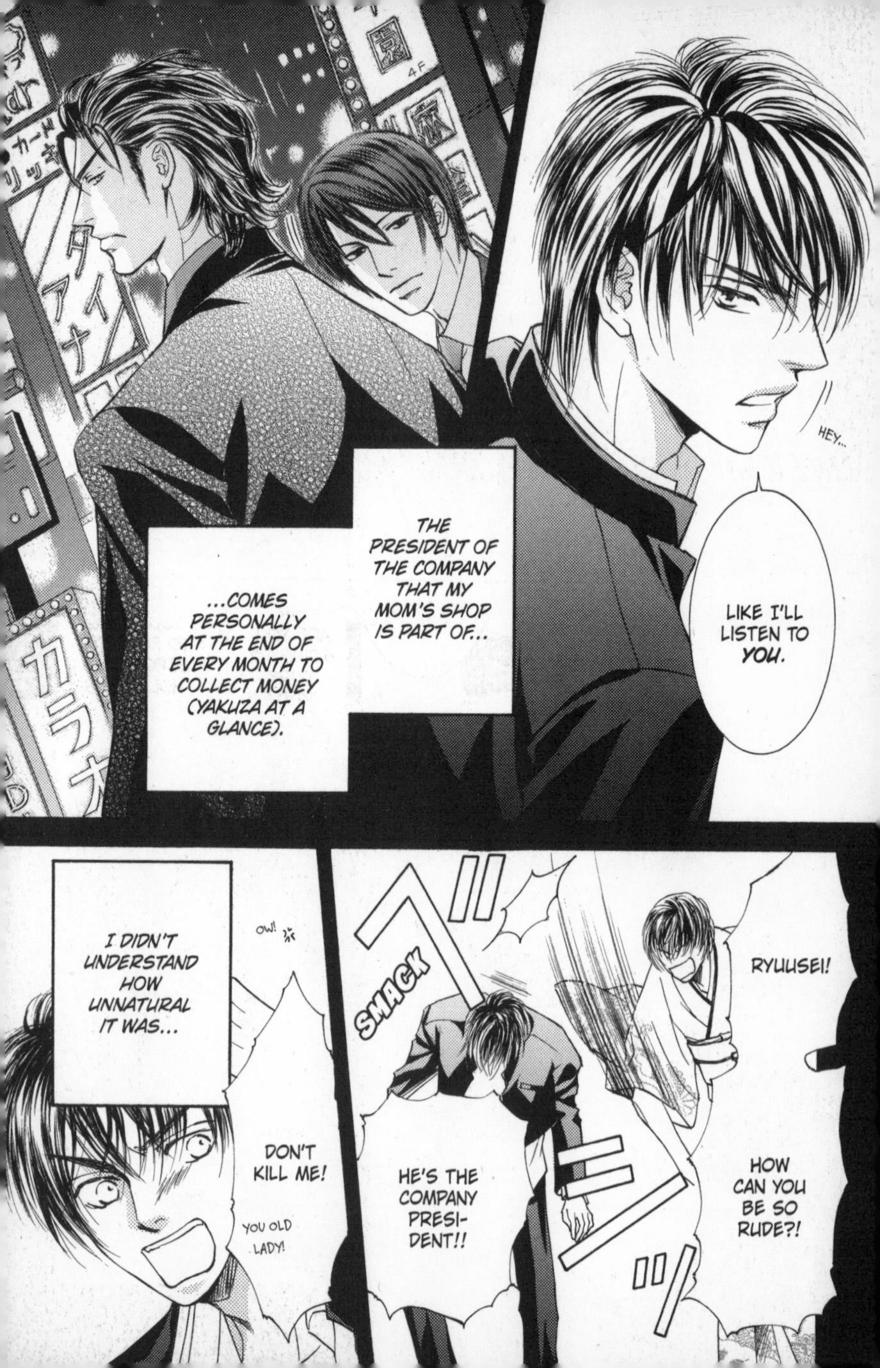
HEY...
LIKE I'LL LISTEN TO YOU.
THE PRESIDENT OF THE COMPANY THAT MY MOM'S SHOP IS PART OF...
...COMES PERSONALLY AT THE END OF EVERY MONTH TO COLLECT MONEY (YAKUZA AT A GLANCE).
RYUUSEI!
HOW CAN YOU BE SO RUDE?!
HE'S THE COMPANY PRESI-DENT!!
SMACK
I DIDN'T UNDERSTAND HOW UNNATURAL IT WAS...
OW!
DON'T KILL ME!
YOU OLD LADY!

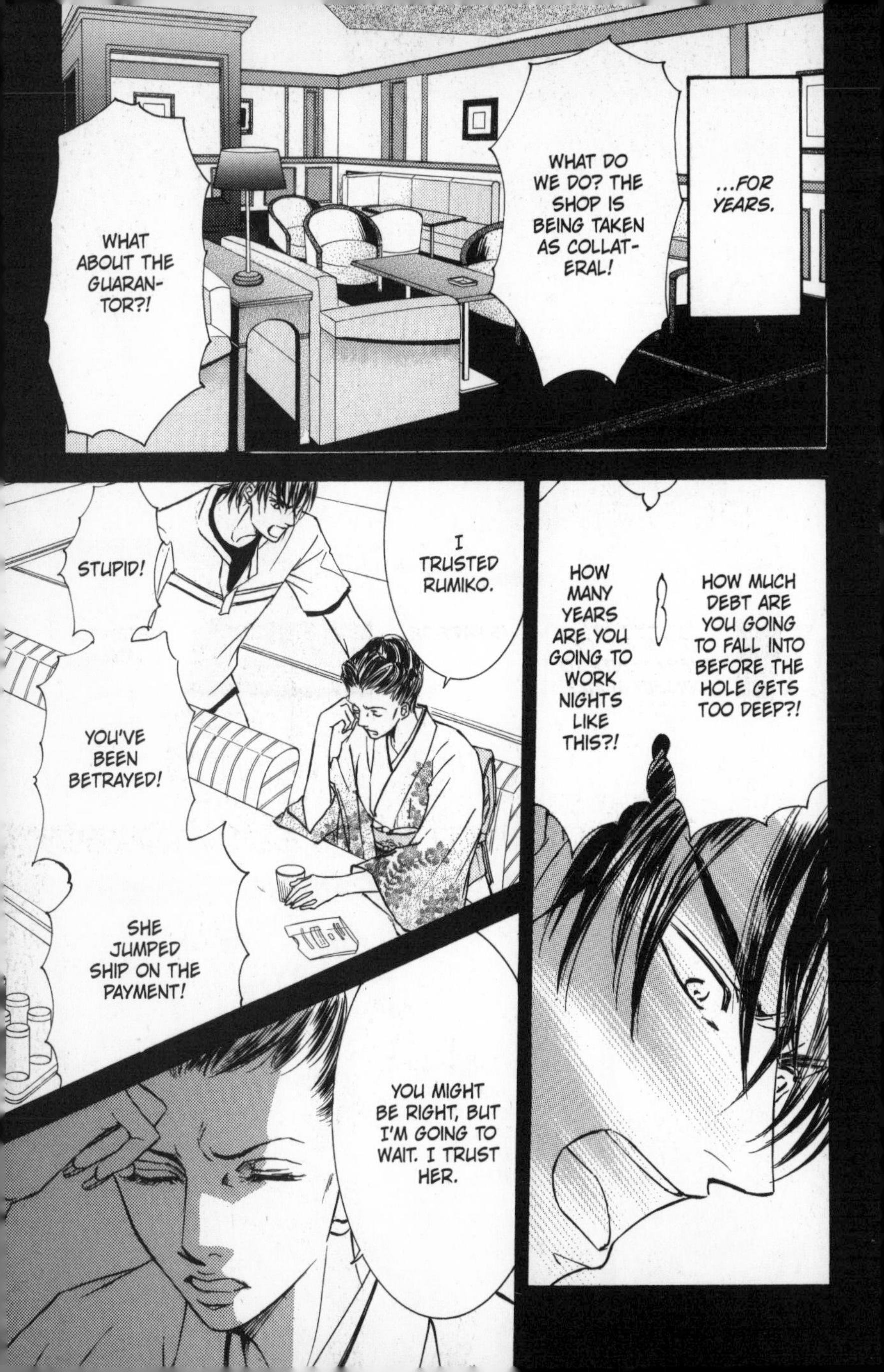
...FOR YEARS.
WHAT DO WE DO? THE SHOP IS BEING TAKEN AS COLLATERAL!
WHAT ABOUT THE GUARANTOR?!
HOW MUCH DEBT ARE YOU GOING TO FALL INTO BEFORE THE HOLE GETS TOO DEEP?!
HOW MANY YEARS ARE YOU GOING TO WORK NIGHTS LIKE THIS?!
I TRUSTED RUMIKO.
STUPID!
YOU'VE BEEN BETRAYED!
SHE JUMPED SHIP ON THE PAYMENT!
YOU MIGHT BE RIGHT, BUT I'M GOING TO WAIT. I TRUST HER.

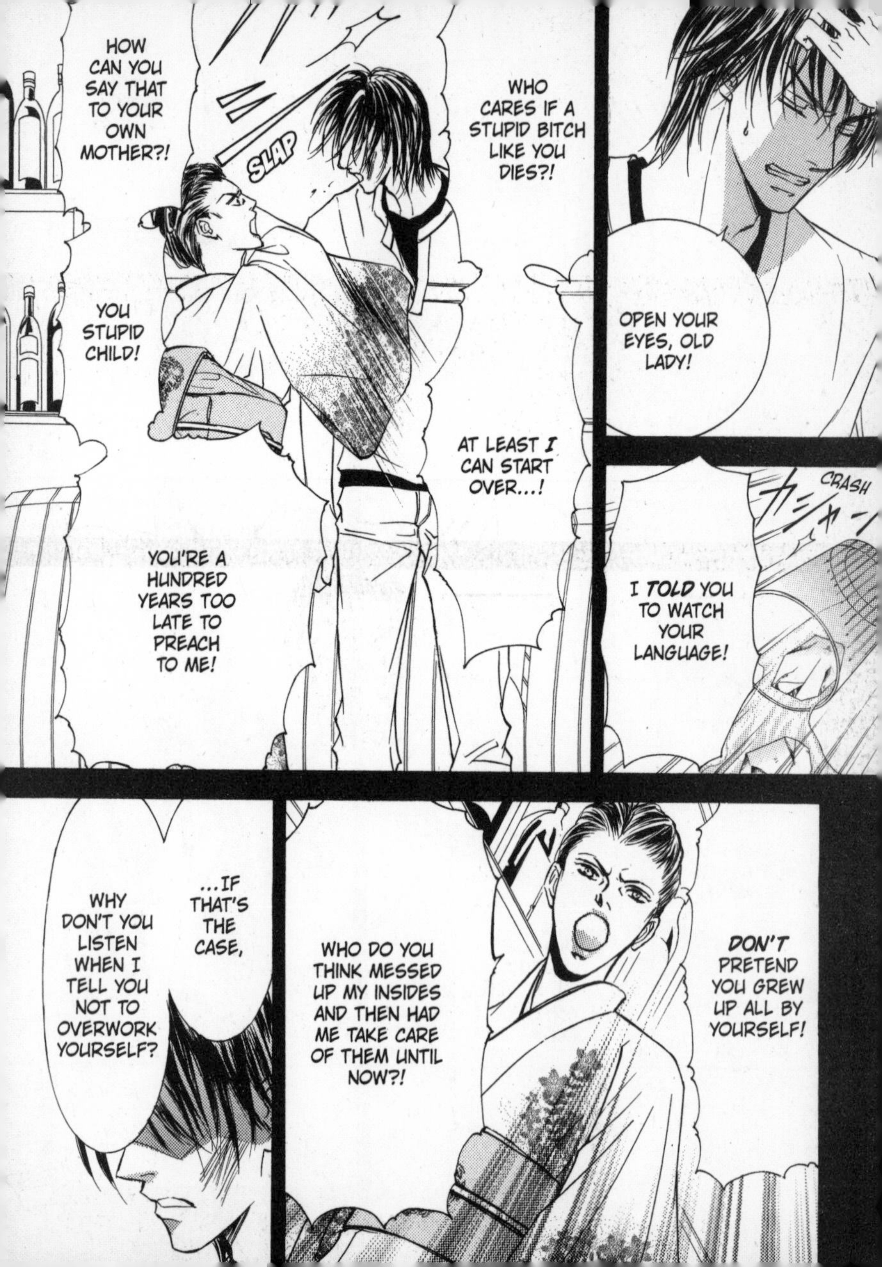
OPEN YOUR EYES, OLD LADY!
CRASH
I TOLD YOU TO WATCH YOUR LANGUAGE!
WHO CARES IF A STUPID BITCH LIKE YOU DIES?!
SLAP
HOW CAN YOU SAY THAT TO YOUR OWN MOTHER?!
AT LEAST I CAN START OVER...!
YOU STUPID CHILD!
YOU'RE A HUNDRED YEARS TOO LATE TO PREACH TO ME!
DON'T PRETEND YOU GREW UP ALL BY YOURSELF!
WHO DO YOU THINK MESSED UP MY INSIDES AND THEN HAD ME TAKE CARE OF THEM UNTIL NOW?!
...IF THAT'S THE CASE,
WHY DON'T YOU LISTEN WHEN I TELL YOU NOT TO OVERWORK YOURSELF?

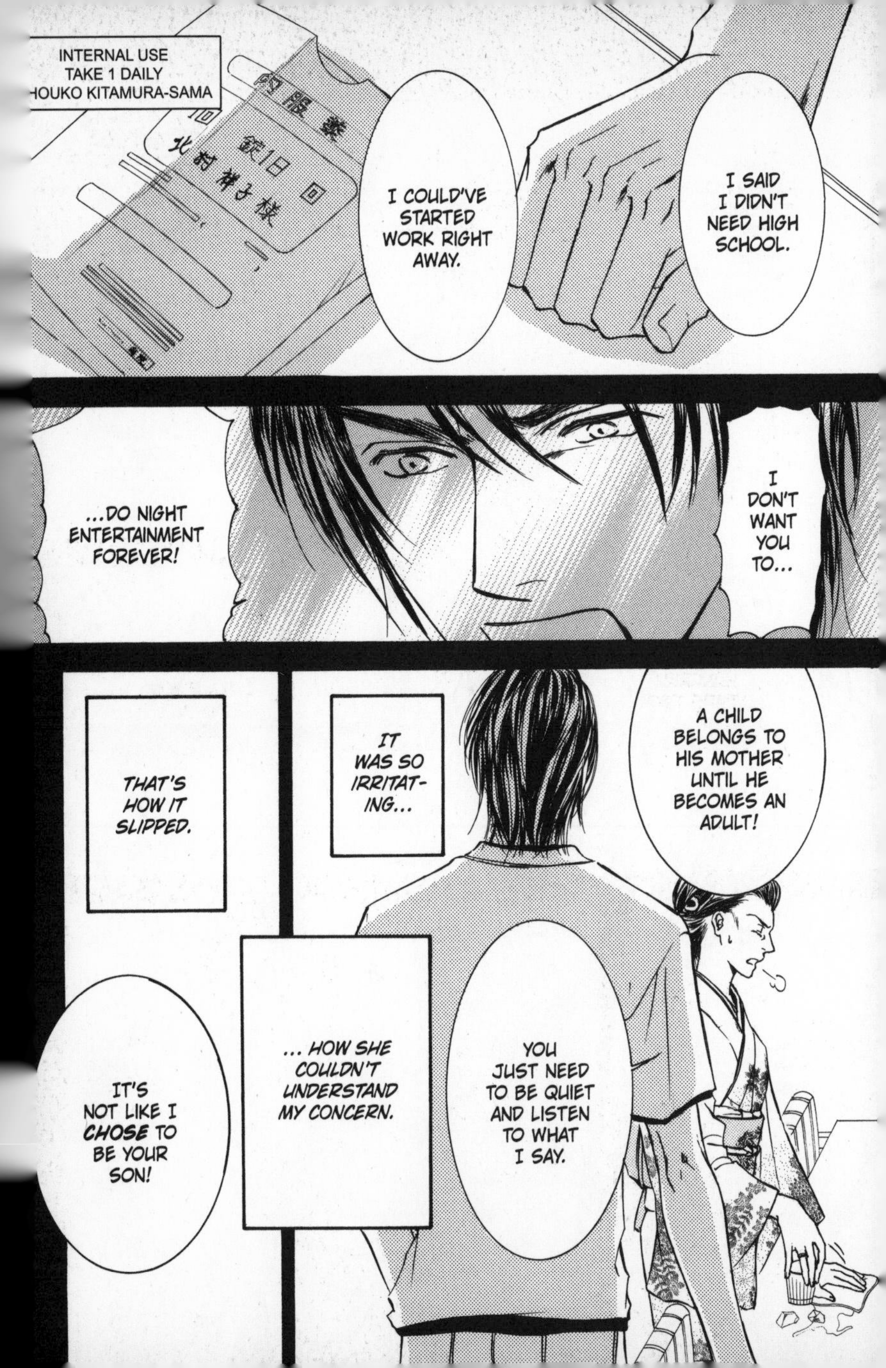
I SAID I DIDN'T NEED HIGH SCHOOL.
I COULD'VE STARTED WORK RIGHT AWAY.
INTERNAL USE
TAKE 1 DAILY
HOUKO KITAMURA-SAMA
I DON'T WANT YOU TO...
...DO NIGHT ENTERTAINMENT FOREVER!
A CHILD BELONGS TO HIS MOTHER UNTIL HE BECOMES AN ADULT!
IT WAS SO IRRITATING...
YOU JUST NEED TO BE QUIET AND LISTEN TO WHAT I SAY.
... HOW SHE COULDN'T UNDERSTAND MY CONCERN.
THAT'S HOW IT SLIPPED.
IT'S NOT LIKE I **CHOSE** TO BE YOUR SON!

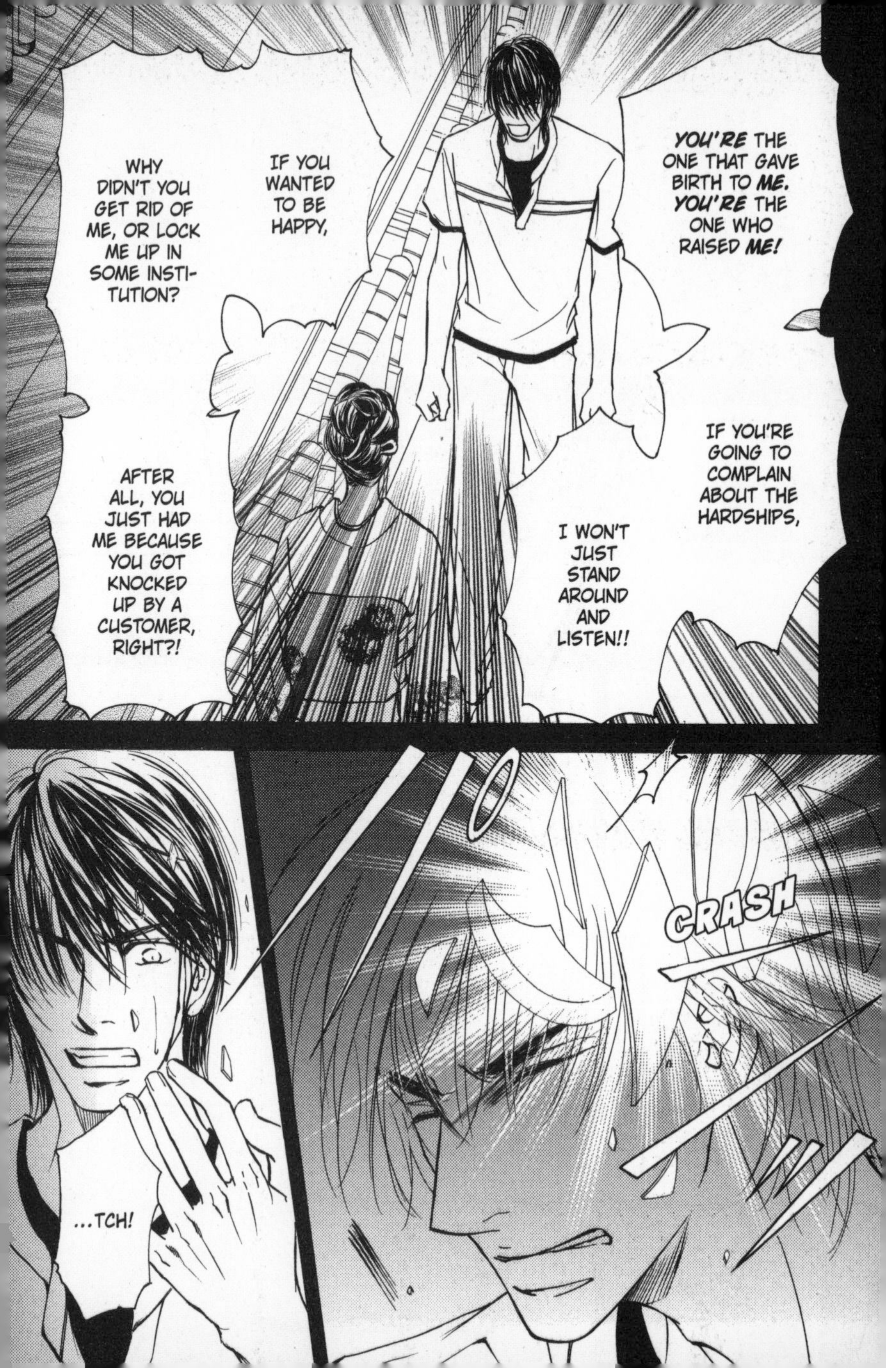
YOU'RE THE ONE THAT GAVE BIRTH TO ME. YOU'RE THE ONE WHO RAISED ME!
IF YOU'RE GOING TO COMPLAIN ABOUT THE HARDSHIPS,
I WON'T JUST STAND AROUND AND LISTEN!!
IF YOU WANTED TO BE HAPPY,
WHY DIDN'T YOU GET RID OF ME, OR LOCK ME UP IN SOME INSTI-TUTION?
AFTER ALL, YOU JUST HAD ME BECAUSE YOU GOT KNOCKED UP BY A CUSTOMER, RIGHT?!
CRASH
...TCH!

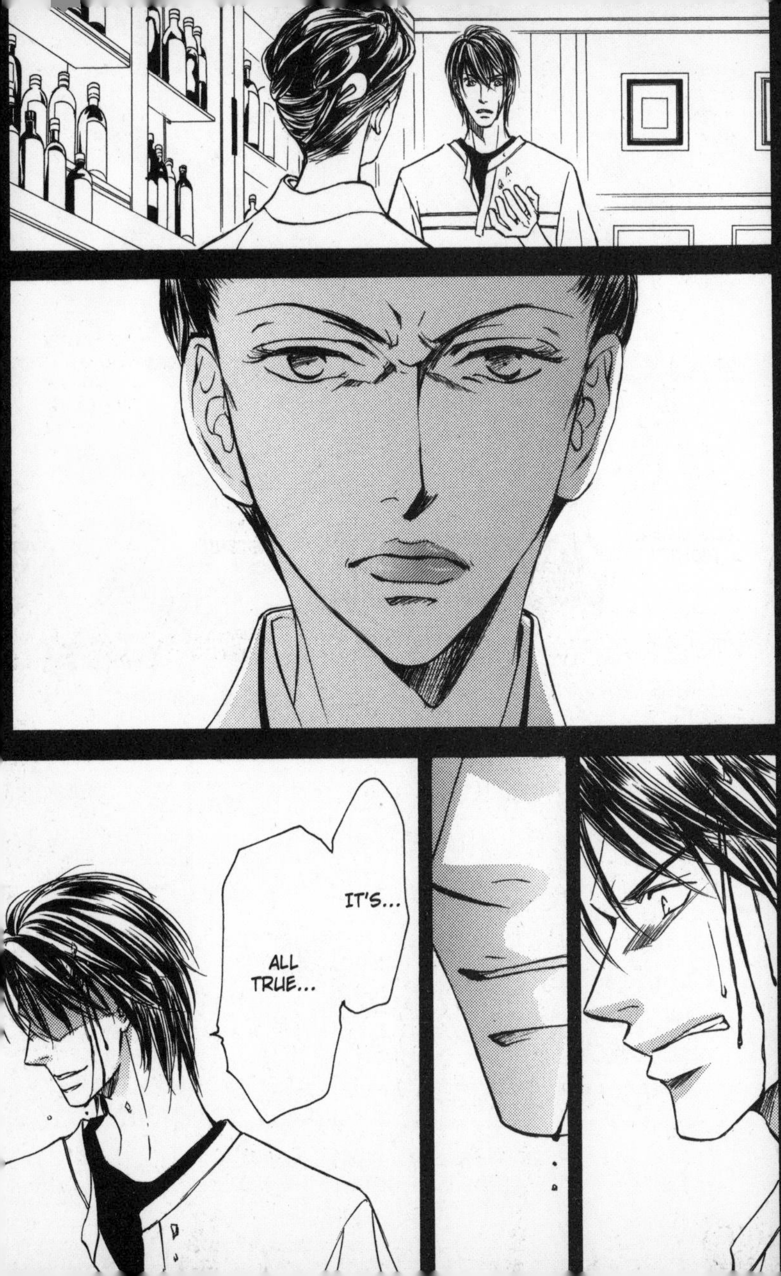
IT'S...
ALL TRUE...

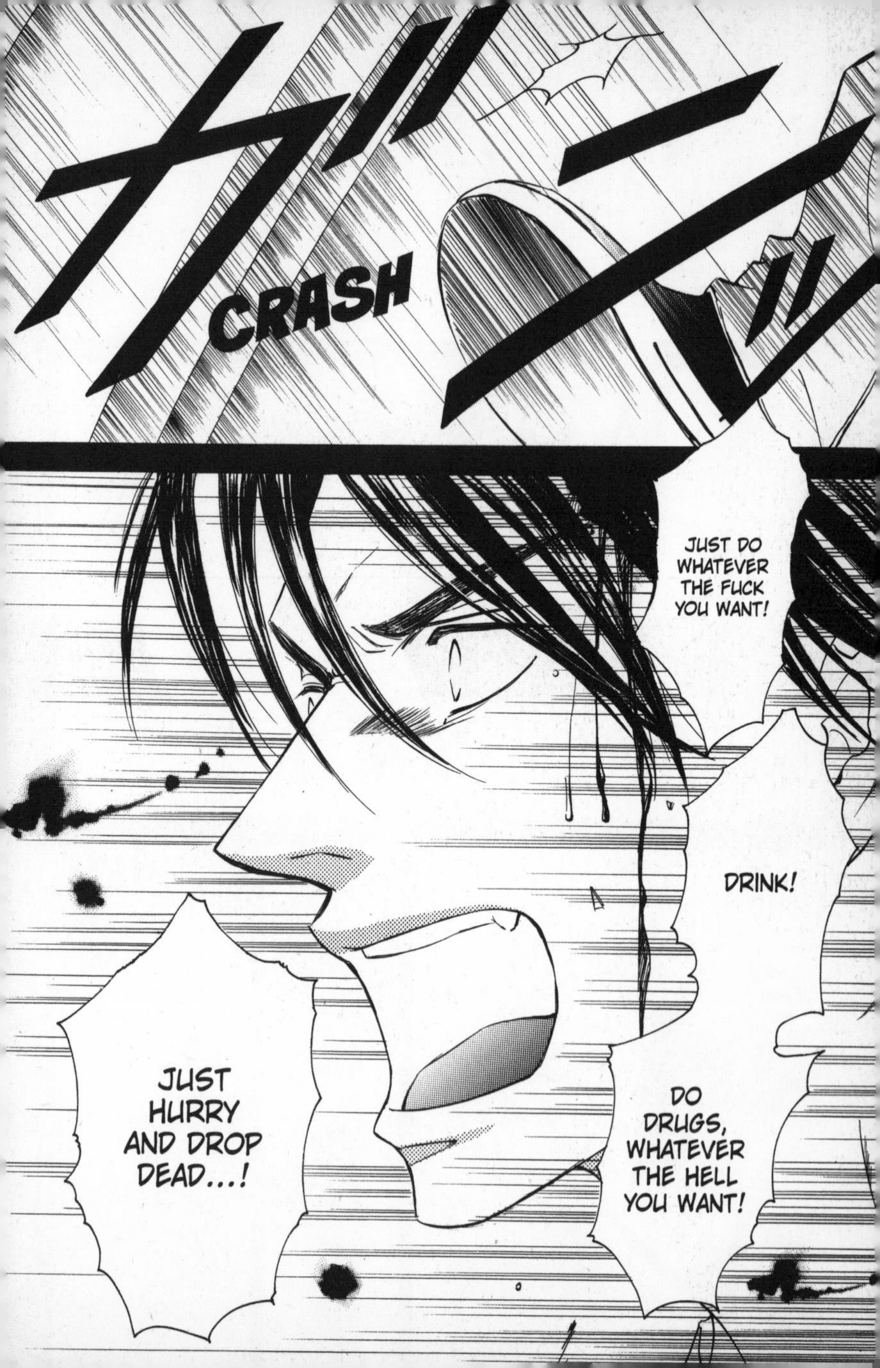
CRASH
JUST DO WHATEVER THE FUCK YOU WANT!
DRINK!
DO DRUGS, WHATEVER THE HELL YOU WANT!
JUST HURRY AND DROP DEAD...!

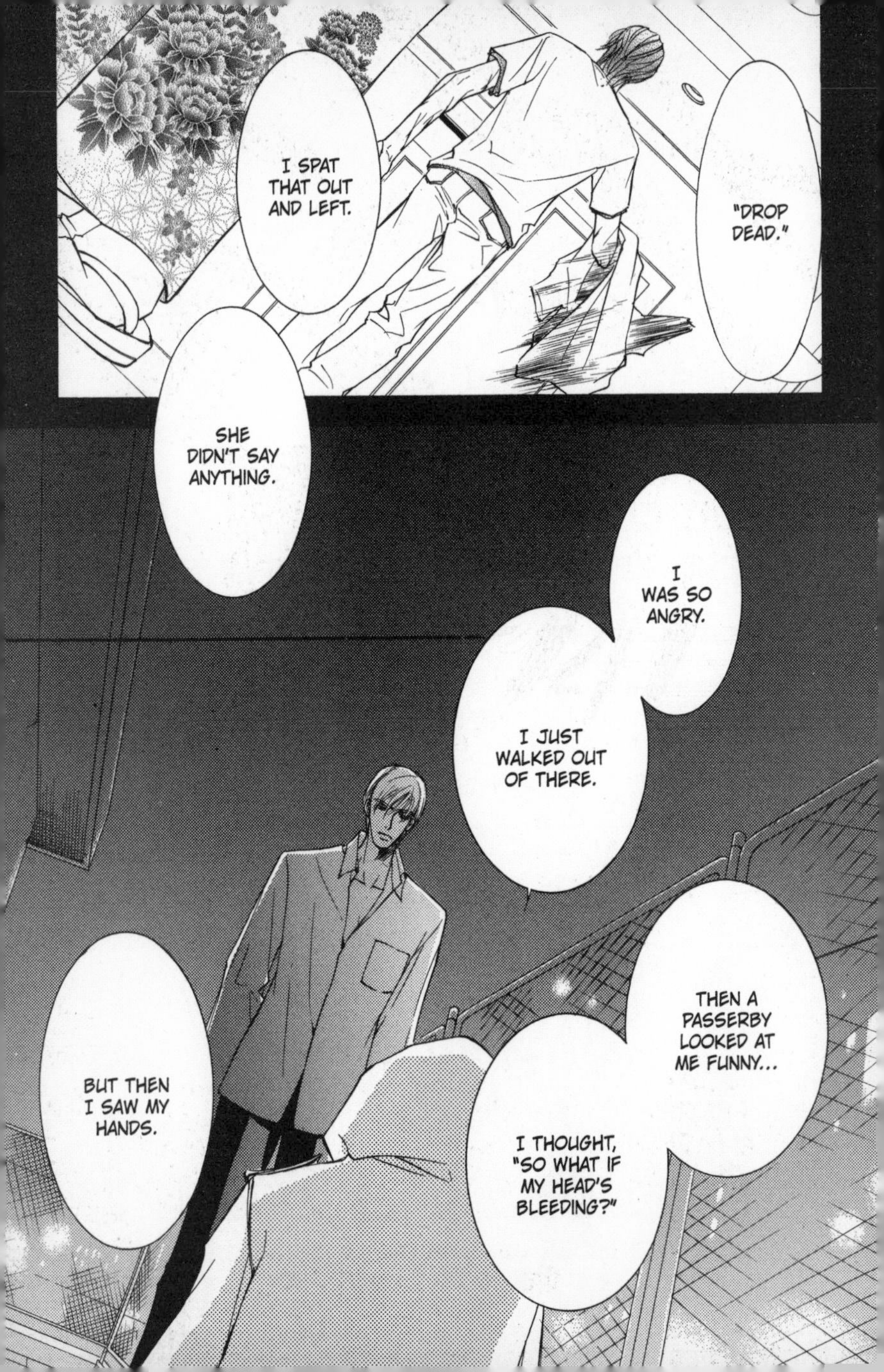
"DROP DEAD."
I SPAT THAT OUT AND LEFT.
SHE DIDN'T SAY ANYTHING.
I WAS SO ANGRY.
I JUST WALKED OUT OF THERE.
THEN A PASSERBY LOOKED AT ME FUNNY...
I THOUGHT, "SO WHAT IF MY HEAD'S BLEEDING?"
BUT THEN I SAW MY HANDS.

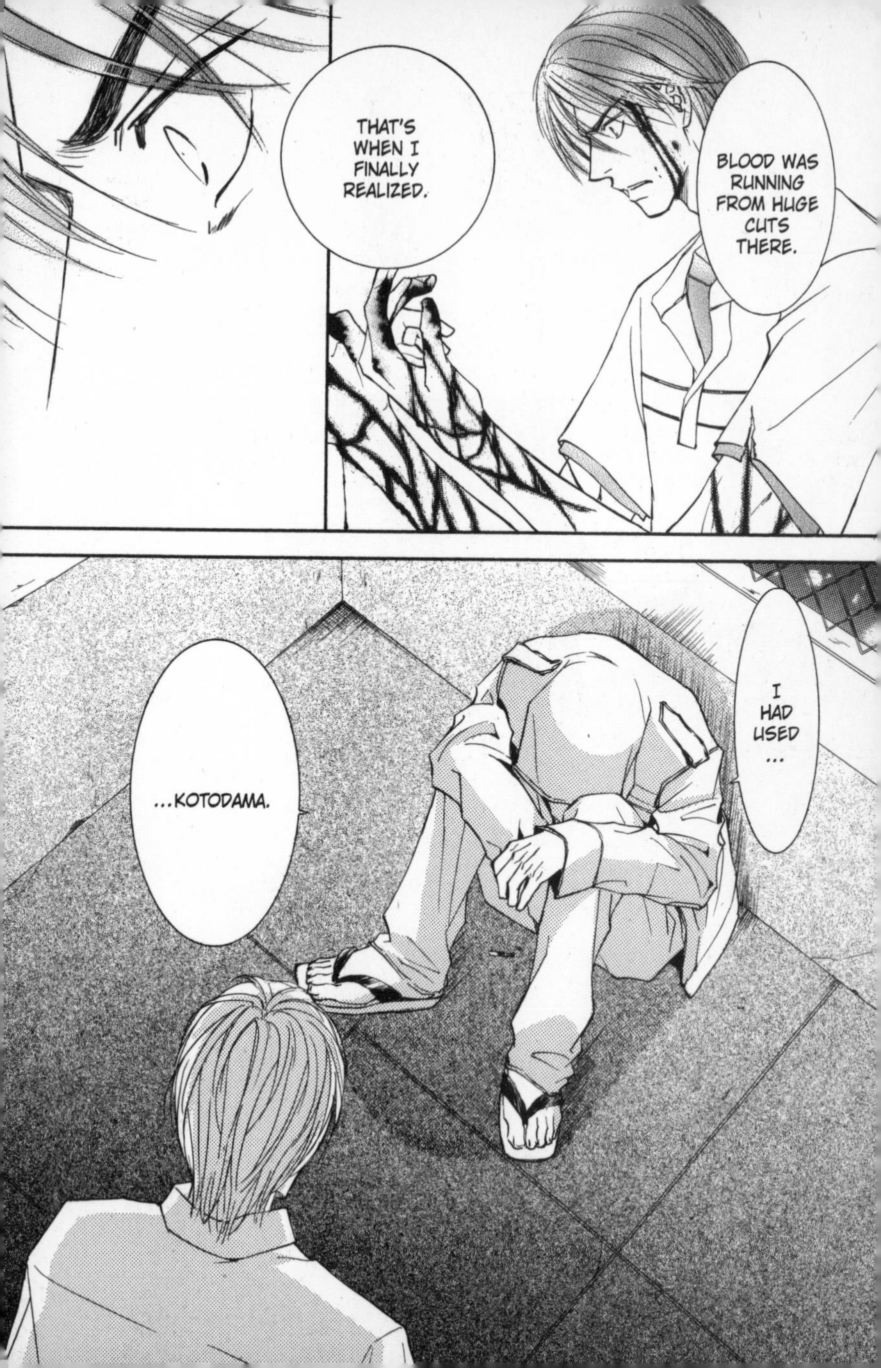
BLOOD WAS RUNNING FROM HUGE CUTS THERE.
THAT'S WHEN I FINALLY REALIZED.
I HAD USED ...
...KOTODAMA.

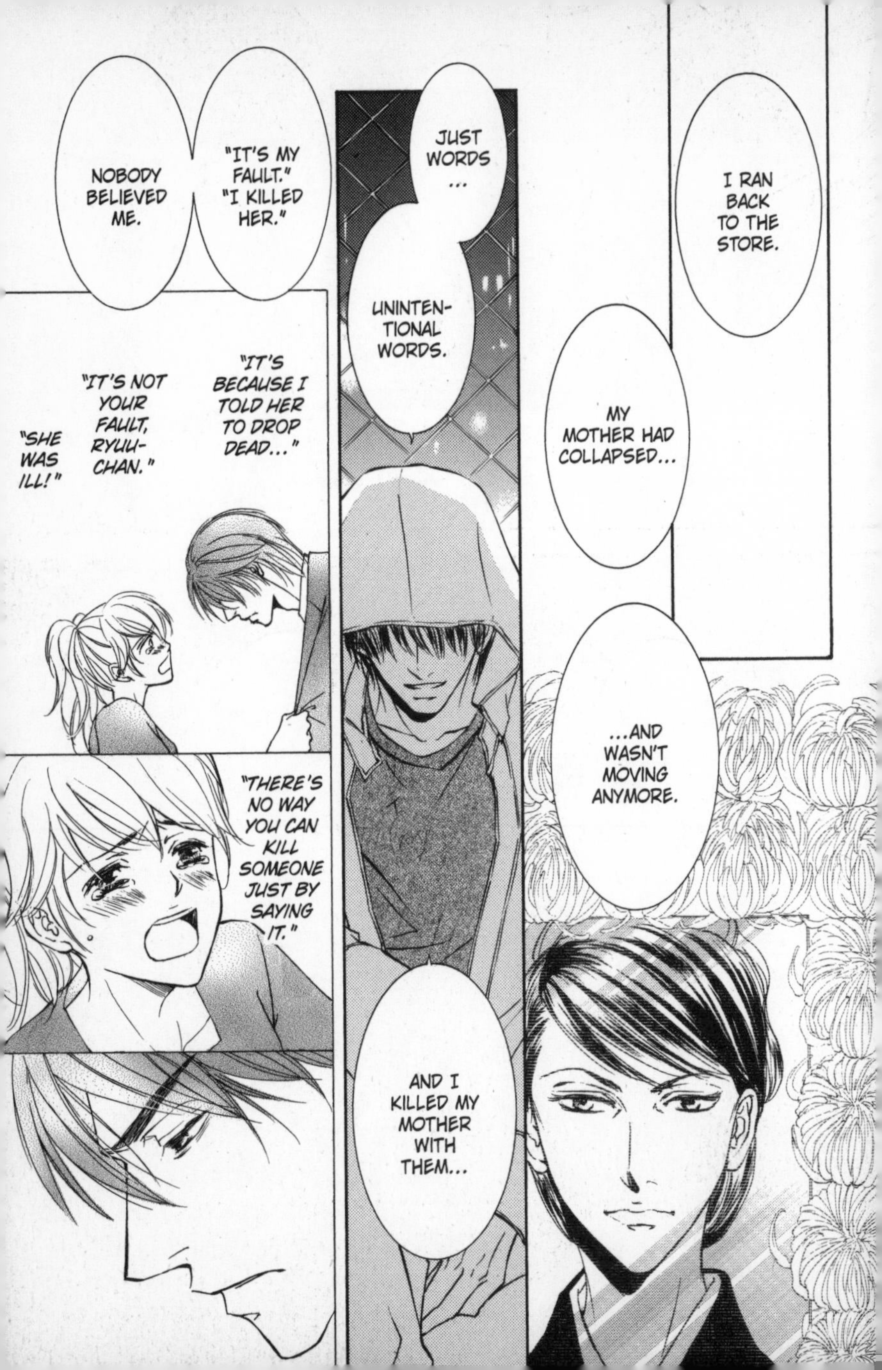
I RAN BACK TO THE STORE.
MY MOTHER HAD COLLAPSED...
...AND WASN'T MOVING ANYMORE.
JUST WORDS...
UNINTEN-TIONAL WORDS.
AND I KILLED MY MOTHER WITH THEM...
"IT'S MY FAULT." "I KILLED HER."
NOBODY BELIEVED ME.
"IT'S BECAUSE I TOLD HER TO DROP DEAD..."
"IT'S NOT YOUR FAULT, RYUU-CHAN."
"SHE WAS ILL!"
"THERE'S NO WAY YOU CAN KILL SOMEONE JUST BY SAYING IT."

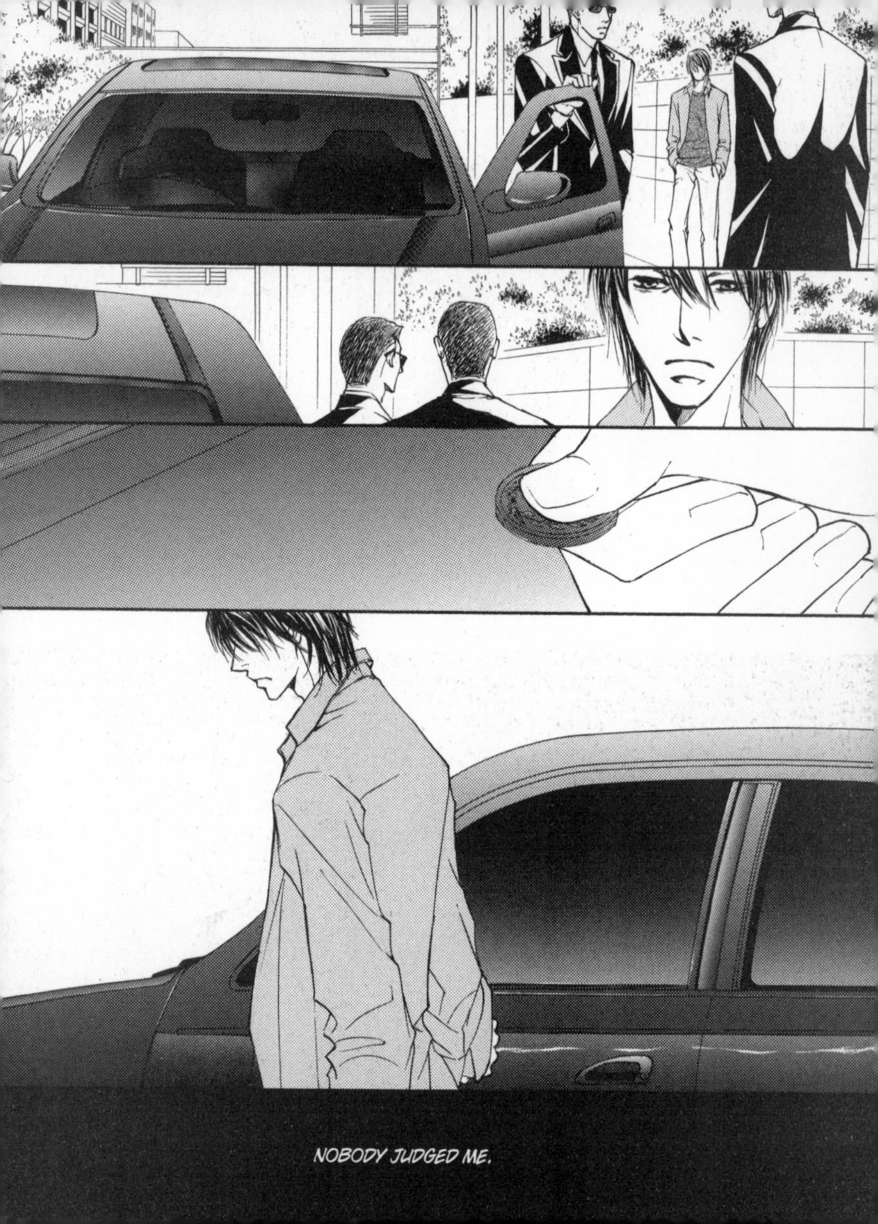
NOBODY JUDGED ME.

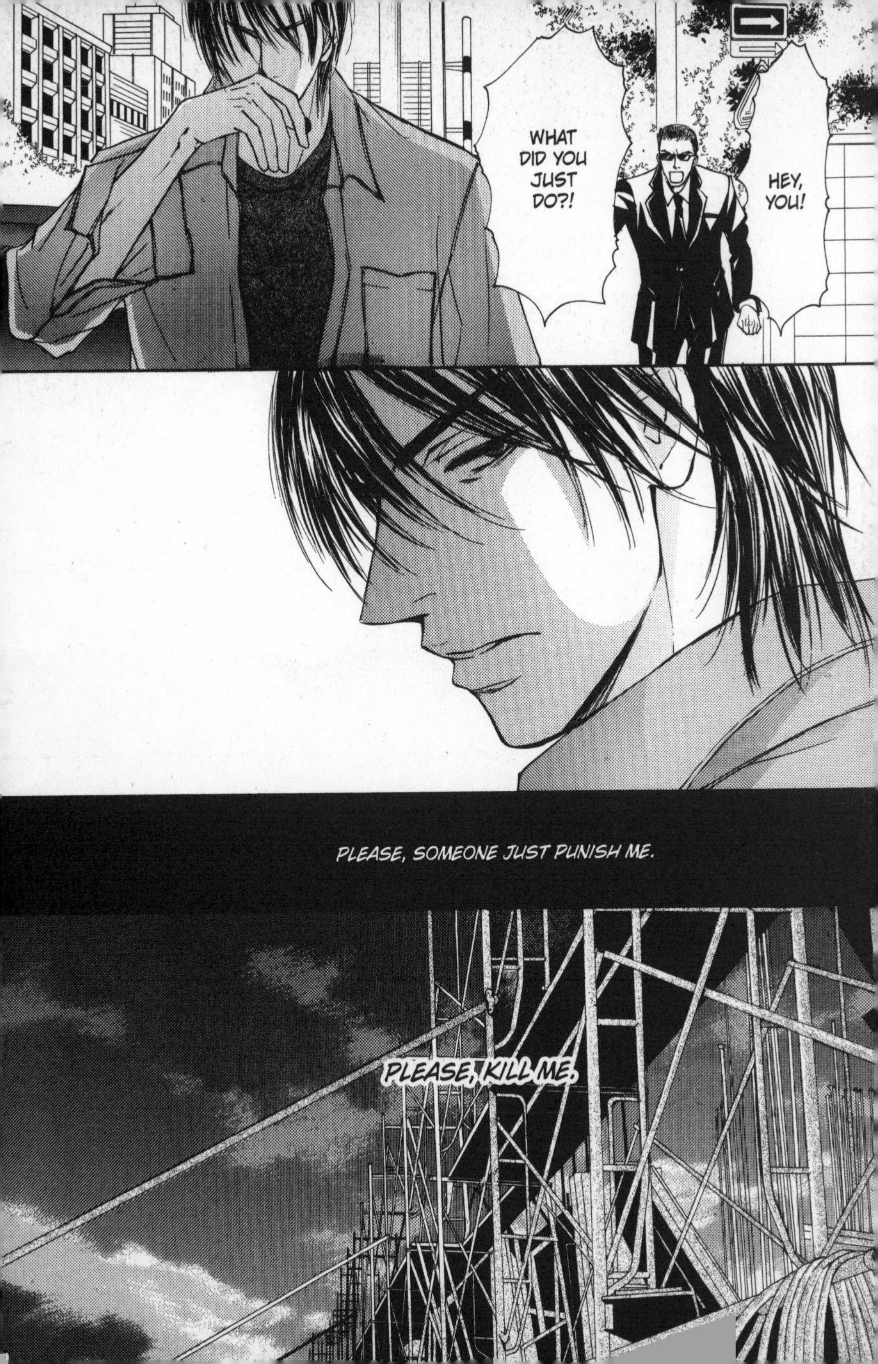
HEY, YOU!
WHAT DID YOU JUST DO?!
PLEASE, SOMEONE JUST PUNISH ME.
PLEASE, KILL ME.

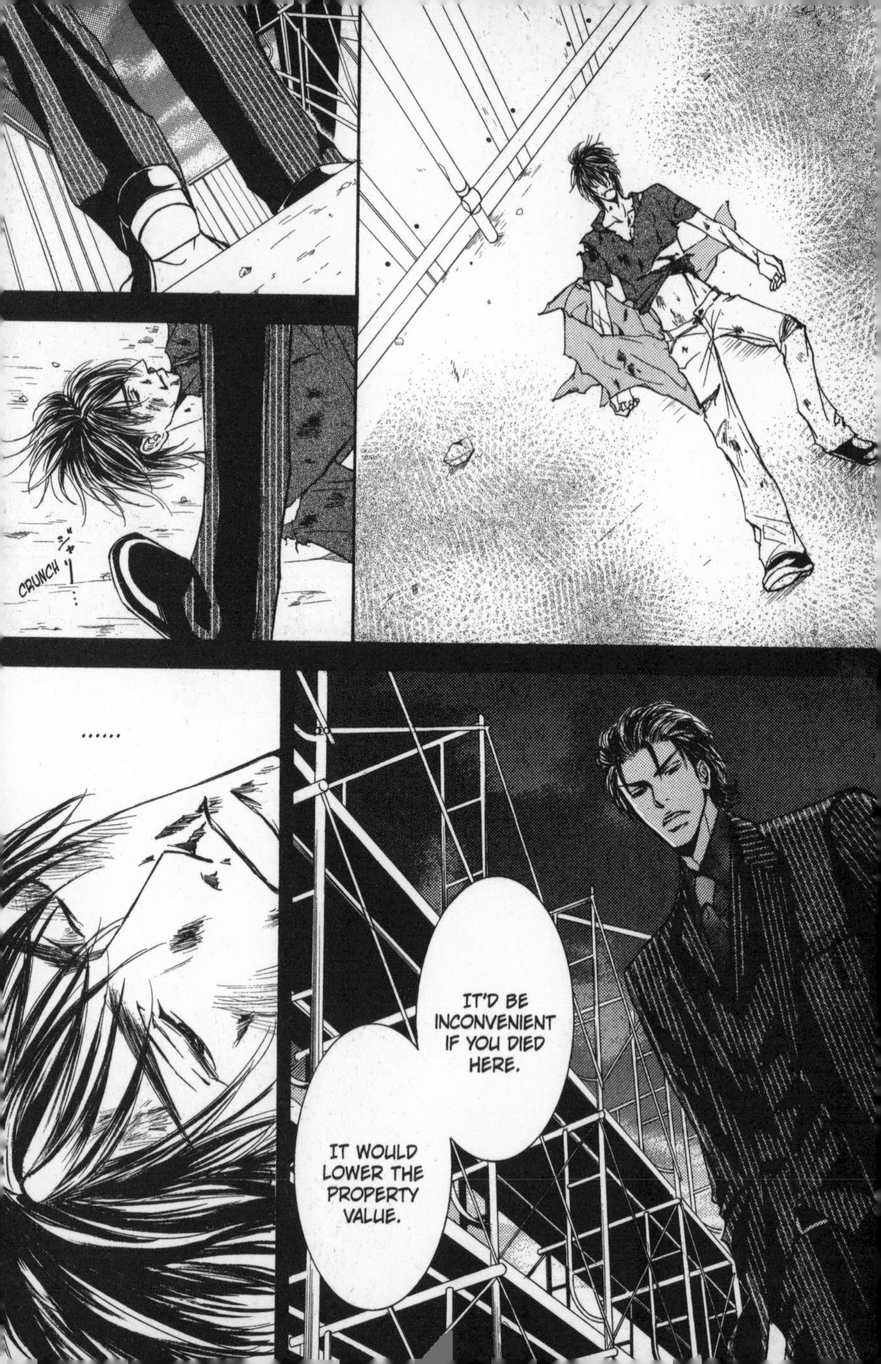
CRUNCH
IT'D BE INCONVENIENT IF YOU DIED HERE.
IT WOULD LOWER THE PROPERTY VALUE.
......

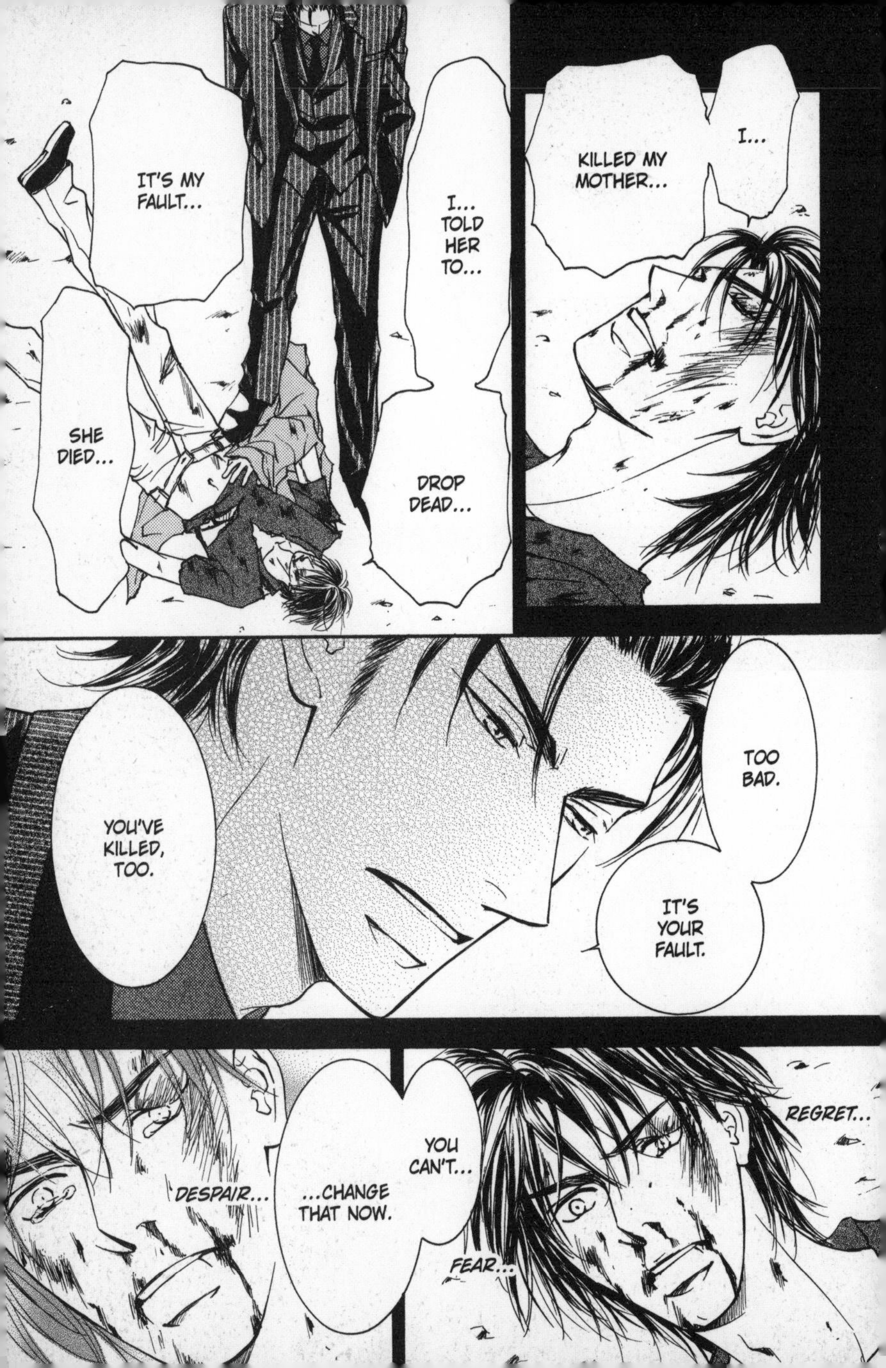
I...
KILLED MY MOTHER...
I... TOLD HER TO...
DROP DEAD...
IT'S MY FAULT...
SHE DIED...
TOO BAD.
IT'S YOUR FAULT.
YOU'VE KILLED, TOO.
REGRET...
FEAR...
YOU CAN'T...
...CHANGE THAT NOW.
DESPAIR...

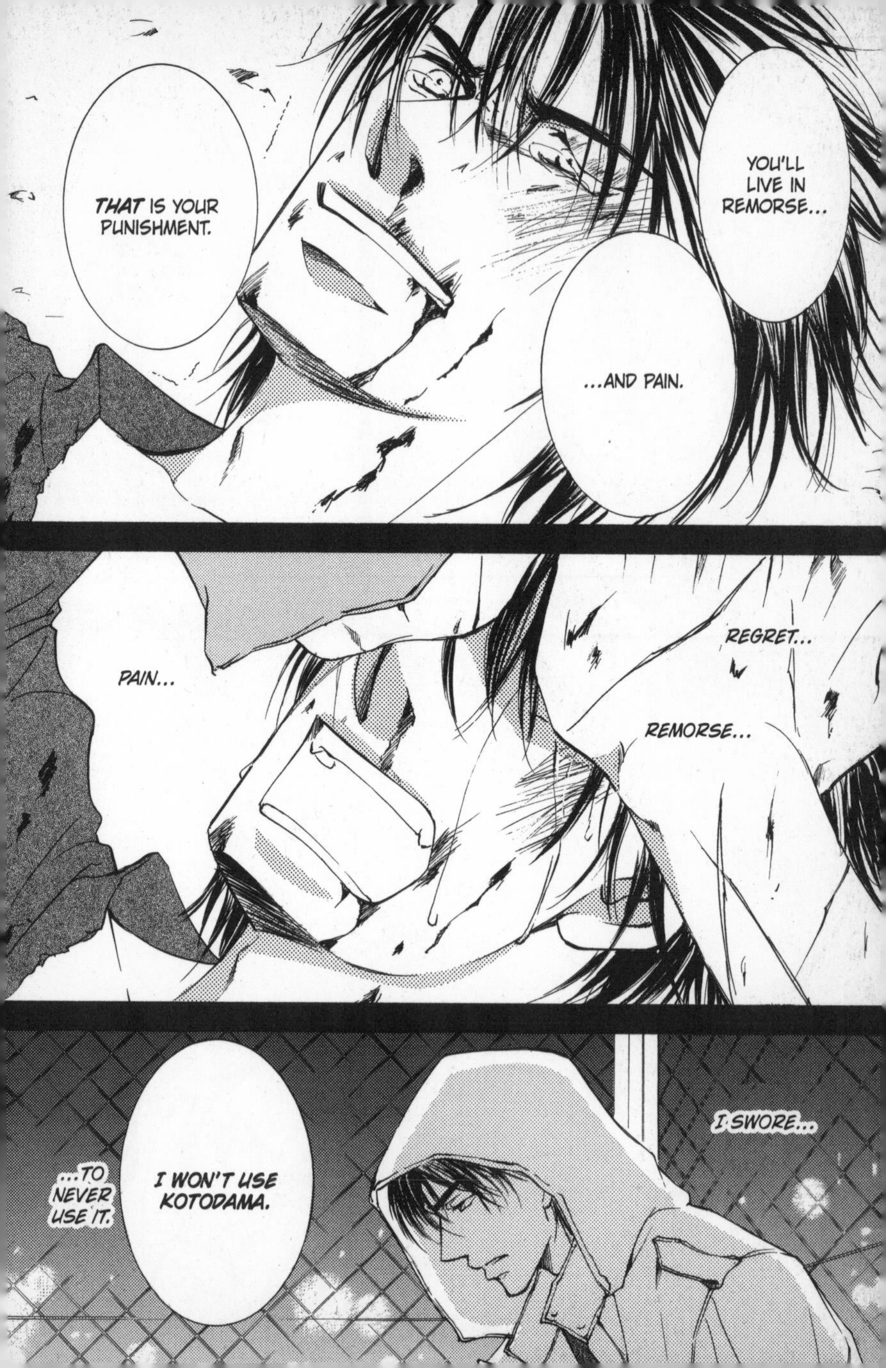
YOU'LL LIVE IN REMORSE...
...AND PAIN.
THAT IS YOUR PUNISHMENT.
REGRET...
REMORSE...
PAIN...
I SWORE...
I WON'T USE KOTODAMA.
...TO NEVER USE IT.

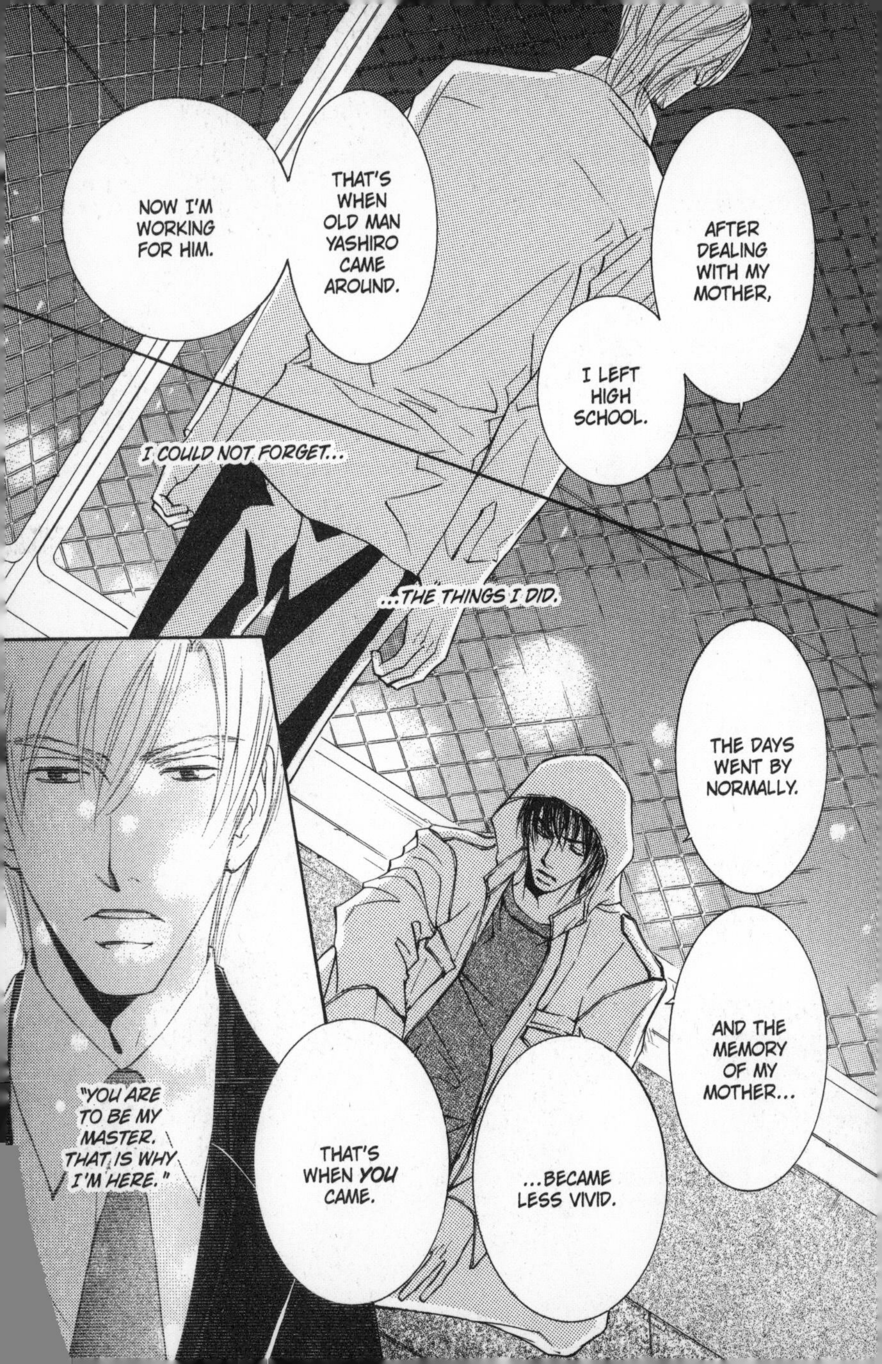
AFTER DEALING WITH MY MOTHER,
I LEFT HIGH SCHOOL.
THAT'S WHEN OLD MAN YASHIRO CAME AROUND.
NOW I'M WORKING FOR HIM.
I COULD NOT FORGET...
...THE THINGS I DID.
THE DAYS WENT BY NORMALLY.
AND THE MEMORY OF MY MOTHER...
...BECAME LESS VIVID.
THAT'S WHEN *YOU* CAME.
"YOU ARE TO BE MY MASTER. THAT IS WHY I'M HERE."

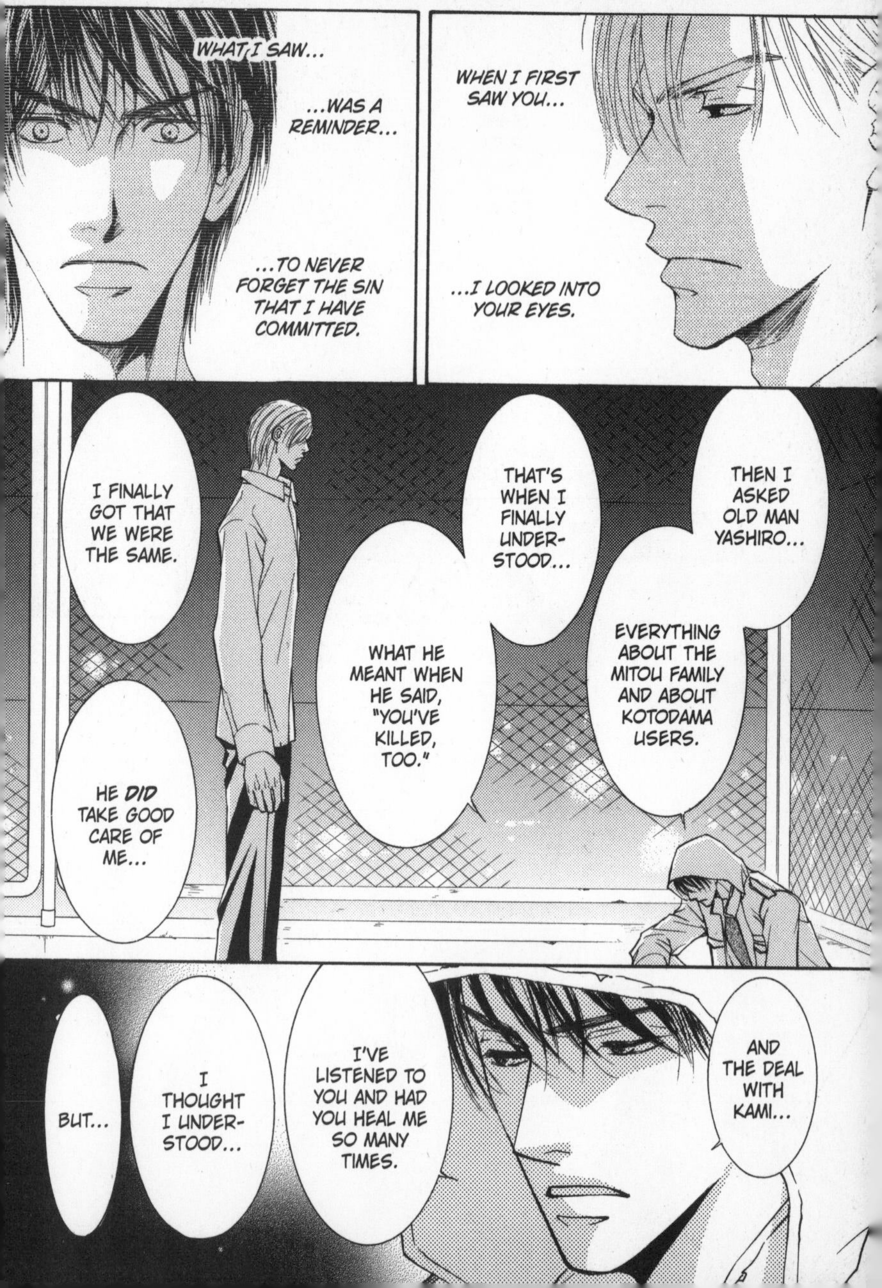
WHEN I FIRST SAW YOU...
...I LOOKED INTO YOUR EYES.
WHAT I SAW...
...WAS A REMINDER...
...TO NEVER FORGET THE SIN THAT I HAVE COMMITTED.
THEN I ASKED OLD MAN YASHIRO...
EVERYTHING ABOUT THE MITOU FAMILY AND ABOUT KOTODAMA USERS.
THAT'S WHEN I FINALLY UNDER-STOOD...
WHAT HE MEANT WHEN HE SAID, "YOU'VE KILLED, TOO."
I FINALLY GOT THAT WE WERE THE SAME.
HE *DID* TAKE GOOD CARE OF ME...
AND THE DEAL WITH KAMI...
I'VE LISTENED TO YOU AND HAD YOU HEAL ME SO MANY TIMES.
I THOUGHT I UNDER-STOOD...
BUT...

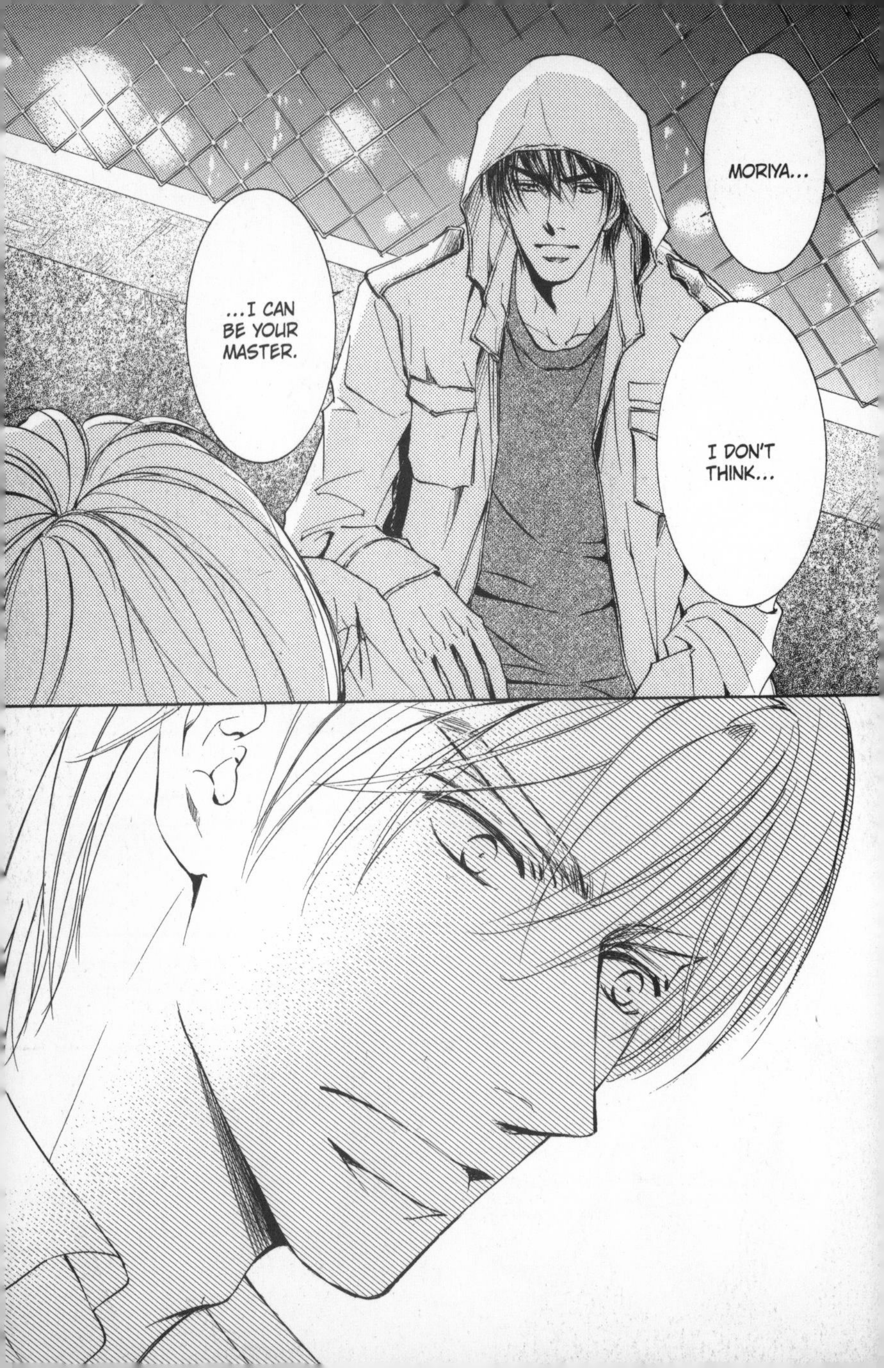
MORIYA...
I DON'T THINK...
...I CAN BE YOUR MASTER.

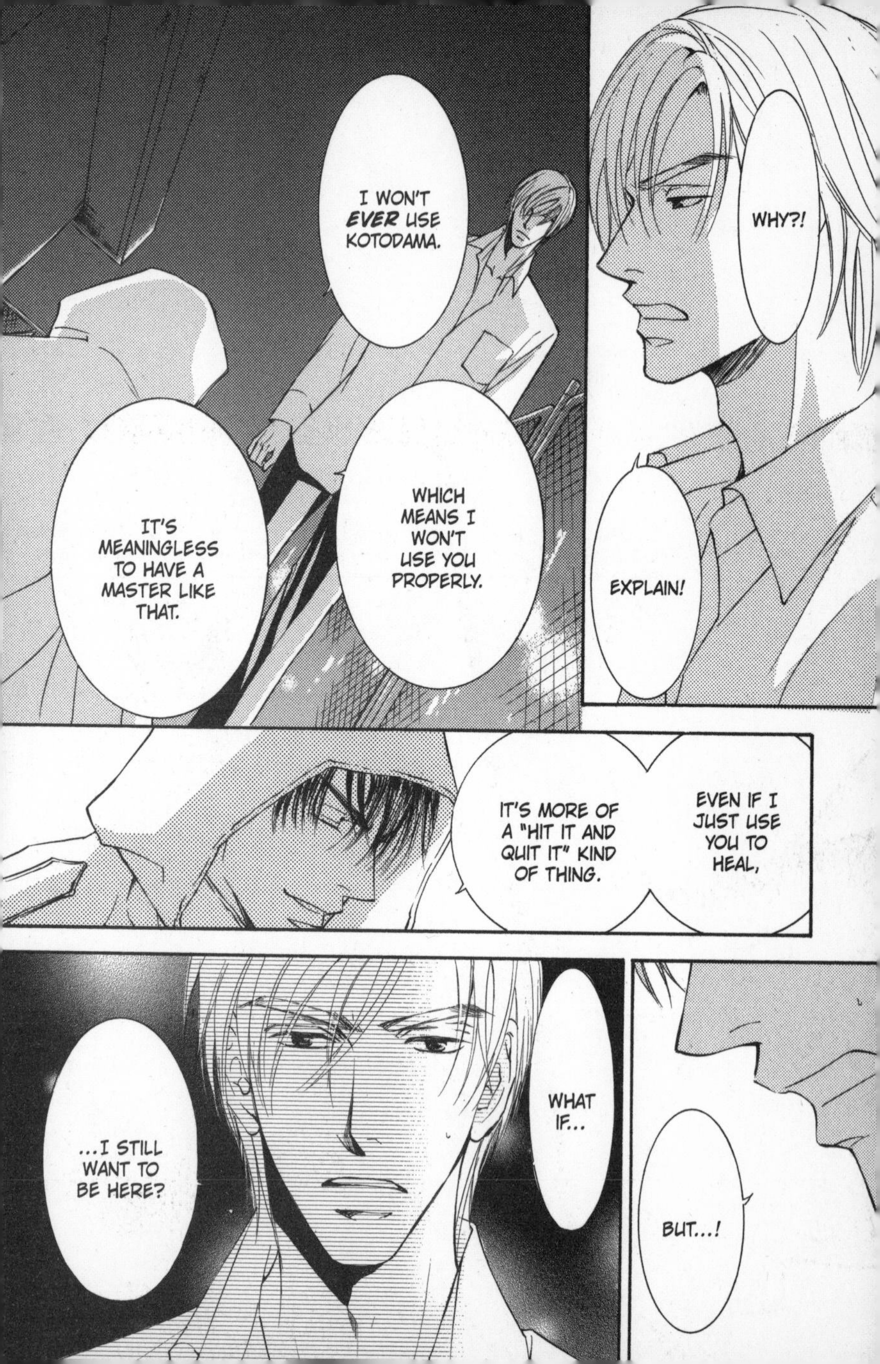
WHY?!
EXPLAIN!
I WON'T **EVER** USE KOTODAMA.
WHICH MEANS I WON'T USE YOU PROPERLY.
IT'S MEANINGLESS TO HAVE A MASTER LIKE THAT.
EVEN IF I JUST USE YOU TO HEAL,
IT'S MORE OF A "HIT IT AND QUIT IT" KIND OF THING.
BUT...!
WHAT IF...
...I STILL WANT TO BE HERE?

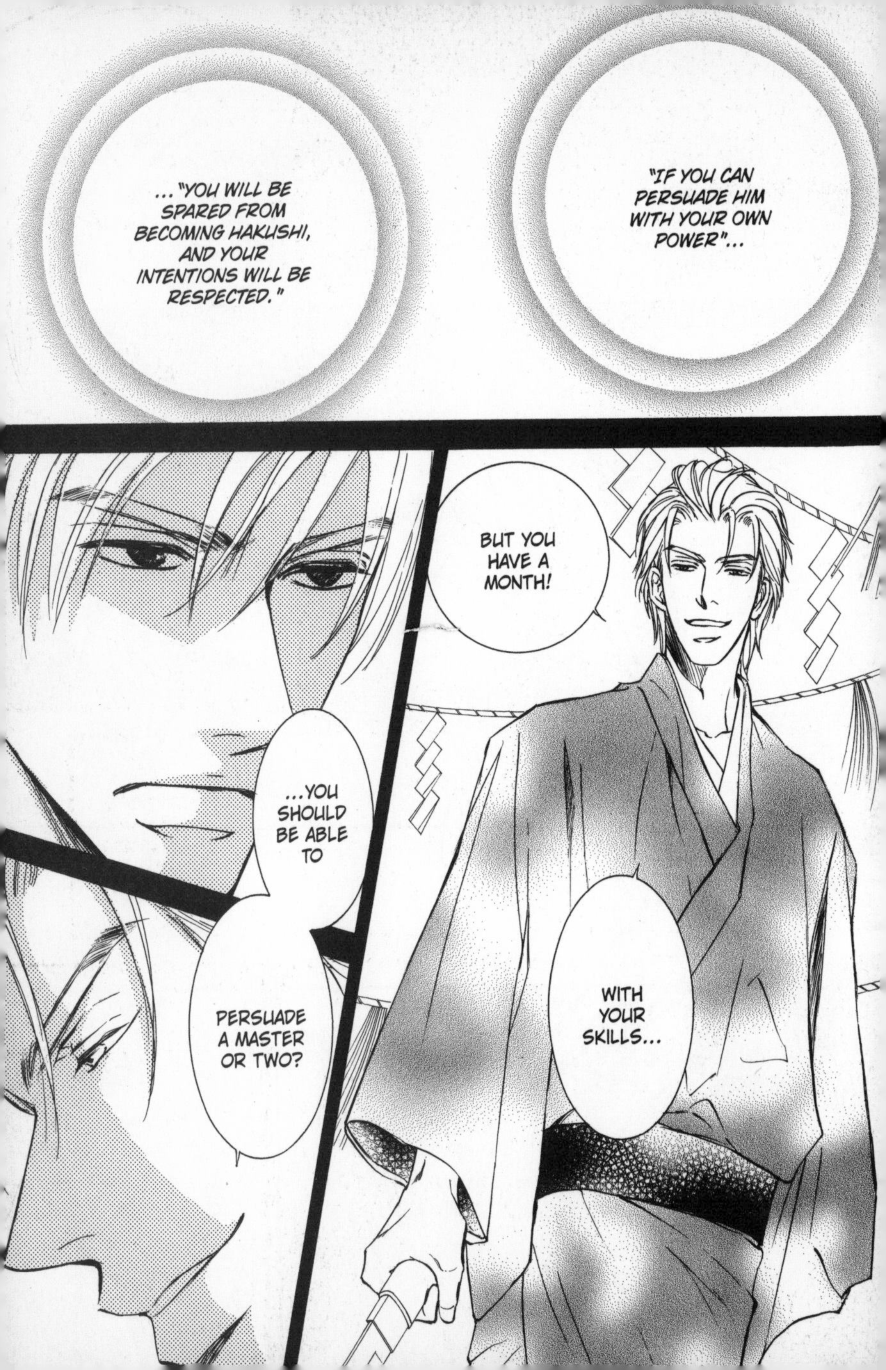
"IF YOU CAN PERSUADE HIM WITH YOUR OWN POWER"...
..."YOU WILL BE SPARED FROM BECOMING HAKUSHI, AND YOUR INTENTIONS WILL BE RESPECTED."
BUT YOU HAVE A MONTH!
WITH YOUR SKILLS...
...YOU SHOULD BE ABLE TO
PERSUADE A MASTER OR TWO?

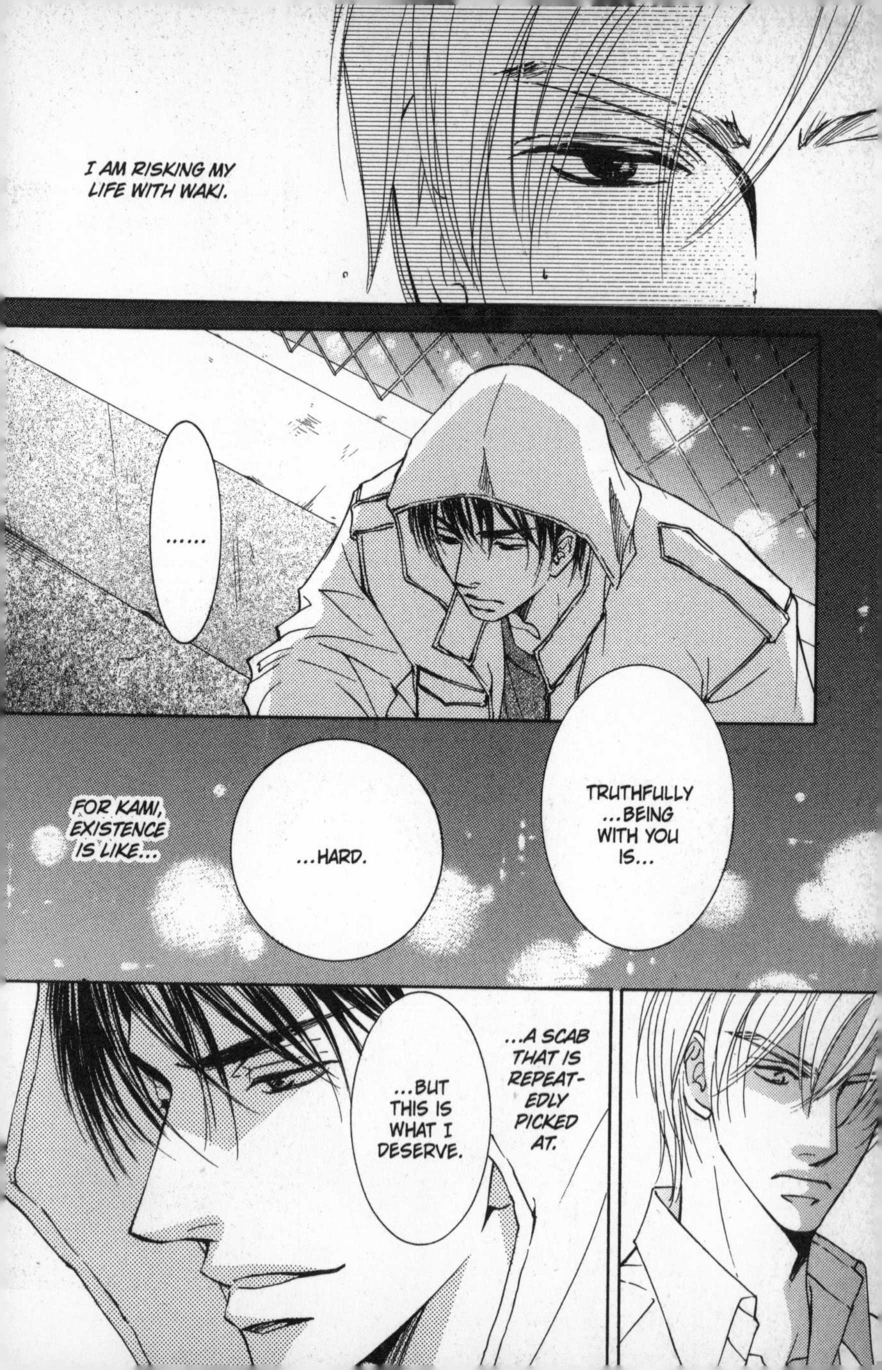
I AM RISKING MY LIFE WITH WAKI.
......
TRUTHFULLY ...BEING WITH YOU IS...
...HARD.
FOR KAMI, EXISTENCE IS LIKE...
...A SCAB THAT IS REPEAT-EDLY PICKED AT.
...BUT THIS IS WHAT I DESERVE.

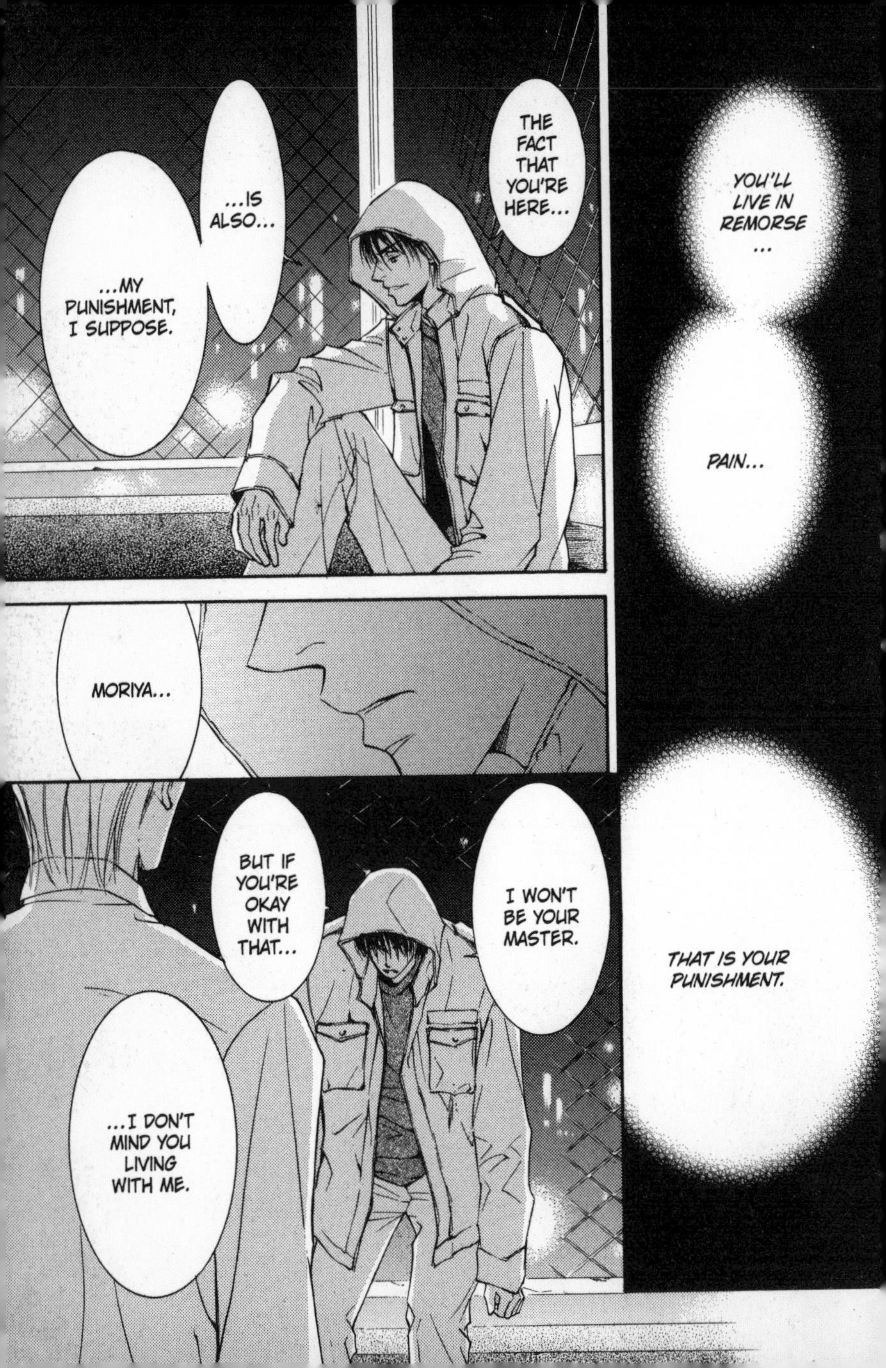
YOU'LL LIVE IN REMORSE ...
PAIN...
THAT IS YOUR PUNISHMENT.
THE FACT THAT YOU'RE HERE...
...IS ALSO...
...MY PUNISHMENT, I SUPPOSE.
MORIYA...
I WON'T BE YOUR MASTER.
BUT IF YOU'RE OKAY WITH THAT...
...I DON'T MIND YOU LIVING WITH ME.

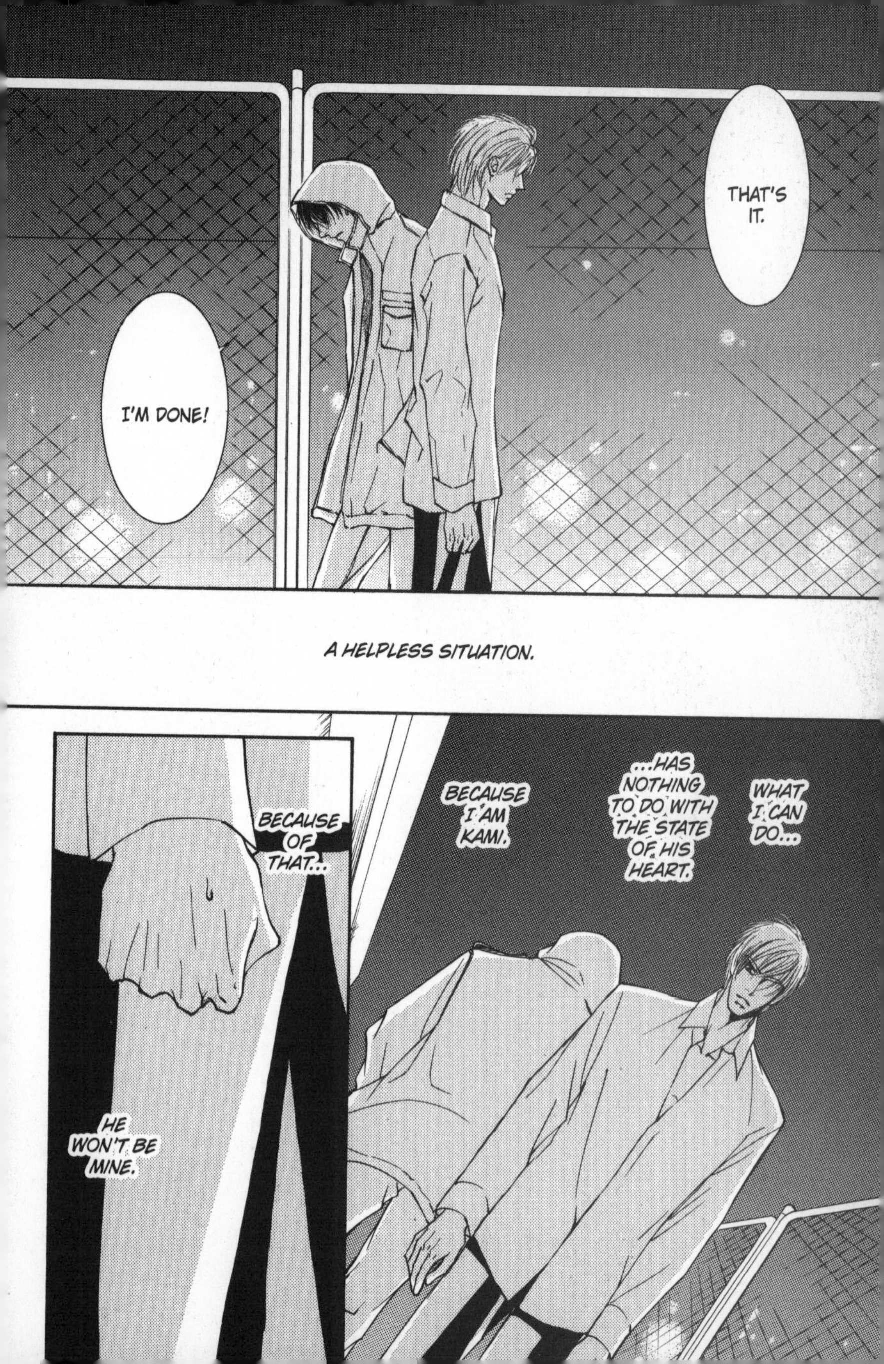
THAT'S IT.
I'M DONE!
A HELPLESS SITUATION.
WHAT I CAN DO...
...HAS NOTHING TO DO WITH THE STATE OF HIS HEART.
BECAUSE I AM KAMI.
BECAUSE OF THAT...
HE WON'T BE MINE.

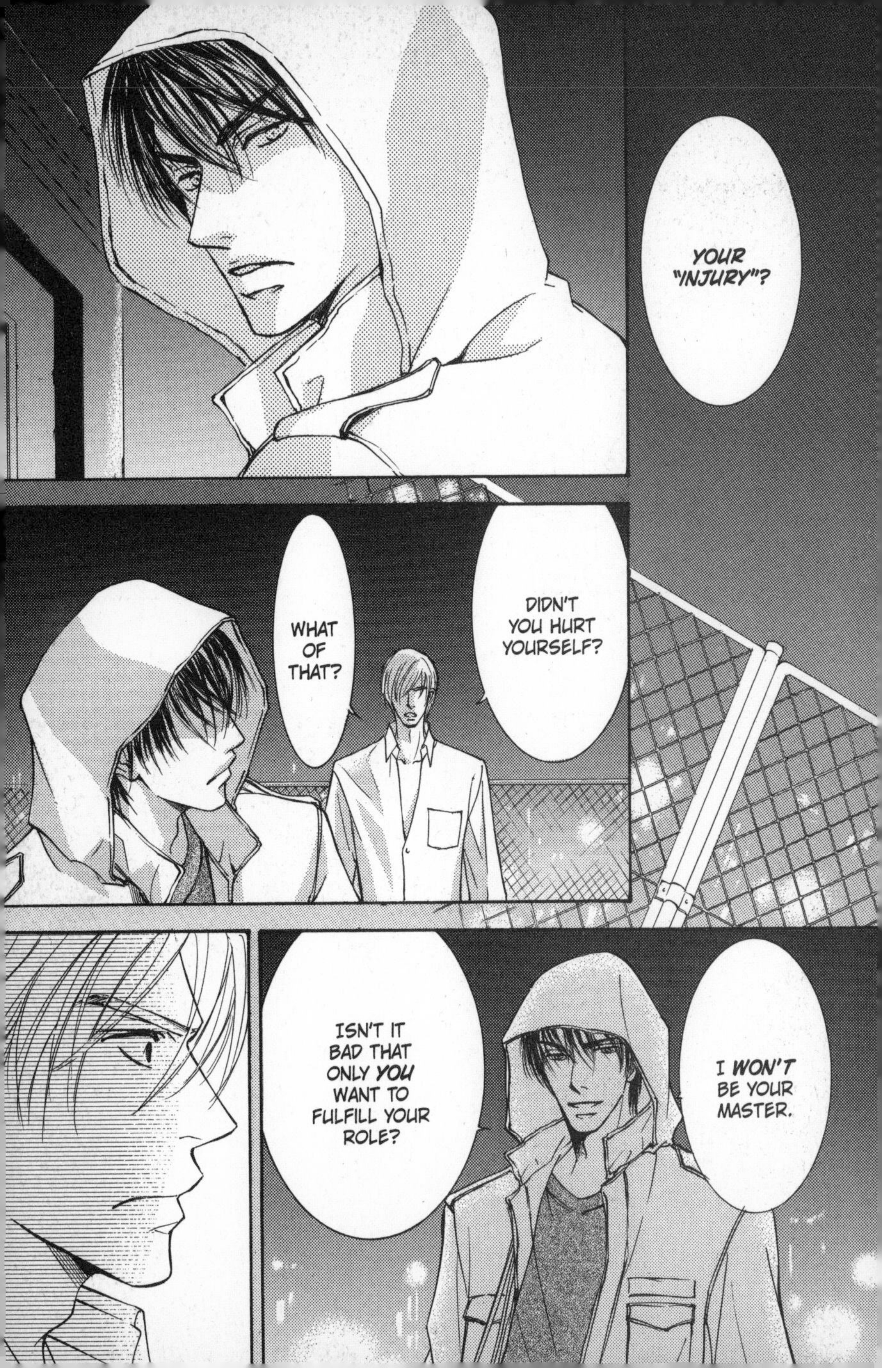
YOUR "INJURY"?
DIDN'T YOU HURT YOURSELF?
WHAT OF THAT?
I *WON'T* BE YOUR MASTER.
ISN'T IT BAD THAT ONLY *YOU* WANT TO FULFILL YOUR ROLE?

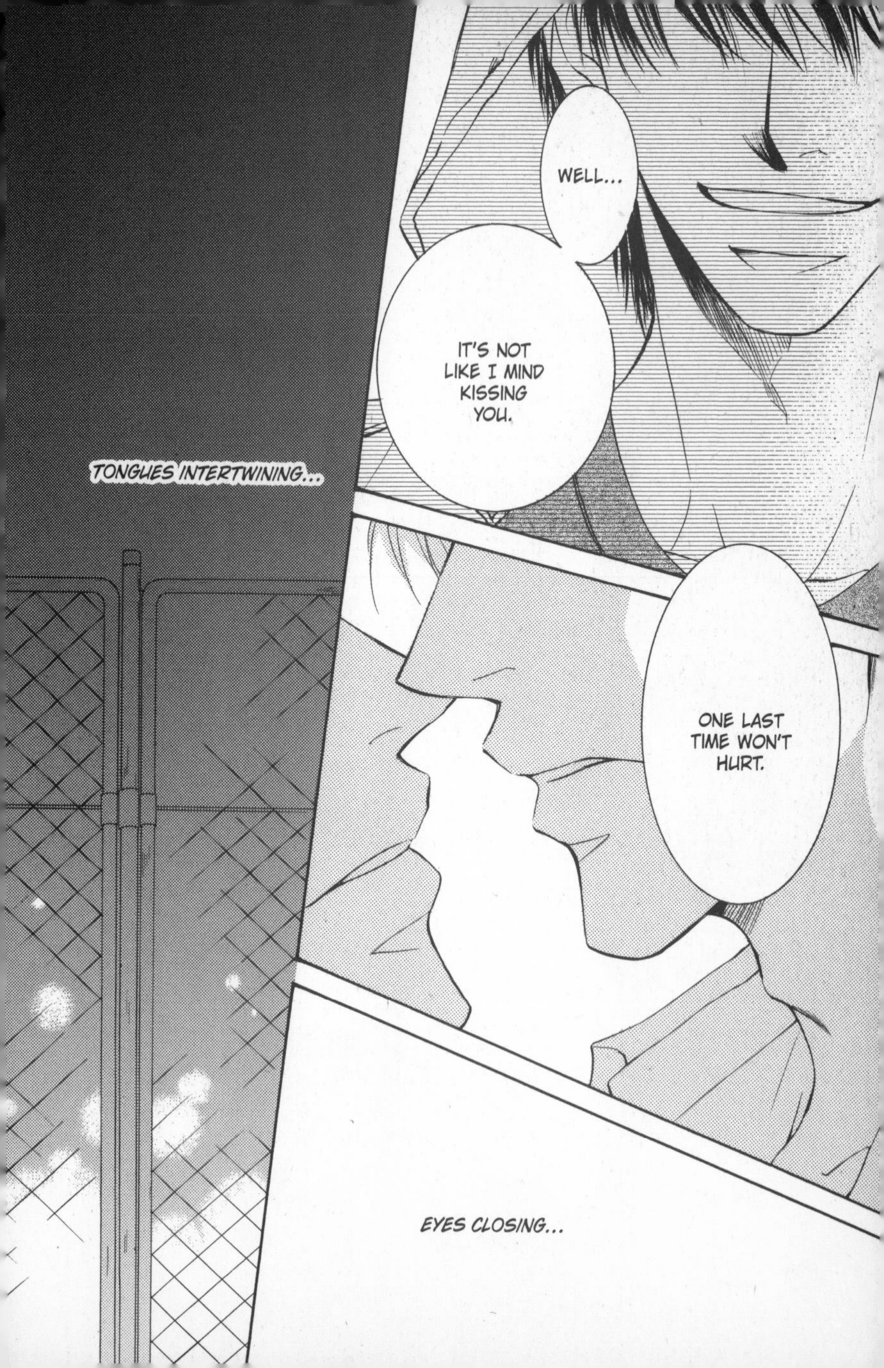
WELL...
IT'S NOT LIKE I MIND KISSING YOU.
ONE LAST TIME WON'T HURT.
EYES CLOSING...
TONGUES INTERTWINING...

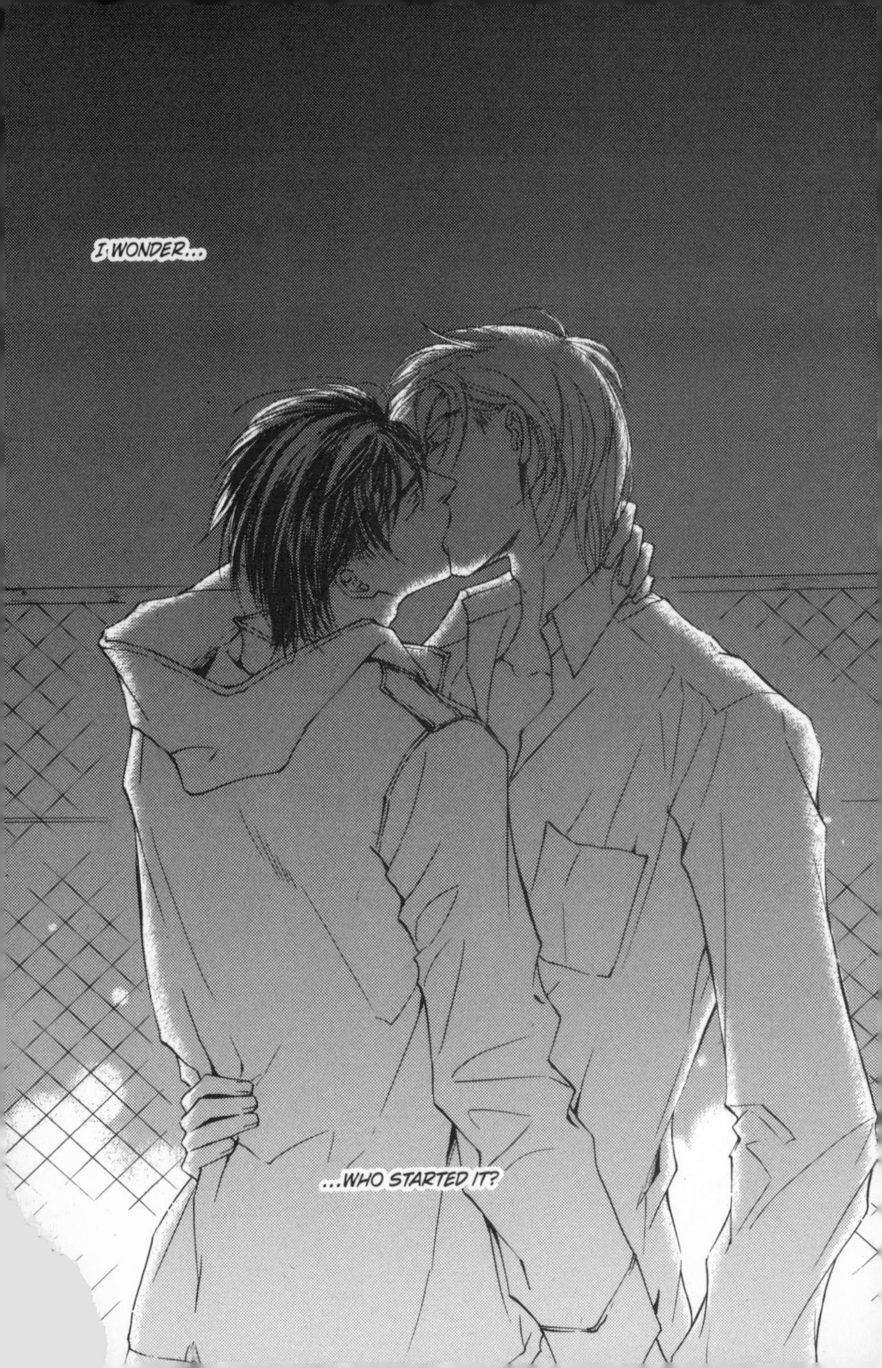
I WONDER...
...WHO STARTED IT?

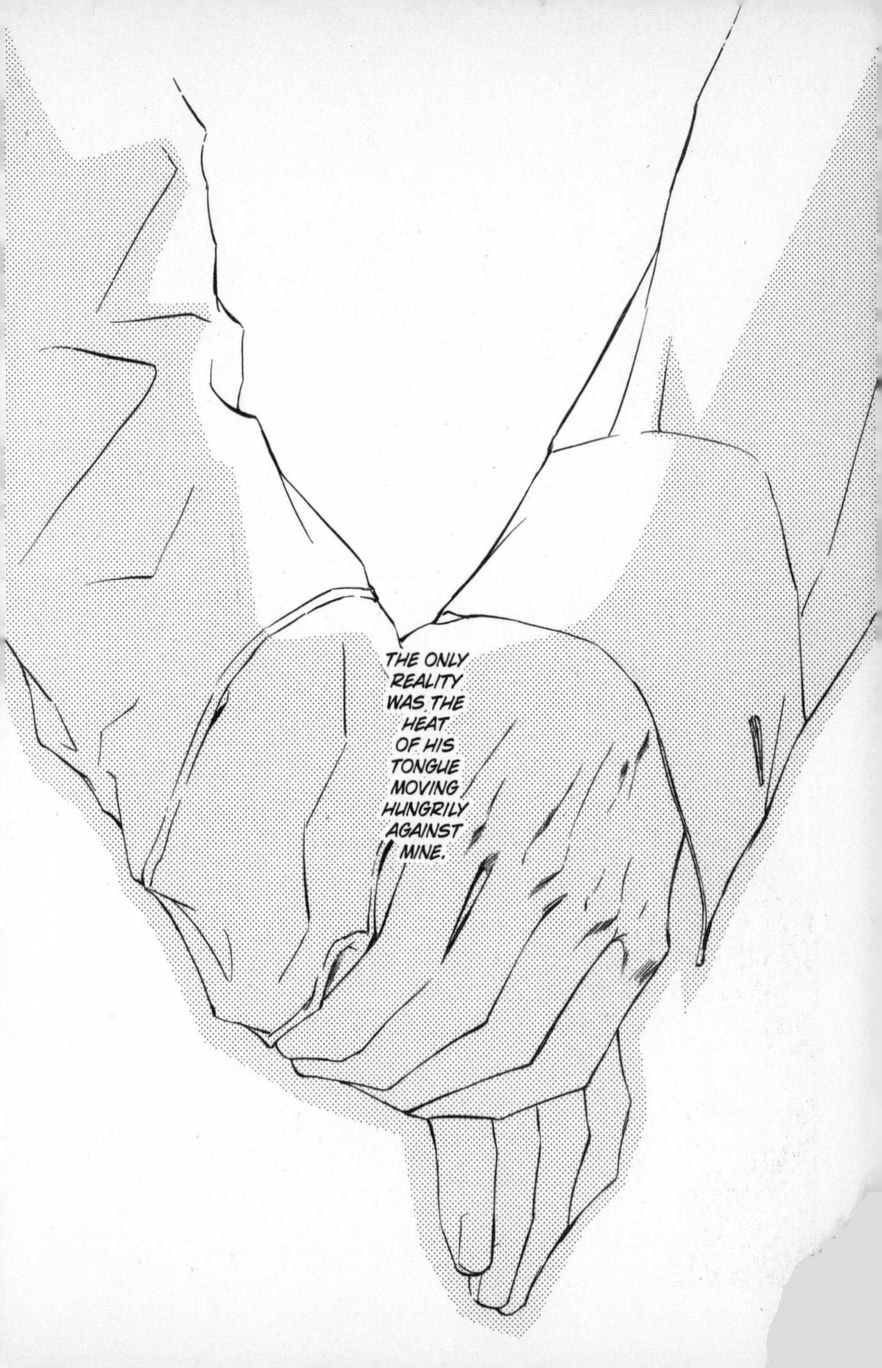
THE ONLY REALITY WAS THE HEAT OF HIS TONGUE MOVING HUNGRILY AGAINST MINE.

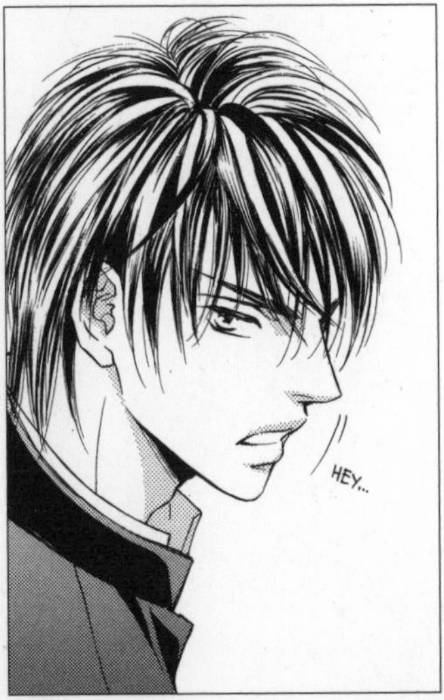
HEY...

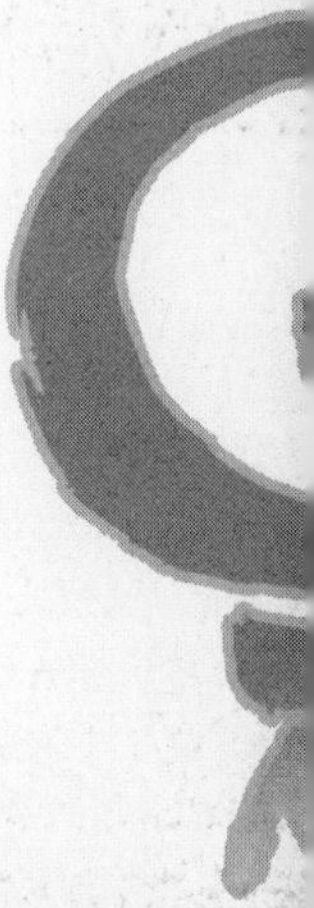

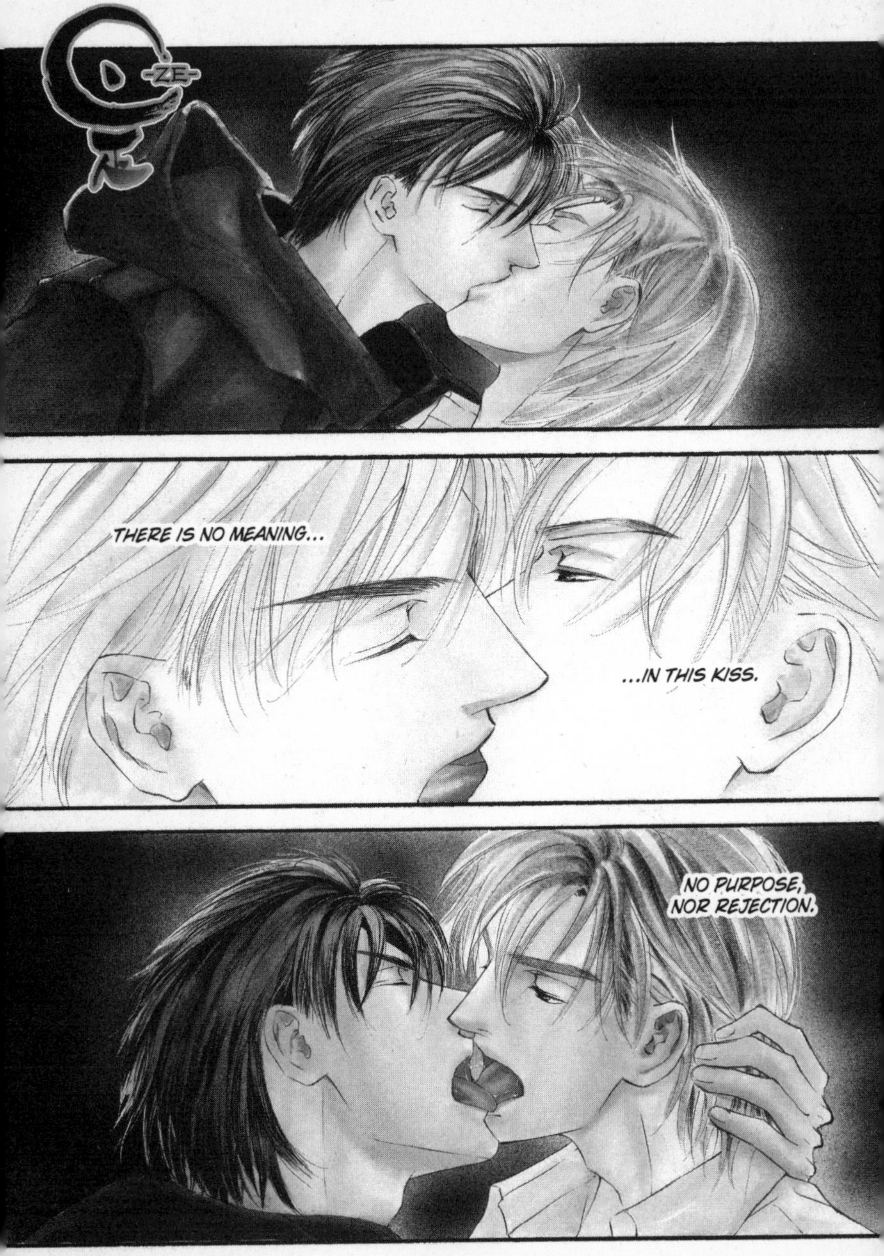
ZE
THERE IS NO MEANING...
...IN THIS KISS.
NO PURPOSE, NOR REJECTION.

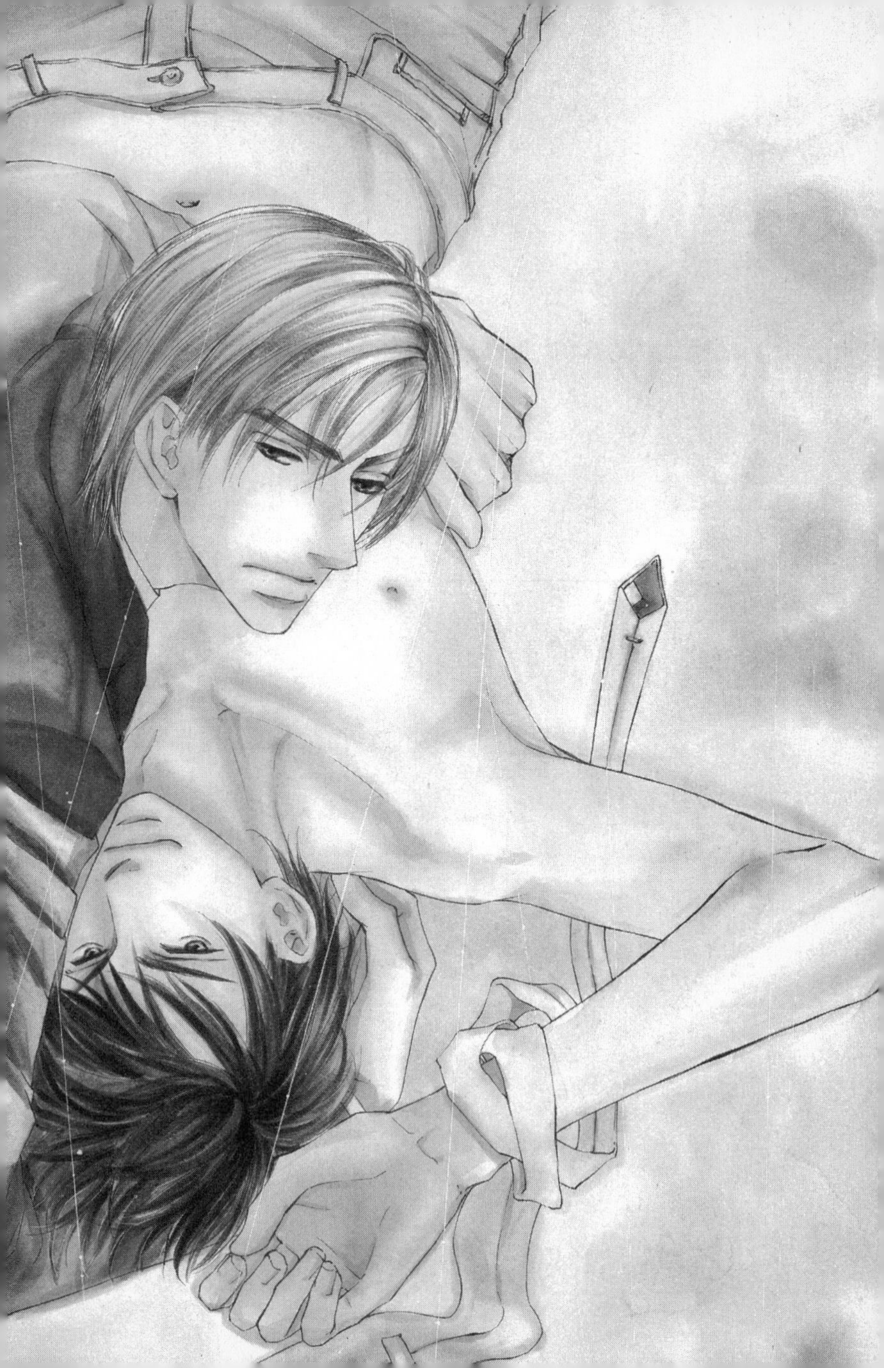

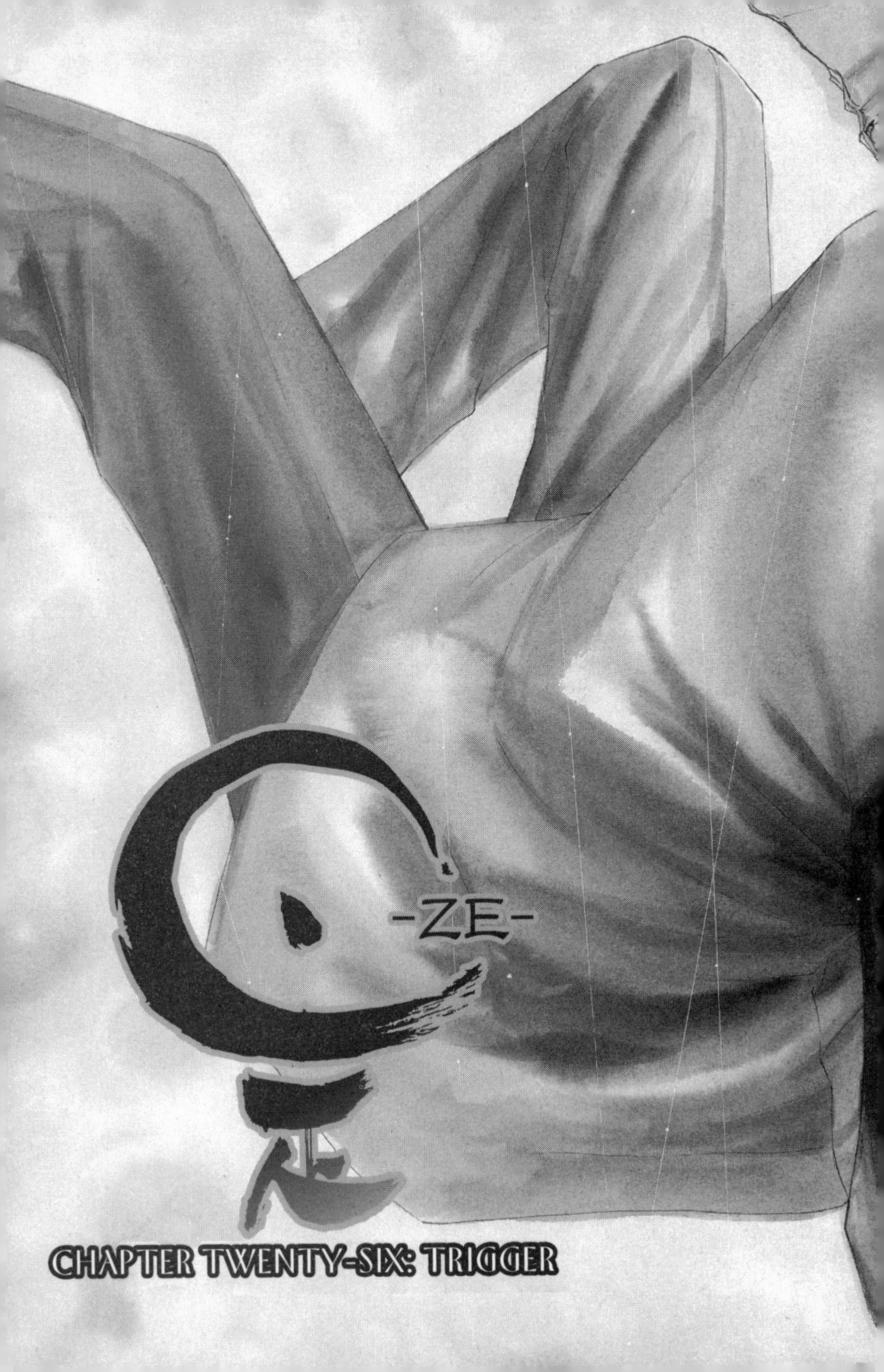

-ZE-
CHAPTER TWENTY-SIX: TRIGGER

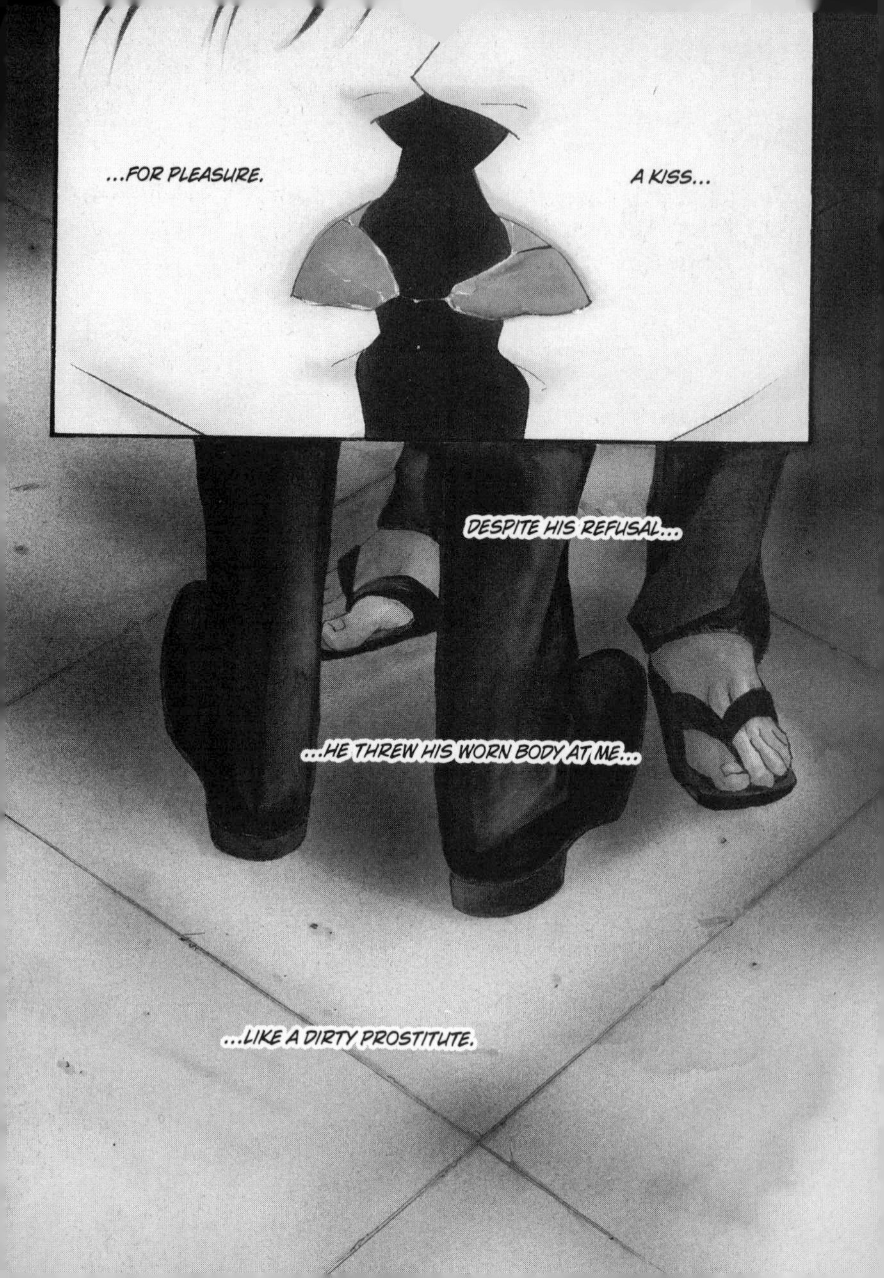
A KISS...
...FOR PLEASURE.
DESPITE HIS REFUSAL...
...HE THREW HIS WORN BODY AT ME...
...LIKE A DIRTY PROSTITUTE.

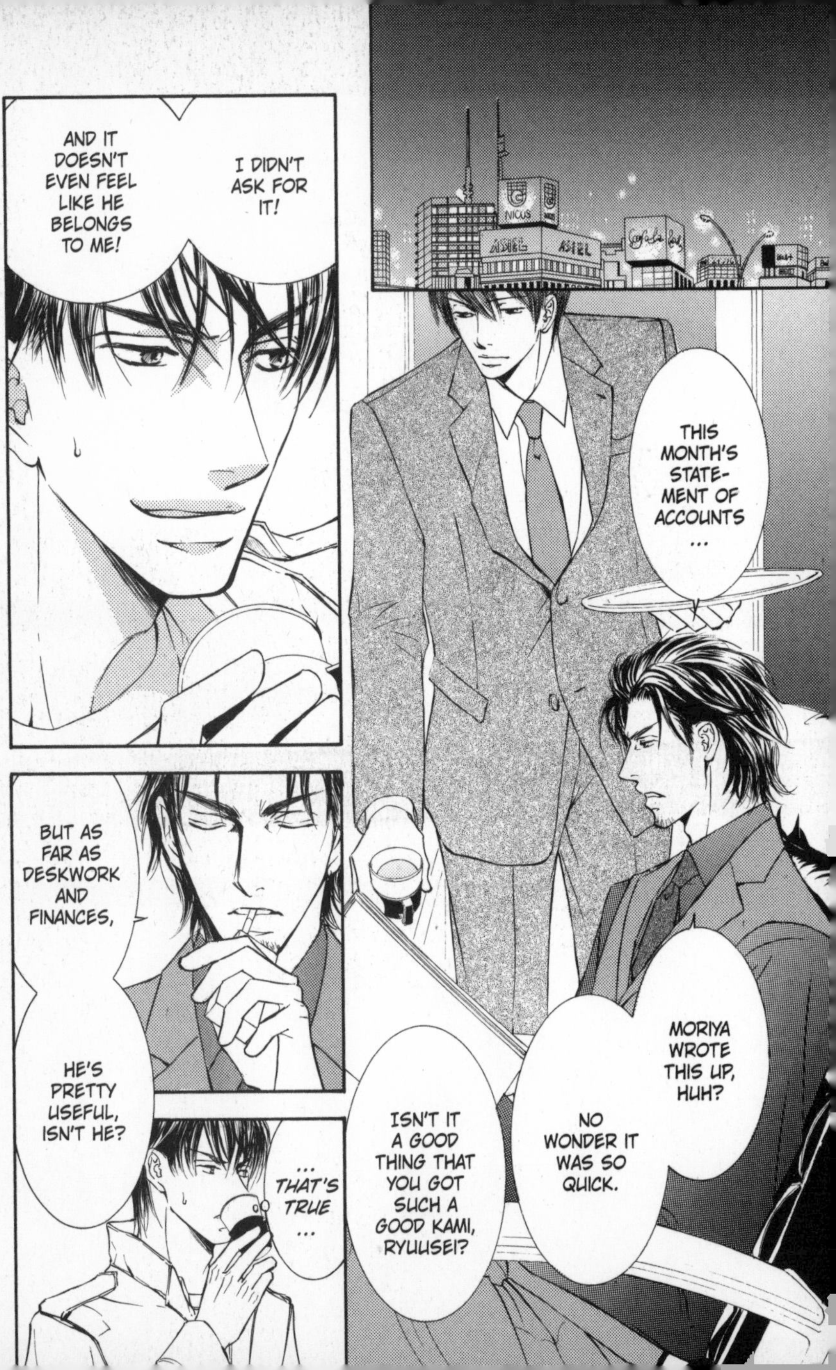

THIS MONTH'S STATE- MENT OF ACCOUNTS ...
MORIYA WROTE THIS UP, HUH?
NO WONDER IT WAS SO QUICK.
ISN'T IT A GOOD THING THAT YOU GOT SUCH A GOOD KAMI, RYUUSEI?
I DIDN'T ASK FOR IT!
AND IT DOESN'T EVEN FEEL LIKE HE BELONGS TO ME!
BUT AS FAR AS DESKWORK AND FINANCES,
HE'S PRETTY USEFUL, ISN'T HE?
... THAT'S TRUE ...

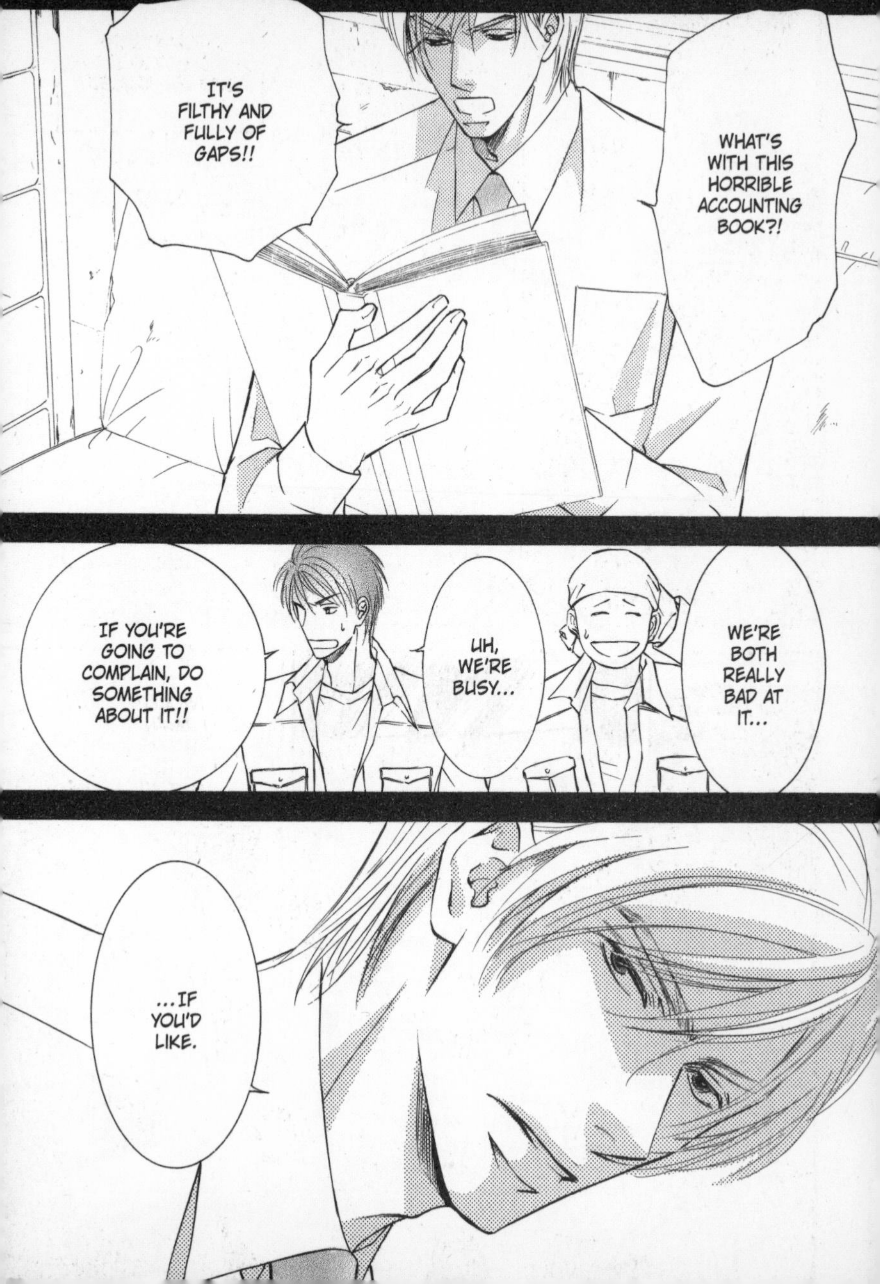
WHAT'S WITH THIS HORRIBLE ACCOUNTING BOOK?!
IT'S FILTHY AND FULLY OF GAPS!!
WE'RE BOTH REALLY BAD AT IT...
UH, WE'RE BUSY...
IF YOU'RE GOING TO COMPLAIN, DO SOMETHING ABOUT IT!!
...IF YOU'D LIKE.

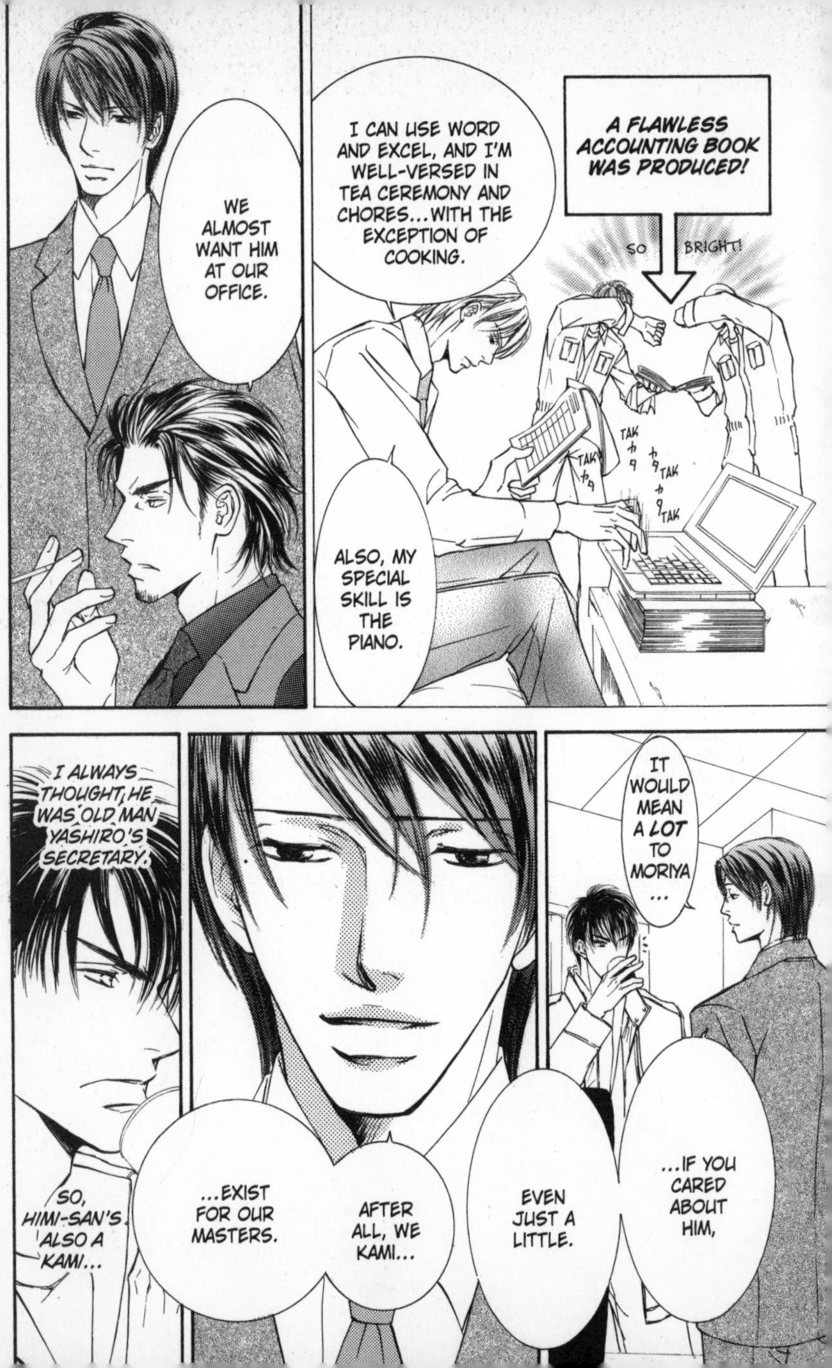
I CAN USE WORD AND EXCEL, AND I'M WELL-VERSED IN TEA CEREMONY AND CHORES...WITH THE EXCEPTION OF COOKING.
A FLAWLESS ACCOUNTING BOOK WAS PRODUCED!
SO BRIGHT!
TAK TAK TAK TAK
ALSO, MY SPECIAL SKILL IS THE PIANO.
WE ALMOST WANT HIM AT OUR OFFICE.
IT WOULD MEAN A LOT TO MORIYA...
...IF YOU CARED ABOUT HIM,
EVEN JUST A LITTLE.
AFTER ALL, WE KAMI...
...EXIST FOR OUR MASTERS.
I ALWAYS THOUGHT HE WAS OLD MAN YASHIRO'S SECRETARY.
SO, HIMI-SAN'S ALSO A KAMI...

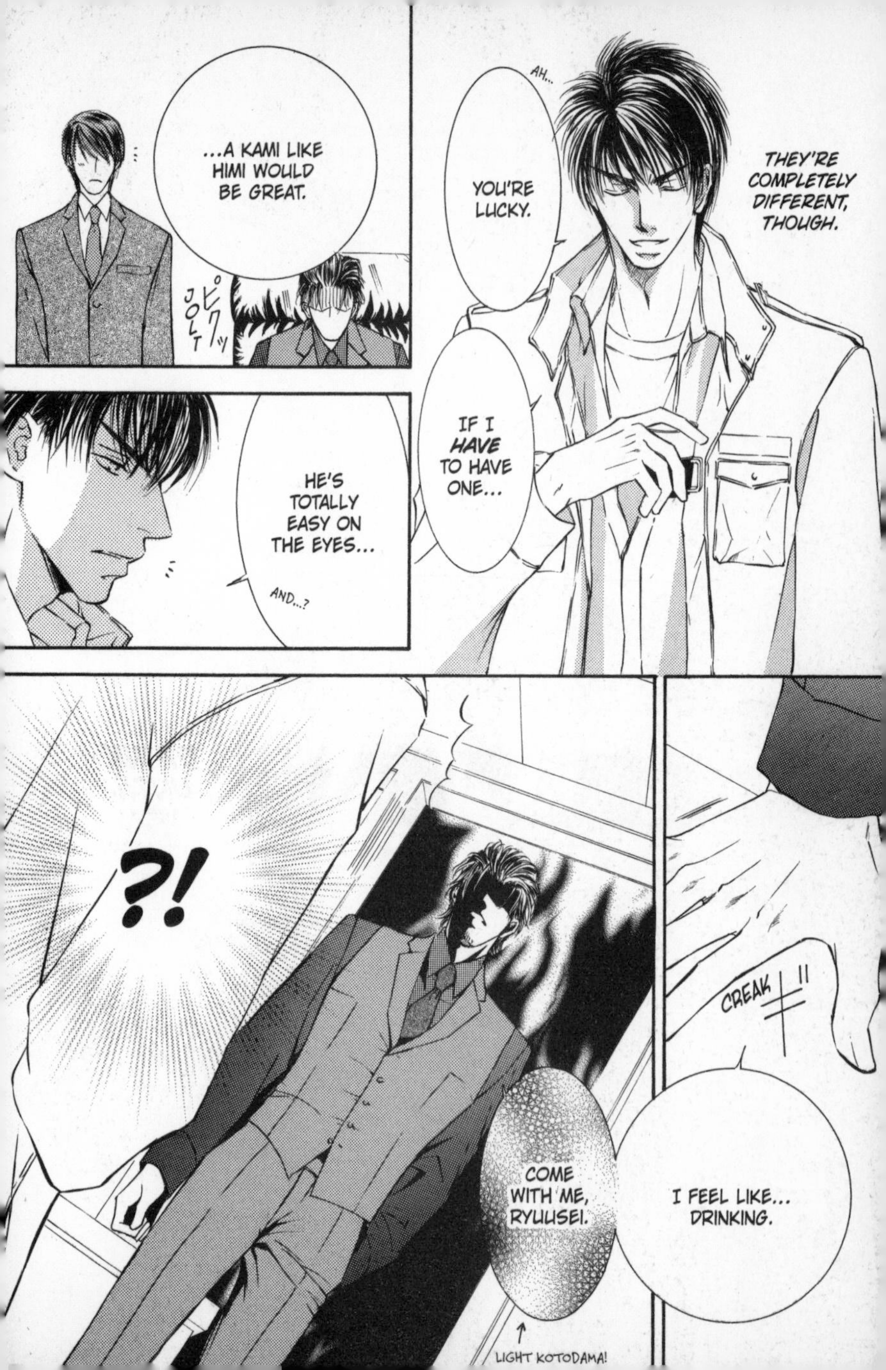
AH...
YOU'RE LUCKY.
THEY'RE COMPLETELY DIFFERENT, THOUGH.
IF I *HAVE* TO HAVE ONE...
...A KAMI LIKE HIMI WOULD BE GREAT.
JOLT
HE'S TOTALLY EASY ON THE EYES...
AND...?
CREAK
I FEEL LIKE... DRINKING.
COME WITH ME, RYUUSEI.
LIGHT KOTODAMA!
?!

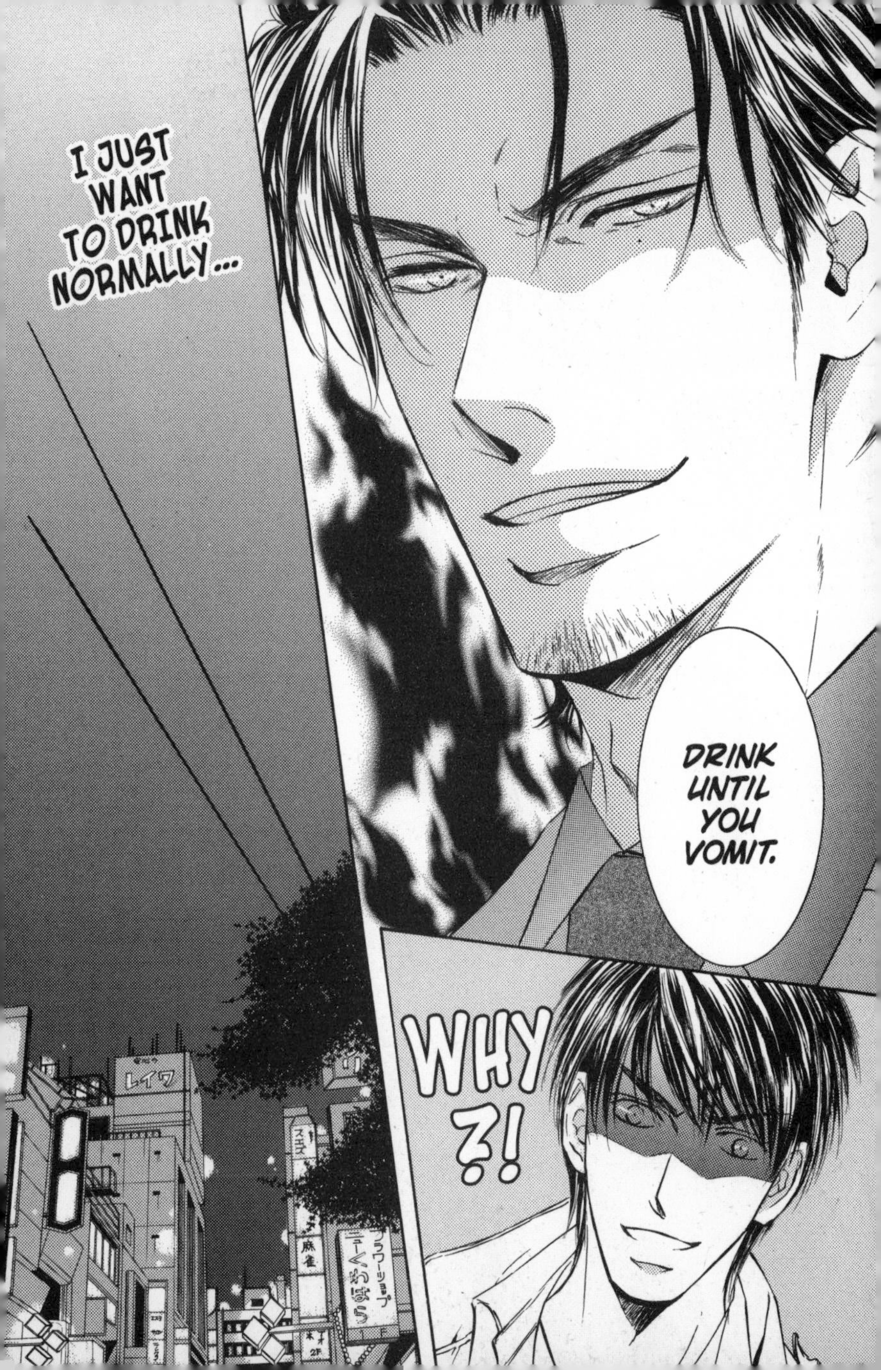
DRINK UNTIL YOU VOMIT.
WHY?!
I JUST WANT TO DRINK NORMALLY...
レイワ

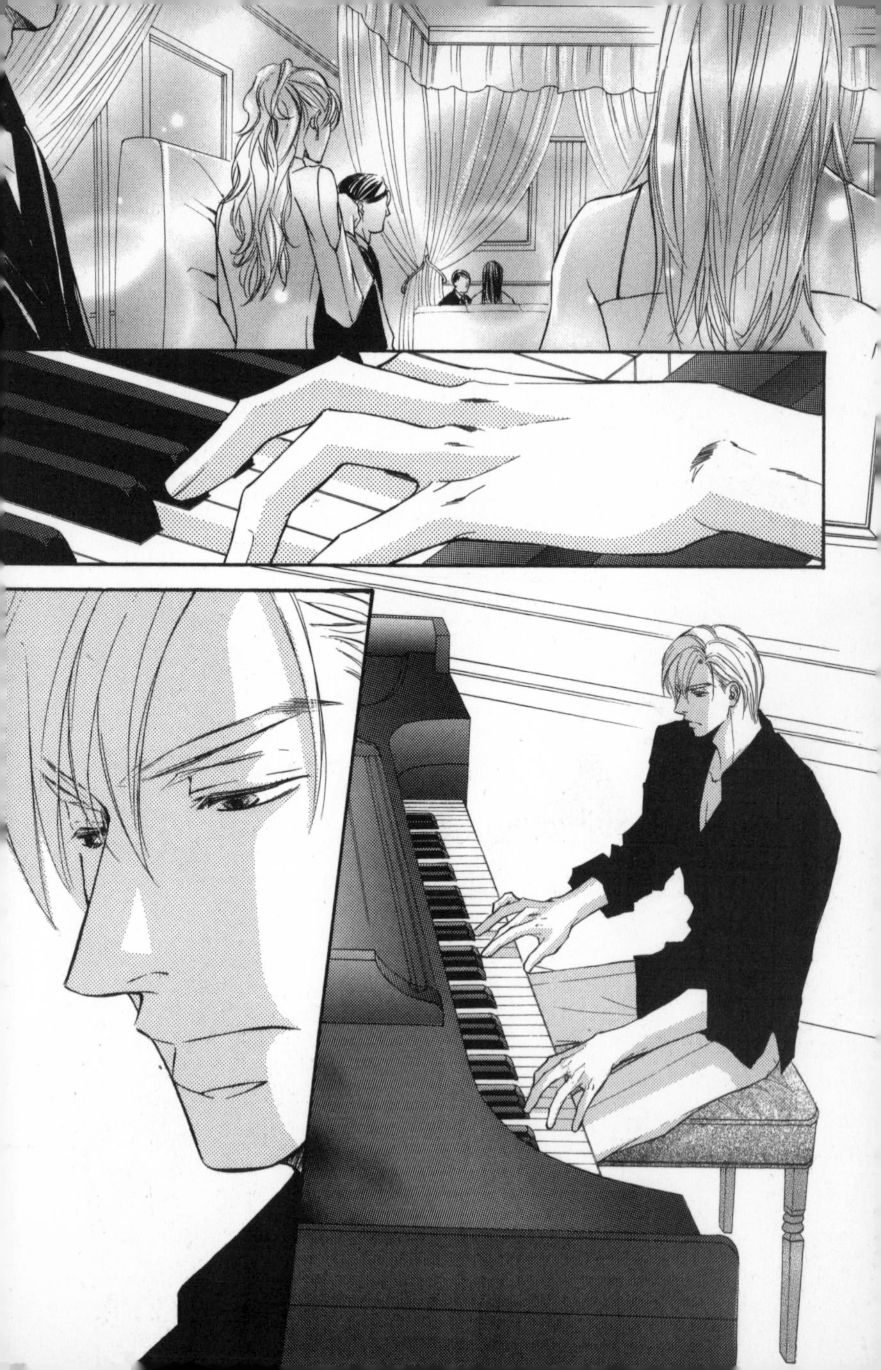

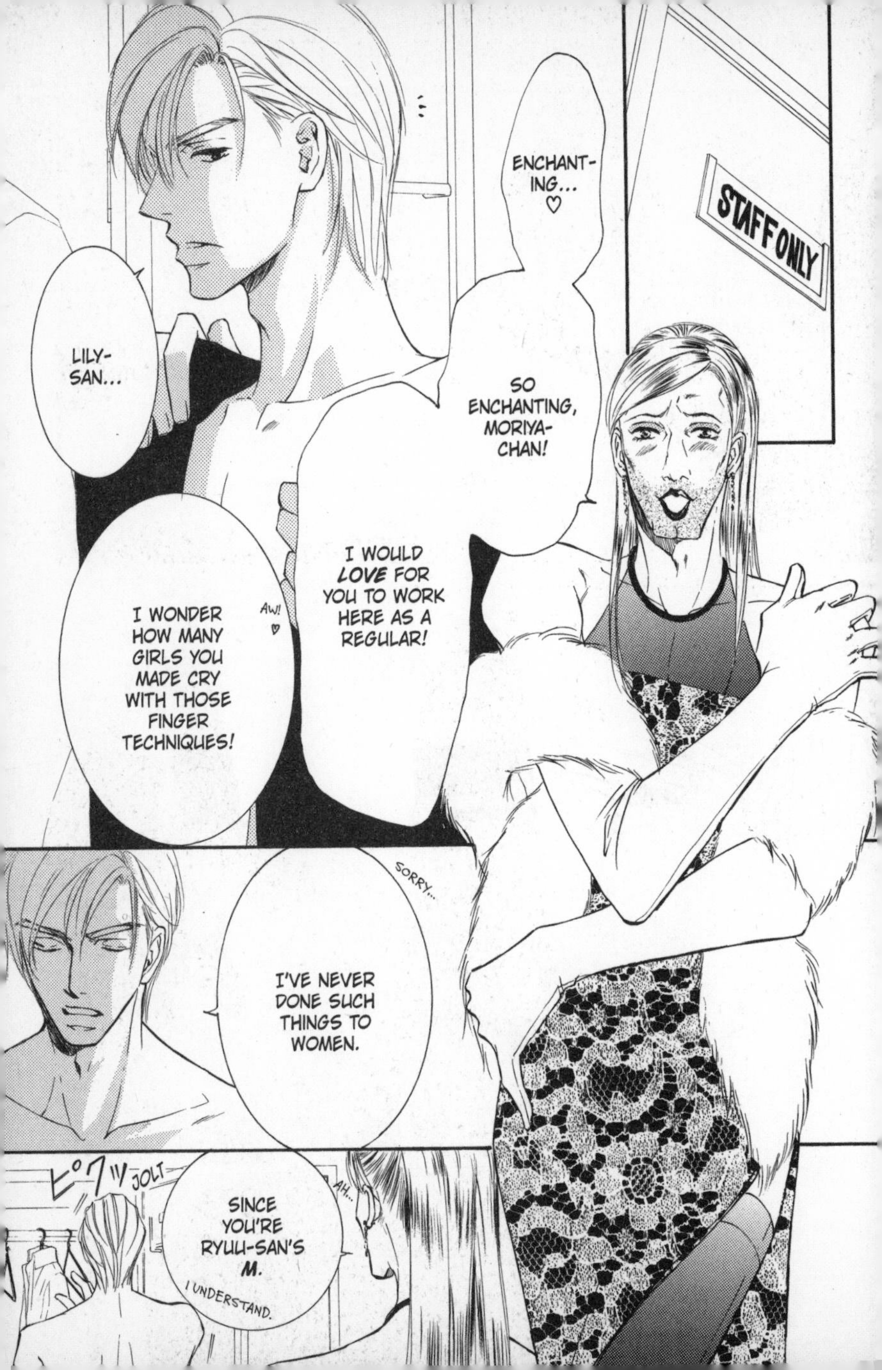
STAFF ONLY
ENCHANTING... ♡
SO ENCHANTING, MORIYA-CHAN!
I WOULD *LOVE* FOR YOU TO WORK HERE AS A REGULAR!
...
LILY-SAN...
AW! ♡
I WONDER HOW MANY GIRLS YOU MADE CRY WITH THOSE FINGER TECHNIQUES!
SORRY...
I'VE NEVER DONE SUCH THINGS TO WOMEN.
ビクッ JOLT
AH...
SINCE YOU'RE RYUU-SAN'S ***M***.
I UNDERSTAND.

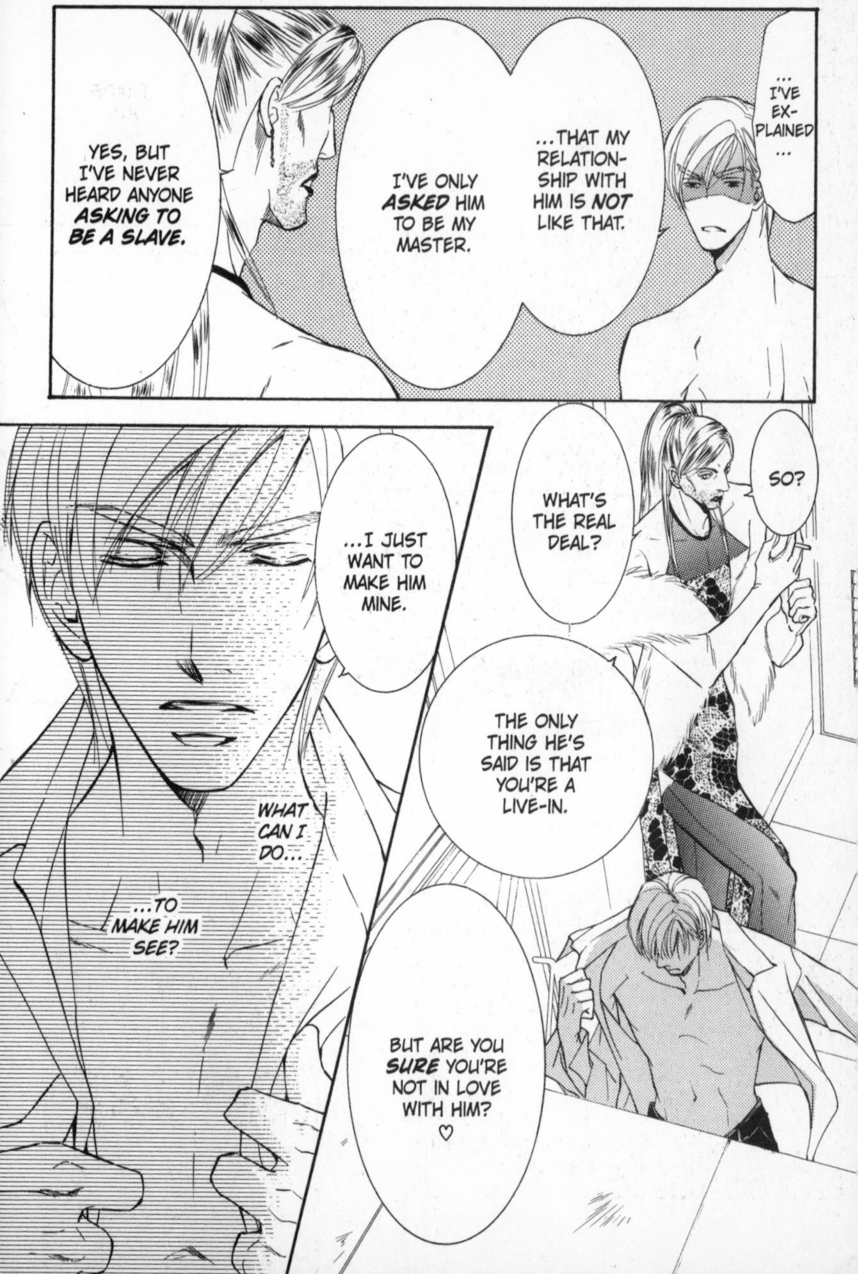
...I'VE EX-PLAINED...
...THAT MY RELATION-SHIP WITH HIM IS **NOT** LIKE THAT.
I'VE ONLY **ASKED** HIM TO BE MY MASTER.
YES, BUT I'VE NEVER HEARD ANYONE ***ASKING TO BE A SLAVE.***
SO?
WHAT'S THE REAL DEAL?
THE ONLY THING HE'S SAID IS THAT YOU'RE A LIVE-IN.
BUT ARE YOU ***SURE*** YOU'RE NOT IN LOVE WITH HIM? ♡
...I JUST WANT TO MAKE HIM MINE.
WHAT CAN I DO...
...TO MAKE HIM SEE?

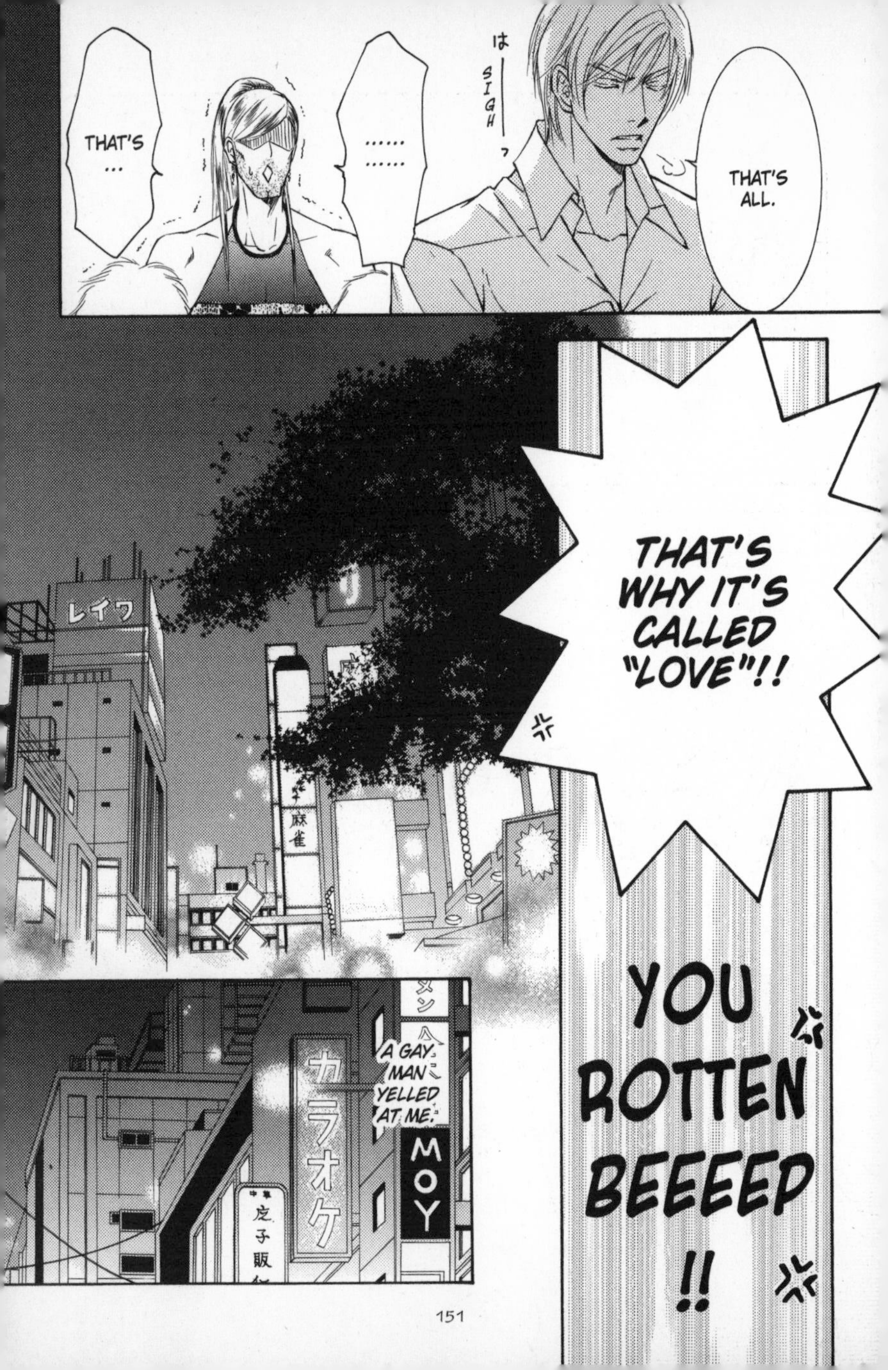

THAT'S ALL.
は―っ SIGH
......
......
THAT'S ...
THAT'S WHY IT'S CALLED "LOVE"!!
YOU ROTTEN BEEEEP!!
レイワ
麻雀
A GAY MAN YELLED AT ME.
カラオケ
MOY

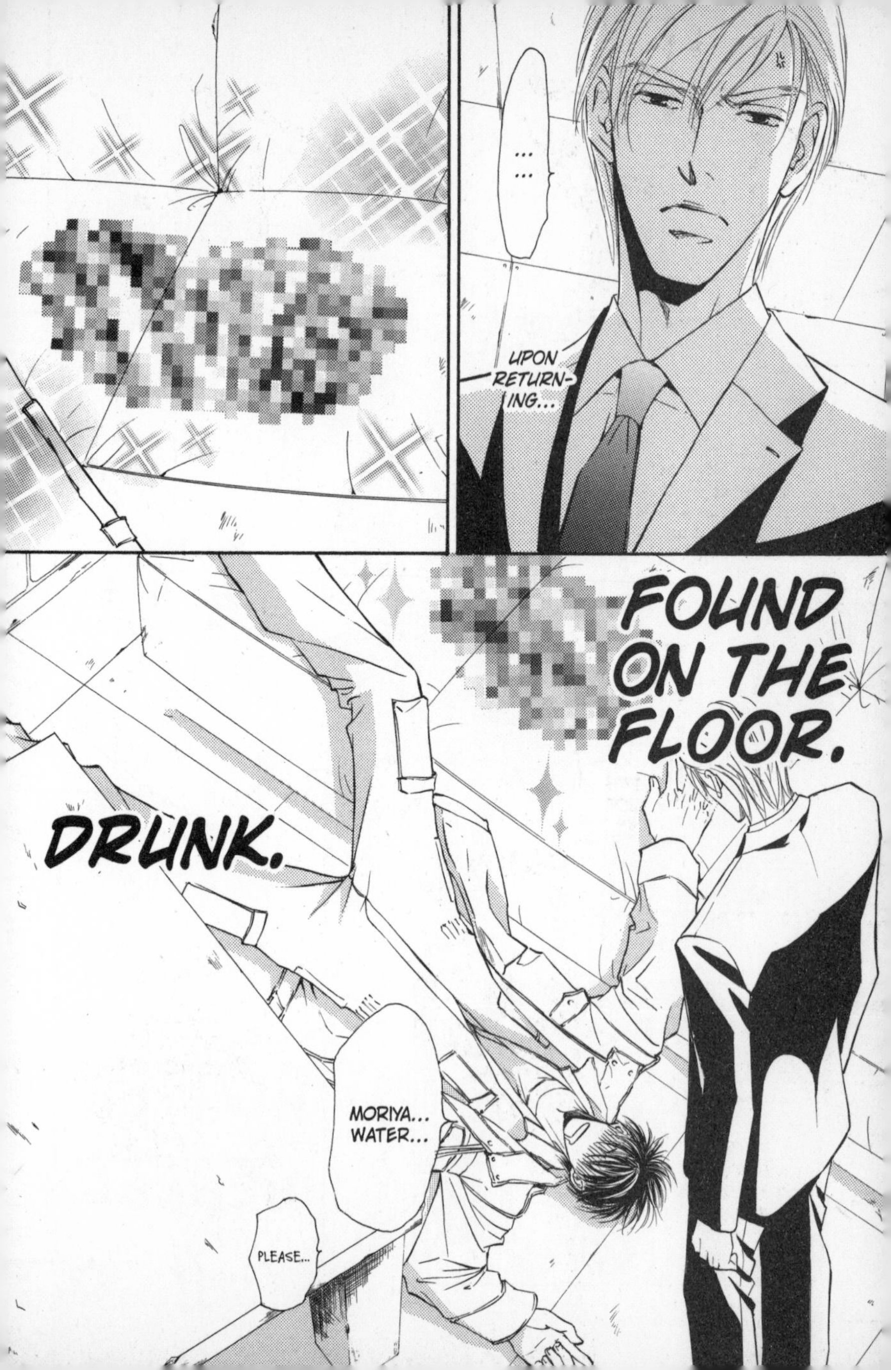
……
UPON RETURNING...
FOUND ON THE FLOOR.
DRUNK.
MORIYA... WATER...
PLEASE...

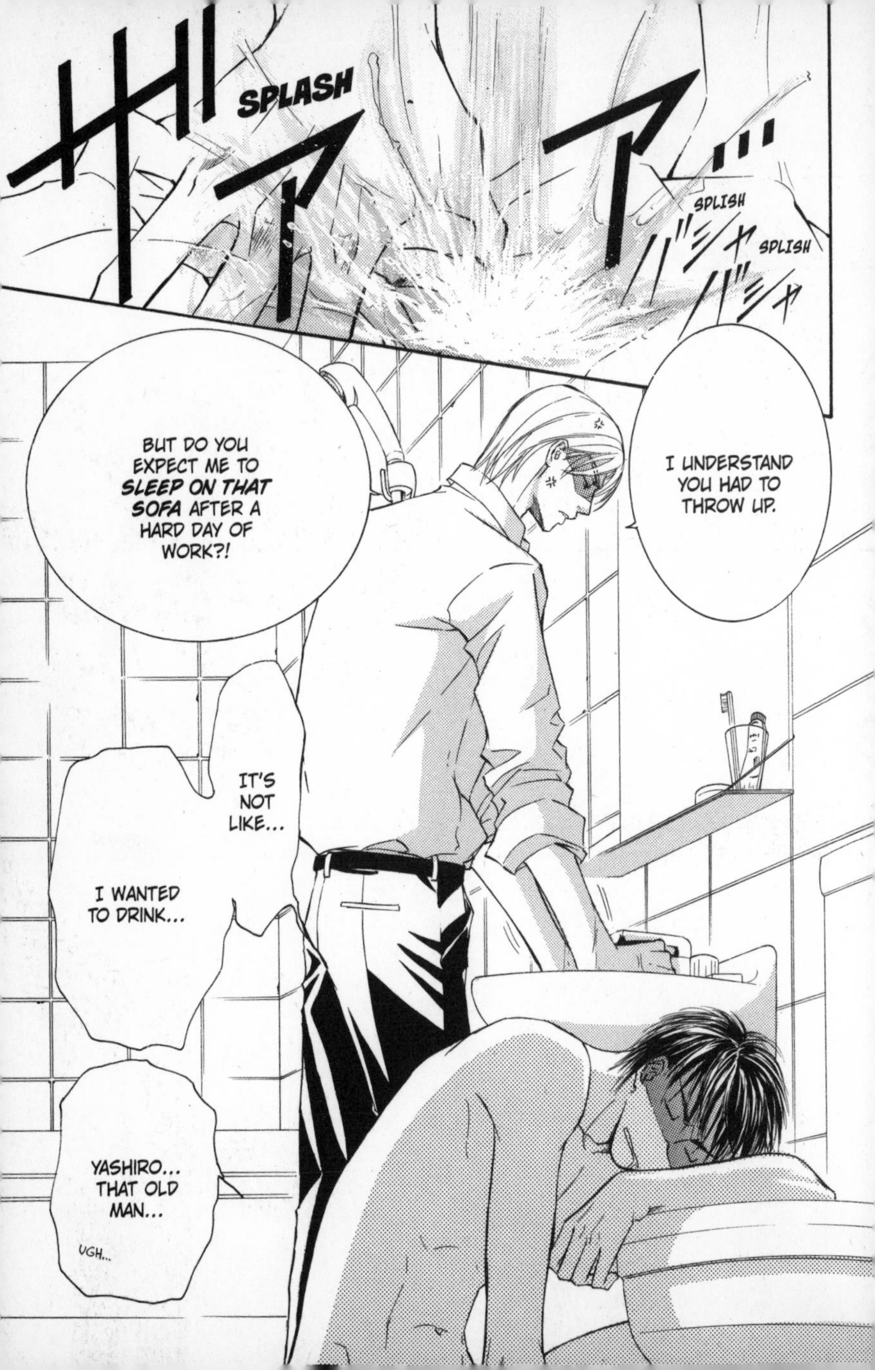
ザアア…
SPLASH
バシャ
SPLISH
バシャ
SPLISH
I UNDERSTAND YOU HAD TO THROW UP.
BUT DO YOU EXPECT ME TO SLEEP ON THAT SOFA AFTER A HARD DAY OF WORK?!
IT'S NOT LIKE...
I WANTED TO DRINK...
YASHIRO... THAT OLD MAN...
UGH...

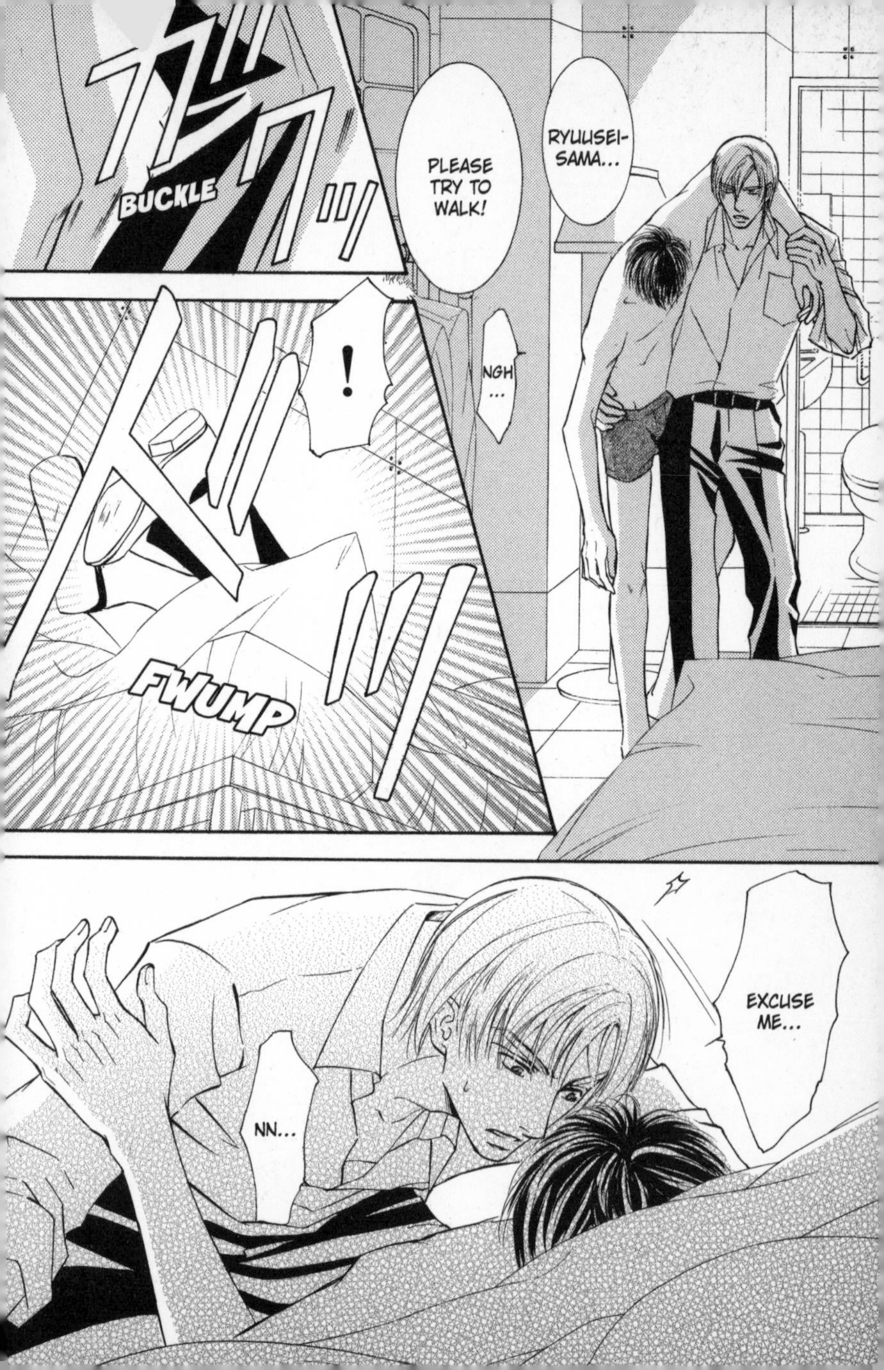
RYUUSEI-SAMA...
PLEASE TRY TO WALK!
NGH...
BUCKLE
!
FWUMP
EXCUSE ME...
NN...

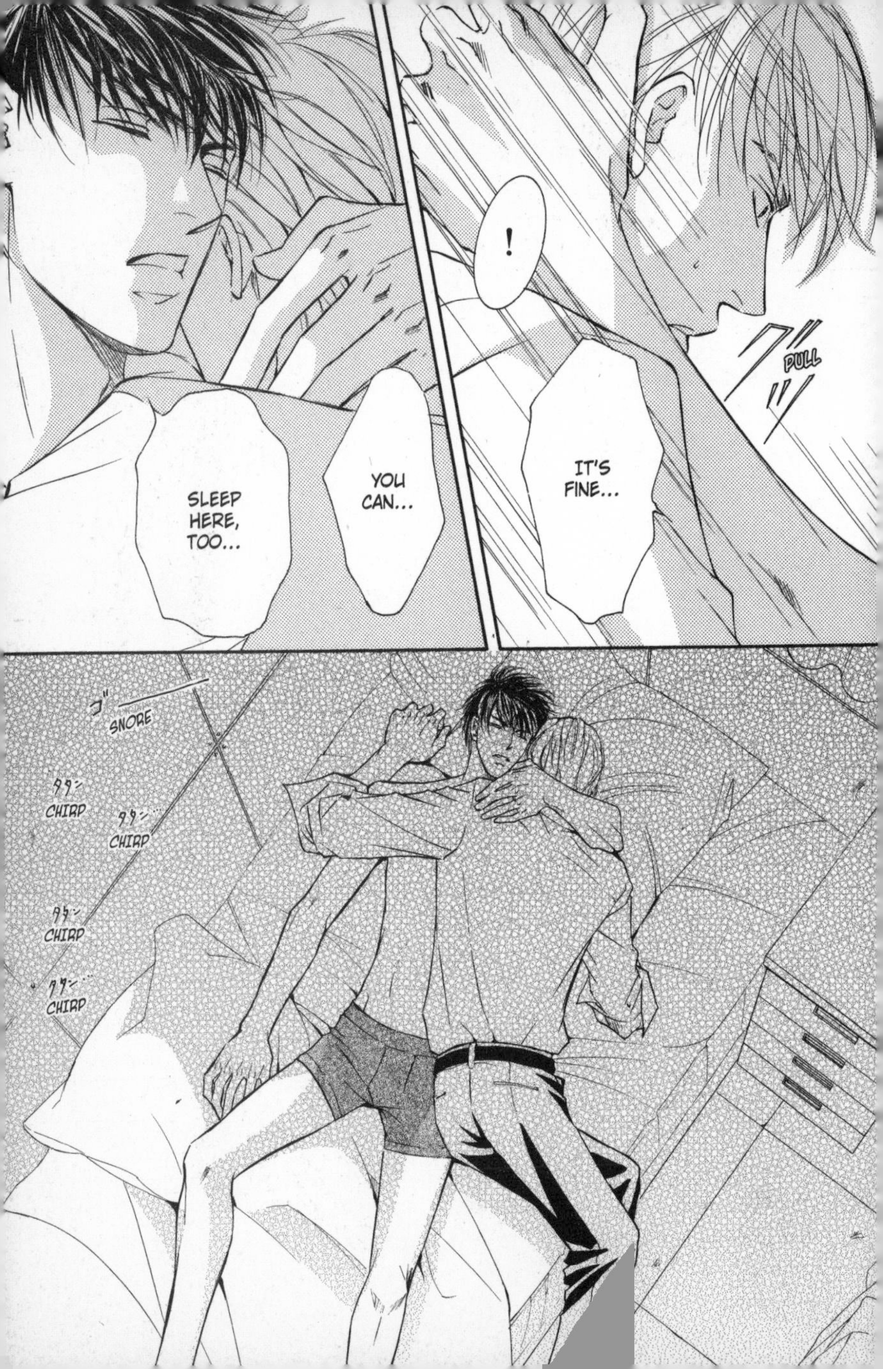
PULL
!
IT'S FINE...
YOU CAN...
SLEEP HERE, TOO...
SNORE
CHIRP
CHIRP
CHIRP
CHIRP

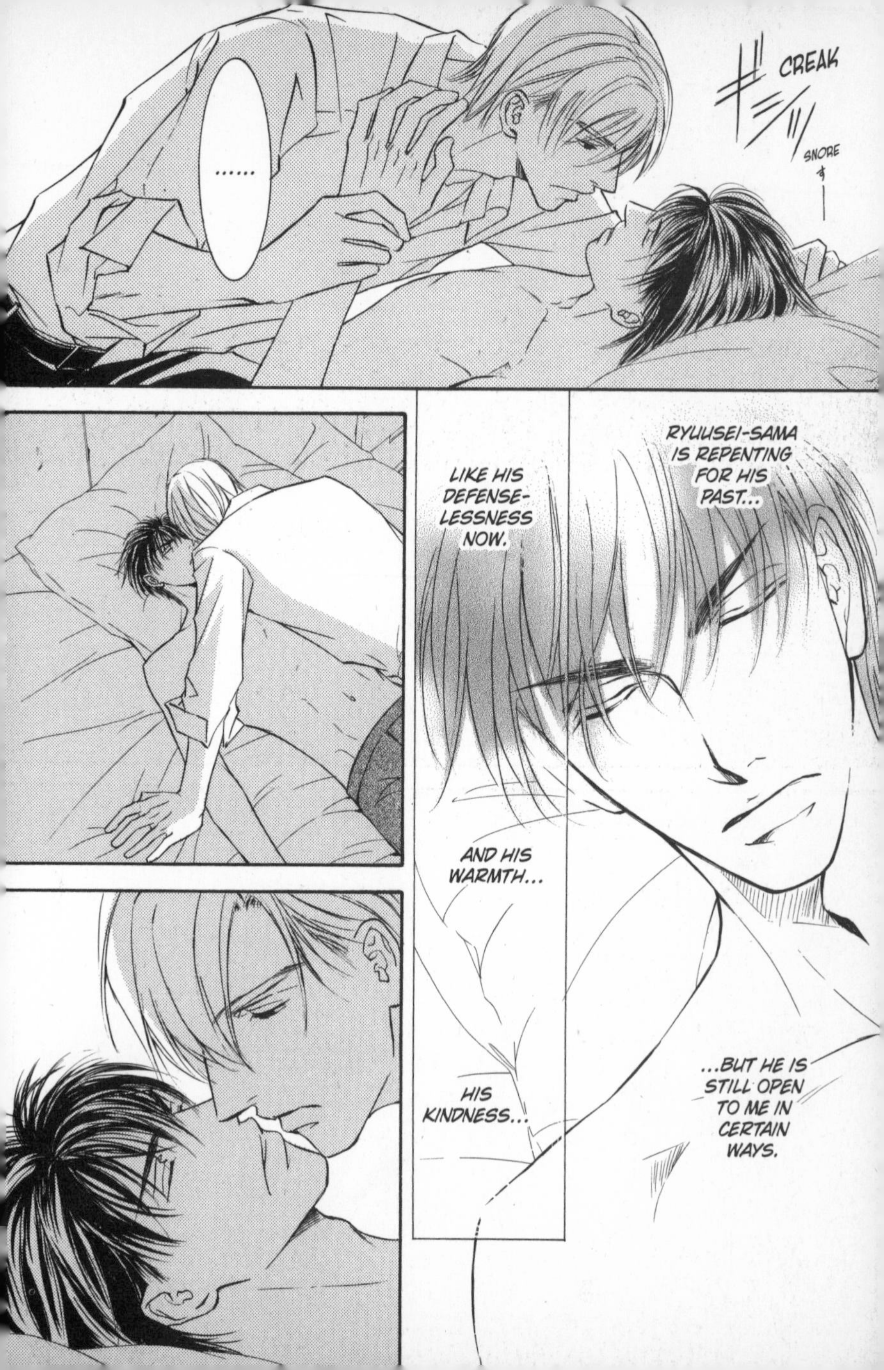
CREAK
SNORE
す
......
RYUUSEI-SAMA IS REPENTING FOR HIS PAST...
...BUT HE IS STILL OPEN TO ME IN CERTAIN WAYS.
LIKE HIS DEFENSE-LESSNESS NOW.
AND HIS WARMTH...
HIS KINDNESS...

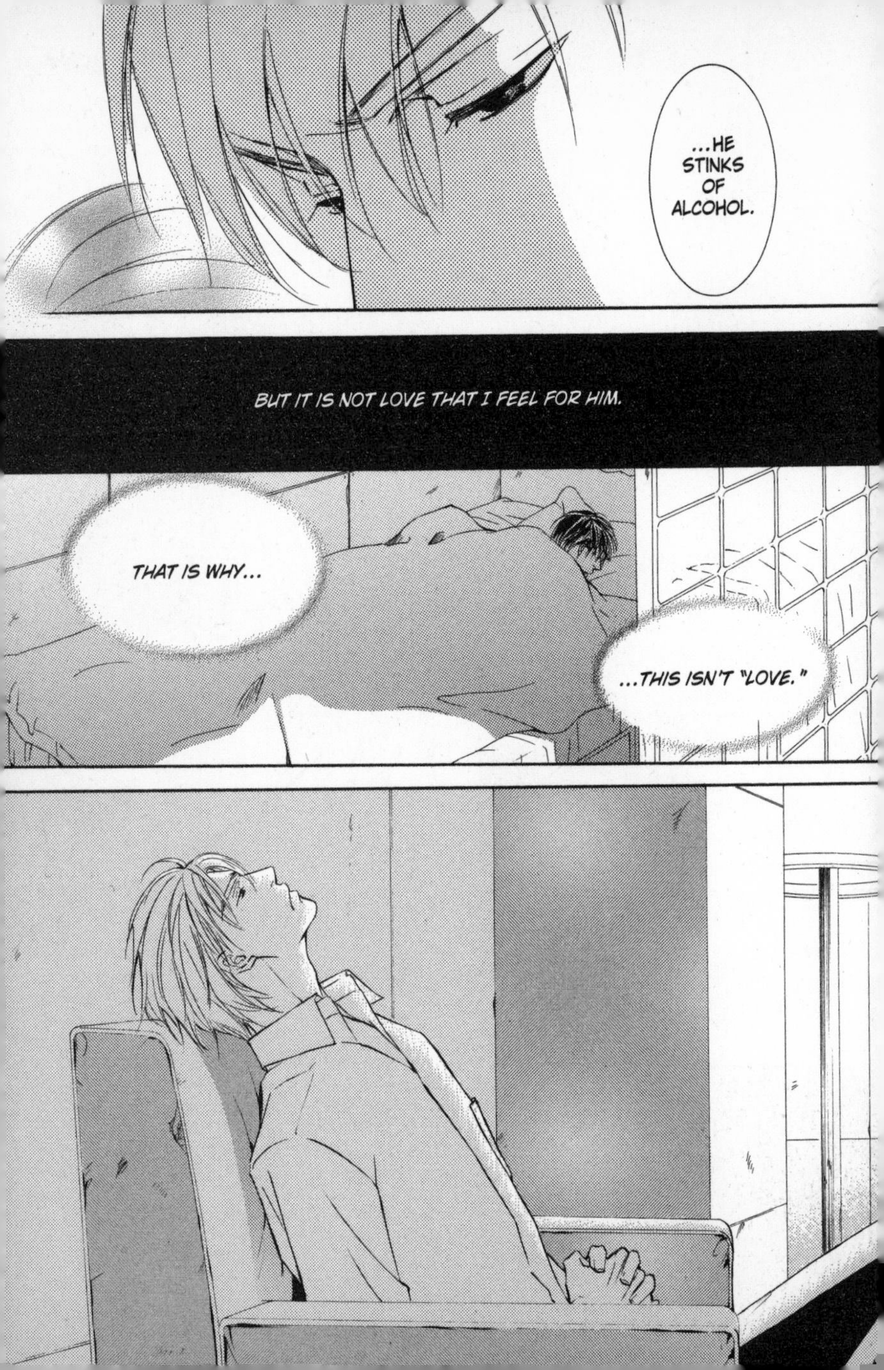
...HE STINKS OF ALCOHOL.
BUT IT IS NOT LOVE THAT I FEEL FOR HIM.
THAT IS WHY...
...THIS ISN'T "LOVE."

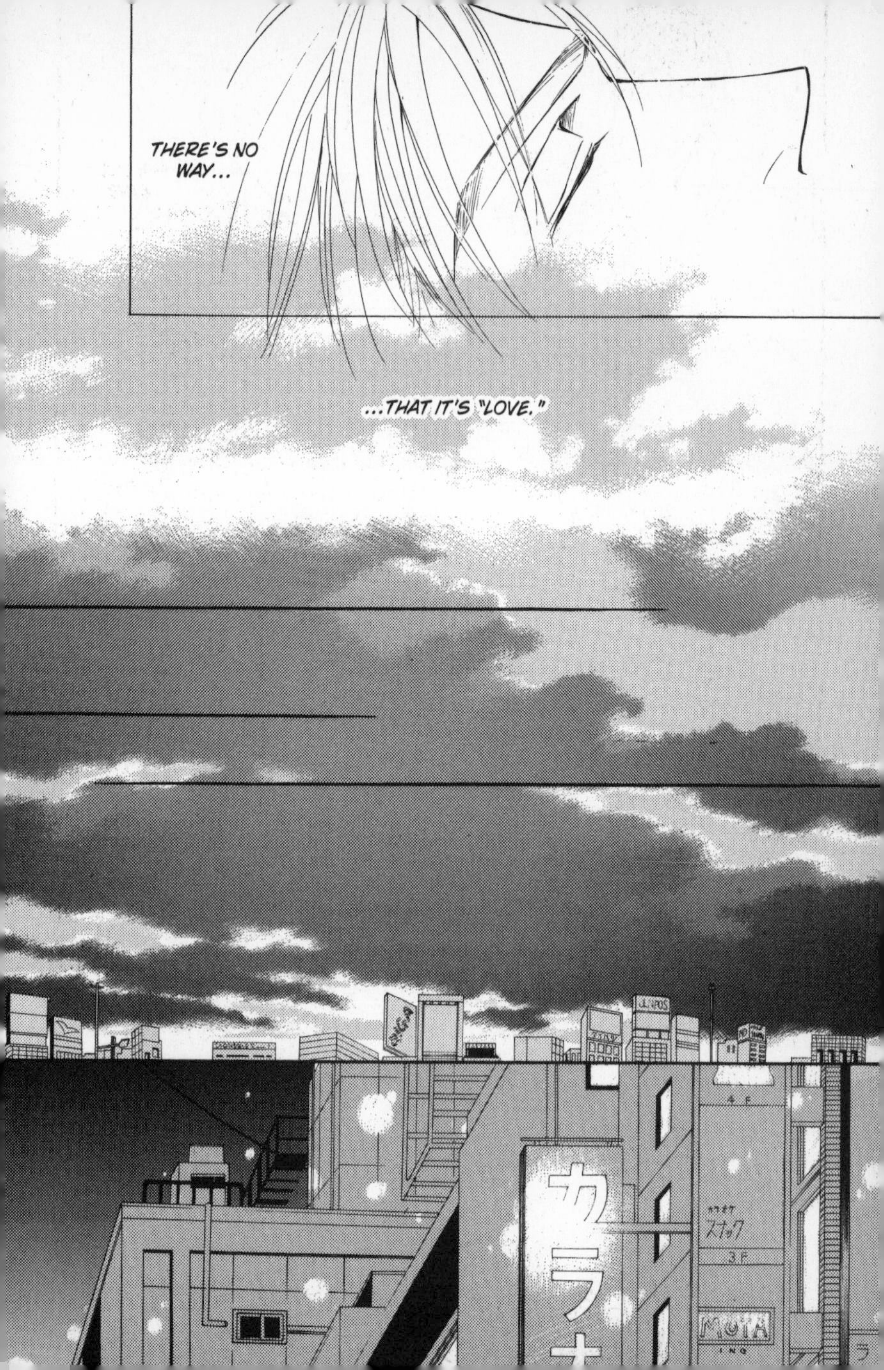
THERE'S NO WAY...
...THAT IT'S "LOVE."

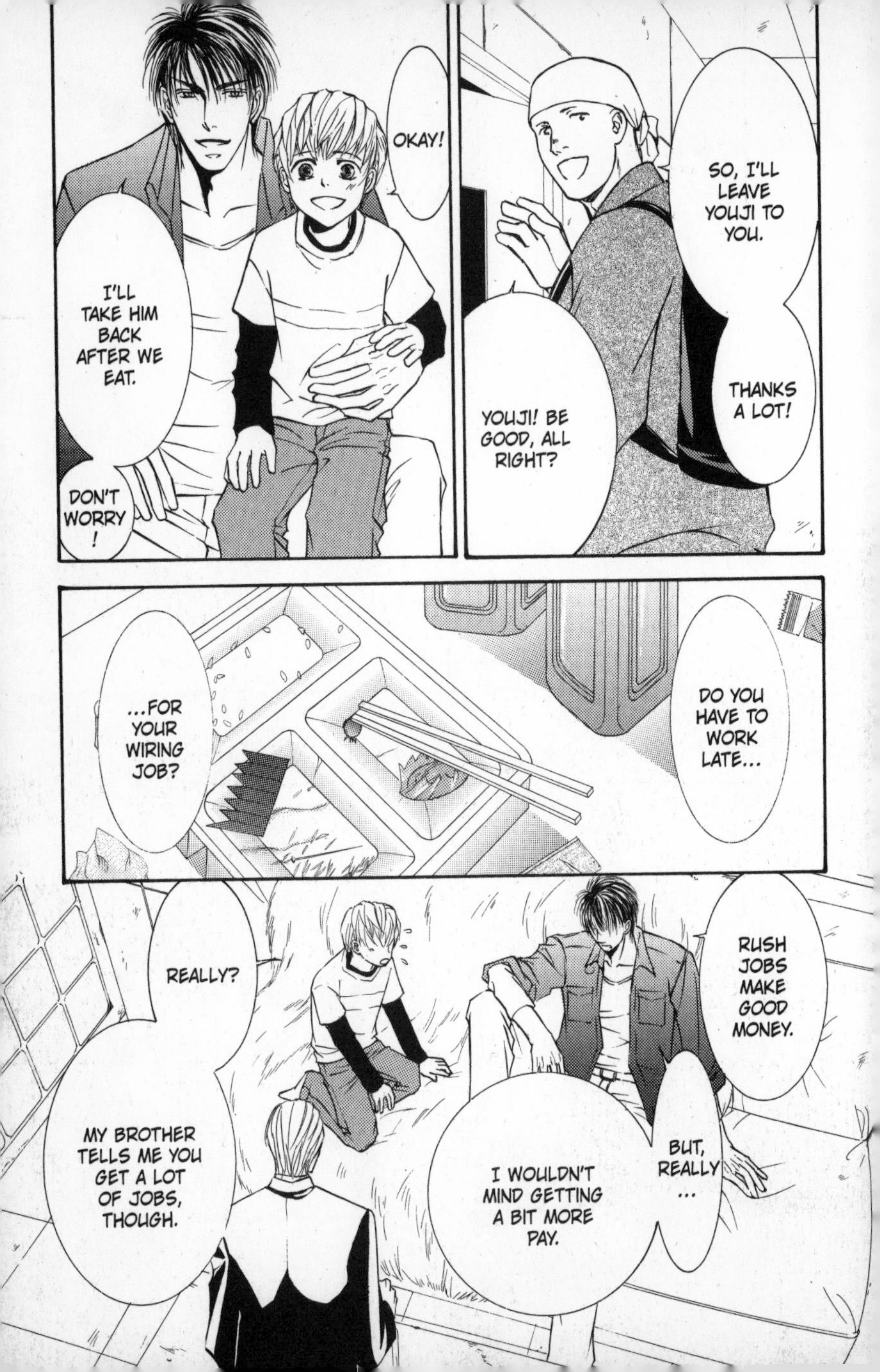
SO, I'LL LEAVE YOUJI TO YOU.
THANKS A LOT!
YOUJI! BE GOOD, ALL RIGHT?
OKAY!
I'LL TAKE HIM BACK AFTER WE EAT.
DON'T WORRY!
DO YOU HAVE TO WORK LATE...
...FOR YOUR WIRING JOB?
RUSH JOBS MAKE GOOD MONEY.
BUT, REALLY...
I WOULDN'T MIND GETTING A BIT MORE PAY.
REALLY?
MY BROTHER TELLS ME YOU GET A LOT OF JOBS, THOUGH.

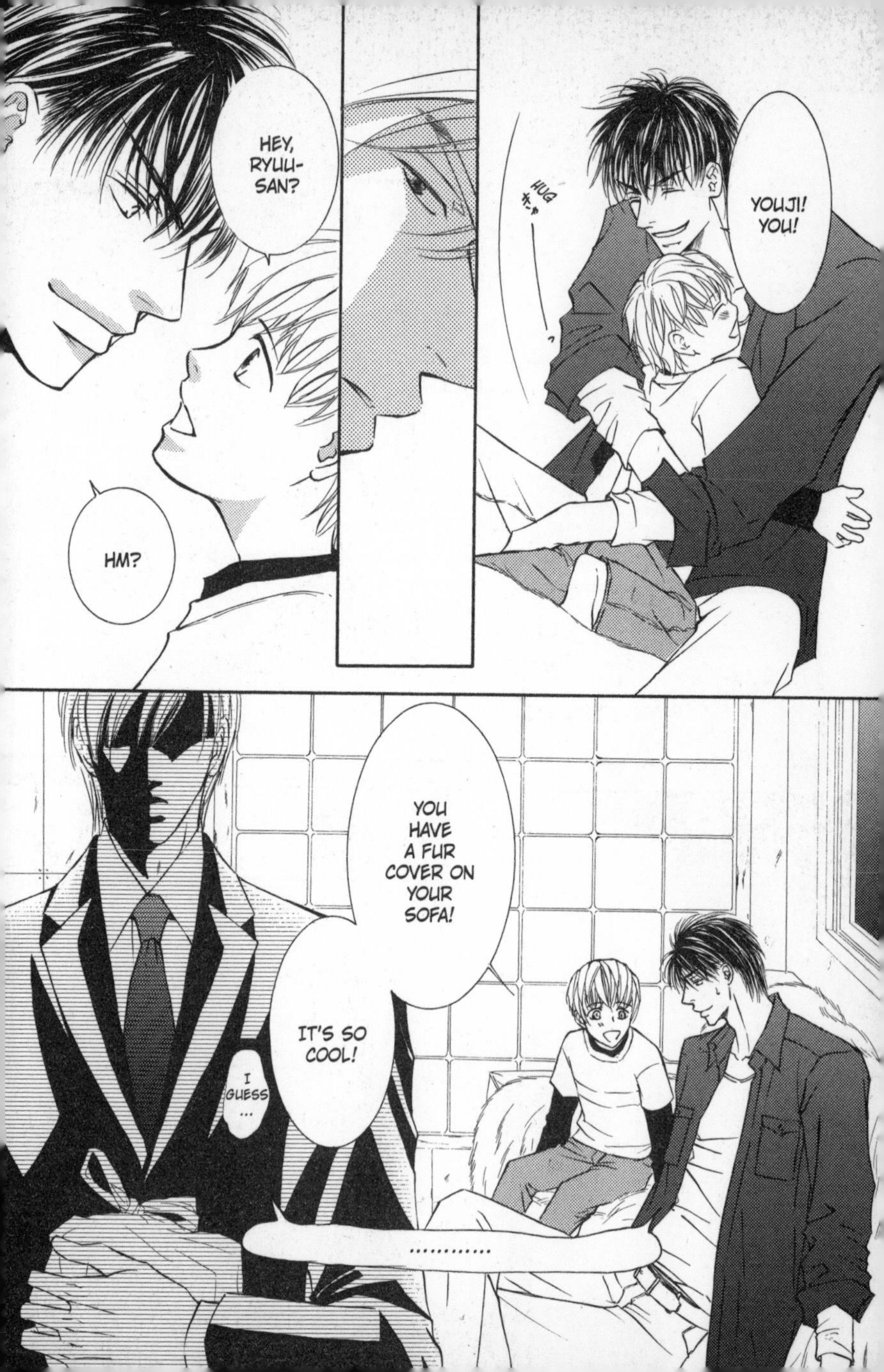
HUG
YOUJI! YOU!
HEY, RYUU-SAN?
HM?
YOU HAVE A FUR COVER ON YOUR SOFA!
IT'S SO COOL!
I GUESS...
....

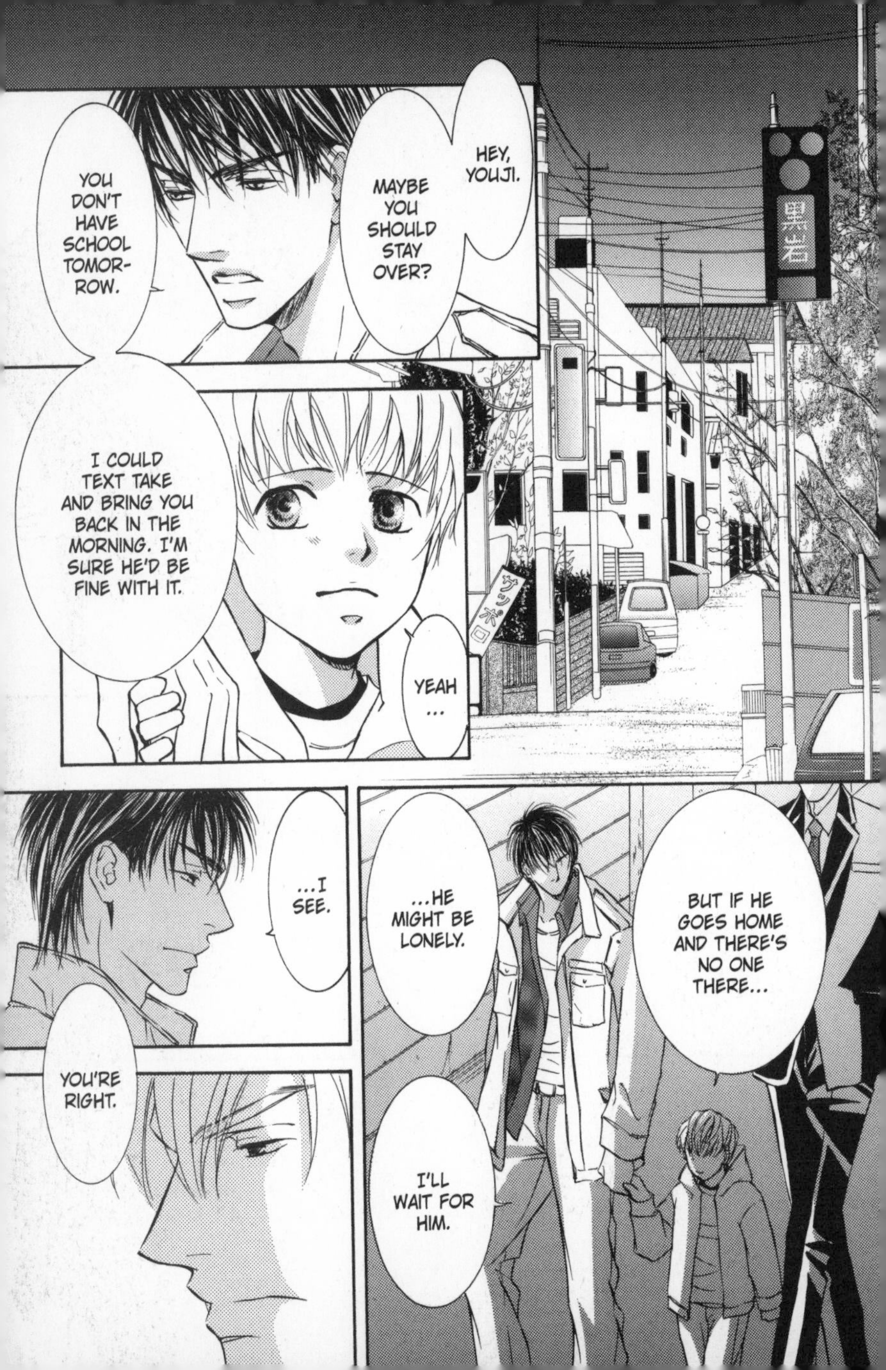
HEY, YOUJI.
MAYBE YOU SHOULD STAY OVER?
黒岩
サッポロ
YOU DON'T HAVE SCHOOL TOMOR-ROW.
I COULD TEXT TAKE AND BRING YOU BACK IN THE MORNING. I'M SURE HE'D BE FINE WITH IT.
YEAH ...
BUT IF HE GOES HOME AND THERE'S NO ONE THERE...
...HE MIGHT BE LONELY.
I'LL WAIT FOR HIM.
...I SEE.
YOU'RE RIGHT.

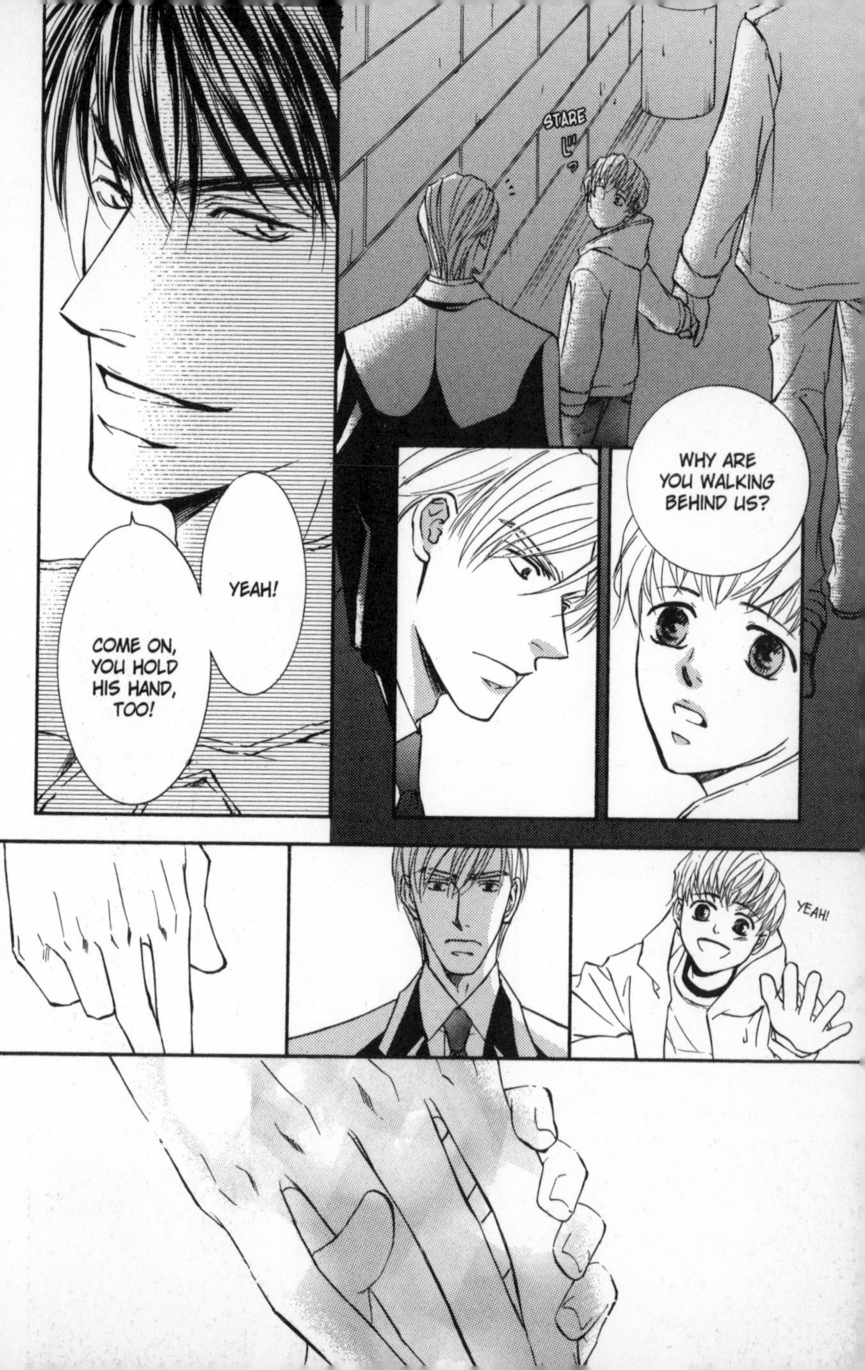
STARE
じっ
WHY ARE YOU WALKING BEHIND US?
YEAH!
COME ON, YOU HOLD HIS HAND, TOO!
YEAH!

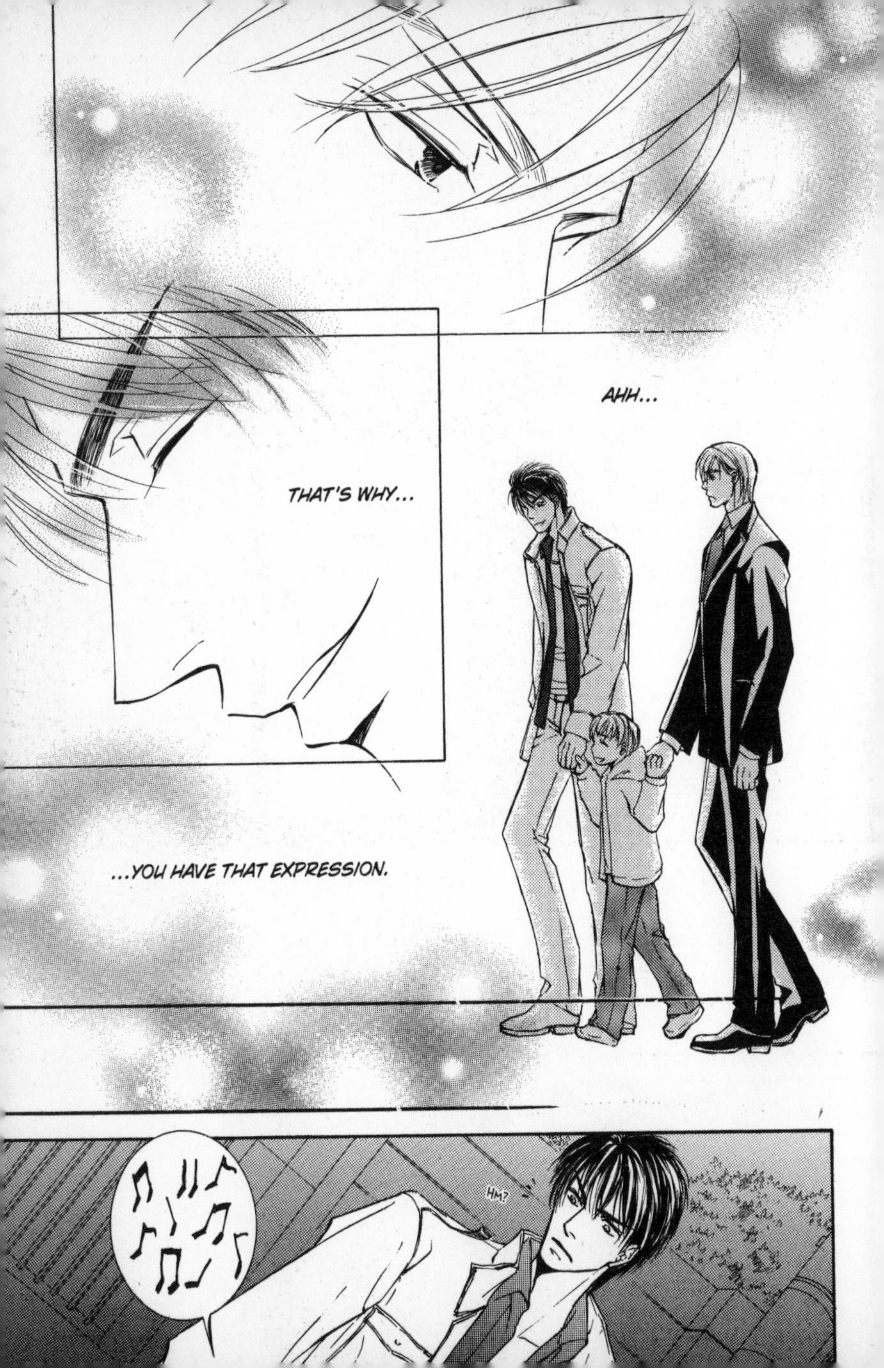

AHH...
THAT'S WHY...
...YOU HAVE THAT EXPRESSION.
HM?

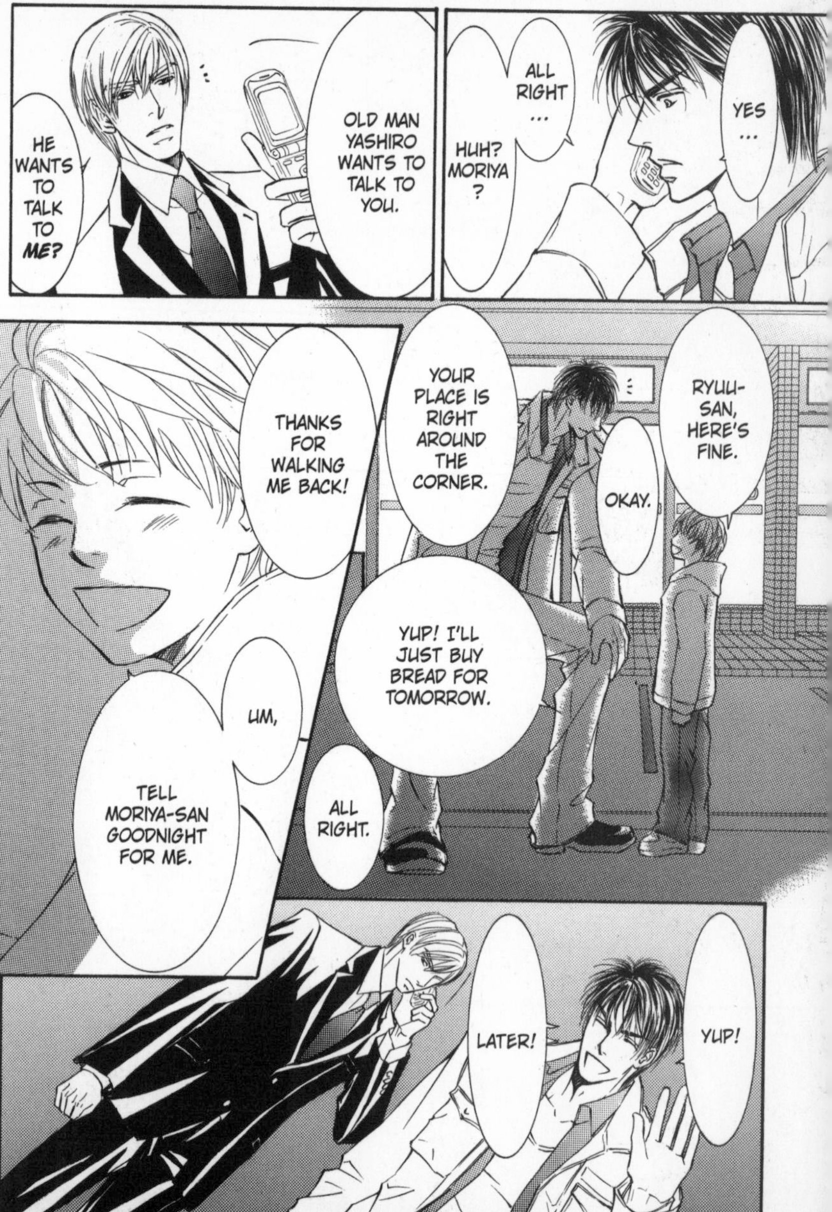
YES ...
ALL RIGHT ...
HUH? MORIYA?
OLD MAN YASHIRO WANTS TO TALK TO YOU.
HE WANTS TO TALK TO *ME?*
RYUU-SAN, HERE'S FINE.
YOUR PLACE IS RIGHT AROUND THE CORNER.
OKAY.
YUP! I'LL JUST BUY BREAD FOR TOMORROW.
THANKS FOR WALKING ME BACK!
UM,
TELL MORIYA-SAN GOODNIGHT FOR ME.
ALL RIGHT.
YUP!
LATER!

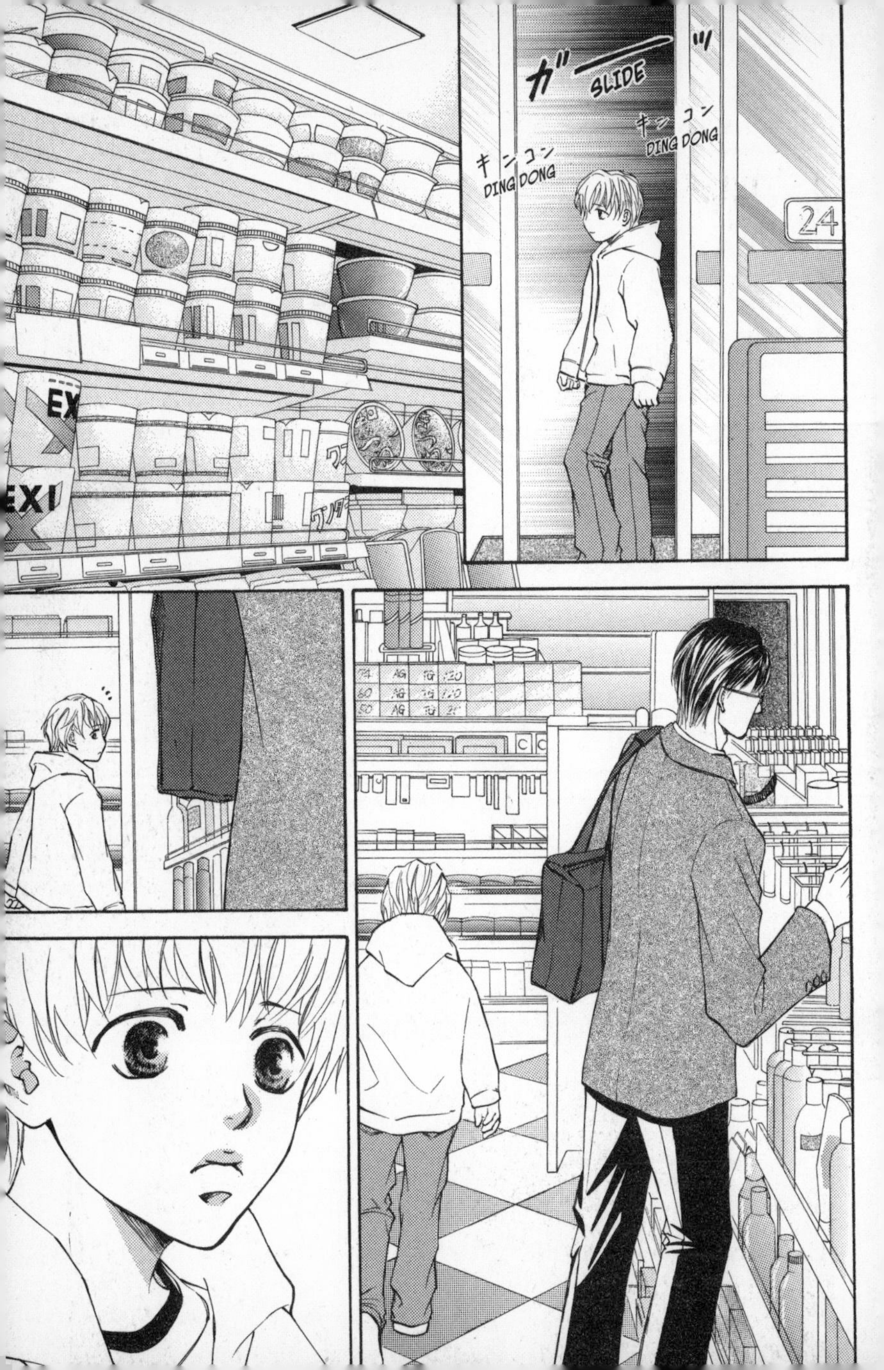
ガーッ
SLIDE
キンコン
DING DONG
キンコン
DING DONG

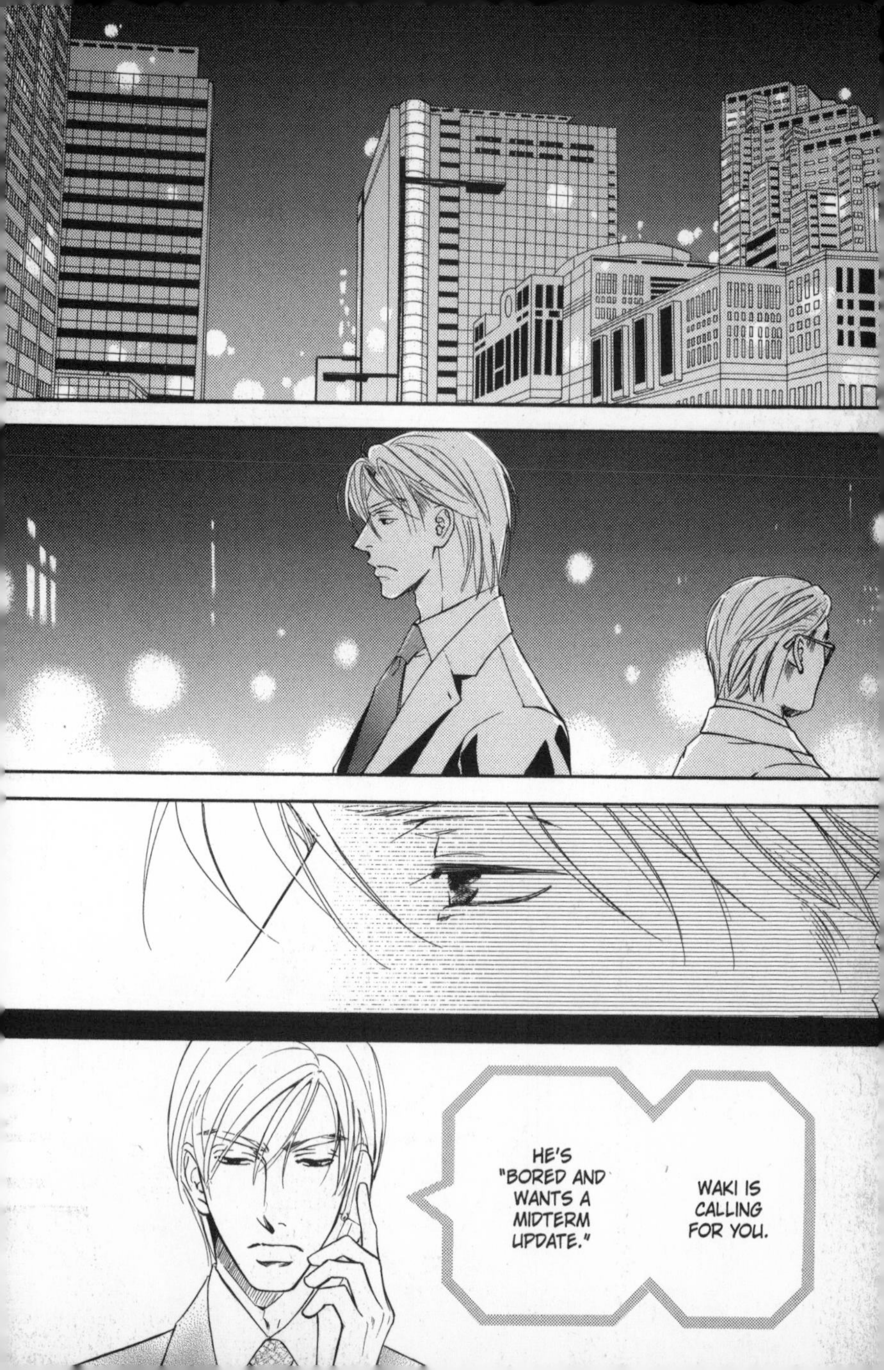
WAKI IS CALLING FOR YOU.
HE'S "BORED AND WANTS A MIDTERM UPDATE."

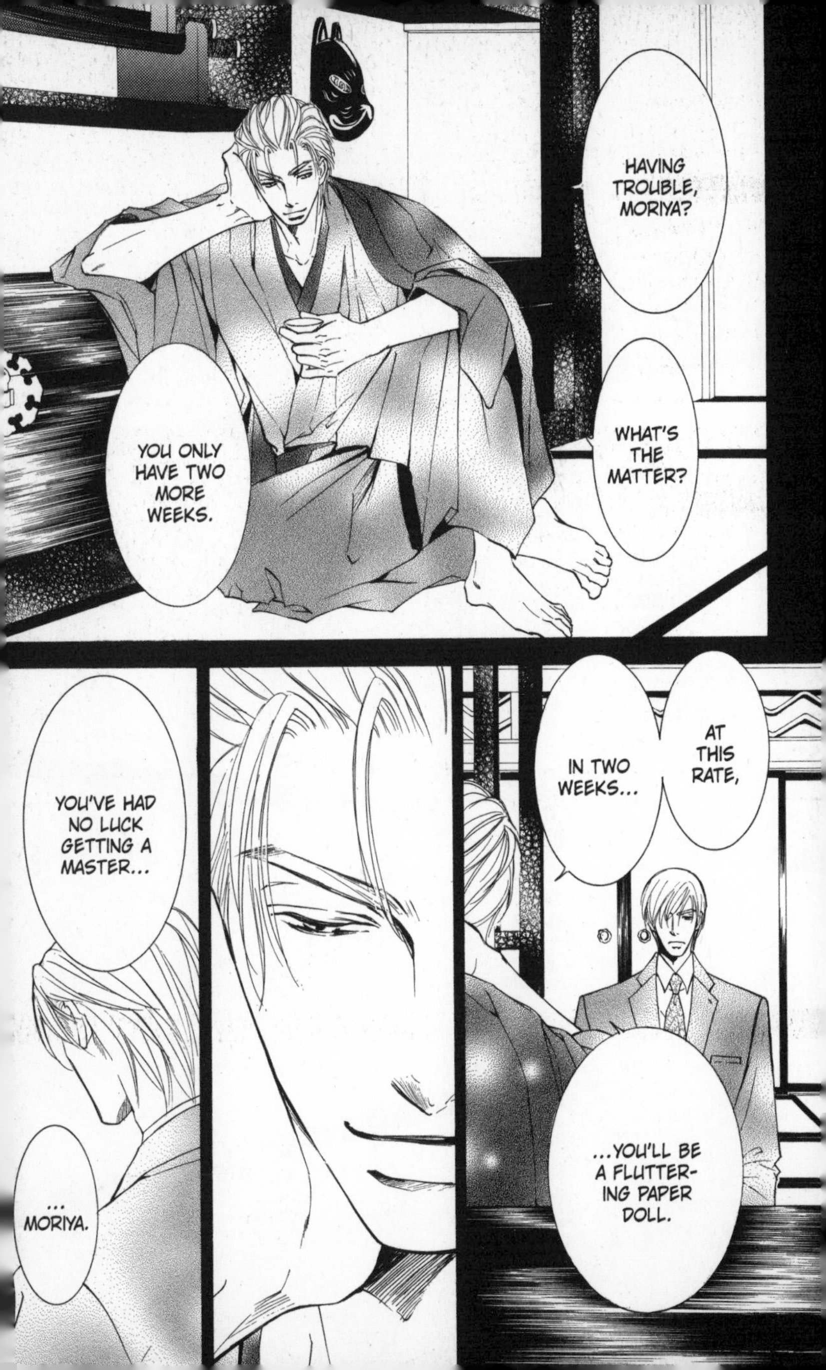
HAVING TROUBLE, MORIYA?
WHAT'S THE MATTER?
YOU ONLY HAVE TWO MORE WEEKS.
AT THIS RATE,
IN TWO WEEKS...
...YOU'LL BE A FLUTTER-ING PAPER DOLL.
YOU'VE HAD NO LUCK GETTING A MASTER...
...MORIYA.

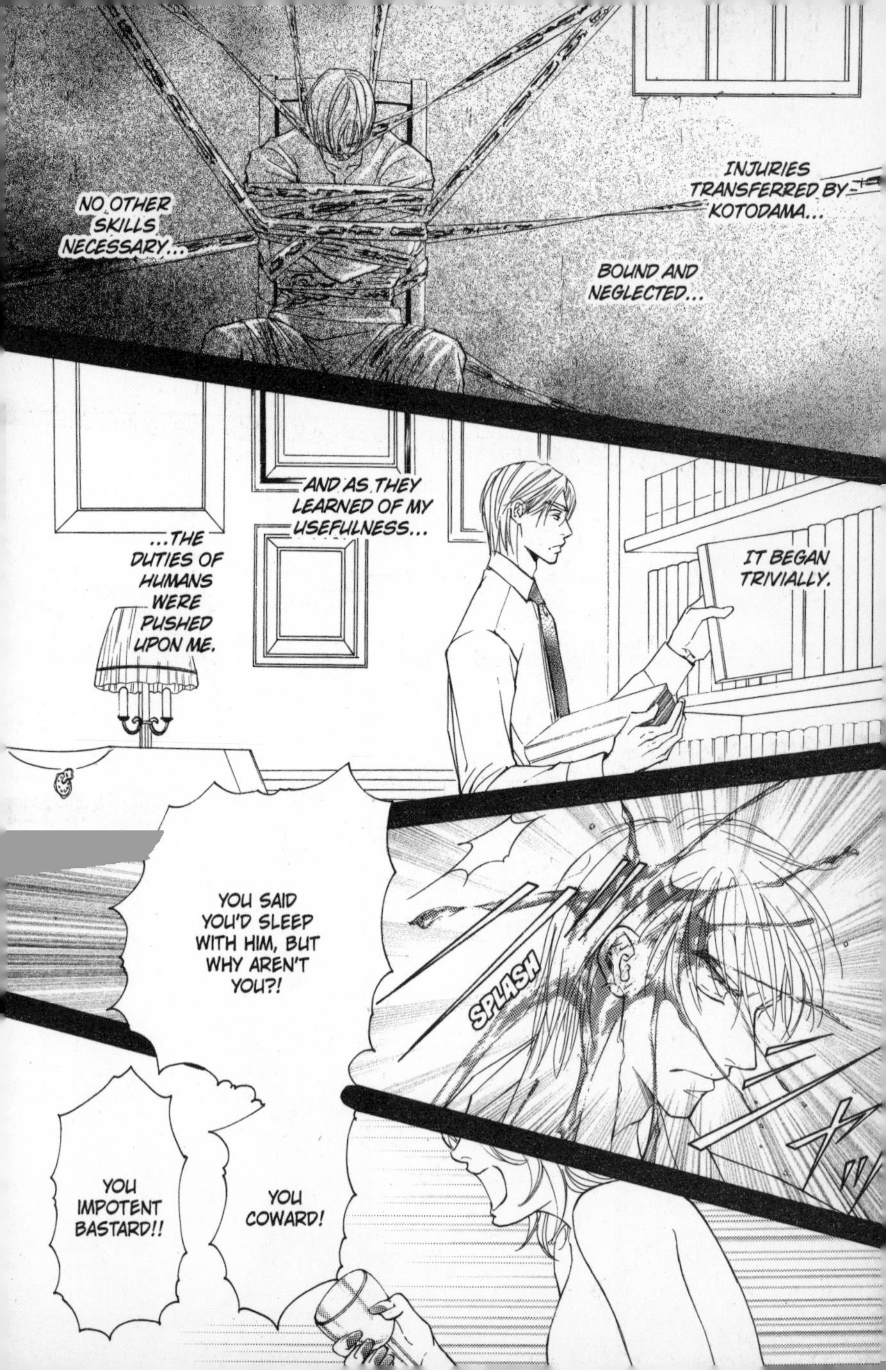
INJURIES TRANSFERRED BY KOTODAMA...
BOUND AND NEGLECTED...
NO OTHER SKILLS NECESSARY...
IT BEGAN TRIVIALLY.
AND AS THEY LEARNED OF MY USEFULNESS...
...THE DUTIES OF HUMANS WERE PUSHED UPON ME.
SPLASH
YOU SAID YOU'D SLEEP WITH HIM, BUT WHY AREN'T YOU?!
YOU COWARD!
YOU IMPOTENT BASTARD!!

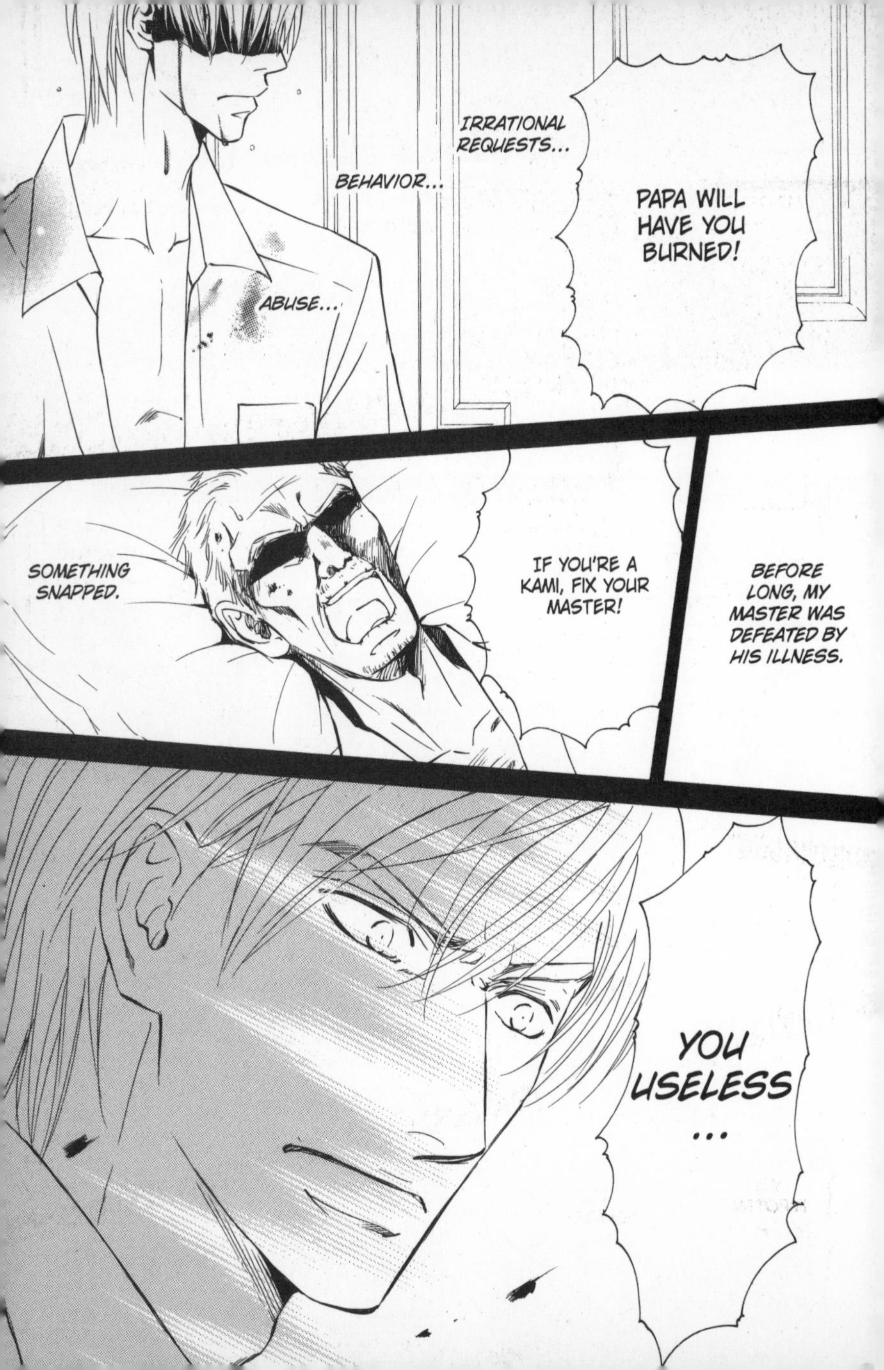
PAPA WILL HAVE YOU BURNED!
IRRATIONAL REQUESTS...
BEHAVIOR...
ABUSE...
BEFORE LONG, MY MASTER WAS DEFEATED BY HIS ILLNESS.
IF YOU'RE A KAMI, FIX YOUR MASTER!
SOMETHING SNAPPED.
YOU USELESS ...

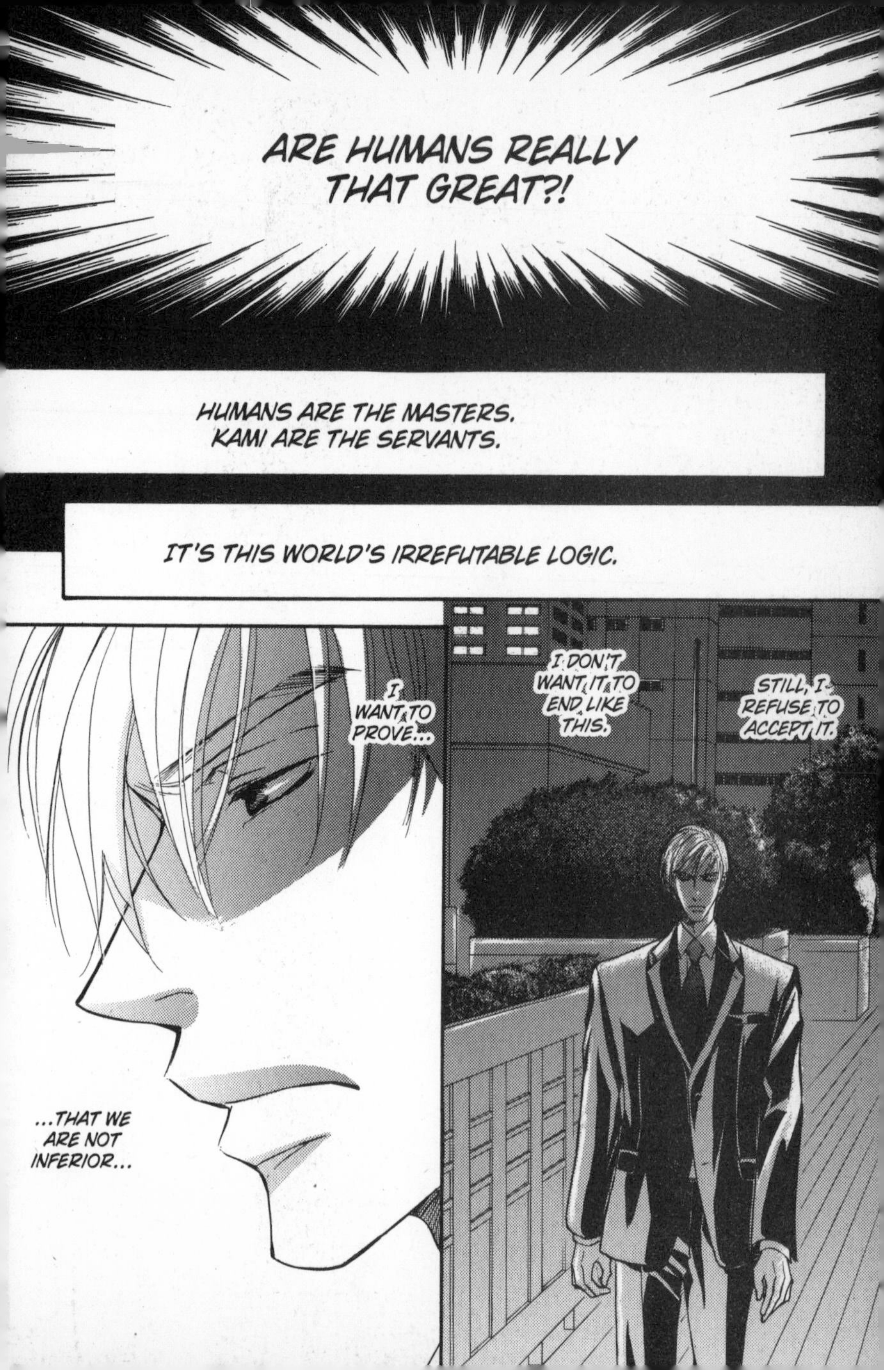
ARE HUMANS REALLY THAT GREAT?!
HUMANS ARE THE MASTERS. KAMI ARE THE SERVANTS.
IT'S THIS WORLD'S IRREFUTABLE LOGIC.
STILL, I REFUSE TO ACCEPT IT.
I DON'T WANT IT TO END LIKE THIS.
I WANT TO PROVE...
...THAT WE ARE NOT INFERIOR...

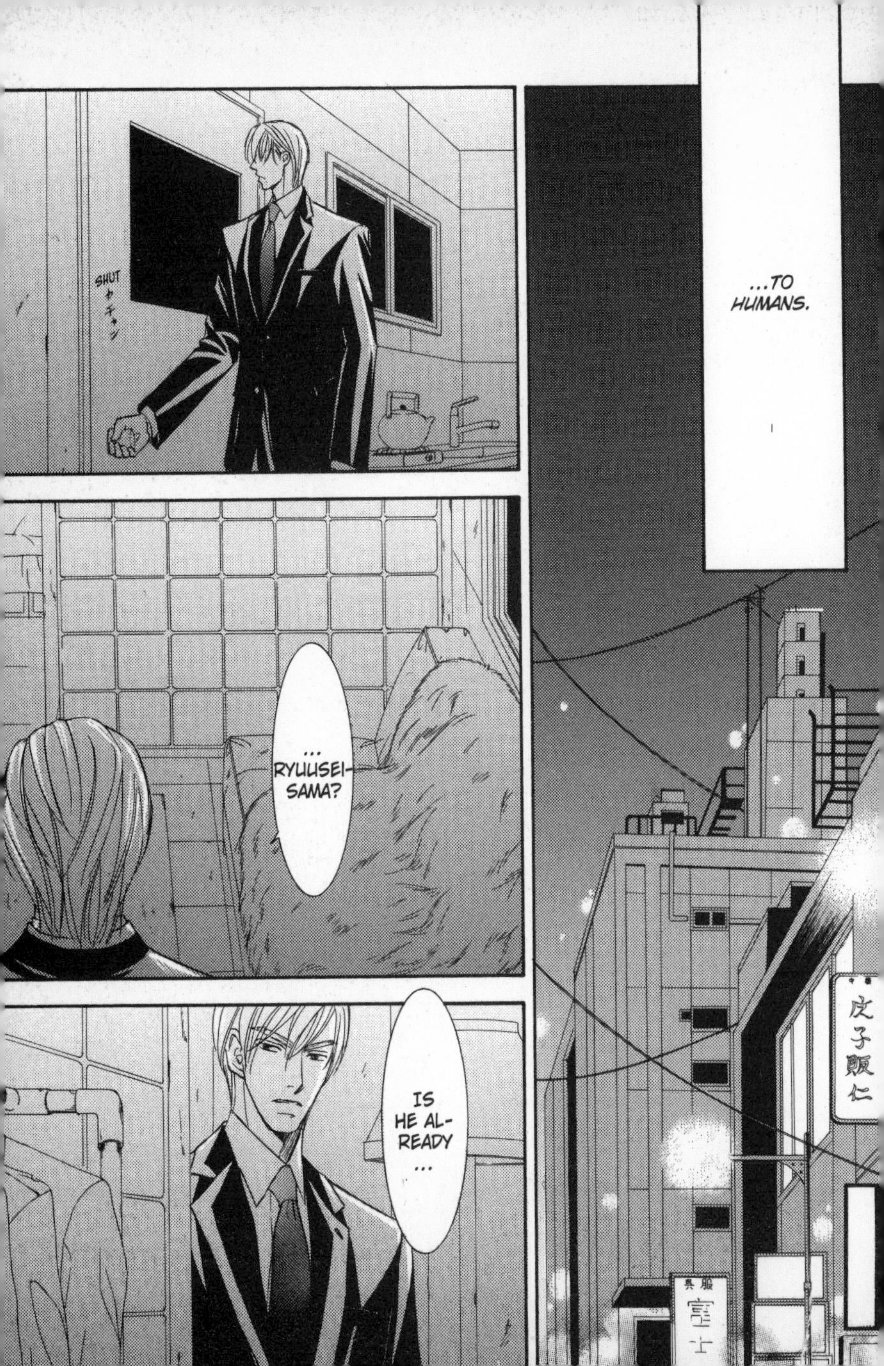

...TO HUMANS.
SHUT
カチャッ
... RYUUSEI-SAMA?
IS HE AL-READY ...

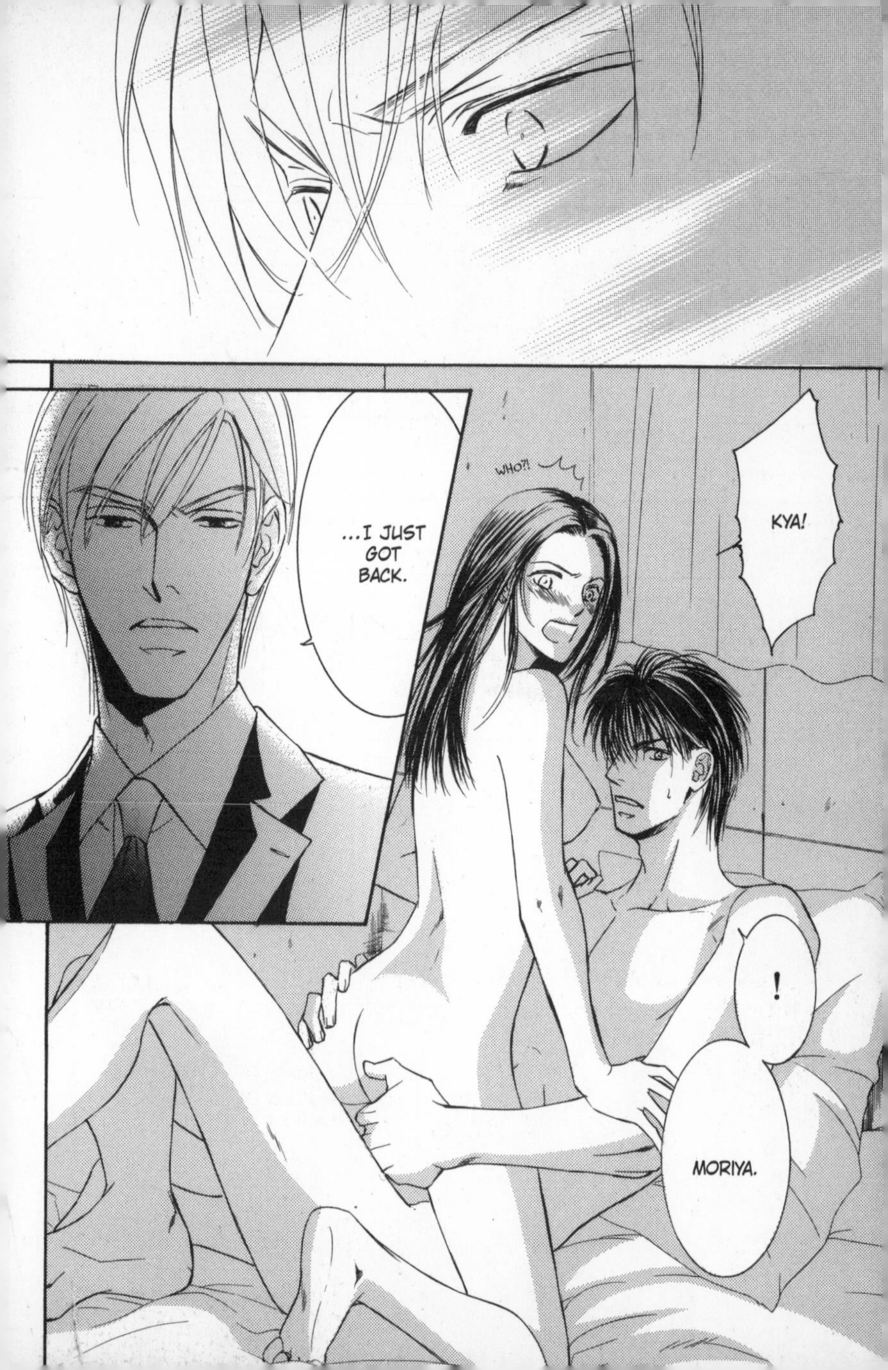
KYA!
WHO?!
...I JUST GOT BACK.
!
MORIYA.

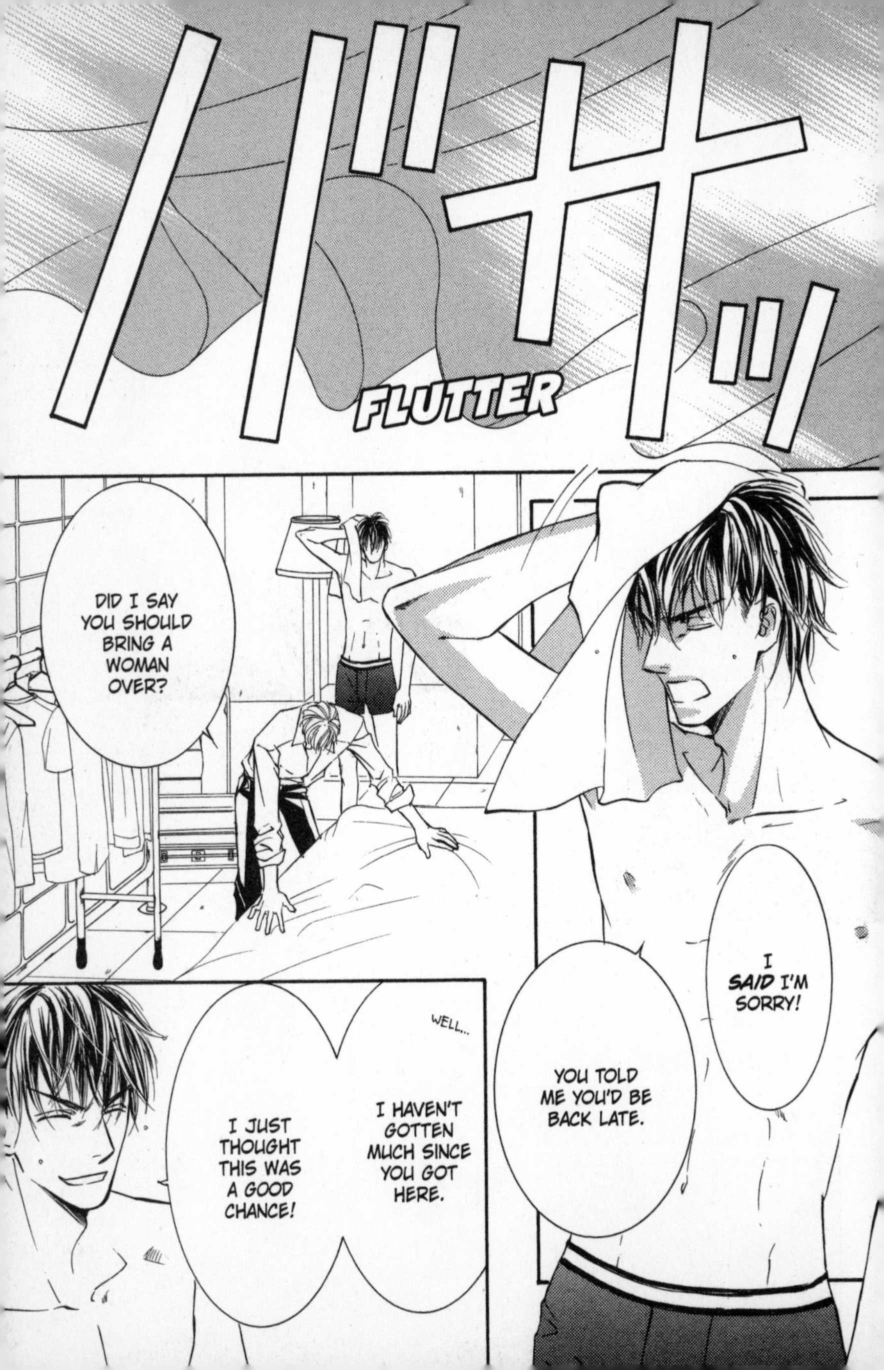
バサッ
FLUTTER
DID I SAY YOU SHOULD BRING A WOMAN OVER?
I SAID I'M SORRY!
YOU TOLD ME YOU'D BE BACK LATE.
WELL...
I HAVEN'T GOTTEN MUCH SINCE YOU GOT HERE.
I JUST THOUGHT THIS WAS A GOOD CHANCE!

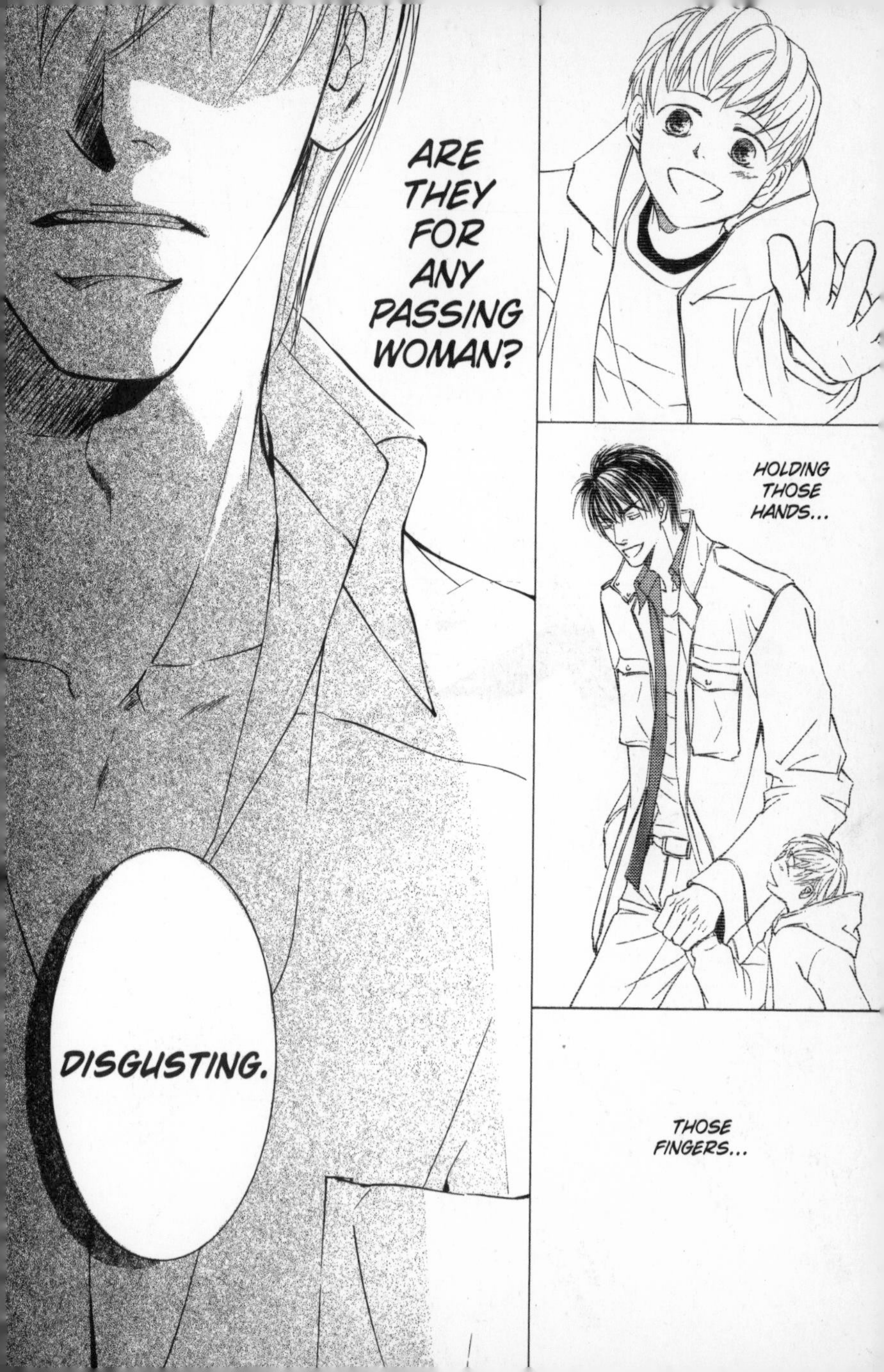
HOLDING THOSE HANDS...
THOSE FINGERS...
ARE THEY FOR ANY PASSING WOMAN?
DISGUSTING.

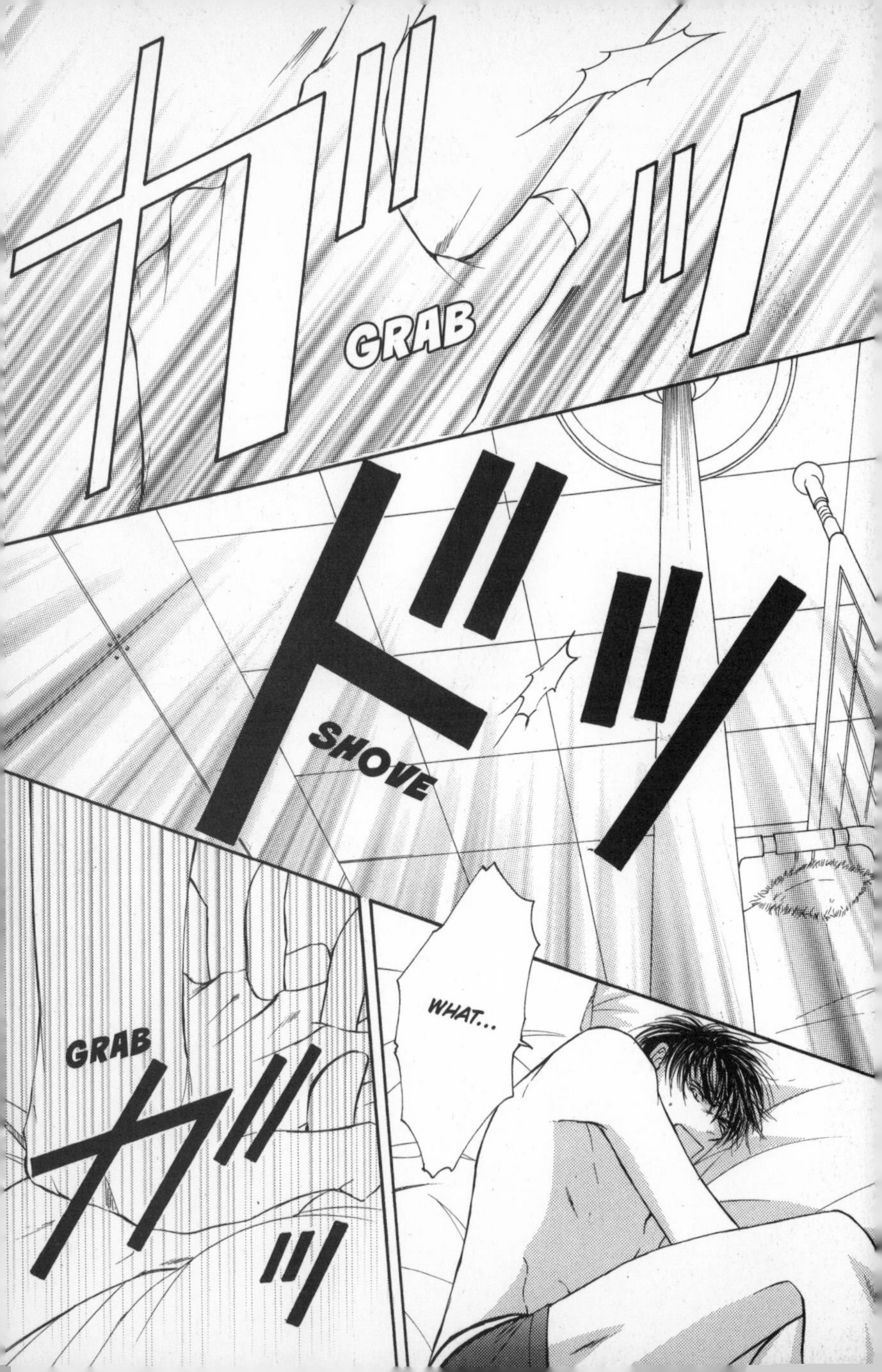
GRAB
SHOVE
WHAT...
GRAB

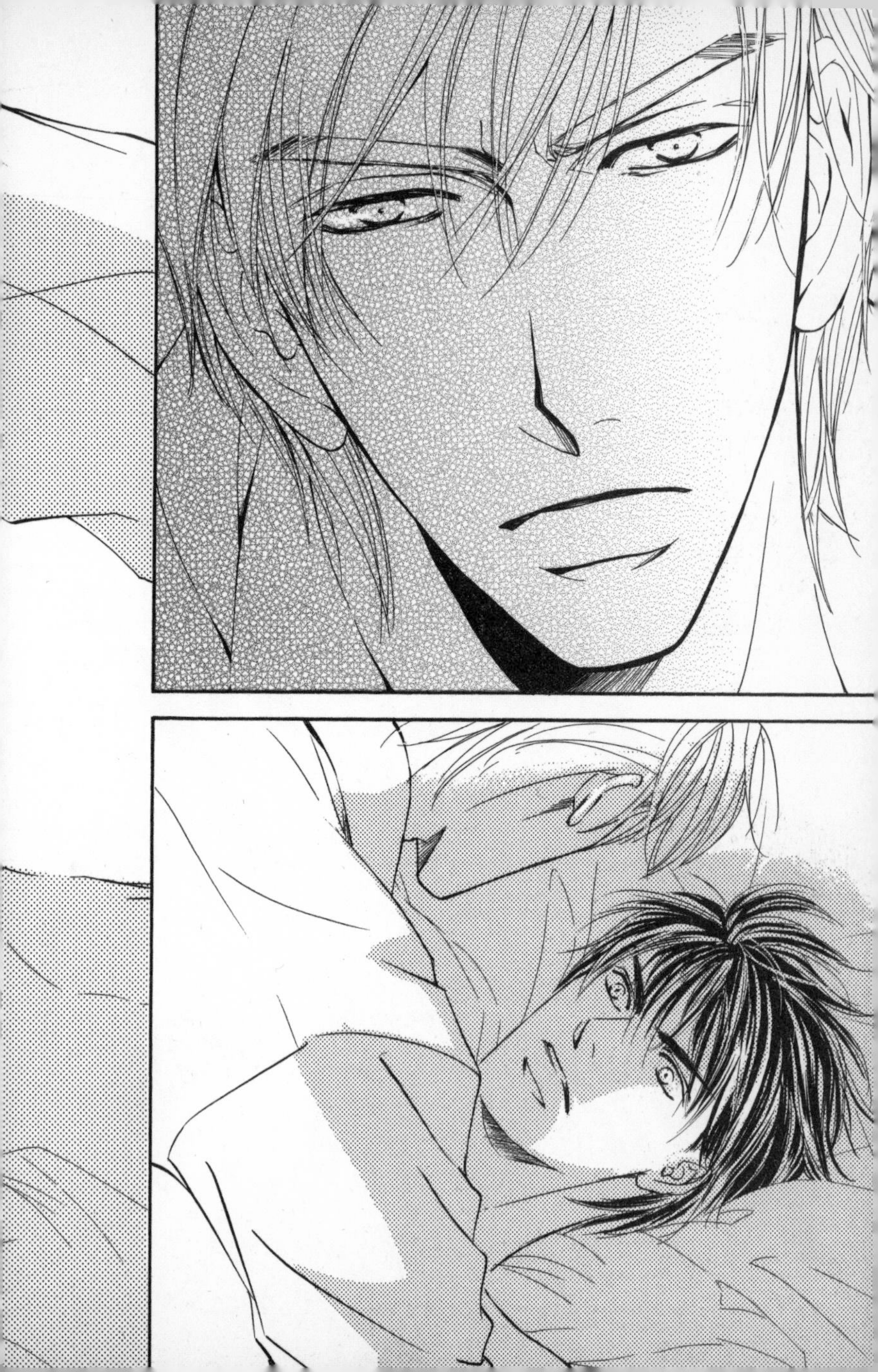

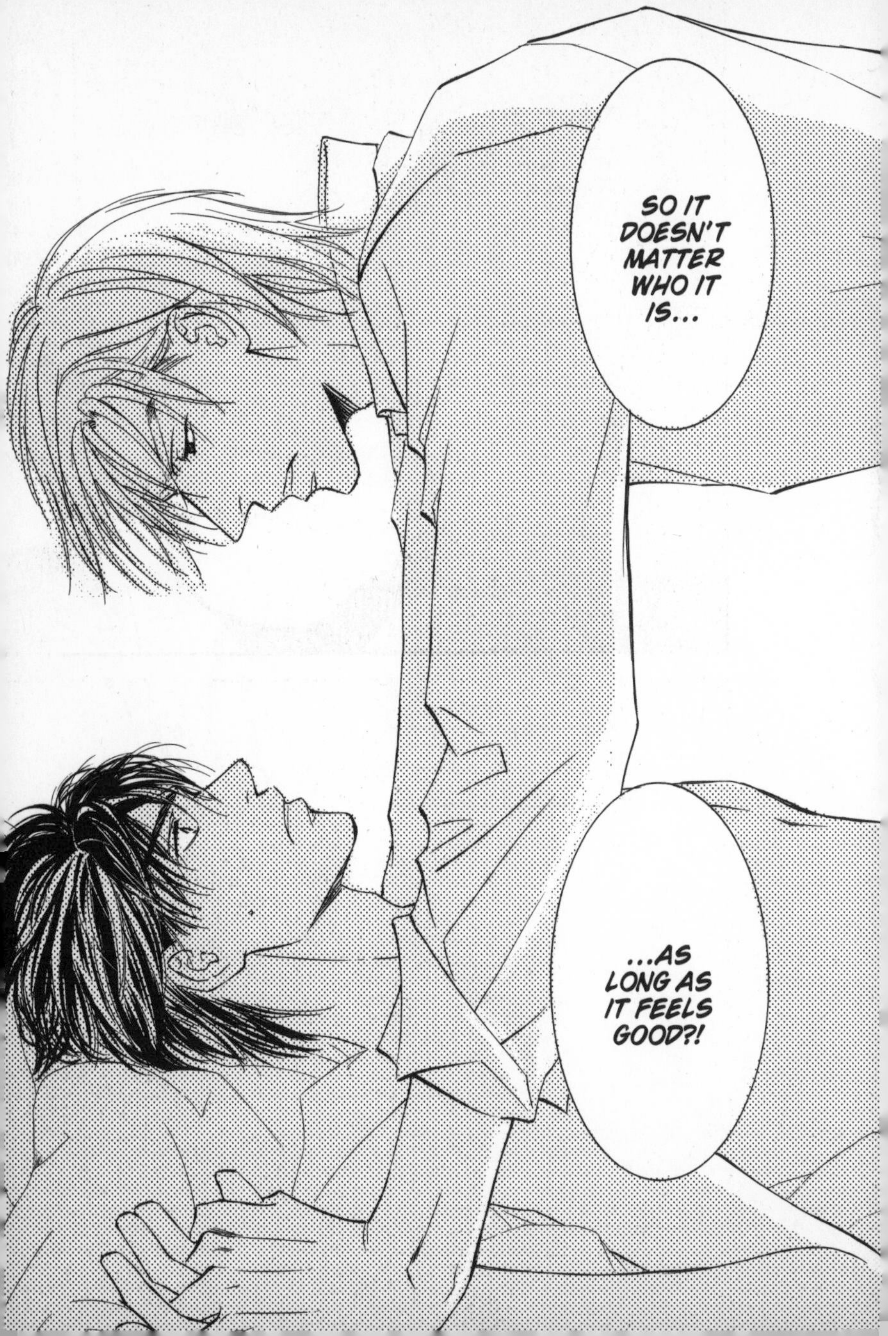
SO IT DOESN'T MATTER WHO IT IS...
...AS LONG AS IT FEELS GOOD?!

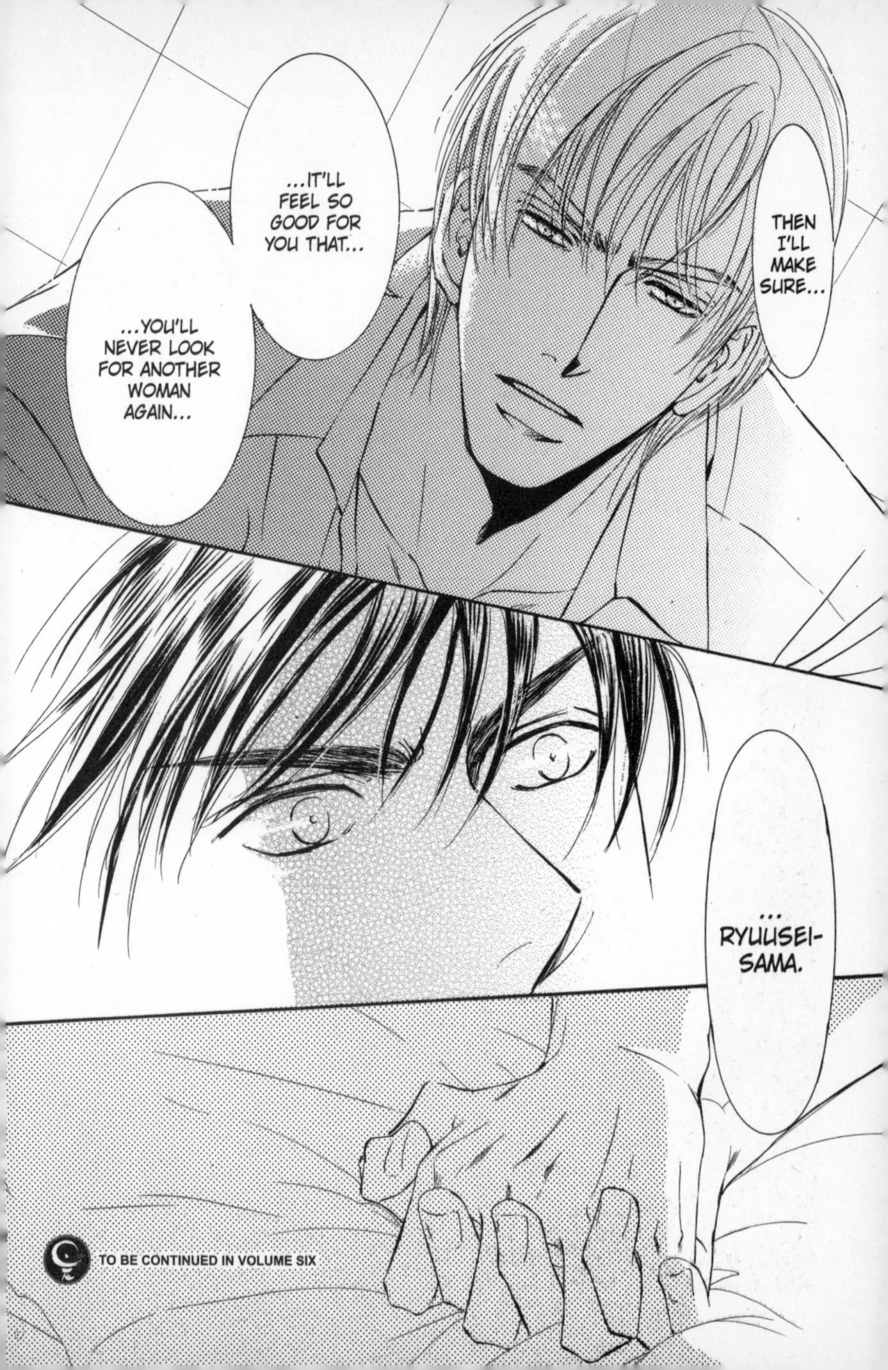
THEN I'LL MAKE SURE...
...IT'LL FEEL SO GOOD FOR YOU THAT...
...YOU'LL NEVER LOOK FOR ANOTHER WOMAN AGAIN...
... RYUUSEI-SAMA.
TO BE CONTINUED IN VOLUME SIX

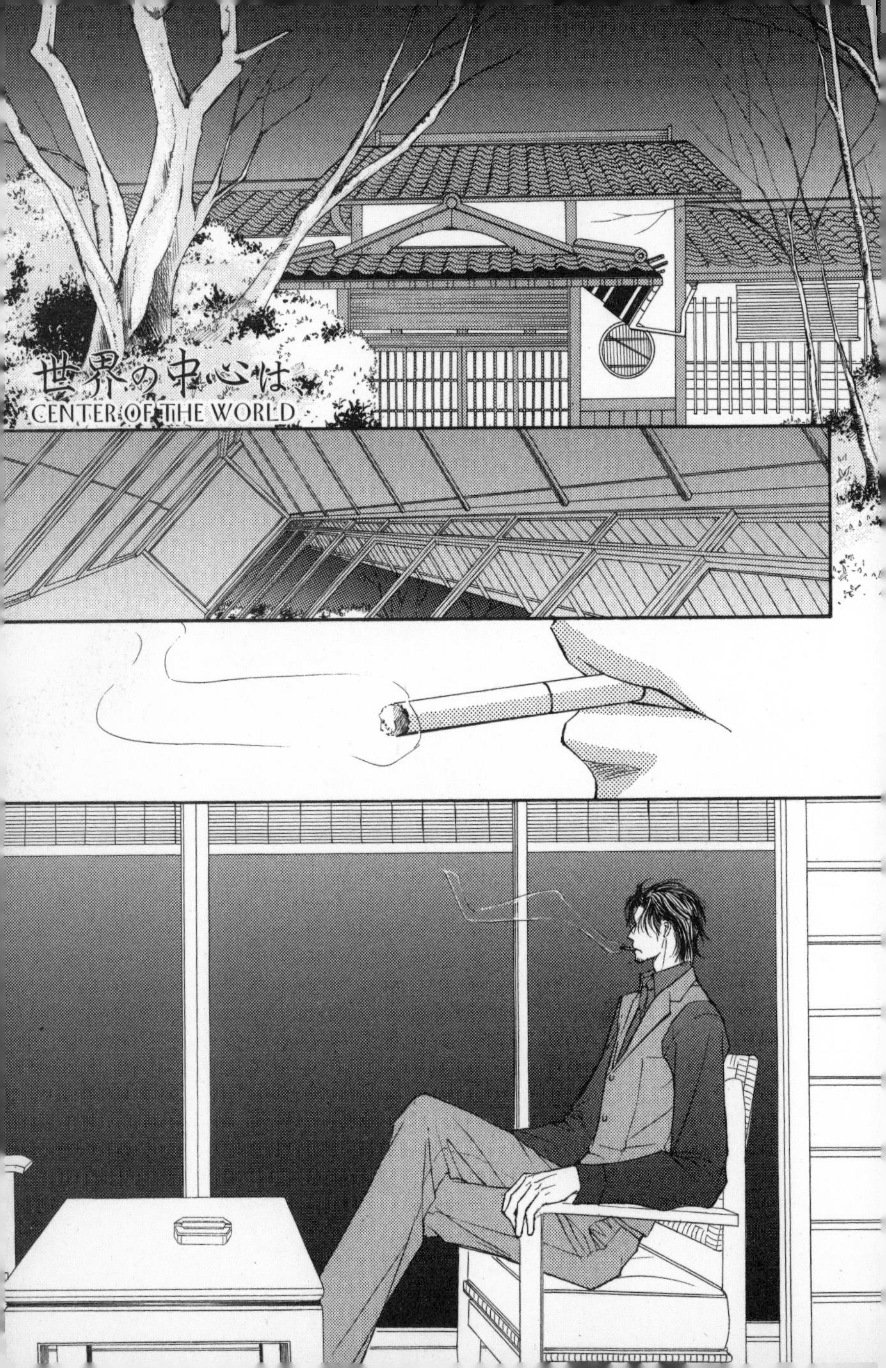
世界の中心は、
CENTER OF THE WORLD

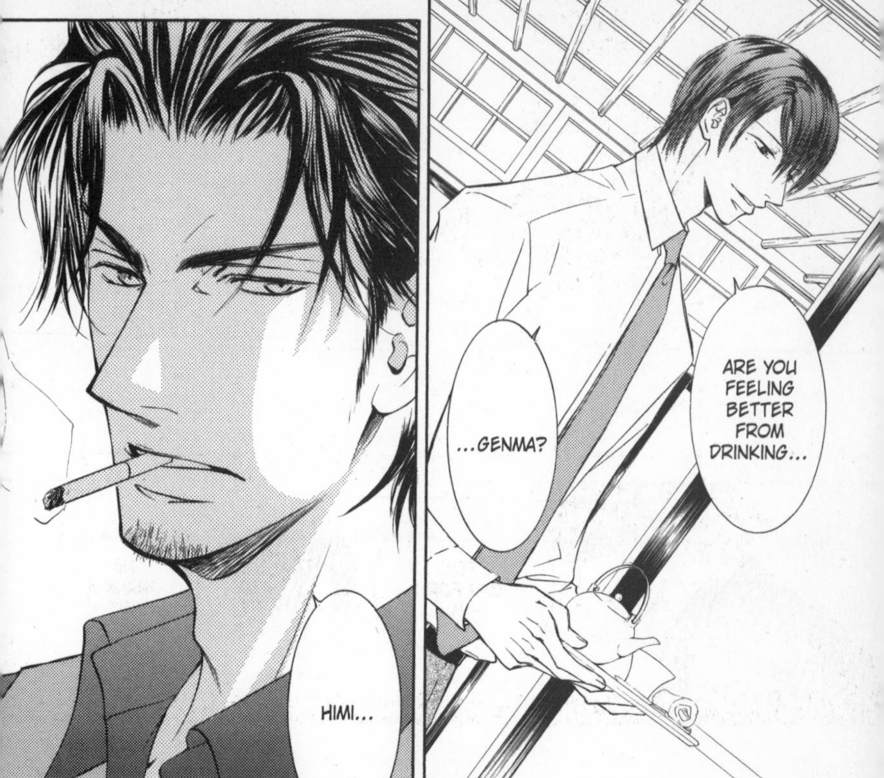
ARE YOU FEELING BETTER FROM DRINKING...
...GENMA?
HIMI...

世界の中心は、

CENTER OF THE WORLD

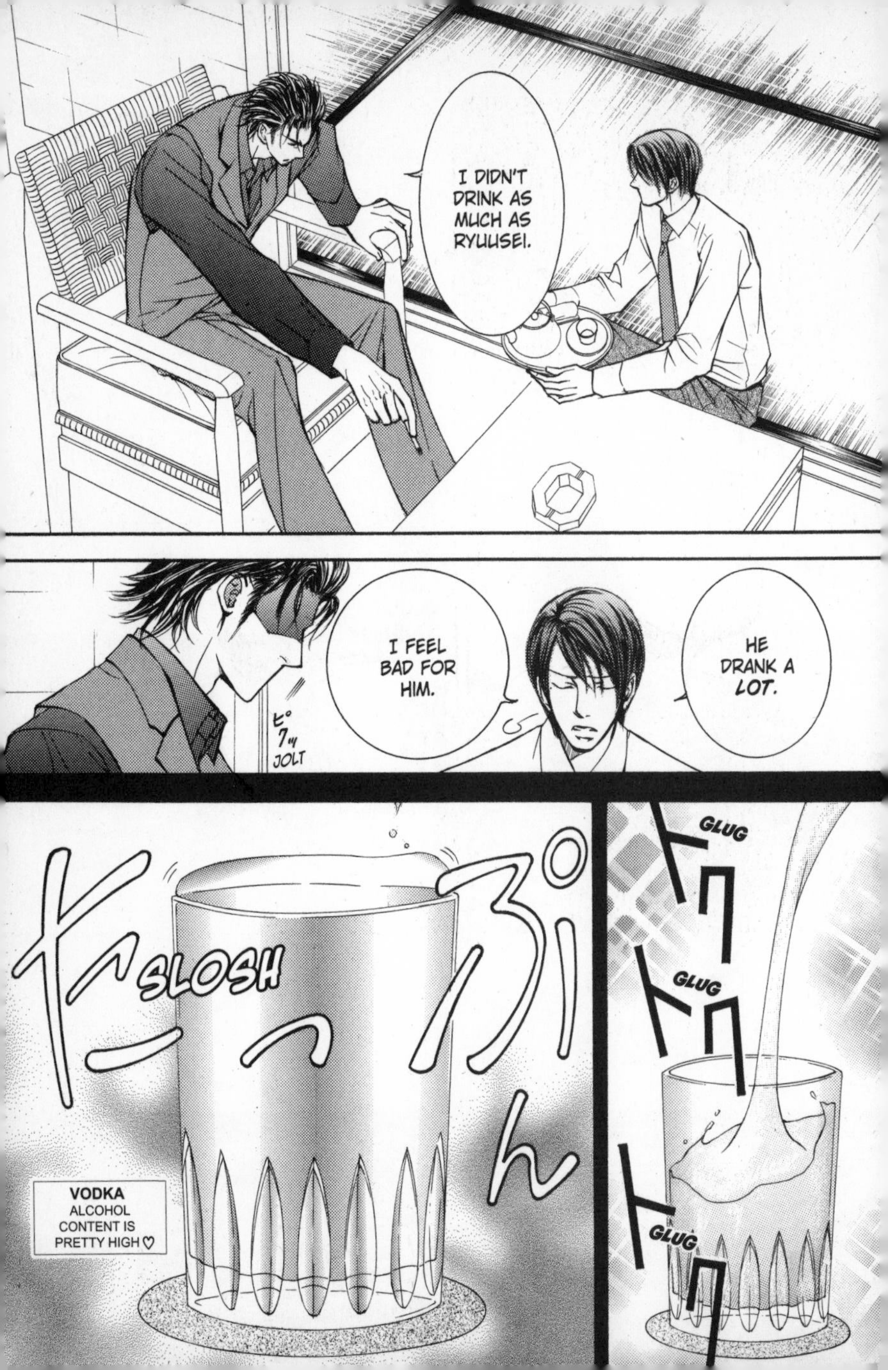
I DIDN'T DRINK AS MUCH AS RYUUSEI.
HE DRANK A LOT.
I FEEL BAD FOR HIM.
ピクッ
JOLT
GLUG
GLUG
GLUG
SLOSH
VODKA ALCOHOL CONTENT IS PRETTY HIGH ♡

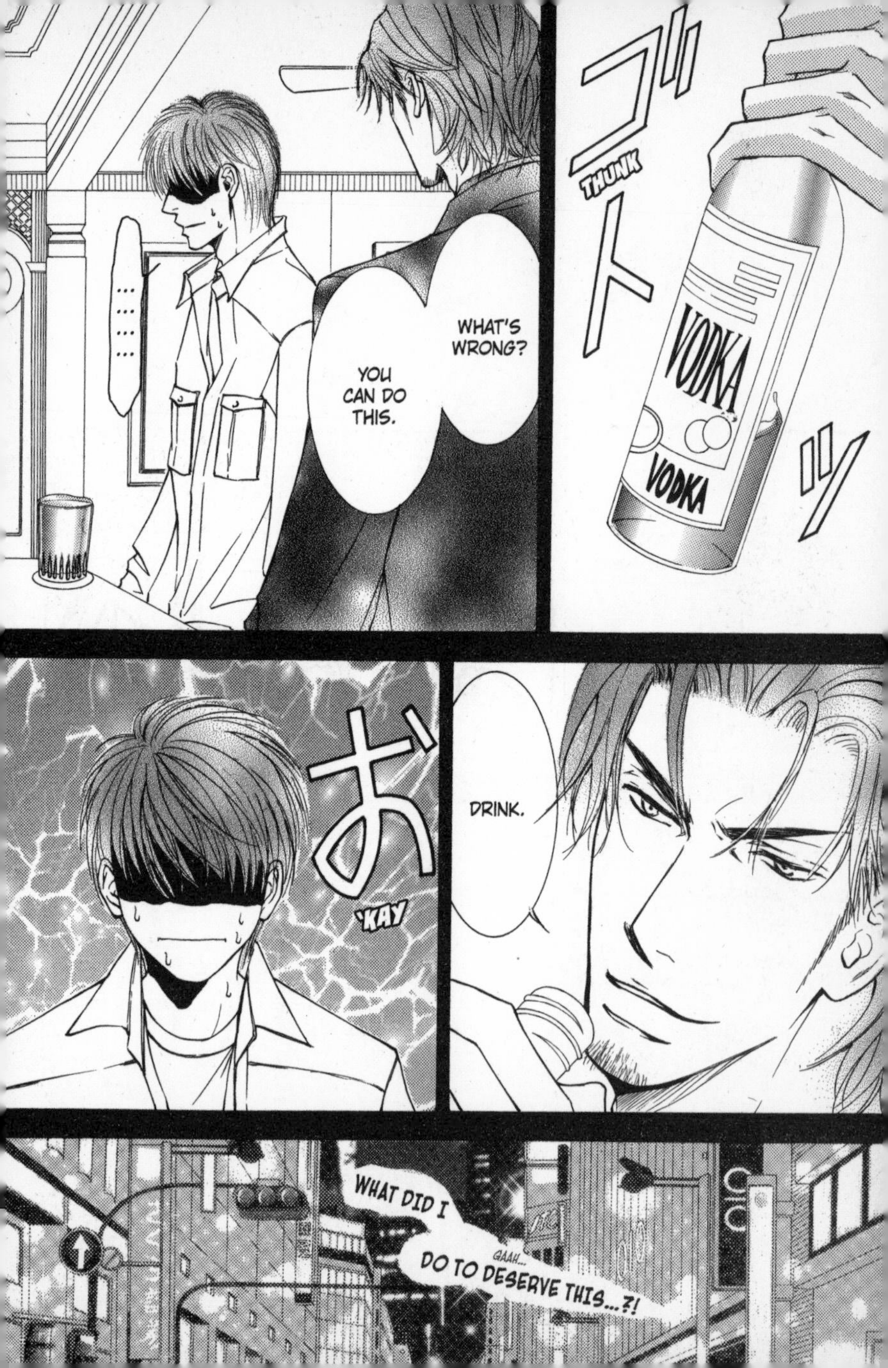
ゴトッ
THUNK
VODKA
VODKA
WHAT'S WRONG?
YOU CAN DO THIS.
......
DRINK.
お
'KAY
WHAT DID I
DO TO DESERVE THIS...?!
GAAH...

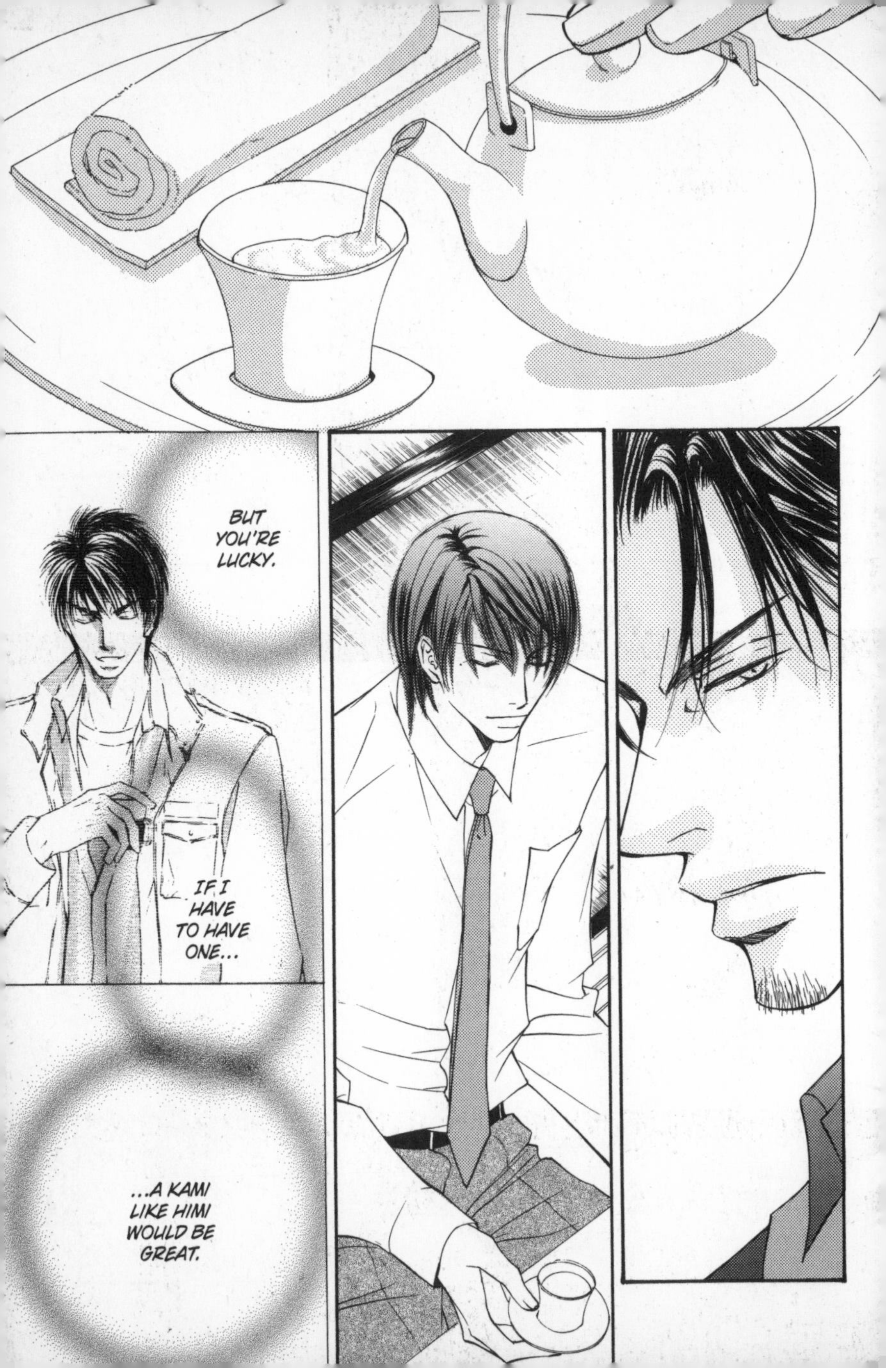
BUT YOU'RE LUCKY.
IF I HAVE TO HAVE ONE...
...A KAMI LIKE HIMI WOULD BE GREAT.

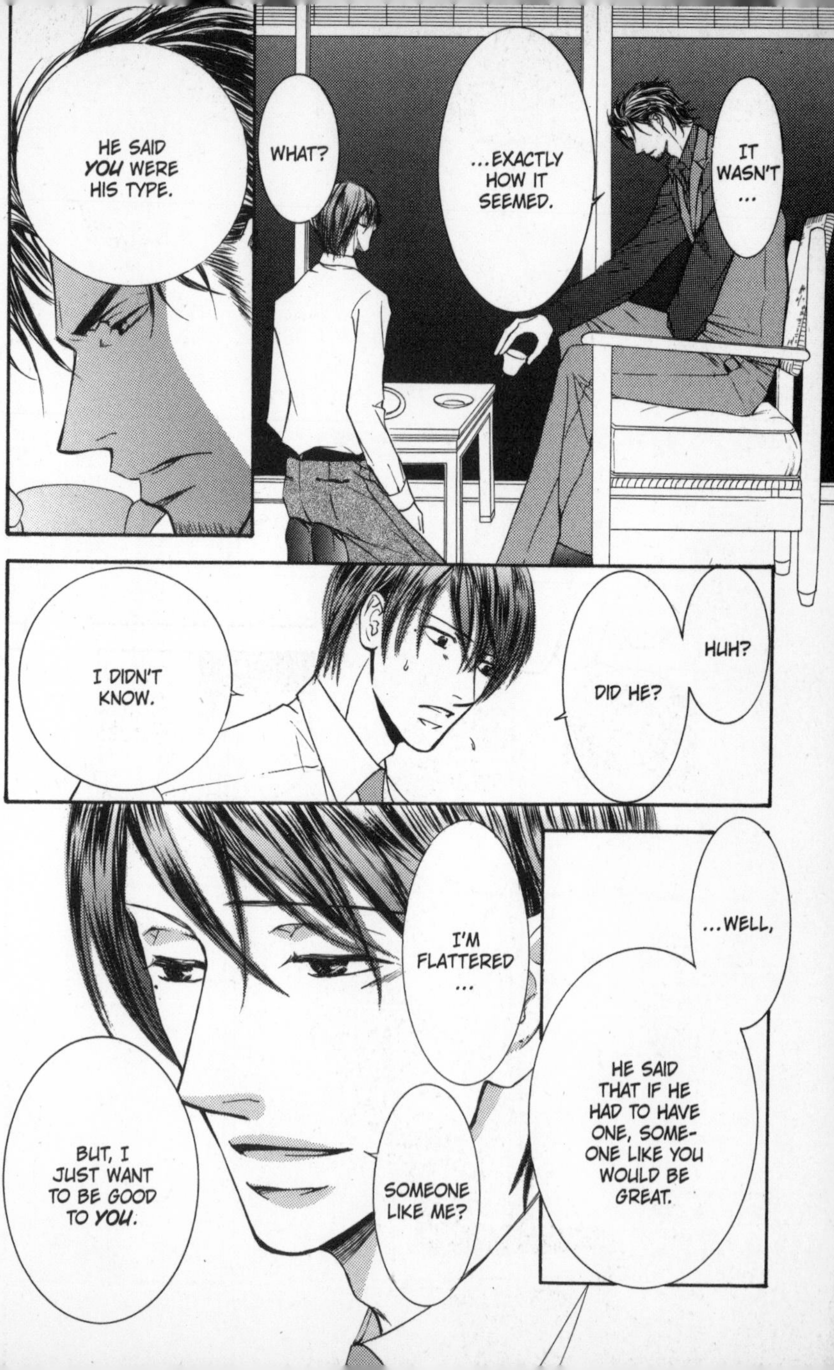
IT WASN'T ...
...EXACTLY HOW IT SEEMED.
WHAT?
HE SAID *YOU* WERE HIS TYPE.
HUH?
DID HE?
I DIDN'T KNOW.
...WELL,
HE SAID THAT IF HE HAD TO HAVE ONE, SOME-ONE LIKE YOU WOULD BE GREAT.
SOMEONE LIKE ME?
I'M FLATTERED ...
BUT, I JUST WANT TO BE GOOD TO *YOU*.

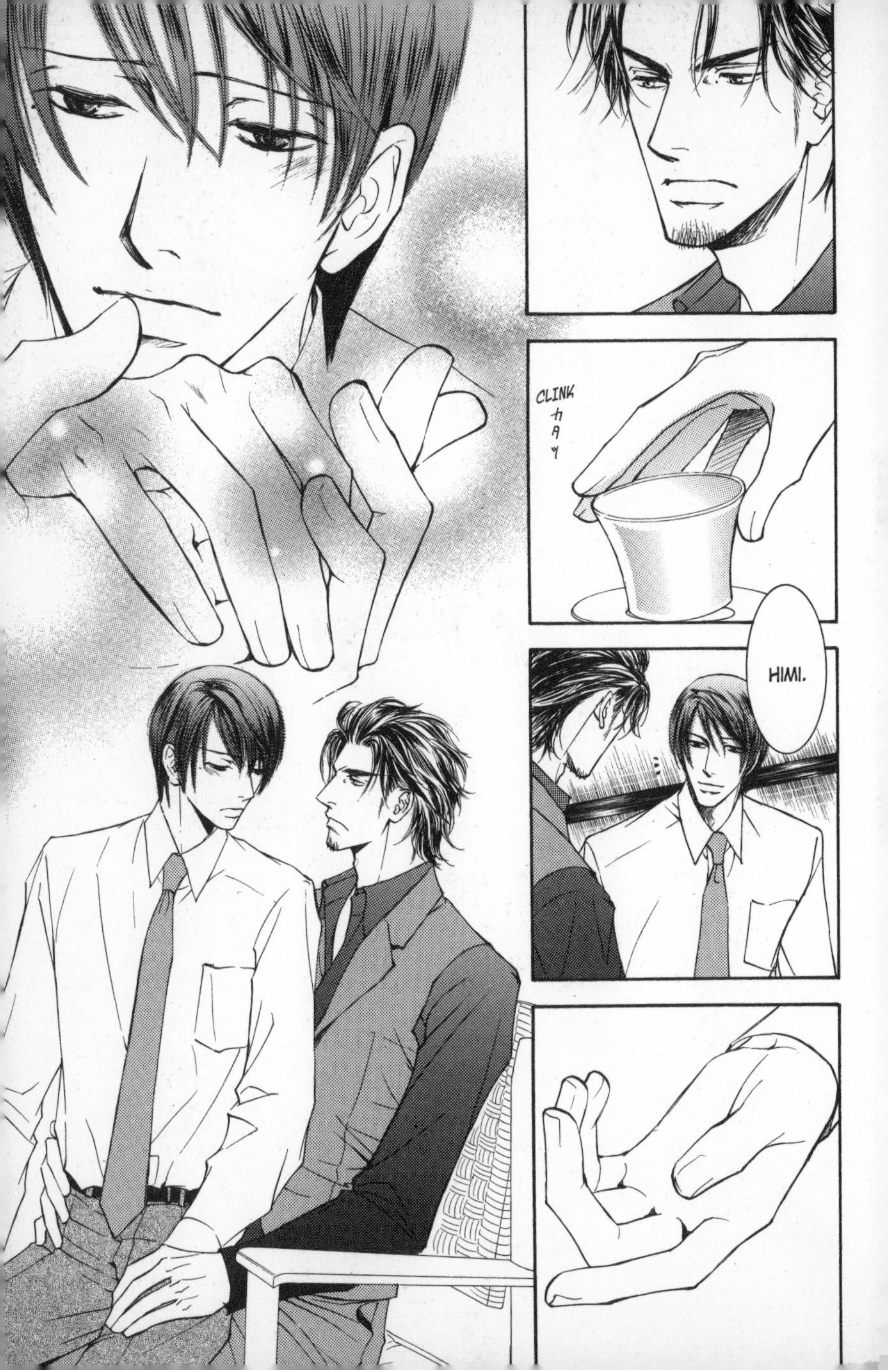
CLINK
カタッ
HIMI.

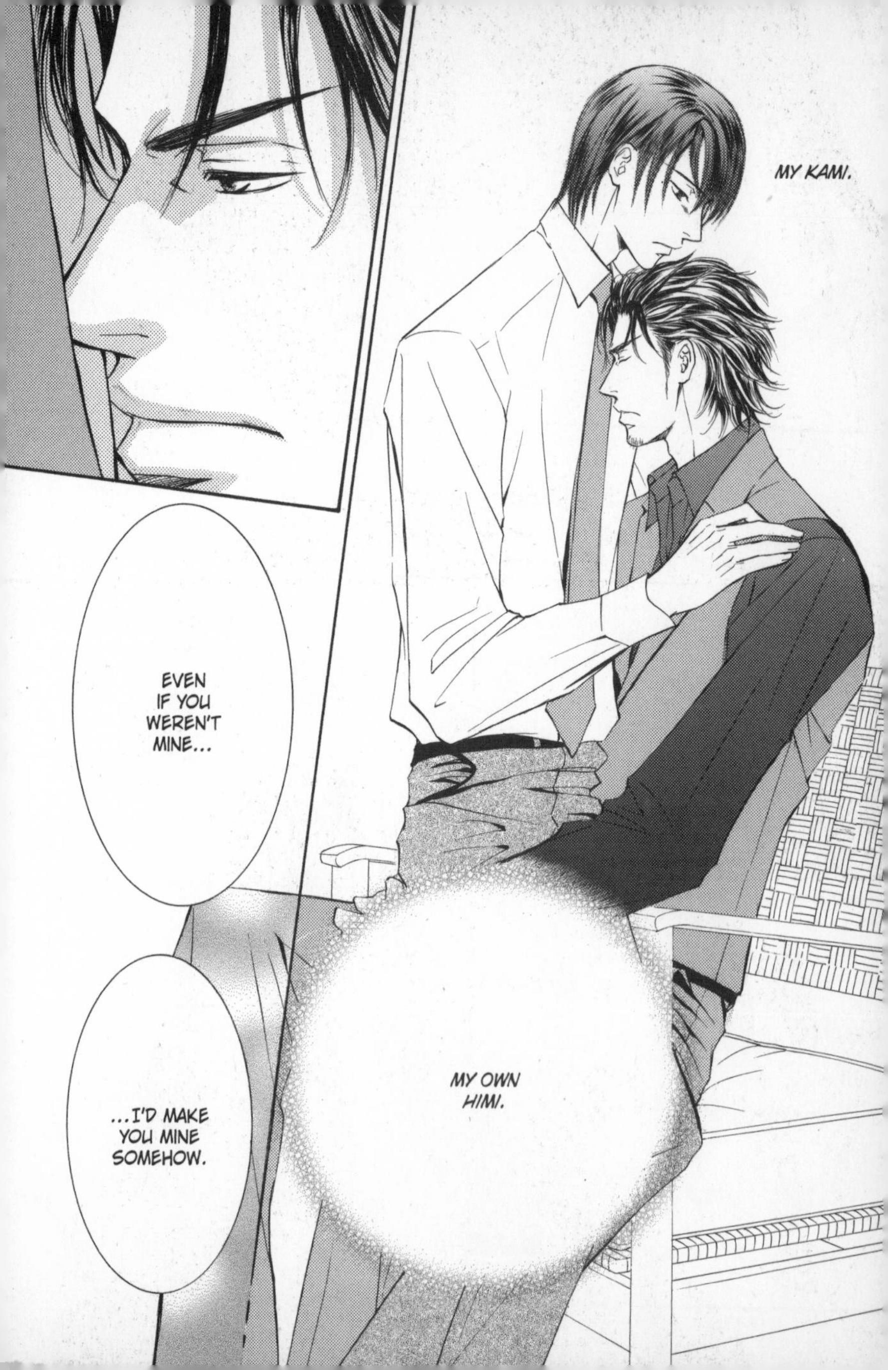
MY KAMI.
MY OWN HIMI.
EVEN IF YOU WEREN'T MINE...
...I'D MAKE YOU MINE SOMEHOW.

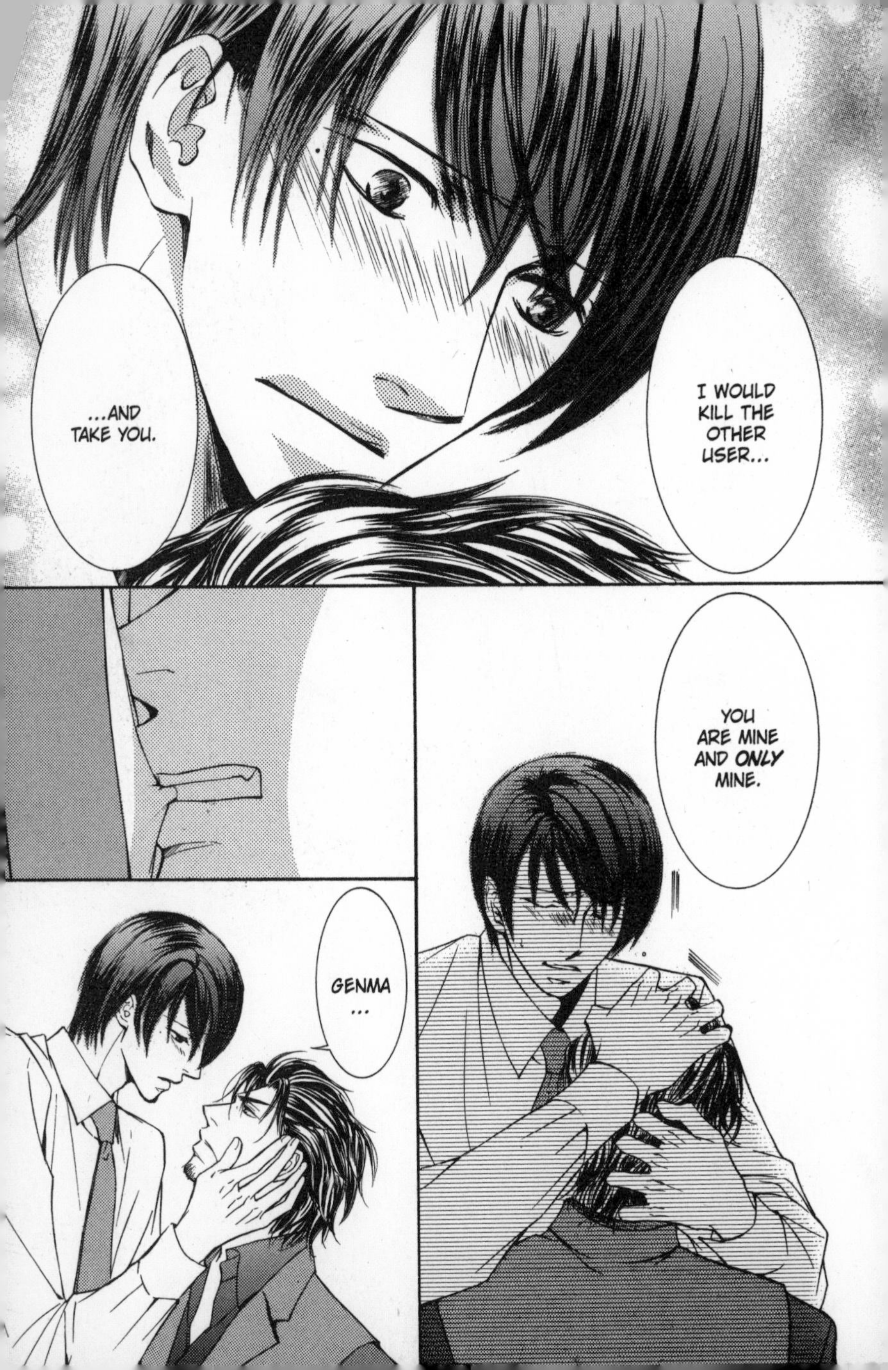
I WOULD KILL THE OTHER USER...
...AND TAKE YOU.
YOU ARE MINE AND *ONLY* MINE.
GENMA ...

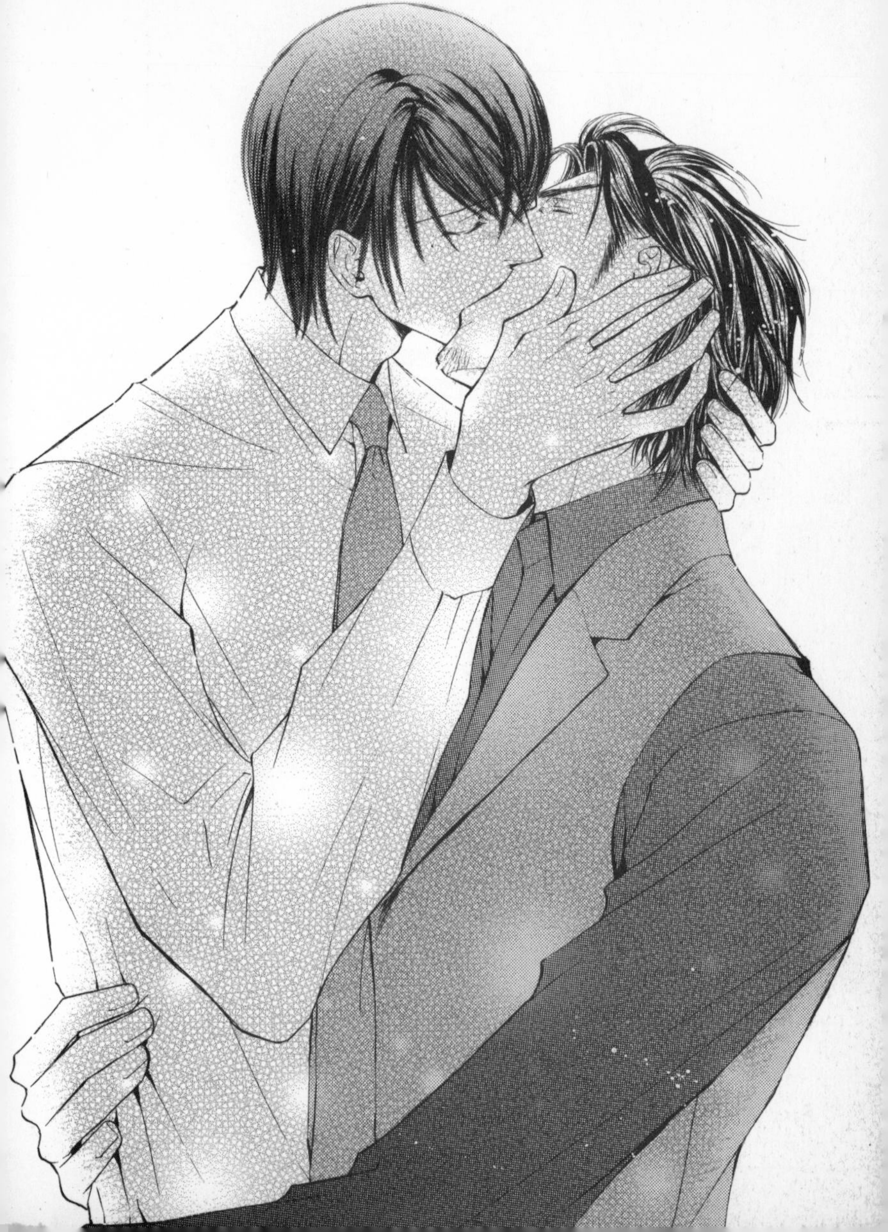

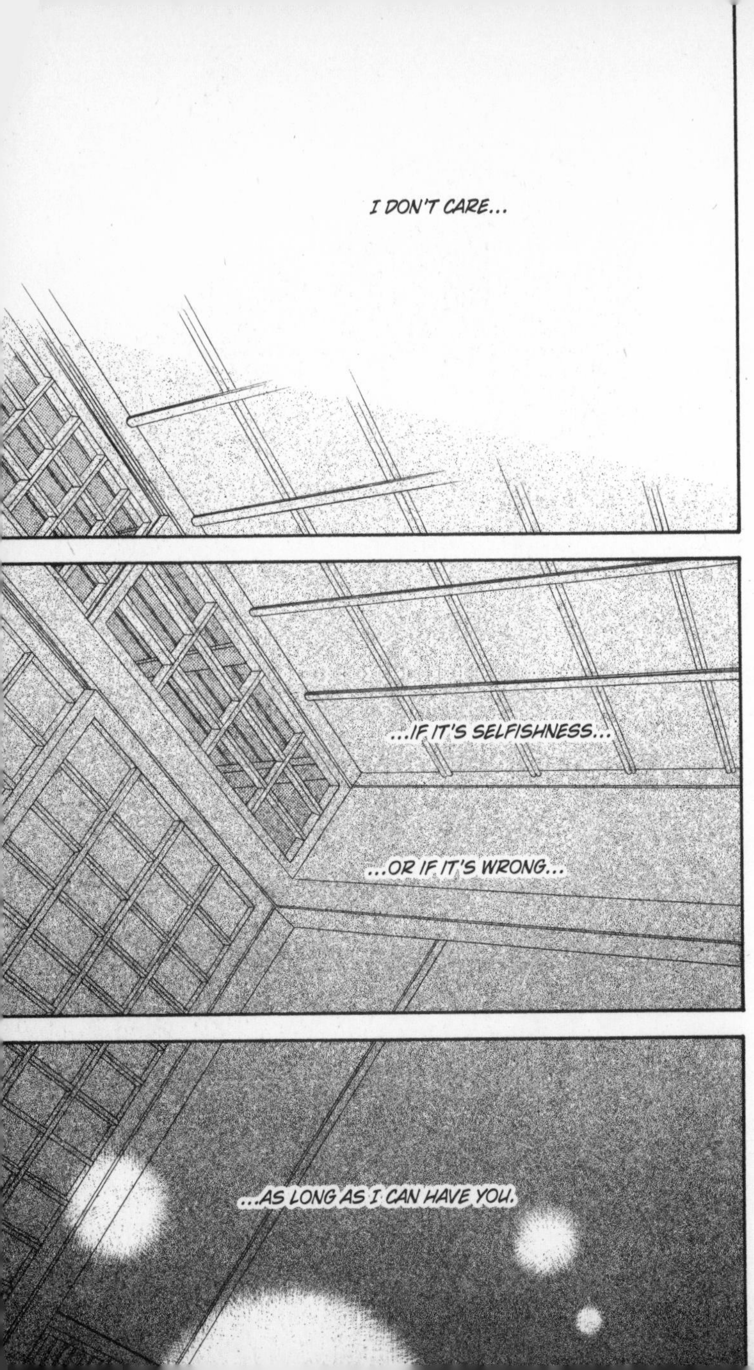
I DON'T CARE...
...IF IT'S SELFISHNESS...
...OR IF IT'S WRONG...
...AS LONG AS I CAN HAVE YOU.

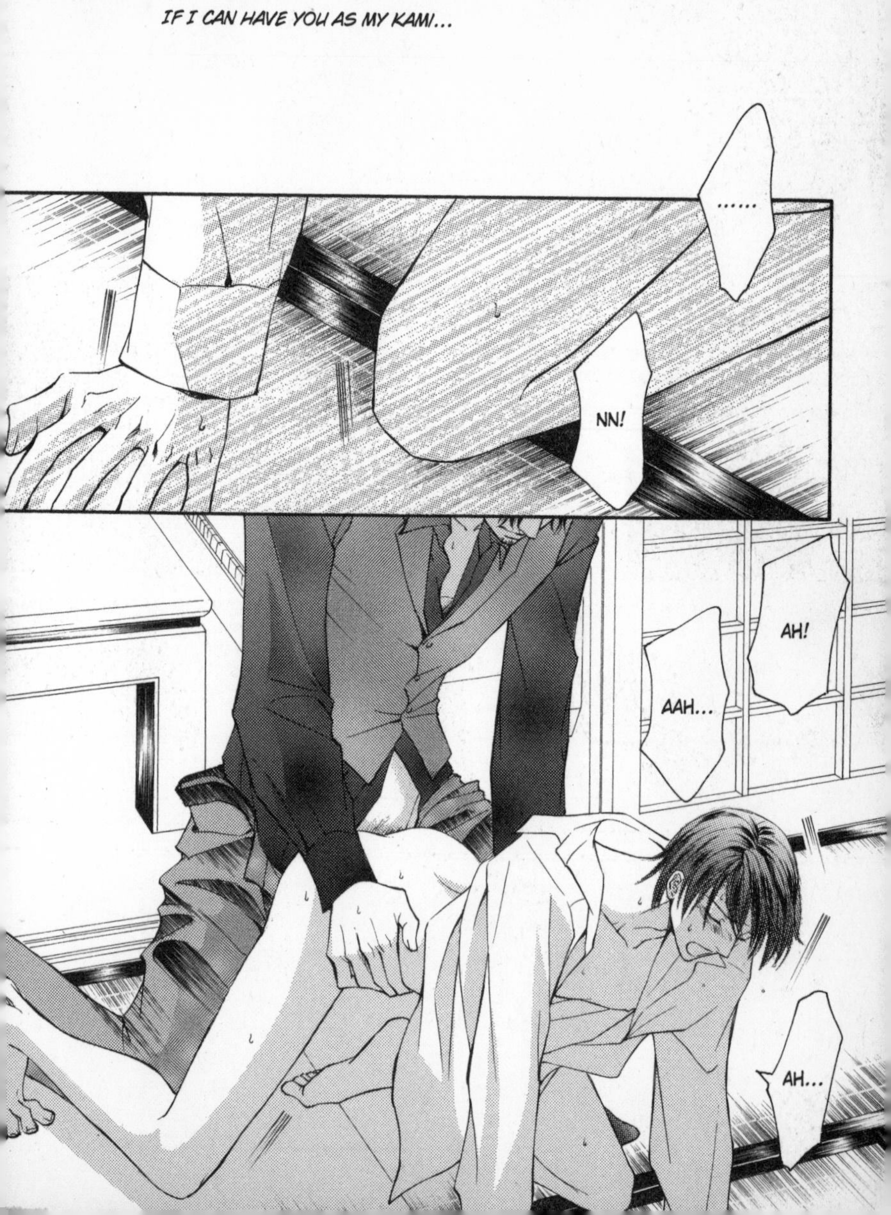
IF I CAN HAVE YOU AS MY KAMI...
......
NN!
AH!
AAH...
AH...

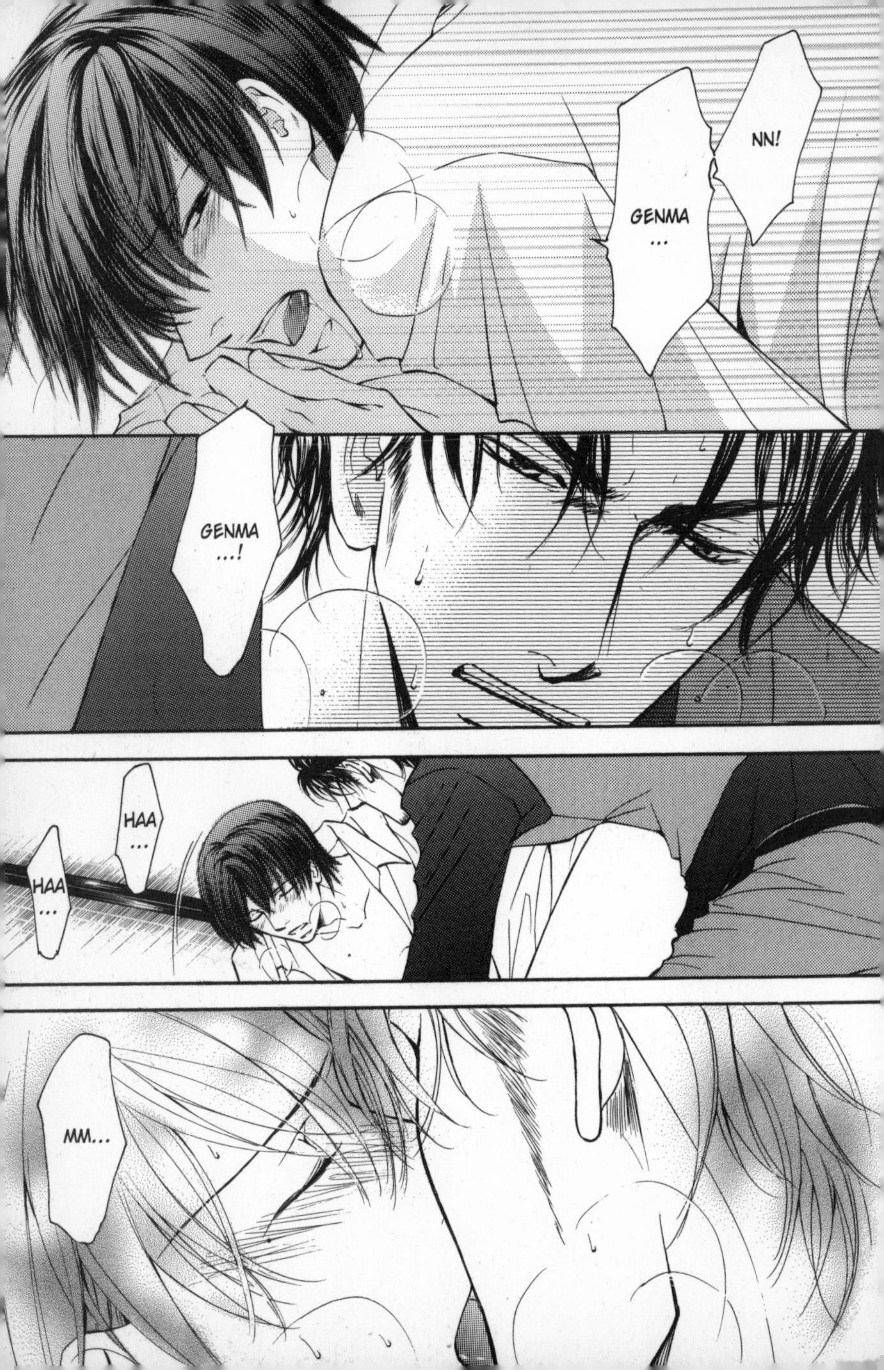
NN!
GENMA ...
GENMA ...!
HAA ...
HAA ...
MM...

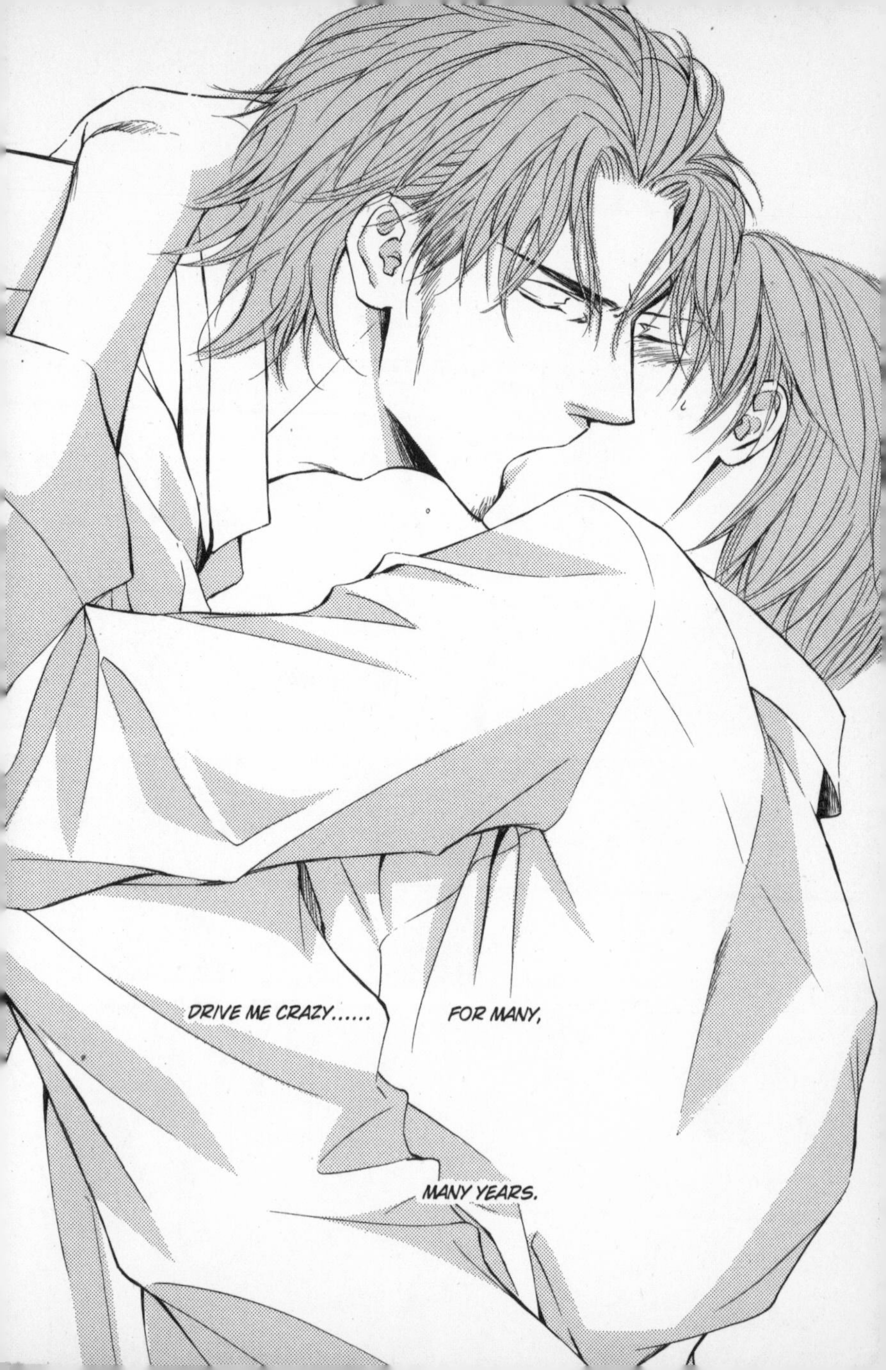
FOR MANY,
DRIVE ME CRAZY......
MANY YEARS.

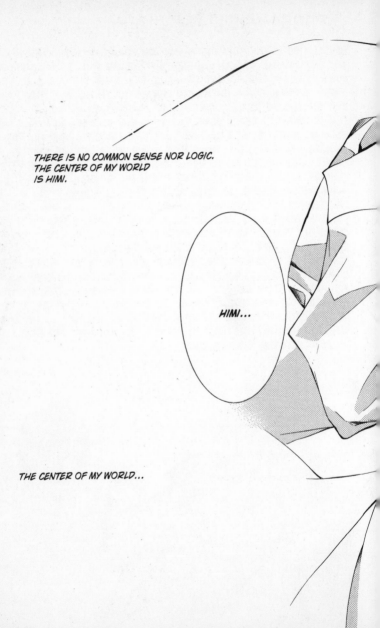

THERE IS NO COMMON SENSE NOR LOGIC.
THE CENTER OF MY WORLD
IS HIMI.

HIMI...

THE CENTER OF MY WORLD...

AFTERWORD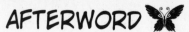

HELLO. THIS IS YUKI SHIMIZU. THANK YOU FOR READING ALL THE WAY TO THE END! THANKS TO YOU, I'VE REACHED VOLUME FIVE. I REALLY APPRECIATE IT! ALSO, THE SECOND DRAMA CD HAS COME OUT, AND I AM VERY HAPPY. I THINK IT'S A GREAT CD. THANKS TO THOSE WHO HAVE PURCHASED IT AND I REALLY WANT YOU TO HEAR GENMA AND HIMI'S VOICES. I ALSO WANT TO THANK EVERYONE WHO SUBSCRIBED FROM THE LAST VOLUME. WAS IT FUN? I RECEIVED LETTERS FROM YOU AND I'M REALLY ENCOURAGED BY THEM. THEY ALSO GAVE ME A LOT OF ENERGY. TO THOSE WHO WANTED ME TO REPLY AND ALSO TO THOSE WHO ARE STILL WAITING, I WILL SEND THEM OUT WHEN MY SCHEDULE ALLOWS. BUT SOMETIMES THERE'S NO RETURN ADDRESS ON SOME OF THEM SO I CAN'T REPLY ~~::. THERE WERE ALSO SOME THAT CAME IN THE SAME ENVELOPE. SO PLEASE RESEND THEM IF YOU'D LIKE. NOW, BOOK FIVE ENDED IN A PRETTY BAD PLACE LIKE IN BOOK THREE... BUT DON'T WORRY ABOUT IT. I'LL LET YOU IN ON SOME THINGS (LAUGH). THE FANSERVICE FOR THE EXTRA CHAPTER IS GENMA X HIMI. I HOPE YOU ENJOY IT. I'M COMING TO THE END, SO I'D LIKE TO THANK EVERYONE. ALWAYS WORKING HARDER THAN ME, I'D LIKE TO THANK MY ASSISTANTS, MY VERY HELPFUL MANAGER, EVERYONE IN THE EDITING AND PRINTING DEPARTMENT, EVERYONE ELSE INVOLVED IN THIS BOOK, AND TO ALL THE READERS, YOU HAVE MY GREATEST THANKS! THANK YOU VERY MUCH! I'LL DO MY BEST FOR THE NEXT VOLUME!

志水ゆき 梓
YUKI SHIMIZU

RYUUSEI IS PROBABLY THE MOST LAIDBACK ONE IN "ZE." HE DOESN'T EVEN FEEL THE NEED TO PUT ON UNDERWEAR...

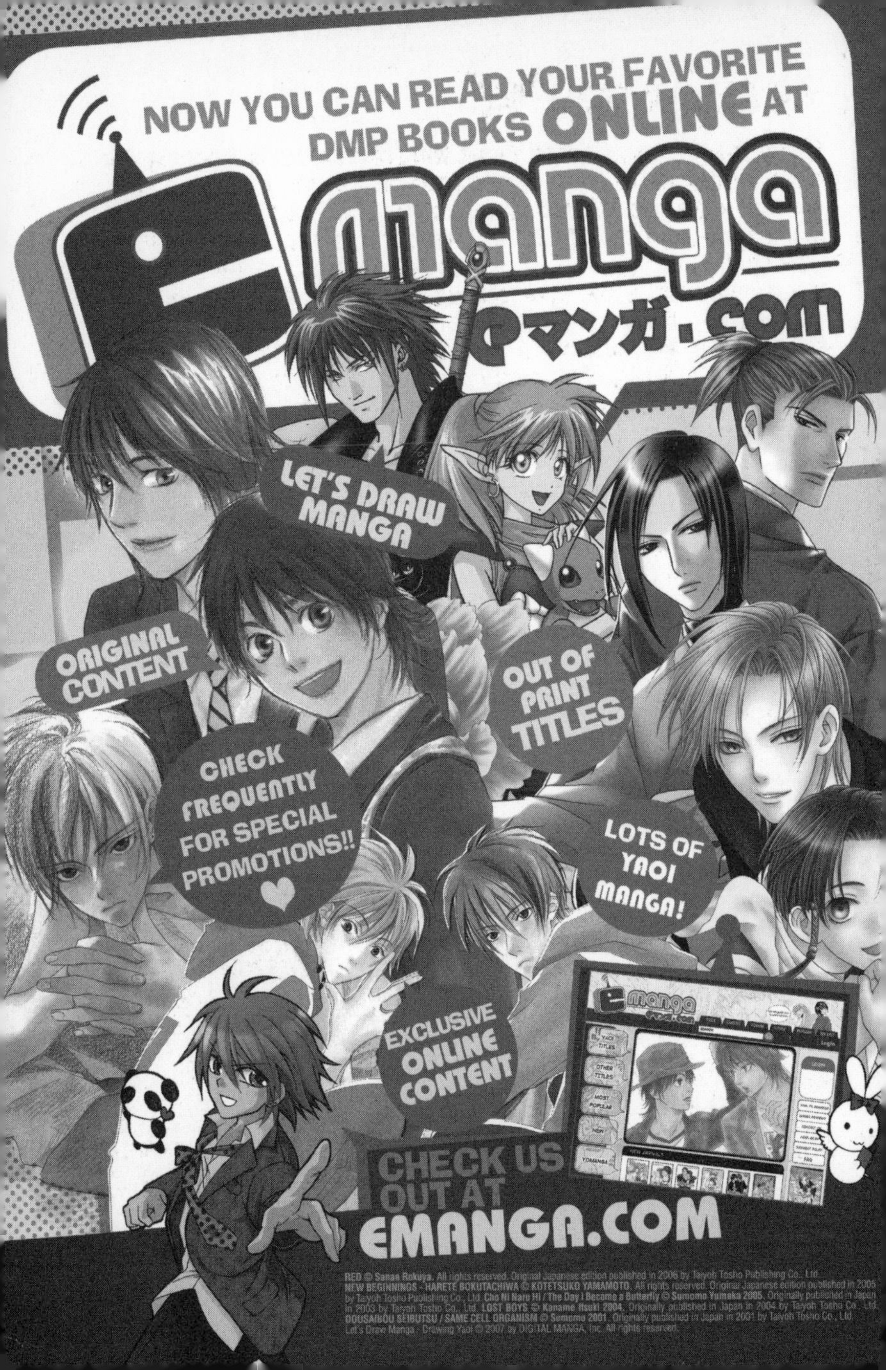
NOW YOU CAN READ YOUR FAVORITE DMP BOOKS ONLINE AT
emanga
@マンガ.com
LET'S DRAW MANGA
ORIGINAL CONTENT
OUT OF PRINT TITLES
CHECK FREQUENTLY FOR SPECIAL PROMOTIONS!!
LOTS OF YAOI MANGA!
EXCLUSIVE ONLINE CONTENT
CHECK US OUT AT
EMANGA.COM
RED © Sanae Rokuya. All rights reserved. Original Japanese edition published in 2006 by Taiyoh Tosho Publishing Co., Ltd.
NEW BEGINNINGS - HARETE BOKUTACHIWA © KOTETSUKO YAMAMOTO. All rights reserved. Original Japanese edition published in 2005 by Taiyoh Tosho Publishing Co., Ltd. Cho Ni Naru Hi / The Day I Become a Butterfly © Sumomo Yumeka 2005. Originally published in Japan in 2003 by Taiyoh Tosho Co., Ltd. LOST BOYS © Kaname Itsuki 2004. Originally published in Japan in 2004 by Taiyoh Tosho Co., Ltd. DOUSAIBOU SEIBUTSU / SAME CELL ORGANISM © Sumomo 2001. Originally published in Japan in 2001 by Taiyoh Tosho CO., Ltd.
Let's Draw Manga - Drawing Yaoi © 2007 by DIGITAL MANGA, Inc. All rights reserved.

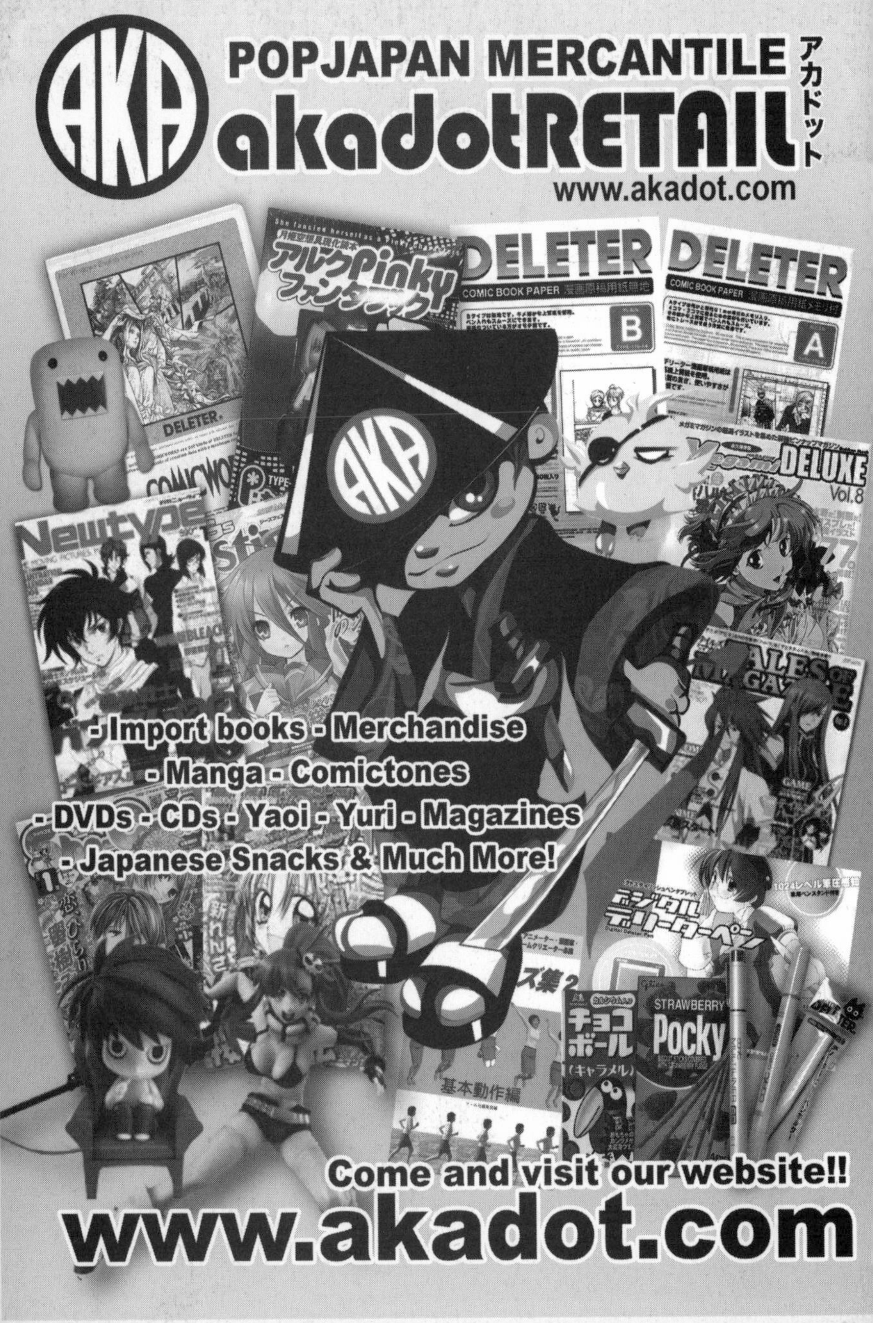

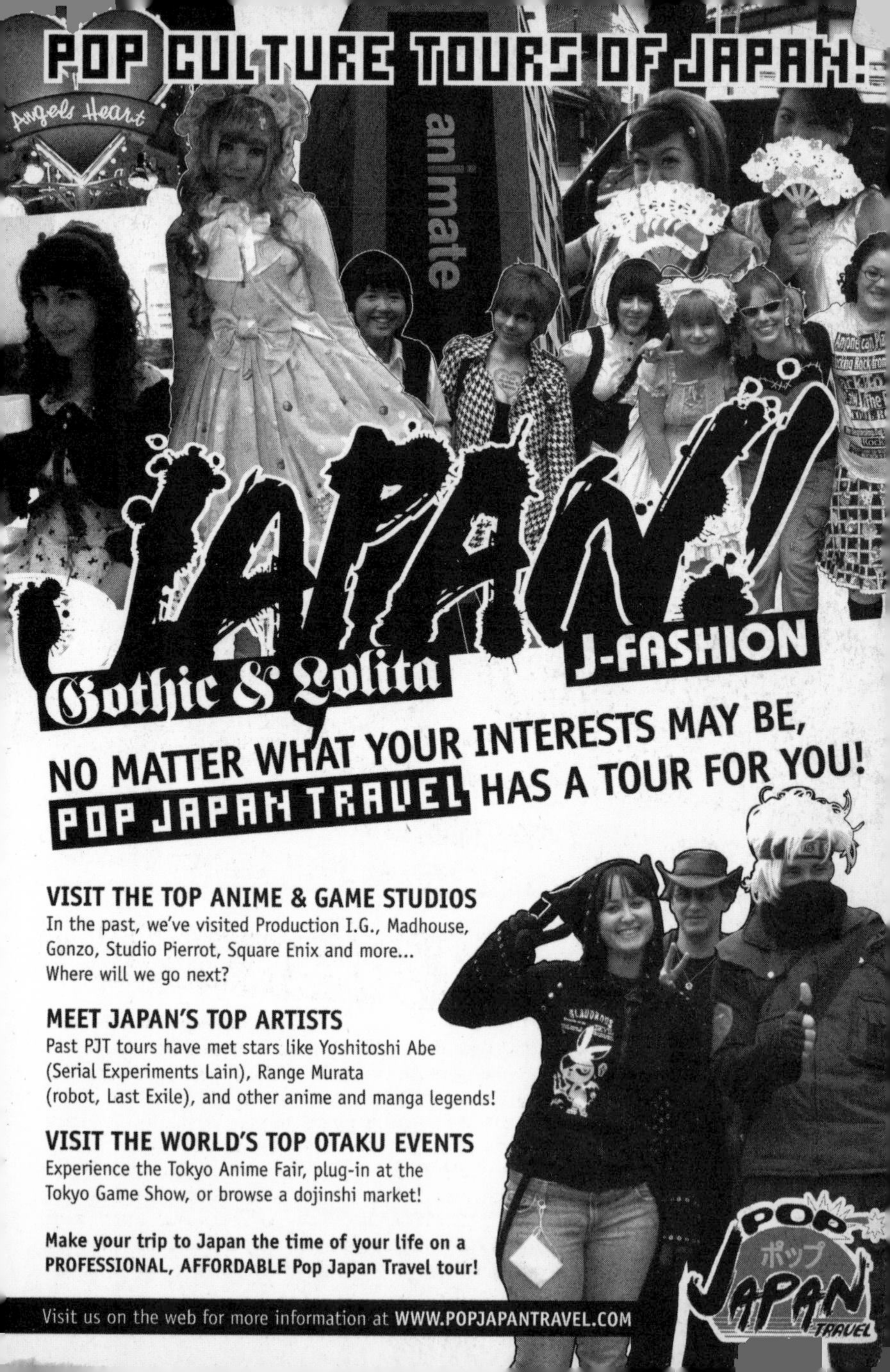

POP CULTURE TOURS OF JAPAN!
Angels Heart
animate
JAPAN!
Gothic & Lolita
J-FASHION
NO MATTER WHAT YOUR INTERESTS MAY BE,
POP JAPAN TRAVEL HAS A TOUR FOR YOU!
VISIT THE TOP ANIME & GAME STUDIOS
In the past, we've visited Production I.G., Madhouse, Gonzo, Studio Pierrot, Square Enix and more... Where will we go next?
MEET JAPAN'S TOP ARTISTS
Past PJT tours have met stars like Yoshitoshi Abe (Serial Experiments Lain), Range Murata (robot, Last Exile), and other anime and manga legends!
VISIT THE WORLD'S TOP OTAKU EVENTS
Experience the Tokyo Anime Fair, plug-in at the Tokyo Game Show, or browse a dojinshi market!
Make your trip to Japan the time of your life on a PROFESSIONAL, AFFORDABLE Pop Japan Travel tour!
Visit us on the web for more information at WWW.POPJAPANTRAVEL.COM
POP ポップ JAPAN TRAVEL